Legal Professional Privilege in Criminal Investigations and Proceedings

Legal Professional Privilege in Criminal Investigations and Proceedings

VIVIEN COCHRANE AND WILL HAYES

OXFORD
UNIVERSITY PRESS

Great Clarendon Street, Oxford, OX2 6DP,
United Kingdom

Oxford University Press is a department of the University of Oxford.
It furthers the University's objective of excellence in research, scholarship,
and education by publishing worldwide. Oxford is a registered trade mark of
Oxford University Press in the UK and in certain other countries

© Oxford University Press 2024

The moral rights of the authors have been asserted

All rights reserved. No part of this publication may be reproduced, stored in
a retrieval system, or transmitted, in any form or by any means, without the
prior permission in writing of Oxford University Press, or as expressly permitted
by law, by licence or under terms agreed with the appropriate reprographics
rights organization. Enquiries concerning reproduction outside the scope of the
above should be sent to the Rights Department, Oxford University Press, at the
address above

You must not circulate this work in any other form
and you must impose this same condition on any acquirer

Public sector information reproduced under Open Government Licence v3.0
(http://www.nationalarchives.gov.uk/doc/open-government-licence/open-government-licence.htm)

Published in the United States of America by Oxford University Press
198 Madison Avenue, New York, NY 10016, United States of America

British Library Cataloguing in Publication Data
Data available
Library of Congress Control Number: 2024931142

ISBN 978–0–19–285917–4

DOI: 10.1093/oso/9780192859174.001.0001

Printed and bound by
CPI Group (UK) Ltd, Croydon, CR0 4YY

Links to third party websites are provided by Oxford in good faith and
for information only. Oxford disclaims any responsibility for the materials
contained in any third party website referenced in this work.

Foreword

Legal Professional Privilege

No one could deny the fundamental significance of the rules on legal professional privilege (LPP). They provide arguably the most important exclusionary rules in the laws of criminal evidence. As Lord Taylor of Gosforth CJ put it in *R v Derby Magistrates' Court, ex p B* [1996] AC 487, at 507: 'Legal professional privilege is ... much more than an ordinary rule of evidence, limited in its application to the facts of a particular case. It is a fundamental condition on which the administration of justice as a whole rests.'

In the digital world, LPP has become ever more important. There is often a significant risk that a digital device will contain privileged material saved amongst the immense volume of other data held on a computer drive or cloud storage. In many cases, there will be no way of discerning at the point of seizure whether material is even likely to be privileged. The consequence is that the, sometimes staggering, volumes of material seized will need to be scrutinized for LPP. The exercise becomes not only technical, but resource intensive, and no less vital for the suspect's protection. It is important also to recognize that the significance of LPP extends beyond the full-blown criminal prosecution arising as it does in regulatory and compliance investigations, including internal investigations (dealt with comprehensively in Chapter 12). In the last decade, LPP has also become a significant issue in the context of voluntary disclosure and cooperation in deferred prosecution agreements (examined in Chapter 7).

Not surprisingly, a sound understanding of the subject is vital for every criminal practitioner. Yet, despite its routine significance and prevalence in criminal trials and investigations, LPP has not generated the volume of *practical* legal scholarship one finds with other areas of criminal evidence. This book, focused exclusively on criminal law, successfully meets that need with its clear analysis of the law and strong emphasis on practical guidance throughout.

The distinctive structure of the book guarantees that practical focus. After a valuable introductory review of the principles of LPP, each chapter deals with a step in the criminal investigation, trial process, and beyond to sentence and appeals. (Chapter 11 offers a clear examination of the particular difficulties arising in appeals with a change of representation.) Within the chapters, the law is set out clearly and concisely. This logical approach helps the reader to find solutions to a particular practical problem more readily than with a text adopting the traditional approach of presenting the material based on each distinct LPP topic.

Although primarily focused on meeting the needs of the defence practitioner, there is a welcome chapter on the prosecution perspective in Chapter 8, including discussion of the relationship between privilege and disclosure obligations. Investigators will be assisted by the clear explanations of the statutory materials and straightforward discussion of relevant case law.

The text is comprehensive and up to date. There is, as one would expect, detailed treatment of the leading cases including *The Director of the Serious Fraud Office v Eurasian Natural Resources Ltd* (in Chapter 12). Offering definitive statements on the law is not always easy when the case law offers apparently contradictory statements and when leading cases leave so many issues unresolved. The authors succeed in presenting a clear picture of the law as it applies in criminal cases, with reliance on civil and comparative materials as necessary.

There is detailed analysis of the problems that may arise in complex white-collar crime and corporate cases (compelled interviews, etc.). But the coverage extends across matters arising in the range of criminal investigations and prosecutions, as with discussion of LPP in the police station in Chapter 6 including, for example, practical advice on LPP and interpreters and appropriate adults. The authors have, sensibly, devoted an entire chapter to the oft-misunderstood but vitally important matter of the crime-fraud exception: Chapter 2. There is also discussion throughout of the implications of digital devices and technology more generally. Chapter 4 includes a timely discussion of the uses and limitations of artificial intelligence, particularly in the LPP review process.

The authors are supremely well-placed to provide the depth of analysis and, most importantly, to address the practical issues based on their vast experience from both branches of the legal profession. Their confident exposition of the subject is founded on expertise derived from years dealing with matters of LPP across a vast range of criminal cases, including the most complex large-scale frauds, as well as their experience in delivering practitioner training on this subject.

I have no doubt that the book will prove a valuable resource for criminal practitioners, investigators, and judges alike. It provides an accessible and practical guide to what is an important and complex subject.

David Ormerod, CBE, KC (Hon)
Professor of Criminal Justice, UCL
9 November 2023

Preface

This is a book about the law of legal professional privilege and its practical application in criminal cases and internal investigations. It is aimed primarily at criminal defence lawyers—both solicitors and barristers—and other lawyers in private practice who deal with corporate investigations and quasi-criminal matters, but it also provides guidance for others involved in the criminal justice system more widely, including prosecution lawyers, investigators, independent counsel undertaking privilege reviews, and members of the judiciary who are asked to determine privilege issues in criminal proceedings. The book is intended to be a single point of reference for all criminal practitioners regardless of the type of case in which they are involved. Whilst certain chapters will be of more relevance to those who specialize in white-collar and financial crime (Chapter 7, on waiver and cooperation, for example), other chapters address issues that are more likely to arise in general criminal practice, including for lawyers undertaking legally aided cases and duty solicitor work (for example, Chapter 6, on privilege at the police station and interviews under caution).

The idea for this book began to develop when our efforts to find solutions to the privilege issues that arose in our own cases identified a lack of clear guidance for criminal lawyers. This, it seems to us, is attributable to several factors. Most significant is the fact that the vast majority of reported cases on privilege arise from civil rather than criminal proceedings. No doubt this is partly a reflection of the disclosure regime in civil litigation, where assertions of privilege are made and challenged far more often than in criminal proceedings, in which a markedly different approach to disclosure is taken. This over-representation in the case law inevitably means that much of the existing commentary focuses mainly on civil rather than criminal cases. Furthermore, as a common law concept that has developed over centuries, privilege exists in the form of a complex body of case law that is at times unclear, ambiguous, and contradictory, with certain decisions difficult to reconcile with each other.

This book differs from other works on privilege in two important respects. First is its focus on the law of privilege as it applies to criminal cases and internal investigations specifically; no other book has yet been written that focuses solely on these areas. Secondly, its content and structure are determined first and foremost by the practical issues that criminal lawyers encounter and the stage in proceedings at which they typically arise. Rather than devoting a whole chapter to litigation privilege, for example, we examine this aspect of privilege across several chapters, looking at how it applies immediately following a suspect's arrest when a legal adviser may be instructed by a third party on the suspect's behalf (Chapter 6), when seeking to obtain evidence from witnesses and experts in the run-up to trial (Chapter 9), and when conducting interviews with witnesses during an internal investigation (Chapter 12). The sequence of chapters broadly reflects the chronology of a typical criminal case, from the very start of a criminal investigation when investigators may exercise powers of compulsion to obtain relevant material (Chapter 3), right through to appeals against conviction in the Court of Appeal (Chapter 11). By structuring the book in this way, we hope to make it as straightforward as possible for the reader to find the guidance they are seeking. Where an issue has not yet come before the courts, we proffer our own opinion on how we believe the matter would be decided were a court to be asked to determine it.

In short, this is the book we wish we had had when dealing with privilege issues in our own cases.

The need for a book of this nature is greater now than at any other point in recent years. Authorities such as the SFO have demonstrated an appetite for challenging what they consider to be ill-founded privilege claims, and the introduction of deferred prosecution agreements and the incentive for companies to waive privilege mean that there is more pressure on the proper maintenance of privilege in criminal cases than ever before. More generally, investigating authorities in all types of criminal cases are gaining access to an ever-increasing volume of data as the storage capabilities of electronic devices continue to expand, increasing the risk of investigators and prosecutors inadvertently encountering privileged material.

The implications of privilege being lost or waived in criminal proceedings, whether deliberately or inadvertently, can be extremely damaging, and it is therefore essential that all involved in the criminal justice system have a proper understanding of this important area of law. This book aims to provide that.

Vivien Cochrane
Will Hayes
January 2024

Acknowledgements

Joint Acknowledgements

We are extremely grateful to our colleagues at Kingsley Napley and Shearman Bowen who shared their thoughts and insight on the topics discussed in this book. Particular thanks are owed to the following for their invaluable assistance proofreading and providing feedback on draft chapters: Mark Bowen of Shearman Bowen, Caroline Day, Jonathan Grimes, Louise Hodges, Alun Milford, Rebecca Niblock, and Aaron Watkins of Kingsley Napley, and Alistair Richardson of 6KBW College Hill.

Thanks also to the team at OUP for allowing us the opportunity to pursue this idea and tolerating the many extensions to our submission date.

Acknowledgements of Vivien Cochrane

Writing this book has been immensely rewarding but not without its challenges. I will forever be grateful to Mark Bowen who has been an unwaveringly supportive employer and friend. My father, Graham Cochrane, provided constant encouragement when finishing felt like a distant goal. And to my children, Lucas and Elliot, who may find that the book does not impress their friends as much as they anticipated, but I hope will be proud nevertheless.

Acknowledgements of Will Hayes

This book would not have been possible without the support of Kathryn Franks, who tolerated an absent partner for the best part of two years and endured many evenings and weekends alone without complaint. Thank you for your incredible patience and for allowing me the space to pursue this project. I am extremely grateful.

Contents

Table of Cases   xiii
Table of Statutes   xix
Table of Statutory Instruments   xxiii

1. Legal Professional Privilege: General Principles   1
   1. Introduction   1.01
   2. Legal Advice Privilege   1.11
   3. Litigation Privilege   1.47
   4. Pre-existing Documents   1.65
   5. Loss of Privilege   1.70
   6. Joint Interest Privilege and Common Interest Privilege   1.112

2. The Crime-Fraud Exception   31
   1. Introduction   2.01
   2. General Principles   2.04
   3. Application in Criminal Cases   2.15
   4. Practical Considerations   2.26

3. Search and Seizure, Compulsion, Surveillance, and Interception   41
   1. Introduction   3.01
   2. Search and Seizure and Compulsion: Main Powers   3.03
   3. Additional Powers of Seizure: Criminal Justice and Police Act 2001   3.14
   4. Seizure and Compelled Production of Privileged Material   3.24
   5. Applying for a Search Warrant   3.38
   6. Executing a Search Warrant   3.61
   7. After Seizure   3.70
   8. Asserting Privilege in Response to Powers of Compulsion   3.88
   9. Impact of Seizure on Fair Trial   3.92
   10. Covert Surveillance and Interception of Communications   3.97

4. Privilege Reviews   73
   1. Introduction   4.01
   2. Privilege Reviews: Seized/Compelled Material   4.05
   3. Privilege Reviews: Other Cases   4.41
   4. Document Types and Practical Issues   4.52

5. Compelled Interviews   93
   1. Introduction   5.01
   2. Compelled Interviews: Main Powers   5.02
   3. Exclusion of Privileged Information   5.06
   4. Failing to Comply without Reasonable Excuse   5.11
   5. During the Interview   5.13
   6. Interviews with Lawyers   5.20

xii CONTENTS

6. The Police Station and Interviews under Caution		101
1 Introduction		6.01
2 Initial Engagement and Instruction		6.06
3 Consultation with the Client		6.22
4 During the Interview		6.37
7. Waiver and Cooperation		117
1 Introduction		7.01
2 Waiving Privilege through Voluntary Disclosure		7.04
3 Deferred Prosecution Agreements and Cooperation with the SFO		7.43
4 Cooperation with Other Authorities		7.76
8. Prosecution Privilege		145
1 Introduction		8.01
2 Availability of Privilege		8.02
3 Examples of Privileged Material		8.11
4 Privilege and Disclosure Obligations		8.12
5 Private Prosecutions		8.29
9. Evidence Gathering and Preparing for Court		155
1 Introduction		9.01
2 Engaging with Third Parties		9.05
3 Engaging with Witnesses		9.23
4 Communications between Co-defendants		9.63
5 Seeking Disclosure of Privileged Material		9.66
6 Deploying Defence Privileged Material		9.78
10. Court Proceedings		177
1 Introduction		10.01
2 Intentional Disclosure of Privileged Documents		10.02
3 Inadvertent Disclosure of Privileged Documents		10.16
4 Oral Evidence		10.26
5 Expert Evidence		10.40
6 Lawyers Giving Evidence		10.41
7 Costs Applications		10.61
8 Interlocutory Hearings		10.62
11. Appeals		199
1 Introduction		11.01
2 Appeals to the Court of Appeal		11.02
3 The Criminal Cases Review Commission		11.40
12. Internal Investigations		213
1 Introduction		12.01
2 Importance of Privilege to Investigations		12.04
3 Legal Advice Privilege		12.07
4 Litigation Privilege		12.36
5 Practical Guidance		12.118
Index		253

Table of Cases

UNITED KINGDOM

A Local Authority v B [2008] EWHC 1017 (Fam), [2009] 1 FLR 289. 6.27, 6.33
Al Sadeq v Dechert LLP [2023] EWHC 795 . . . . 4.57, 4.58
Al Sadeq v Dechert LLP [2024] EWCA Civ 28 . . . 1.55, 1.57, 2.13, 2.19, 2.20, 9.22, 12.08, 12.34, 12.117
Al-Fayed v Commissioner of Police of the Metropolis [2002]
    EWCA Civ 780, [2002] All ER (D) 450. . . . . .8.06
Anderson v Bank of British Columbia (1876) 2 Ch D 644. . . . . 1.24, 6.21
Auten v Rayner (No 2) [1960] 1 QB 669. . . . . .8.05
AXA Seguros SA de CV v Allianz Insurance Plc (T/A Allianz Global Risks)
    [2011] EWHC 268 (Comm), [2011] Lloyd's Rep IR 544. . . . . 12.67, 12.68, 12.80, 12.86

B v Auckland District Law Society [2003] UKPC 38, [2003] 2 AC 736 . . . . 1.01, 1.87
Balabel v Air India [1988] Ch 317. . . . . 1.25, 1.26, 1.28, 1.29, 1.36, 1.37, 1.43, 1.42, 12.33
Bank of Nova Scotia v. Hellenic Mutual War Risks Association (Bermuda) Ltd. (Note)
    (No. 2) [1992] 2 Lloyd's Rep. 540 . . . . .4.57
Banque Keyser Ullman SA v Skandia (UK) Insurance Company Limited [1986]
    1 Lloyd's Rep 336 . . . . .2.10
Bates v Chief Constable of Avon and Somerset [2009] EWHC 942 (Admin),
    [2009] All ER (D) 59 . . . . .3.41
BBGP Managing General Partner Ltd v Babcock & Brown Global Partners [2010]
    EWHC 2176 (Ch), [2011] Ch 296. . . . . .2.08
Berezovsky v Hine & Ors [2011] EWCA Civ 1089, [2011] All ER (D) 61 . . . . 1.85, 1.87, 7.05
Bilta (UK) Ltd v Royal Bank of Scotland [2017] EWHC 3535 (Ch), [2018]
    Lloyd's Rep FC 202 . . . . 12.102, 12.108
Bourns Inc v Raychem Corp (No 3) [1999] CLC 1029, [1999] 3 All ER 154. . . . . 1.51, 1.73, 9.50
Brennan v Sunderland City Council [2008] UKEAT/ 349/ 08, [2009] ICR 479 . . . . 1.88, 1.89, 1.91
British Coal Corp v Dennis Rye (No 2) [1988] 1 WLR 1113. . . . . 7.08, 7.06, 7.11, 7.20
BSA International SA v Irvine [2009] CSOH 77, 2009 SLT 1180 . . . . .9.50
Butler v Board of Trade [1971] Ch 680 (Ch) 1.104, 1.105, 5.25, 10.16, 10.19
Buttes Gas & Oil Co v Hammer (No 3) [1981] QB 223 . . . . .1.116

C v C (Privilege) [2006] EWHC 336 (Fam), [2008] 1 FLR 115 . . . . .2.14
Calcraft v Guest [1898] 1 QB 759 . . . . .10.24
Carpmael v Powis (1846) 1 Ph 687 . . . . .6.25
Causton v Mann Egerton (Johnsons) Ltd [1974] 1 WLR 162 . . . . .6.41
China National Petroleum Corp v Fenwick Elliott [2002] EWHC 60 (Ch), [2002] TCLR 19. . . . . .9.25
Citic Pacific Ltd v Secretary for Justice [2012] HKCA 153. . . . . 7.12, 7.18
Clough v Tameside and Glossop HA [1998] 1 WLR 1478 (QB) 9.49–9.53
Collidge v Freeport Plc [2007] EWHC 645 (QB) 12.67, 12.73, 12.80

D (A Child) (Care Proceedings Legal Privilege) [2011] EWCA Civ 684,
    [2011] 4 All ER 434 . . . . .10.17
Dickinson v Rushmer [2001] All ER (D) 369 (Dec) (Ch) 1.42
Dickinson v Rushmer [2002] 1 Costs LR 128 (Ch). 9.18
Digicel Ltd v Cable & Wireless Plc [2009] EWHC 1437 (Ch), [2009] All ER (D) 44 . . . . .1.82
Director of the Serious Fraud Office v AB Limited and CD Limited
    (Southwark CC, 19 July 2021) 7.69

Director of the Serious Fraud Office v Airbus SE [2021] Lloyd's Rep FC 159 ....7.65
Director of the Serious Fraud Office v Airline Services Ltd [2021] Lloyd's Rep FC 42............7.67
Du Barre v Livette 170 ER 96..6.24
Dunlop Slazenger International Ltd v Joe Bloggs Sports Ltd [2003] EWCA Civ 901,
  [2003] All ER (D) 137 .... 1.88, 1.97, 10.62

Edwardian Group Ltd, Re [2017] EWHC 2805 (Ch), [2017] All ER (D) 109 ....1.40
Eurasian Natural Resources Corp Ltd v Dechert LLP [2022]
  EWHC 1138 (Comm)..................1.104, 1.105, 5.23, 5.24, 5.25, 6.12, 7.40, 7.42, 10.16

Fitzpatrick v Commissioner of Police of the Metropolis [2012] EWHC 12 (Admin),
  [2012] Lloyd's Rep FC 361 .... 3.52, 3.56
FM Capital Partners Ltd v Marino [2017] EWHC 3700 (Comm),
  [2017] All ER (D) 140 .... 12.62, 12.64, 12.110
Fulham Leisure Holdings Limited v Nicholson Graham & Jones [2006]
  EWHC 158 (Ch), [2006] 2 All ER 599... 1.95, 1.96
Fyffes v DCC [2005] IESC 3 ....7.11

GE Capital Corporate Finance Group v Bankers Trust Co [1995] 1 WLR 172 (CA) 4.57
General Accident Fire & Life Assurance Corp Ltd v Tanter (The Zephyr)
  [1984] 1 WLR 100 (Com Ct) 115..1.95
Gerrard v Eurasian Natural Resources Corp Ltd [2020] EWHC 3241 (QB), [2021] EMLR 8......2.12
Gittins v Central Criminal Court [2011] EWHC 131 (Admin), [2011]
  Lloyd's Rep FC 219 .... 3.38, 3.57, 3.60, 3.62
Goodridge v Chief Constable of Hampshire [1999] 1 WLR 1558...................... 8.07, 8.08
Gotha City v Sotheby's (No 1) [1998] 1 WLR 114................. 1.77, 1.78, 6.16, 6.26, 9.07
Government of Ukraine v Kononko [2014] EWHC 1420 (Admin)..........................8.10
Great Atlantic Insurance Co v Home Insurance Co [1981] 1 WLR 529................... 1.93, 9.75
Greenough v Gaskell [1824- 34] All ER Rep 767 .... 1.21, 1.36

Harmony Shipping Co SA v Saudi Europe Line Ltd [1979] 1 WLR 1380 ....9.41
Hellenic Mutual War Risks Association (Bermuda) Ltd v Harrison (The Sagheera)
  [1997] 1 Lloyd's Rep 160 (QB) 1.114
Henderson and Jones Ltd v Ross [2022] EWHC 2560 (Ch), [2022] All ER (D) 50...............1.88
Highgrade Traders Ltd, Re [1984] BCLC 151 .... 1.24, 1.60, 12.95, 12.101, 12.108
Hoare & Pierce [2004] EWCA Crim 784...10.33
Howes v Hinckley and Bosworth BC [2008] UKEAT/ 0213/ 08/ MAA, [2008] All ER (D) 112....1.98
Hughes v Biddulph (1827) 38 ER 777..1.41

IBM v Phoenix International (Computers) Ltd [1995] 1 All ER 413 (Ch).....................9.18
In the Estate of Fuld (deceased) (No 2 A) [1965] 3 WLR 162 ....9.27
Istil Group Inc v Zahoor [2003] EWHC 165 (Ch), [2003] 2 All ER 252.....................9.29
Jinxin Inc v Aser Media Pte Limited [2022] EWHC 2856 (Comm), [2023] 1 WLR 1084 ....1.74

Jones v Great Central Railway Co [1910] AC 4...1.24
JSC BTA Bank v Ablyazov [2014] EWHC 2788 (Comm), [2014] 2 CLC 263 .... 2.08, 2.17, 2.18

Kupe Group v Seamar Holdings [1993] 3 NZLR 209...9.18
Kuruma v The Queen [1955] AC 197..10.24
Kuruma, son of Kanui v R [1955] A.C. 197..10.19
Kuwait Airways Corp v Iraqi Airways Co [2005] EWCA Civ 286, [2005] 1 WLR 2734 ..... 2.04, 2.19
Kyla Shipping Co Ltd v Freight Trading Ltd [2022] EWHC 376 (Comm)................. 1.60, 1.89

London Fire and Emergency Planning Authority (LFEPA) v Halcrow Gilbert & Co Ltd
  [2004] EWHC 2340 (TCC), [2005] BLR 18 ....12.89
Lord Ashburton v Pape [1913] 2 Ch 469 ....10.24

Lucas v Barking [2003] EWCA Civ 1102, [2004] 1 WLR 220 ....9.50
Lyell v Kennedy (No 3) (1884) 27 Ch D 1, 26 (CA)....................................1.40, 1.69

MAC Hotels Ltd v Rider Levett Bucknall UK Ltd [2010] EWHC 767 (TCC) 1.97
McE v Prison Service of Northern Ireland [2009] UKHL 15, [2009] 1 AC 908...... 1.10, 3.100, 3.101
Medcalf v Mardell [2002] UKHL 27, [2003] 1 AC 120.......................................10.61
Minter v Priest [1930] AC 558.. 1.21, 1.29, 12.33

Nationwide Anglia Building Society v Various Solicitors (No 1) [1999] PNLR 52 (Ch) 69........1.04
Nea Karteria Maritime Co Ltd v Atlantic & Great Lakes Steamship Corp (No 2)
 [1981] Com LR 138...1.94, 10.12
Nederlandse Reassurantie Groep Holding NV v Bacon & Woodrow (No 1)
 [1995] 1 All ER 976 ....11.34

O'Rourke v Darbishire [1920] AC 581..2.16, 2.18
Oceanic Finance Corp Ltd v Norton Rose (QB, 26 March 1997) 9.18

Paragon Finance v Freshfields [1999] 1 WLR 1183 .... 1.110, 11.33, 11.34
Parry v News Group Newspapers Ltd [1990] NLJR 1719, [1990] 11 WLUK 267 ..... 1.42, 6.38, 12.22
Patrick v Capital Finance Corporation (Australasia) Pty Ltd [2004] FCA 1249..................9.65
PCP Capital Partners LLP v Barclays Bank plc [2020] EWHC 1393 (Comm) 1.90, 1.92, 7.27
Pearce v Foster (1885) 15 QBD 114 ....6.09
PJSC Tatneft v Gennady Bogolyubov [2020] EWHC 2437 (Comm), [2021] 1 WLR 403 ....1.17
Price Waterhouse v BCCI Holdings (Luxembourg) SA [1992] BCLC 583 .... 1.24, 12.87, 12.92
Property Alliance Group Ltd v Royal Bank of Scotland Plc [2015] EWHC 1557 (Ch),
 [2016] 1 WLR 361 .... 7.09, 7.12, 7.32

R (A) v Central Criminal Court [2017] EWHC 70 (Admin), [2017] 1 WLR 3567...........3.34, 3.57
R (AL) v Serious Fraud Office [2018] EWHC 856 (Admin), [2018]
 1 WLR 4557 .... 1.82, 3.91, 7.21, 7.24, 7.34, 7.52, 7.54, 7.58, 7.72, 12.25
R (B) v Huddersfield Magistrates' Court [2014] EWHC 1089 (Admin),
 [2015] 1 WLR 4737 ....3.44, 3.65
R (Bozkurt) v Thames Magistrates' Court [2001] EWHC Admin 400, [2002] RTR 15 ....6.24
R (Cabot Global Ltd) v Barkingside Magistrates' Court [2015] EWHC 1458 (Admin),
 [2015] 2 Cr App R 26...3.34
R (F) v Blackfriars Crown Court [2014] EWHC 1541 (Admin) 3.57–3.60
R (Firth) v Epping Magistrates' Court [2011] EWHC 388 (Admin), [2011] 1 WLR 1818.........9.12
R (Ford) v Financial Services Authority [2011] EWHC 2583 (Admin), [2012] 1 All ER 1238 ....1.114
R (Glenn & Co (Essex) Ltd) v HM Commissioners for Revenue and Customs [2011]
 EWHC 2998 (Admin), [2012] 1 CR App R 22 ....3.34
R (Goode) v Nottingham Crown Court [2013] EWHC 1726 (Admin),
 [2013] All ER (D) 281 ....3.57
R (Hallinan Blackburn Gittings and Nott) v Middlesex Guildhall Crown Court [2004]
 EWHC 2726 (Admin), [2005] 1 WLR 766 .... 2.20, 2.21, 2.23–2.26, 10.58, 10.59
R (Jet2.com Ltd) v Civil Aviation Authority [2020] EWCA Civ 35,
 [2020] QB 1027 .... 1.12, 1.26, 1.31, 1.33, 4.63, 4.65, 9.18
R (Kay) v Leeds Magistrates' Court [2018] EWHC 1233 (Admin), [2018] 4 WLR 91 ....8.29
R (Kelly) v Warley Magistrates' Court [2007] EWHC 1836 (Admin), [2008] 1 WLR 2001........9.25
R (Lord) v Director of the Serious Fraud Office [2015] EWHC 865 (Admin),
 [2015] 2 Cr App R 5.13
R (McKenzie) v Director of the Serious Fraud Office [2016] EWHC 102 (Admin),
 [2016] 1 WLR 1308 .... 3.62, 4.12, 4.13
R (Miller Gardner Solicitors) v Minshull Street Crown Court [2002]
 EWHC 3077 (Admin), [2002] All ER (D) 338..1.42
R (Morgan Grenfell & Co Ltd) v Special Commissioner of Income Tax [2002]
 UKHL 21, [2003] 1 AC 563 .... 1.01, 1.09, 3.33, 8.23, 11.41

xvi TABLE OF CASES

R (National Council for Civil Liberties) v Secretary of State for the Home
 Department [2023] EWCA Civ 926 .... 3.105
R (on the application of Her Majesty's Commissioners of Customs & Excise) v Nottingham
 Magistrates' Court [2004] EWHC 1922(Admin), [2004] All ER (D) 241 .... 3.95, 6.14
R (Prudential Plc) v Special Commissioner of Income Tax [2013] UKSC 1,
 [2013] 2 AC 185 .... 1.17, 1.23, 9.22
R (Rawlinson & Hunter Trustees) v Central Criminal Court [2012]
 EWHC 2254 (Admin), [2013] 1 WLR 1634 .... 3.62
R (S) v Chief Constable of the British Transport Police [2013]
 EWHC 2189 (Admin), [2014] 1 WLR 1647 .... 3.42, 3.45, 3.65, 3.68
R (Sharer) v City of London Magistrates' Court [2016]
 EWHC 1412 (Admin), (2017) 181 JP 48 .... 3.40
R (the Health and Safety Executive) v Jukes [2018] EWCA Crim 176, [2018] 2 Cr App R 9 .... 9.27
R (United States) v Bow Street Magistrates' Court [2006] EWHC 2256 (Admin),
 [2007] 1 WLR 1157 .... 8.09
R v Achogbuo [2014] EWCA Crim 567 .... 11.04, 11.08, 11.11, 11.19
R v Bowden [1999] 1 WLR 823 .... 6.42, 6.46, 10.28, 10.31, 10.33, 10.35
R v Braham and Mason [1976] VR 547 .... 6.07, 6.09, 9.10
R v Brown [2015] EWCA Crim 1328, [2016] 1 WLR 1141 .... 2.09, 6.29, 6.33, 6.34
R v Bunting & Others [2002] SASC 412 .... 8.27
R v Central Criminal Court, ex p Francis & Francis [1989] AC 346 .... 2.10, 2.11, 2.17, 3.28, 3.29, 5.09
R v Chesterfield Justices, ex p Bramley [2000] QB 576 .... 3.36, 3.68, 3.69
R v Clinton [1993] 1 WLR 1181 .... 11.05
R v Condron [1997] 1 WLR 827 .... 6.40, 10.30, 10.29
R v Cottrill [1997] Crim LR 56 (CA) 1.104, 10.16
R v Cox and Railton (1884) 14 QBD 153 .... 2.05, 2.16, 2.21
R v Crozier (1990) 12 Cr App R (CA) 9.27, 9.29, 9.39, 10.40
R v Customs and Excise Commissioners, ex p Popely [2000] Crim LR 388 .... 3.62
R v Davies [2002] EWCA Crim 85, (2002) 166 JP 243 .... 9.46, 9.51, 9.52
R v Derby Magistrates' Court, ex p B [1996] AC 487 ...... 1.01, 1.03, 1.04, 1.08, 3.31, 5.06, 6.32, 8.25,
                                                                  9.71, 10.10, 10.28, 11.48
R v Devani [2007] EWCA Crim 1926, [2008] 1 Cr App R 4 .... 6.51, 9.79, 10.47, 10.58, 10.60
R v DPP ex p Lee [1999] 1 WLR 1950 .... 9.69
R v G [2004] EWCA Crim 1368, [2004] 1 WLR 2932 .... 10.23, 10.25
R v Grant [2005] EWCA Crim 1089, [2006] QB 60 .... 3.96, 6.13, 6.14
R v Grant-Murray [2017] EWCA Crim 1228, [2018] Crim LR 71 .... 11.21
R v Guildhall Magistrates' Court, ex p Primlaks Holdings Co (Panama) Inc
 [1990] 1 QB 261 (QB) 3.51, 3.55, 3.56
R v Hall [2015] EWCA Crim 581, [2015] All ER (D) 41 .... 10.15
R v Hall-Chung [2007] EWCA Crim 3429, [2007] All ER (D) 429 .... 6.46, 10.36, 10.35
R v Inglis [2021] EWCA Crim 1545, All ER (D) 54 .... 10.39
R v Jukes [2018] EWCA Crim 176, [2018] 2 Cr App R 9 .... 6.19, 6.20, 12.50, 12.54, 12.66, 12.116
R v K (A) [2009] EWCA Crim 1640, [2010] QB 343 .... 1.104–1.106, 10.16
R v King [1983] 1 WLR 411 .... 9.42–9.45
R v Kular (8 April 2000) 3.92
R v Lea [2021] EWCA Crim 65, [2021] 4 WLR 38 .... 11.23
R v Lee [2014] EWCA Crim 2928 .... 11.15
R v Loizou [2006] EWCA Crim 1719, [2006] All ER (D) 215 (Jul) 1.95, 10.28, 10.33
R v Manchester Crown Court ex p Rogers [1999] 1 WLR 832 (QB) 1.45
R v McCook [2014] EWCA Crim 734, [2016] 2 Cr App R 30 .... 11.02–11.04, 11.07, 11.10, 11.12,
                                                                  11.14, 11.20–11.24, 11.31
R v Middlesex Guildhall Crown Court, ex p Tamosius & Partners [2000] 1 WLR 453 .... 3.62
R v Minchin, Dwyer and Healey [2013] EWCA Crim 2412 .... 2.22, 2.25, 2.26, 10.59
R v Pearce [2013] EWCA Crim 808 .... 10.37
R v R (Blood Sample: Privilege) [1994] 1 WLR 758 .... 9.43
R v Roberts [2016] EWCA Crim 71, [2016] 1 WLR 324 .... 11.23

R v Rochford [2010] EWCA Crim 1928, [2011] 1 WLR 534..............................9.15
R v Sally Jones [1984] Crim LR 357 ....6.15
R v Seaton [2010] EWCA Crim 1980, [2011] 1 WLR 623 ....10.15, 10.28
R v Secretary of State for Transport, ex p Factortame Ltd (1997) 9 Admin LR 591...............1.97
R v Singh [2017] EWCA Crim 466, [2018] 1 WLR 1425 .... 11.12, 11.19, 11.20
R v Snaresbrook Crown Court, ex p DPP [1988] QB 532 .... 2.17, 9.20, 9.21
R v Southampton Crown Court, ex p J [1993] Crim LR 962 (QB) 3.43
R v Tompkins (1978) 67 Cr App R 181 (CA)...................... 1.104, 1.107, 1.108, 6.10–6.13,
    10.18, 10.16, 10.20
R v Uljee [1982] 1 NZLR 561... 6.09–6.12, 6.14
R v Ungvari [2003] EWCA Crim 2346, [2003] All ER (D) 335 ....7.19
R v Wishart [2005] EWCA Crim 1337...10.32
R. v Doherty and McGregor [1997] 2 Cr. App. R. 218 ....11.09
R. v. Frost-Helmsing [2010] EWCA Crim 1200 .... 11.25, 11.32
Reg. v. Wilmot (1988) 89 Cr.App.R. 341 ....10.30

Sands v Gardner [2012] NIQB 29..9.50
Schneider v Leigh [1955] 2 QB 195..9.38, 10.40
Serdar Mohammed v Ministry of Defence [2013] EWHC 4478...... 1.71, 1.73, 1.74, 1.76, 1.80, 1.81,
    1.100, 7.26
Serious Fraud Office v Amec Foster Wheeler Energy Ltd [2021] Lloyd's Rep FC 353 ....7.68
Serious Fraud Office v G4S Care and Justice Services (UK) Ltd [2021] Crim LR 138 ....7.66
Serious Fraud Office v Glencore Energy UK Ltd (Southwark CC, 3 November 2022)............7.75
Serious Fraud Office v Guralp Systems Ltd [2020] Lloyd's Rep FC 90
    (Southwark CC, 22 October 2019) 7.73
Serious Fraud Office v Rolls-Royce Plc [2017] Lloyd's Rep FC 249 ....7.62
Serious Fraud Office v Sarclad Limited (Southwark CC, 8 July 2016) 7.72
Serious Fraud Office v Serco Geografix Limited [2020] Crim LR 66 ....7.64
Serious Fraud Office v Standard Bank PLC [2016] Lloyd's Rep FC 102......................7.70
Serious Fraud Office v Tesco Stores Ltd [2019] Lloyd's Rep FC 283 ....7.63
SL Claimants v Tesco Plc [2019] EWHC 3315 (Ch),
    [2019] All ER (D) 30 .... 1.75, 1.76, 7.26, 7.29, 10.04
SRJ v Persons Unknown [2014] EWHC 2293 (QB), [2014] All ER (D) 129 ....3.29
Stanford International Limited, Re [2010] 3 WLR 941 ....3.42
Starbev GP Ltd v Interbrew Central European Holding BV [2013]
    EWHC 4038 (Comm), [2014] All ER (D) 116......................... 1.60, 12.66, 12.77
Sumitomo Corpn v Credit Lyonnais Rouse Ltd [2001] EWCA Civ 1152,
    [2002] 1 WLR 479 ....1.69
Svenska Handelsbanken v Sun Alliance and London Insurance plc [1995]
    2 Lloyd's Rep 84 (Com Ct) 88..1.116

Taylor v Director of the Serious Fraud Office [1999] 2 AC 177.............................10.03
Tesco Stores Ltd v Office of Fair Trading [2012] CAT 6, [2012] Comp AR 188............12.39, 12.58
The Director of the Serious Fraud Office v Eurasian Natural Resources Corporation
    Limited (SFO v ENRC Ltd) [2017] EWHC 1017 (QB), [2017] 1 WLR 4205, [2018]
    EWCA Civ 2006, [2019] 1 WLR 791 ....1.20, 1.37, 1.61, 3.28, 3.88, 4.34, 5.09, 6.20, 7.22,
    7.42, 7.45, 7.50, 12.04, 12.16, 12.21, 12.22,
    12.29, 12.30, 12.43, 12.45, 12.46, 12.50,
    12.54, 12.61, 12.66, 12.80, 12.100,
    12.108, 12.109, 12.125, 12.127
The Palermo (1883) 9 PD 6 (CA) 1.66, 1.67
The RBS Rights Issue Litigation [2016] EWHC 3161 (Ch),
    [2017] 1 WLR 1991 .... 1.36, 1.37, 7.22, 12.14, 12.18, 12.22
The Southwark and Vauxhall Water Company v Quick (1878) 3 QBD 315....................1.39
The State of Qatar v Banque Havilland SA & Another [2021]
    EWHC 2172 (Comm)... 12.55, 12.58, 12.112

Three Rivers District Council v Governor and Co of the Bank of England
  (Three Rivers (No 5)) [2003] EWCA Civ 474, [2003] QB 1556 .....1.17, 1.20, 1.34, 1.36–1.38,
  1.46, 5.17, 6.49, 12.04, 12.11–12.13,
  12.15, 12.16, 12.23, 12.120, 12.121
Three Rivers District Council v Governor and Company of the Bank of England
  (Three Rivers (No 6)) [2004] UKHL 48, [2005] 1 AC 610 ....1.01, 1.03, 1.08, 1.11, 1.25,
  1.27, 1.29, 1.47, 1.54, 1.60,
  6.17, 9.05, 10.40, 12.33

United States of America v Philip Morris Inc [2004] EWCA Civ 330,
  [2004] 1 CLC 811...1.55, 1.56, 6.18, 12.41
USP Strategies Plc v London General Holdings Ltd (No 2) [2004] EWHC 373 (Ch),
  [2004] All ER (D) 132 ....1.34, 1.38, 1.44, 1.46, 1.77, 6.49

Ventouris v Mountain (The Italia Express) (No 1) [1991] 1 WLR 607, 615F (CA).....1.40, 1.66, 1.69

W v Edgell [1990] Ch 359 (CA) 9.45
Watson v Cammell Laird & Co [1959] 1 WLR 702 (CA)...............................1.66, 1.68
Waugh v British Railways Board [1980] AC 521.......1.50, 1.60, 1.62, 9.23, 9.37, 12.83, 12.88, 12.92,
  12.98, 12.99
WH Holding Limited v E20 Stadium LLP [2018] EWCA Civ 2652,
  [2018] All ER (D) 17 (Dec)...1.60, 1.61
Wheeler v Le Marchant (1881) 17 Ch D 675..1.18, 1.24
Winterthur Swiss Insurance Co v AG (Manchester) Ltd (In Liquidation)
  [2006] EWHC 839 (Comm), [2006] All ER (D) 196...............................1.116
WXY v Gewanter [2012] EWHC 1071 (QB)..9.64

Yurov, Re [2022] EWHC 2112 (Ch), [2022] BPIR 1616.....................................1.97

EUROPEAN UNION

Akzo Nobel Chemicals Ltd v Commission of the European Communities
  Case C-550/ 07 P [2011] 2 AC 338..1.18

NATIONAL COURTS

Autralia
AWB v Terence Cole [2006] FCA 571 ....1.40
Commissioner of Taxation v Coombes [1999] FCA 842.....................................1.43
Farrow Mortgage Services Pty Ltd v Webb (1996) 39 NSWLR 601 ....9.65
Grant v Downs (1976) 135 CLR 674..1.50, 1.60, 1.62, 6.14
Trade Practices Commission v Sterling (1979) 36 FLR 244..................................1.41

Canada
Visx Inc v Nidex Co [1999] FSR 91..1.38, 9.18

Hong Kong
Citic Pacific Ltd..7.37

Ireland
Ainsworth v Wilding (No 2) [1900] 2 Ch 315 (Ch) 323....................................1.36
Ahern v Judge Mahon [2008] IEHC 119, [2008] 4 IR 704....................................9.37

Table of Statutes

Constables Protection Act 1750
    s 6 . . . . .3.53
Crime and Courts Act 2013
    s 45 . . . . 7.01, 7.43
    Sch 17 . . . . 7.01, 7.43
Crime (International Co-operation)
    Act 2003
    s 15(2) 3.12
    s 16 . . . . .3.12
    s 17 . . . . .3.12
Criminal Appeal Act 1968
    s 20 . . . . 11.08
    s 23(2)(d) 11.19
Criminal Appeal Act 1995 . . . . 11.40, 11.48
    s 17 . . . . 11.40, 11.42
    s 17(4) 11.40
    s 18A 11.40, 11.42
    s 25 . . . . 11.42, 11.45, 11.47
    s 25(3) 11.44
Criminal Justice Act 1967 (CJA 1967)
    s 9 . . . . 9.24, 12.53
Criminal Justice Act 1987
        (CJA 1987) 3.30, 7.27
    s 2 . . . . 3.06, 3.12, 3.30, 5.11, 5.13
    s 2(2) 5.02, 5.07
    s 2(3) 3.06, 3.88, 4.41
    s 2(4) 3.06
    s 2(9) 3.29, 3.88, 5.07, 5.08
    s 3(5) 7.36
Criminal Justice Act 2003 . . . . .9.60
Criminal Justice and Police Act 2001
        (CJPA) 1.108, 3.16, 3.17, 3.37, 3.41,
        3.69, 3.70, 4.05, 4.06, 4.24
    s 50 . . . . 3.15, 3.17–3.19, 3.24, 3.34, 3.40, 3.52,
        3.62, 3.63, 3.67, 3.68, 3.70, 3.71,
        3.76, 3.79, 3.81, 3.85,
        3.87, 3.89, 4.05
    s 50(1) 3.19, 3.22
    s 50(2) 3.19, 3.23, 3.35
    s 50(3) 3.21
    s 50(4) 3.35
    s 51 . . . . 3.15, 3.17, 3.18, 3.24, 3.63, 3.67,
        3.68, 3.70, 3.71, 3.76, 3.79,
        3.81, 3.85, 3.87, 4.05
    s 51(1) 3.20
    s 51(2) 3.20, 3.35
    s 51(3) 3.21
    s 51(4) 3.35
    s 52(1) 3.67
    s 52(2) 3.67
    s 52(3) 3.67
    s 52(4) 3.67
    s 53 . . . . 3.70, 3.81, 3.82, 4.05
    s 53(2)(a) 3.71
    s 53(2)(b) 3.71
    s 53(2)(c) 3.74, 3.79, 3.81
    s 53(2)(d) 3.74
    s 53(3) 3.71, 3.74
    s 53(3)(a) 3.71, 3.81
    s 53(3)(b) 3.71, 3.81
    s 53(3)(c) 3.71, 3.72, 3.79
    s 53(4) 3.73
    s 53(5) 3.72
    s 54 . . . . 3.71, 3.75–3.77, 3.79, 3.85, 3.87,
        4.05, 4.33, 4.35
    s 54(1)(b) 3.77
    s 54(2) 3.77
    s 54(3) 3.77
    s 55 . . . . 3.77, 3.79
    s 56 . . . . 3.71, 3.77
    s 59 . . . . 3.64, 3.85–3.87, 4.33, 4.34
    s 59(3)(b) 3.85
    s 59(4)–(5) 3.86
    s 59(6)–(7) 3.86
    s 59(11)–(12) 3.85
    s 60(1)–(2) 3.87
    s 61 . . . . .3.87
    s 61(1) 3.87
    s 62 . . . . 3.78–3.82, 4.05, 4.34, 4.35
    s 62(2) 3.80
    s 62(3)–(4) 3.80
    s 62(5)–(8) 3.79
    s 65 . . . . .3.75
    Sch 1
        Pt 1 . . . . 3.15, 3.19, 3.70, 3.76, 3.79, 3.85
        Pt 2 . . . . 3.15, 3.70, 3.76, 3.79, 3.85
Criminal Justice and Public Order
    Act 1994 (CJPOA)
    s 34 . . . . 10.28, 10.32
Criminal Procedure and Investigations
    Act 1996 (CPIA) 7.22, 8.12, 8.13,
        8.17, 8.21, 8.24–8.29, 9.15,
        9.66, 9.68–9.70, 9.77, 10.21
    s 3 . . . . .8.22
    s 3(6) 8.22
    s 3(7) 8.22
    s 5 . . . . .9.14
    s 6A 9.15, 9.72

s 6C 9.25, 9.33
s 6D 9.60
s 6D(1) 9.60
s 7A 8.22
s 7A(8) 8.22
s 7A(9) 8.22
s 8 . . . . 7.33, 8.22, 8.28
s 8(5) 8.22
s 8(6) 8.22
s 17 . . . . 7.06, 10.03
s 17(3) 10.03
s 23(1) Code of Practice 9.71
    para 6.15 . . . . 9.71
Criminal Procedure (Attendance of Witnesses)
    Act 1965
    s 2 . . . . 3.11, 3.31, 5.05, 7.45
Enterprise Act 2002
    s 193 . . . . 5.05
Financial Services and Markets
    Act 2000 (FSMA) 3.10, 3.30, 5.09
    s 165 . . . . 3.10, 3.12
    s 169 . . . . 3.12
    ss 171–173 . . . . 3.10, 5.04, 5.11
    s 171 . . . . 5.11
    s 172 . . . . 5.11
    s 173 . . . . 5.11
    s 175 . . . . 3.10
    s 175(4) 3.30
    s 176 . . . . 3.10
    s 177(2) 5.11
    s 413 . . . . 3.30, 5.09
Health and Safety at Work Act 1974
    s 20 . . . . 5.05
Insolvency Act 1986 . . . . 1.97
Investigatory Powers Act 2016
    (IPA) 1.10, 3.97, 3.103–3.105
    Pt 2 . . . . 3.103
    Pt 6, Ch 1 . . . . 3.103
    s 15(2) 3.103
    s 15(3) 3.103
    s 18(1) 3.103
    s 19 . . . . 3.103
    s 19(2) 3.103
    s 23 . . . . 3.103
    s 27(4)(a) 3.106
    s 27(6) 3.106
    s 27(8) 3.107
    s 27(11)–(13) 3.107
    s 53(3) 3.108
    s 55 . . . . 3.108
    s 136 . . . . 3.103
    s 138 . . . . 3.103
Magistrates' Court Act 1980
    s 97 . . . . 3.11, 3.31, 5.05

Police and Criminal Evidence
    Act 1984 (PACE) 3.03, 3.05, 5.01,
        6.01, 6.04, 6.05
    s 2(9) 3.29
    s 8 . . . . 3.04, 3.12, 3.39, 3.40, 3.41, 3.44,
        3.50–3.52, 3.65
    s 8(1)(d) 3.39, 3.40, 3.51, 3.53, 3.55, 3.65
    s 9 . . . . . . 3.04, 3.22, 3.42, 3.43, 3.50, 3.51, 3.53,
        3.56, 3.58
    s 10 . . . . 3.28, 3.29, 3.30, 3.75, 5.09
    s 10(1) 3.26, 9.20, 9.44
    s 10(2) 2.11, 2.20, 3.27, 3.51, 9.44
    s 18 . . . . 3.05
    s 19 . . . . 3.05
    s 19(6) 3.25, 3.35, 3.36, 3.57
    s 32 . . . . 3.05
    s 37A(3) 8.08
    s 37B(4) 8.08
    s 37B(5) 8.08
    s 37B(6) 8.08
    s 54 . . . . 3.05
    s 78 . . . . 1.106, 1.108, 4.35, 6.14, 7.17, 9.51,
        9.73, 10.20, 10.36
    Sch 1 . . . . 3.04, 3.12, 3.22, 3.42, 3.43, 3.45,
        3.48, 3.50, 3.51, 3.53, 3.56, 3.58
        para 2(b) 3.46
        para 2(c) 3.47
        para 4 . . . . 3.86
Proceeds of Crime Act 2002
    (POCA) 3.07–3.09, 3.30, 5.03, 5.12
    s 345 . . . . 3.07, 3.30, 4.41
    s 348 . . . . 3.30
    s 352 . . . . 3.07, 3.30
    s 352(4) 3.75
    s 354 . . . . 3.30
    s 357 . . . . 3.07, 3.30
    s 361(1) 3.30
    s 378 . . . . 3.07
Regulation of Investigatory Powers
    Act 2000 (RIPA) 1.10, 3.97, 3.100,
        3.104–3.106, 6.35
    Pt II 3.98, 3.101
    s 26(2) 3.98
    s 26(3) 3.98
    s 27 . . . . 3.100
    s 28 . . . . 3.98, 3.100
    s 32 . . . . 3.98, 3.100
    s 32(6) 3.99
    s 41(1) 3.99
    s 71 . . . . 3.100
    Sch 1
        Pt A1 . . . . 3.99
        Pt I 3.99
        Pt II 3.99

Serious Organised Crime and Police
    Act 2005 (SOCPA 2005)... 3.09, 3.30, 3.89
  s 62 .... 3.09, 3.30, 5.03, 5.08, 5.11
  s 64 ....5.08
  s 66 ....3.09, 3.30
  s 64(1) 3.30
  s 66(9) 3.30
  s 67(1) 5.11

Table of Statutory Instruments

Civil Procedure Rules....................9.50
    Pt 8..........................3.88, 4.34
    r 35.10(3)..........................9.47
    r 35.10(4)..........................9.47
Criminal Procedure Rules.............. 10.06
    r 3.2................................9.12
    r 16.................................9.24
    r 19.4(b)...........................9.47
    r 19.4(c)...........................9.47
    r 19.7..............................9.61
    r 19.8..............................9.61
    r 39.3(1)...........................11.02
    r 39.2(2)...........................11.02
    Crim PD 2015................11.13, 11.18
        para 5B.14......................10.06
    Crim PD 2023
        para 10.4.4..................11.02, 11.12
        para 10.4.4.a..................... 11.12
        para 10.4.4.b................11.12, 11.24
        para 10.4.4.c..................... 11.12
        para 10.4.4.d..................... 11.12
        para 10.4.4.e......11.12, 11.19, 11.22, 11.24
Prosecution of Offences Regulations
    1978 (SI 1978/1357)
    reg 6(1).............................8.07
Regulation of Investigatory Powers
    (Extension of Authorisation
    Provisions: Legal Consultations)
    Order 2010 (SI 2010/461)........ 3.101

CODES

Covert Surveillance and Property
    Interference: Revised Code of
    Practice (August 2018) (RIPA
    2000 Code)....3.100, 3.102, 3.105, 3.108
    para 2.10 ....3.99
    para 3.21 ....3.98

para 9.50 .... 3.102
para 9.51 .... 3.106
para 9.52 .... 3.106
para 9.54 .... 3.107
paras 9.55–9.57.................... 3.107
para 9.74 .... 3.108
para 9.80 .... 3.108
para 9.81 .... 3.108
Deferred Prosecution Agreements
    Code of Practice (DPA Code
    of Practice)
    para 2.8.2(i).................. 7.44, 7.47
    para 2.9.1...........................7.47
Interception of Communications
    Code of Practice (December
    2022) (IPA 2016 Code).....3.105, 3.106
    para 4.5 .... 3.103
    paras 6.1–6.2..................... 3.103
    para 9.54 .... 3.106
    para 9.55 .... 3.106
    para 9.67 .... 3.108
    para 9.72 .... 3.108
    para 9.73 .... 3.108
Police and Criminal Evidence
    Act 1984 Code of Practice
    Code B................. 3.69, 3.72, 3.80
        para 7.7 ....3.69
        para 7H 3.72, 3.80
    Code C...........................6.15
    Code H, Annex B, para 4..............6.15
SRA Code of Conduct
    para 6.3 ....1.02

INTERNATIONAL INSTRUMENTS

European Convention on Human
    Rights (ECHR)............3.100, 3.101
    Art 8........................3.100, 3.105

1
Legal Professional Privilege: General Principles

1 Introduction

What Is Legal Professional Privilege?

Legal professional privilege is a common law concept that protects certain types of confidential communications between a lawyer and their client or, in the context of litigation, between a lawyer or their client and a third party. Where it applies, it enables the privilege holder to withhold disclosure of material or information to another party in circumstances where they would otherwise be required to provide it.[1] It is more than just a rule of evidence: in *R (Morgan Grenfell & Co Ltd) v Special Commissioner of Income Tax*, Lord Hoffmann described it as 'a fundamental human right long established in the common law',[2] and it has been expressed in similar terms elsewhere.[3] It has been developed by the courts over several centuries and is a continually evolving area of law to this day.

1.01

Whilst it overlaps significantly with the concept of confidentiality, it is not identical. Lawyers owe a professional duty to their clients to keep their affairs confidential. This is broader in scope than legal professional privilege. However, it is a qualified obligation and can be overridden in certain circumstances. The SRA Code of Conduct for solicitors, for example, states at paragraph 6.3 that solicitors must 'keep the affairs of current and former clients confidential unless disclosure is required or permitted by law or the client consents.'[4] Legal professional privilege, however, provides an absolute form of protection. It can be waived by the privilege holder and, in exceptional circumstances, overridden by statute, but it is otherwise an inviolable right that will exist indefinitely (often expressed as 'once privileged, always privileged'), even in the face of law enforcement agencies exercising powers of compulsion in connection with a criminal investigation.

1.02

An inevitable corollary of the absolute nature of privilege is that opponents in litigation, law enforcement agencies, prosecutors, public authorities, courts, and other parties may be denied access to potentially relevant material. However, the courts have repeatedly emphasized that this is an acceptable consequence of maintaining so fundamental a right as legal professional privilege, and there is no balancing exercise to be carried out between

1.03

---

[1] In *B v Auckland District Law Society* [2003] UKPC 38, [2003] 2 AC 736 [67], privilege was described as 'a right to resist the compulsory disclosure of information'.
[2] [2002] UKHL 21, [2003] 1 AC 563 [7].
[3] See eg *R v Derby Magistrates' Court, ex p B* [1996] AC 487 (HL); *Three Rivers District Council v Governor and Company of the Bank of England (Three Rivers (No 6))* [2004] UKHL 48, [2005] 1 AC 610.
[4] Similarly, r C15.5 of the Bar Standards Board Handbook requires barristers to 'protect the confidentiality of each client's affairs, except for such disclosures as are required or permitted by law or to which your client gives informed consent'.

competing public interests. The public interest in maintaining privilege cannot be overridden by some supposedly greater public interest, such as ensuring that the guilty are convicted.[5]

1.04 Legal professional privilege belongs to the client, not their lawyer.[6] A lawyer is professionally obliged to assert their client's privilege unless and until it has been waived,[7] and it applies just as much to former clients as to current clients. Although only the client is entitled to waive privilege,[8] the actions of their lawyer can cause privilege to be lost or waived inadvertently, the consequences of which can be extremely detrimental to the client's interests, especially in a criminal investigation or prosecution. This in turn can have serious professional and regulatory repercussions on the lawyer and their practice.

1.05 Under the law of England and Wales, there are two types of legal professional privilege: legal advice privilege and litigation privilege.

Rationale for Legal Professional Privilege

1.06 Legal professional privilege is a fundamental aspect of the rule of law. It has at its foundation the principle that a person should be free to consult a lawyer for legal advice safe in the knowledge that anything passing between them is confidential and will not be disclosed to a third party under any circumstances unless the client consents. Without this protection, the administration of justice would be seriously impaired. A client might withhold information from their lawyer, thereby undermining the quality of legal advice they would receive.

1.07 Another core principle underpinning legal professional privilege (more specifically, litigation privilege) is that a person should be free to prepare for litigation in which they are or may become a party by gathering information and evidence without the risk of that material being disclosed to their opponent. A litigant might otherwise be more reluctant to make certain enquiries or attempt to obtain evidence if there was a risk that any unhelpful material uncovered in the process would have to be disclosed to an adverse party.

1.08 In *R v Derby Magistrates' Court, ex p B*, Lord Taylor described the principle as such:

> [A] man must be able to consult his lawyer in confidence, since otherwise he might hold back half the truth. The client must be sure that what he tells his lawyer in confidence will never be revealed without his consent. Legal professional privilege is thus much more than an ordinary rule of evidence, limited in its application to the facts of a particular case. It is a fundamental condition on which the administration of justice as a whole rests.[9]

---

[5] See eg *Three Rivers (No 6)* (n 3) [25] (Lord Scott); *R v Derby Magistrates' Court, ex p B* (n 3) 511–12.
[6] *R v Derby Magistrates' Court, ex p B* (n 3) 504–05.
[7] See eg *Nationwide Anglia Building Society v Various Solicitors (No 1)* [1999] PNLR 52 (Ch) 69; see also The Law Society, 'Legal Professional Privilege' Practice Note (12 August 2021) https://www.lawsociety.org.uk/topics/client-care/legal-professional-privilege#sub-menu-dy21 (accessed 9 June 2023).
[8] *R v Derby Magistrates' Court, ex p B* (n 3) 504–05.
[9] ibid 507.

Lord Rodger expressed the rationale for litigation privilege in the following terms in *Three Rivers District Council v Governor and Co of the Bank of England (Three Rivers (No 6))*:

> It is based on the idea that legal proceedings take the form of a contest in which each of the opposing parties assembles his own body of evidence and uses it to try to defeat the other, with the judge or jury determining the winner. In such a system each party should be free to prepare his case as fully as possible without the risk that his opponent will be able to recover the material generated by his preparations.[10]

Overriding Privilege by Statute

Notwithstanding the absolute nature of privilege, it can be overridden (or 'abrogated', as it is sometimes expressed in the case law) by Parliament in exceptional cases if an intention to override privilege is expressly stated in a statute or appears by 'necessary implication'.[11] Lord Hobhouse defined 'necessary implication' in *R (Morgan Grenfell & Co Ltd) v Special Commissioners of Income Tax* in the following terms: **1.09**

> A necessary implication is not the same as a reasonable implication ... A necessary implication is one which necessarily follows from the express provisions of the statute construed in their context. It distinguishes between what it would have been sensible or reasonable for Parliament to have included or what Parliament would, if it had thought about it, probably have included and what it is clear that the express language of the statute shows that the statute must have included. A necessary implication is a matter of express language and logic not interpretation.[12]

It is very rare for a statutory provision expressly to limit or override a person's right to privilege, and it is even rarer for this to be interpreted by 'necessary implication'. As discussed at paras 3.24–3.30, all of the main powers of search and seizure and compulsion in criminal investigations contain express prohibitions on seizing or compelling the production of privileged material. There are, however, provisions under the Regulation of Investigatory Powers Act 2000 (RIPA 2000) and the Investigatory Powers Act 2016 (IPA 2016) that allow investigating agencies and other public authorities access to privileged communications in exceptional circumstances by way of covert surveillance and interception.[13] The relevant provisions of the RIPA 2000 are an example of privilege being overridden by 'necessary implication',[14] whereas the IPA 2016 contains express wording to that effect. **1.10**

2 Legal Advice Privilege

In *Three Rivers (No 6)*, Lord Rodger described legal advice privilege in the following terms: '[Legal advice privilege] attaches to all communications made in confidence between **1.11**

---

[10] *Three Rivers (No 6)* (n 3) [52].
[11] *R (Morgan Grenfell & Co Ltd) v Special Commissioners of Income Tax* (n 2).
[12] ibid [45].
[13] See ch 3, s 10.
[14] *McE v Prison Service of Northern Ireland* [2009] UKHL 15, [2009] 1 AC 908.

solicitors and their clients for the purpose of giving or obtaining legal advice even at a stage where litigation is not in contemplation.'[15]

1.12 With one important clarification arising from the more recent case of *R (Jet2.com Ltd) v Civil Aviation Authority*,[16] this can be broken down into the following requirements, each of which is discussed below:

- There must be a communication;[17]
- The communication must be confidential;
- The communication must be between a client and their lawyer; and
- The dominant purpose of the communication must be giving or obtaining legal advice.

Communications

1.13 For the purposes of legal advice privilege, this has the broadest possible definition and can include any type of communication. The most obvious examples are conversations in person, phone calls, emails, and letters, but privilege can also cover text messages, other forms of instant messaging, annotations on a document, handwritten notes, and voicemail messages. Essentially, any form of communication that is capable of transmitting a message confidentially between a lawyer and their client is sufficient.

1.14 Whilst legal advice privilege is primarily concerned with communications, it also extends more broadly to certain types of documents which are not strictly communications per se, but are created by the lawyer or their client for the dominant purpose of giving or obtaining legal advice. These are discussed in more detail at paras 1.35–1.41.

Confidentiality

1.15 Confidentiality is the bedrock of legal professional privilege. If there is no confidentiality in the communication in question, there can be no privilege.

1.16 A conversation between a solicitor and their client at a police station in the presence of a police officer will not be sufficiently confidential to enable privilege to apply, even though the lawyer may be providing legal advice. However, the same conversation in a private consultation room at the police station where only the lawyer and client are present will be confidential. Privilege in the context of the police station is discussed in more detail in Chapter 6.

---

[15] *Three Rivers (No 6)* (n 3) [50].
[16] [2020] EWCA Civ 35, [2020] QB 1027, confirming that a dominant purpose test applies to legal advice privilege.
[17] Although certain categories of documents can also attract legal advice privilege; see paras 1.35–1.41.

Between a Client and their Lawyer

Who is a lawyer?
A lawyer for these purposes is a solicitor, barrister, or legal executive qualified to practise in England and Wales,[18] or a foreign qualified lawyer. The precise status of a foreign lawyer in their home jurisdiction, including how they are regulated and their level of training and experience, is not relevant for the purposes of legal advice privilege. It is their *function* that matters, and the only requirement in order for privilege to apply is that they must be acting in the capacity or function of a lawyer.[19]

1.17

Legal advice privilege applies equally to lawyers in private practice as to in-house lawyers.[20] It covers communications with and advice from counsel irrespective of whether they are instructed through a solicitor or on a direct access basis. Communications between a client and 'a clerk or subordinate' of a lawyer, such as a trainee solicitor, pupil barrister, paralegal, or secretary, can also be privileged if that person is acting in place of the lawyer and under their direction.[21]

1.18

Who is a client?
A client for these purposes can be an individual, a corporate entity or any other type of organization.

1.19

In the case of a corporate client, the contractual and professional relationship will be between the lawyer and the corporate entity itself, but a corporate entity can only operate through its employees and officers. Rather than applying to communications between all such persons and the corporate's lawyers, the effect of *Three Rivers District Council v Governor and Co of the Bank of England*[22] (*Three Rivers (No 5)*) is that legal advice privilege will only apply to communications to or from individuals within the company who are authorized to seek and receive legal advice on behalf of the corporate entity.[23] This is not the same as an employee who is only authorized to speak to the company's lawyers or to provide information to them, for example an employee who is interviewed as a witness by the company's lawyers during the course of an internal investigation.[24]

1.20

Relationship between client and lawyer
A lawyer must be acting in a professional capacity as legal adviser to a client in order for legal advice privilege to apply. This means, for example, that a situation in which a lawyer is consulted by a friend in a social context will not give rise to a privileged relationship.[25]

1.21

---

[18] *R (Prudential Plc) v Special Commissioner of Income Tax* [2013] UKSC 1, [2013] 2 AC 185 [29].
[19] *PJSC Tatneft v Gennady Bogolyubov* [2020] EWHC 2437 (Comm), [2021] 1 WLR 403 [36], [57].
[20] Although note the exception for in-house lawyers in respect of anti-competition investigations conducted by the European Commission—Case C-550/07 P *Akzo Nobel Chemicals Ltd v Commission of the European Communities* [2011] 2 AC 338.
[21] *Wheeler v Le Marchant* (1881) 17 Ch D 675, 682 (Lord Jessel MR) (CA).
[22] [2003] EWCA Civ 474, [2003] QB 1556.
[23] Confirmed in *The Director of the Serious Fraud Office v Eurasian Natural Resources Corporation Limited (SFO v ENRC Ltd)* [2018] EWCA Civ 2006, [2019] 1 WLR 791 [123].
[24] See paras 12.11–12.16.
[25] *Greenough v Gaskell* [1824-34] All ER Rep 767.

However, a lawyer does not need to have been formally instructed by a client in order for their communications to be privileged. Legal advice privilege will apply to a prospective client who has not yet decided whether to instruct the lawyer, even if the client ultimately decides not to instruct them or the lawyer declines to accept them as a client.[26]

Third parties

1.22 It follows from the above that legal advice privilege does not extend to communications with third parties, even if a lawyer communicates with a third party for the dominant purpose of advising their client.

1.23 If a non-lawyer provides legal advice to their client, such as an accountant providing advice on a tax avoidance scheme,[27] their communications will not be protected by legal advice privilege.[28]

Agents

1.24 Either client or lawyer may communicate through an agent and still maintain a claim to privilege.[29] However, the agent's involvement must be limited simply to passing on the communication between lawyer and client with no input of their own.[30]

Made for the Dominant Purpose of Giving or Obtaining Legal Advice

Legal advice

1.25 Advice must have a 'relevant legal context' in order for legal advice privilege to apply.[31] In most cases, this will not be difficult to identify, but in more marginal cases, relevant considerations will include whether:

- the advice relates to the rights, liabilities, obligations, or remedies of the client (or a third party[32]) under private or public law;[33]
- the communication falls within the policy underlying the justification for legal advice privilege, ie the occasion on which the communication takes place and the purpose for which it takes place are such as to make it reasonable to expect privilege to apply;[34]
- the lawyer is being consulted in their capacity as a lawyer and is being asked to 'put on legal spectacles';[35] and

---

[26] *Minter v Priest* [1930] AC 558, 584 (Lord Atkin) (HL).
[27] See eg *R (Prudential Plc) v Special Commissioner of Income Tax* (n 18).
[28] The advice is, however, likely to be covered by that person's duty of professional confidence, the difference being that this is a qualified right, as discussed at para 1.02 in respect of a lawyer's duty of confidentiality.
[29] *Anderson v Bank of British Columbia* (1876) 2 Ch D 644, 649 (CA); *Wheeler v Le Marchant* (n 21) 682.
[30] *Jones v Great Central Railway Co* [1910] AC 4, 6 (HL); *Re Highgrade Traders Ltd* [1984] BCLC 151, 164 (CA); *Price Waterhouse v BCCI Holdings (Luxembourg) SA* [1992] BCLC 583, 589 (Ch).
[31] *Balabel v Air India* [1988] Ch 317, 330 (CA); *Three Rivers (No 6)* (n 3) [38] (Lord Scott).
[32] *Three Rivers (No 6)* (n 3) [56] (Lord Scott).
[33] ibid [38] (Lord Scott).
[34] ibid.
[35] ibid [58], [60] (Lord Scott).

- the context is one in which it is reasonable for the client to consult the special professional knowledge and skills of a lawyer, so that the lawyer can give the client sound advice as to what they should do and how to do it, or what they should not do.[36]

1.26 Legal advice privilege will cover advice about not only what the law is, but also the application of the law[37] and 'what should prudently and sensibly be done in the relevant legal context'.[38]

1.27 Advice provided by a criminal defence lawyer will almost always have a relevant legal context, usually because their client will be seeking legal advice as a suspect in an investigation or a defendant in a prosecution or otherwise in relation to their potential liability under the criminal law.[39]

Broad range of communications

1.28 The scope of legal advice privilege is broader than applying only to communications conveying legal advice from a lawyer to their client or explicit requests from the client for advice.[40] As long as there is a relevant legal context, it will also extend to communications that do not expressly seek or provide legal advice but form part of the 'continuum of communication' between the lawyer and their client, with information being 'passed by the solicitor or client to the other as part of the continuum aimed at keeping both informed so that advice may be sought and given as required'.[41] Confirming this principle in *Balabel v Air India*, Taylor LJ said that: '[a] letter from the client containing information may end with such words as "please advise me what I should do". But, even if it does not, there will usually be implied in the relationship an overall expectation that the solicitor will at each stage, whether asked specifically or not, tender appropriate advice'.[42]

1.29 In *Three Rivers (No 6)*, Lord Carswell expressed the scope of legal advice privilege in similarly broad terms:

> [A]ll communications between a solicitor and his client relating to a transaction in which the solicitor has been instructed for the purpose of obtaining legal advice will be privileged, notwithstanding that they do not contain advice on matters of law or construction, provided that they are directly related to the performance by the solicitor of his professional duty as legal adviser of his client.[43]

1.30 The effect of these decisions is that the vast majority of communications passing between a client and their lawyer will be covered by legal advice privilege.

---

[36] ibid [62] (Baroness Hale).
[37] *R (Jet2.com Ltd) v Civil Aviation Authority* (n 16) [68].
[38] *Balabel v Air India* (n 31) 330.
[39] Should it be needed, confirmation that legal advice privilege applies to criminal law advice can be found in the judgment of Lord Rodger in *Three Rivers (No 6)* (n 3) [56]: 'Legal advice privilege also applies to advice on criminal matters, which it may not always be easy to characterise as relating, strictly speaking, to rights and obligations of the client.'
[40] *Balabel v Air India* (n 31) 330.
[41] ibid.
[42] ibid.
[43] *Three Rivers (No 6)* (n 3) [111], summarizing the principle affirmed in an earlier case, *Minter v Priest* (n 26), which he considered to be unaffected by *Balabel v Air India* (n 31).

Dominant purpose

1.31 Following the Court of Appeal's decision in *R (Jet2.com Ltd) v Civil Aviation Authority*,[44] there is no longer any doubt that a dominant purpose test applies to legal advice privilege. The giving or obtaining of legal advice must be the *dominant* (or sole) purpose of the communication rather than just *a* purpose.

1.32 The dominant purpose test can present difficulties in two important areas. The first concerns the in-house lawyer, whose role will often stray outside the confines of pure legal adviser. Their input may be sought on quasi-legal or non-legal issues, perhaps through membership of an internal group or committee. For example, general counsel might be a member of the board or management team of their company, and, in a meeting, they might be asked for advice on a particular issue that draws on their expertise not only as a lawyer but also as a manager. Depending on the circumstances, it is unlikely that this advice would satisfy the dominant purpose test if their ability to analyse the issue whilst wearing 'legal spectacles' is only part of the reason why their advice is being sought.

1.33 The second issue arising from *Jet2* concerns multi-recipient emails sent to lawyers and non-lawyers. A client may email their lawyer and another professional adviser, such as an accountant, asking them both for advice on a particular issue. If the email were to be sent to the lawyer only, it would be privileged. However, when sent in identical terms in one email to both the lawyer and the other professional adviser, it will most likely have a dual purpose and therefore fail to satisfy the dominant purpose requirement.[45]

Other Aspects of Legal Advice Privilege

Evidence of privileged communications

1.34 Legal advice privilege applies not only to privileged communications themselves, but also to documents evidencing such communications and anything that reveals the substance of legal advice, including in a paraphrased or summarized form.[46] An obvious example is a solicitor's attendance note of a privileged conversation with their client. It is the conversation recorded in the note that is the communication attracting privilege, not the note itself. Another example is where legal advice received by a company is disseminated more widely within the organization beyond the client group on a confidential basis, such as at a board or committee meeting. In this case, the communication through which the advice is conveyed is not itself covered by legal advice privilege as it is a communication between the client and a third party or between one third party and another. However, privilege continues to apply to the advice that is being shared.[47] This means that if there is a note of the meeting, the section recording the legal advice is treated as privileged and can be redacted if, for example, it is later disclosed in the course of legal proceedings.

---

[44] *R (Jet2.com Ltd) v Civil Aviation Authority* (n 16).
[45] See further discussion at paras 4.63–4.65.
[46] *Three Rivers (No 5)* (n 22) [19]; *USP Strategies Plc v London General Holdings Ltd (No 2)* [2004] EWHC 373 (Ch), [2004] All ER (D) 132 (Mar) [20].
[47] Although subject to the principles concerning loss of confidentiality discussed at paras 1.77–1.79.

Documents

Although essentially concerned with communications, legal advice privilege also applies to certain types of documents which are not strictly communications per se, but which arise out of the client-lawyer relationship and are created for the dominant purpose of seeking or providing legal advice.

1.35

Lawyers' working papers

One such category of documents is lawyers' working papers, such as their own confidential notes and documents relating to the matter on which they are instructed.[48] These documents might never be shared with the client, but they are nevertheless placed on the same footing as communications between the client and their lawyer.[49] Examples include comments on and analysis of prosecution evidence, a legal research note relating to a client's case, and notes setting out the areas on which instructions are needed and disclosure to request from the prosecution.

1.36

In the first instance decision of *The Director of the Serious Fraud Office v Eurasian Natural Resources Corp Ltd*, it was suggested by Andrews J that a claim for privilege over lawyers' working papers would only succeed if the documents betrayed the trend of the legal advice.[50] Whilst much of Andrews J's decision was subsequently overturned by the Court of Appeal, the Court declined to give an opinion on this particular issue. The authors' view is that this is not an accurate reflection of the law. As others have noted, the two key Court of Appeal authorities that confirmed the application of legal advice privilege to lawyers' working papers, *Balabel* and *Three Rivers (No 5)*, imposed no such requirement.[51] The authors suggest that Andrews J's comments (and similar comments by Hildyard J in *The RBS Rights Issue Litigation*[52]) should be understood as applying only to notes of non-privileged internal investigation interviews prepared by lawyers rather than lawyers' working papers generally.[53]

1.37

Draft documents

Legal advice privilege applies to draft documents prepared by a lawyer in relation to the matter on which they are instructed.[54] This includes drafts of documents that will not be privileged in their final form, such as a letter of representations to the CPS or a defence case statement. Even once the non-privileged final version has been submitted or served on the opposing party, draft versions will remain privileged.[55]

1.38

---

[48] *Balabel v Air India* (n 31); *Three Rivers (No 5)* (n 22) [30]; *The RBS Rights Issue Litigation* [2016] EWHC 3161 (Ch), [2017] 1 WLR 1991 [99]; older authorities include *Greenough v Gaskell* (n 25); *Ainsworth v Wilding (No 2)* [1900] 2 Ch 315 (Ch) 323.
[49] *Ainsworth v Wilding (No 2)* (n 48) 323.
[50] [2017] EWHC 1017 (QB), [2017] 1 WLR 4205 [97].
[51] See eg Colin Passmore, *Privilege* (4th edn, Sweet & Maxwell 2020) paras 2-322–2-323; Tamara Oppenheimer KC, Rebecca Loveridge, and Samuel Rabinowitz, 'Privilege: The UK Perspective' in Judith Seddon and others (eds), *The Practitioner's Guide to Global Investigations* (7th edn, Law Business Research Ltd 2023) vol 1, fn 84.
[52] *The RBS Rights Issue Litigation* (n 48) [105].
[53] See discussion at para 12.23.
[54] *USP Strategies Plc v London General Holdings Ltd (No 2)* (n 46) [48], referring to *Three Rivers (No 5)* (n 22) [29].
[55] See eg *Visx Inc v Nidex Co* [1999] FSR 91, 106–07 (CA).

Documents prepared by the client

1.39 If a client creates a document that relates to the matter on which legal advice is being sought and the dominant purpose of its creation is so that it can be provided to a lawyer in order for legal advice to be obtained, the document will be privileged.[56]

Other documents indicating substance of advice

1.40 More generally, legal advice privilege will extend to other documents whose disclosure would 'give a clue' to or 'betray the trend' of advice which the lawyer has provided to their client.[57] It has been suggested that this can include an *inference* as to the substance of the advice, but only if there is a 'definite and reasonable foundation in the contents of the document for the suggested inference as to the substance of the legal advice given' rather than 'merely something which would allow one to wonder or speculate whether legal advice had been obtained and as to the substance of that advice'.[58]

Communications between lawyers

1.41 Communications between two or more sets of lawyers instructed by the same client are covered by legal advice privilege if they relate to the provision of legal advice to their common client.[59] This includes lawyers of different disciplines, such as a criminal defence solicitor contacting their client's divorce solicitor, as well as communications with counsel and foreign lawyers. This is a separate concept from joint interest privilege and common interest privilege (see Section 6 below).

Items Not Covered by Legal Advice Privilege

1.42 Notwithstanding the broad scope of legal advice privilege, it does not extend to everything generated as part of the lawyer-client relationship. A non-exhaustive list of examples of what will not, without more, be covered by legal advice privilege includes:

- Details of a client's name, address and telephone number, and other information that is recorded by a solicitor as a formality before legal advice is sought or given and which merely creates the channel through which advice may later flow.[60]
- A client care or engagement letter, insofar as it goes no further than merely setting out the terms on which a solicitor is to act for a client.[61]
- Emails between a lawyer and their client concerning compliance, anti-money laundering and other 'on-boarding' matters.

---

[56] *The Southwark and Vauxhall Water Company v Quick* (1878) 3 QBD 315, 322–23 (CA).
[57] *Lyell v Kennedy (No 3)* (1884) 27 Ch D 1, 26 (CA); *Ventouris v Mountain (The Italia Express) (No 1)* [1991] 1 WLR 607, 615F (CA); *Re Edwardian Group Ltd* [2017] EWHC 2805 (Ch), [2017] All ER (D) 109 (Nov) [34], [37].
[58] *Re Edwardian Group Ltd* (n 57) [37], adopting the distinction from the Australian case of *AWB v Terence Cole* [2006] FCA 571.
[59] See eg *Hughes v Biddulph* (1827) 38 ER 777, which confirmed this principle in the context of communications between a client's country and town solicitors, and the Australian case of *Trade Practices Commission v Sterling* (1979) 36 FLR 244 [4] (FCA). In the view of Colin Passmore, this principle is justified on the basis that the solicitor contacting the other lawyer is in effect acting as the client's agent for the purpose of communicating instructions and/or receiving advice. See Passmore (n 51) para 2-207.
[60] *R (Miller Gardner Solicitors) v Minshull Street Crown Court* [2002] EWHC 3077 (Admin), [2002] All ER (D) 338 (Dec).
[61] *Dickinson v Rushmer* [2001] All ER (D) 369 (Dec) (Ch).

- Records showing dates and times of calls and meetings with a client.⁶²
- A lawyer's attendance note recording nothing more than what happened in open court or in a meeting with an opposing party.⁶³
- Correspondence between a lawyer and their client which does no more than acknowledge receipt of a document or suggest a date for a meeting.⁶⁴

1.43 It has been suggested that instructions to a lawyer to do a particular thing, for example to prepare a legal document, are generally not privileged, because instructions to do something do not necessarily amount to a request for advice.⁶⁵ However, this reflects too narrow an interpretation of 'legal advice'. In preparing a legal document for a client, a lawyer is effectively advising them (by implication at the very least) that the document they have prepared and the information they have included reflects what is most appropriate for their client's purposes. Furthermore, if preparing the document or doing whatever else the client has asked will be contrary to the client's interests or there is some other important issue of which they should be made aware, the lawyer will be expected (and obliged) to advise them accordingly. As such, a request for a lawyer to do something ought to be seen as a communication that falls within the broad scope of legal advice privilege confirmed in *Balabel*.⁶⁶

1.44 There is some uncertainty over whether a reference to the subject matter of legal advice is privileged. The case of *USP Strategies Plc v London General Holdings Ltd (No 2)*⁶⁷ would suggest not. In that case, privilege was claimed over documents or parts of documents that indicated the subject matter of legal advice that had been obtained but not its content or the instructions given. Ultimately, Mann J did not need to reach a firm view on the issue as he held that any privilege that may have existed had been waived in any event. However, he indicated his instinct that such references would not, as a matter of principle, be privileged.

1.45 In *R v Manchester Crown Court ex p Rogers*,⁶⁸ however, in the course of dismissing an argument that a solicitor's record of an appointment with a client was privileged, Lord Bingham suggested that a reference to the subject matter of legal advice in such a record would be: 'Production is sought of nothing relating to legal advice or the subject matter of legal advice. Any such reference in, for example, an attendance note can be covered up, blacked out or obliterated.'⁶⁹

1.46 The authors suggest that a more appropriate way to approach this issue is not simply to ask whether references to the subject matter of legal advice can ever, as a matter of principle, be covered by privilege, but rather to consider the extent to which the reference reveals the actual request for legal advice that the client has communicated to their lawyer. A reference to the subject matter may amount to nothing more than 'advice on criminal case', but it could include something more detailed, such as 'advice on whether a money laundering offence

---

⁶² *R (Miller Gardner Solicitors) v Minshull Street Crown Court* (n 60).
⁶³ *Parry v News Group Newspapers Ltd* [1990] NLJR 1719 (CA).
⁶⁴ *Balabel v Air India* (n 31) 330.
⁶⁵ *Commissioner of Taxation v Coombes* [1999] FCA 842 [31].
⁶⁶ See para 1.28.
⁶⁷ *USP Strategies Plc v London General Holdings Ltd (No 2)* (n 46).
⁶⁸ [1999] 1 WLR 832 (QB).
⁶⁹ ibid 839.

has been committed by handling the proceeds of the sale of X property'. In this example, the subject matter essentially sets out the request for advice that the client will have communicated to their lawyer. If privilege can also cover *evidence* of privileged communications passing between a client and their lawyer, it would seem logical for references such as these to be included within its scope. Whilst this approach does not fully align with Mann J's indication in *USP Strategies*, the authors consider it to be more consistent with what was stated by the Court of Appeal in *Three Rivers (No 5)*, discussed at para 1.34.

3 Litigation Privilege

1.47 In *Three Rivers (No 6)*, Lord Carswell set out what is considered to be the authoritative definition of litigation privilege:

> [C]ommunications between parties or their solicitors and third parties for the purpose of obtaining information or advice in connection with existing or contemplated litigation are privileged, but only when the following conditions are satisfied: (a) litigation must be in progress or in contemplation; (b) the communications must have been made for the sole or dominant purpose of conducting that litigation; (c) the litigation must be adversarial, not investigative or inquisitorial.[70]

The key distinctions between legal advice privilege and litigation privilege are that: (1) litigation privilege is chiefly concerned with communications with third parties rather than between a lawyer and their client; and (2) litigation privilege only arises in the context of litigation (in progress or reasonably in contemplation).

1.48 Each component of Lord Carswell's definition is considered below.

Communications

1.49 'Communication' has the same broad meaning as with legal advice privilege (see para 1.13).

1.50 Litigation privilege also covers documents which are not, strictly speaking, communications but which are created for one or more of the purposes set out at para 1.60.[71]

Confidentiality

1.51 Although not expressly stated by Lord Carswell, confidentiality is an essential requirement for both legal advice privilege and litigation privilege. The authors of *The Law of Privilege*

---

[70] *Three Rivers (No 6)* (n 3) [102].
[71] *Waugh v British Railways Board* [1980] AC 521, 544 (Lord Edmund-Davies) (HL), quoting with approval the Australian case of *Grant v Downs* (1976) 135 CLR 674, 677 (High Court (Australia)).

suggest that, for the purposes of litigation privilege, confidentiality does not mean a legal or equitable duty of confidence but rather simply that the communication or document is 'not properly available for use'.[72]

Between a Party or their Lawyer and a Third Party

1.52 Litigation privilege is principally concerned with a party to existing or contemplated litigation or their lawyer communicating with a third party in order to prepare for/conduct that litigation. Third parties in this context will typically include experts, witnesses of fact, character witnesses, and family and friends of the party to the litigation, but litigation privilege will not apply to communications with adverse parties or potential opponents in litigation, such as a prosecutor or the police.

1.53 'Lawyer' for these purposes has the same meaning as with legal advice privilege (see paras 1.17–1.18).

Litigation

1.54 Litigation for the purposes of litigation privilege means proceedings that are adversarial rather than investigative or inquisitorial.[73] In criminal cases, this means a prosecution (ie charges brought by the police, CPS, SFO, FCA, etc.) rather than merely an investigation. It also includes extradition proceedings, confiscation proceedings, applications for a variety of orders relating to the proceeds of crime, such as account freezing or account forfeiture orders, and potentially any other ancillary applications or proceedings that come before the criminal courts and involve two (or more) adverse parties.

1.55 Certain types of application which are made to the court during the course of a criminal investigation, such as applications for search warrants or production orders, could be said to be sufficiently adversarial in and of themselves to engage litigation privilege, at least as far as communications made for the dominant purpose of the conduct of that particular application (as opposed to the wider investigation) are concerned. However, the Court of Appeal in *United States of America v Philip Morris Inc* appears to have shut down the possibility of such an argument being made, holding that:

> There is ... a clear distinction to be made between adversarial proceedings (pending or contemplated) between two or more parties which are destined, in theory at any rate, for a contested hearing in a court or court-like body, and proceedings whereby a party may compel a non-party to produce relevant documents for the purposes of the main proceedings. The non-party may well wish to seek legal advice about his obligations in this regard, but all that will be in issue is whether he is or is not legally obliged to do what is required of

---

[72] Bankim Thanki (ed), *The Law of Privilege* (3rd edn, OUP 2018) para 3.34, referring to *Bourns Inc v Raychem Corp (No 3)* [1999] CLC 1029, 1041 (CA).
[73] *Three Rivers (No 6)* (n 3) [102].

him. In this context there is never any question of collecting evidence from third parties as part of the material for the brief in the action, or of seeking information which might lead to the obtaining of such evidence.[74]

Reasonably in Contemplation

1.56 Litigation must already be underway or reasonably in contemplation at the time the relevant communication is made. 'Reasonably in contemplation' is not clearly defined, although the authorities do provide some guidance as to what will *not* suffice:

- a 'mere possibility' of litigation;
- a 'distinct possibility that sooner or later someone might make a claim'; or
- a 'general apprehension of future litigation'.[75]

What is not required, however, is a greater than 50 per cent chance of litigation.[76]

1.57 Although litigation privilege will usually be claimed by a party to the litigation in question or, if the litigation is not yet underway, a prospective party to the litigation that is reasonably in contemplation, it is possible for litigation privilege to arise in favour of a non-party, such as a complainant in a criminal case, provided the necessary conditions for litigation privilege are otherwise satisfied.[77]

1.58 Although a criminal investigation itself will not constitute litigation for the purposes of privilege, just because a case has not yet progressed beyond the investigation stage does not mean that litigation cannot reasonably be in contemplation. It may be clear to a solicitor who attends the police station immediately after a client has been arrested that they will be charged, even if it is unlikely to happen for many months. The evidence put to the client in interview may be of such strength that, irrespective of the client's instructions and what, if any, account they put forward in interview, the solicitor's professional opinion is that a prosecution is likely. Care is still needed, however, when relying on litigation privilege at this early stage of a case. This is discussed in more detail at paras 6.17–6.20.

1.59 Ultimately, the stage at which litigation can be said to be reasonably in contemplation will vary from one case to the next and will be fact-specific. A detailed review of the case law relating to reasonable contemplation of litigation in the context of internal investigations (but also of relevance to criminal investigations more generally) can be found at paras 12.38–12.80.

---

[74] *United States of America v Philip Morris Inc* [2004] EWCA Civ 330, [2004] 1 CLC 811 [72]. Note that in *Al Sadeq v Dechert LLP* [2024] EWCA Civ 28, Popplewell LJ did not consider *United States of America v Philip Morris Inc* (*Philip Morris*) to be authority for the submission (which he rejected) that a non-party to litigation cannot rely on litigation privilege.
[75] *Philip Morris* (n 74) [68].
[76] ibid.
[77] *Al Sadeq v Dechert LLP* (n 74).

Purpose

Lord Carswell's formulation as to the purpose of the relevant communication can cause some confusion, since reference is made to two purposes ('for the purpose of obtaining information or advice in connection with existing or contemplated litigation' and 'for the sole or dominant purpose of conducting that litigation'), only one of which is expressed in terms of dominance. However, from the various formulations that have been expressed in other cases, the authors suggest that it should be understood as a statement to the effect that, once litigation is in progress or in reasonable contemplation, litigation privilege will apply if the sole or dominant purpose of the relevant communication or document is: **1.60**

1. to enable legal advice to be sought or given in connection with the conduct of the litigation;
2. to obtain evidence or information to be used in or in connection with the conduct of the litigation; or
3. to conduct or aid in the conduct of the litigation (insofar as not covered by the above).[78]

Note the inclusion of 'in connection with' in point 2. This reflects the fact that litigation privilege is not limited only to documents that are intended to be used as evidence in the litigation.[79]

'Conducting litigation' includes avoiding or settling litigation or deciding whether to do so,[80] although it does not extend to documents which are concerned with the settlement or avoidance of litigation but which neither seek advice or information for the purpose of conducting litigation nor reveal the nature of such advice or information.[81] **1.61**

It is not enough if the relevant litigation purpose is only *a* purpose and of no more than equal importance to one or more other purposes; it must be the sole or dominant purpose.[82] It is the purpose of the creator/sender of the document/communication or of the person or authority under whose direction it is created/sent that is relevant,[83] and it must be assessed by reference to the purpose of that party at the time it is created/sent. **1.62**

In criminal cases, once a prosecution is underway, examples of communications that will satisfy the test for litigation privilege include speaking to potential defence witnesses to take their account of events, instructing experts to produce reports on issues in the case, and **1.63**

---

[78] See eg Hamblen J's formulation in *Starbev GP Ltd v Interbrew Central European Holding BV* [2013] EWHC 4038 (Comm), [2014] All ER (D) 116 (Jan) [11], cited with approval by Charles Hollander QC (sitting as a Deputy Judge of the High Court) in *Kyla Shipping Co Ltd v Freight Trading Ltd* [2022] EWHC 376 (Comm) [20]. Hamblen J's formulation does not refer to the 'conduct of litigation', but it is clear from *Three Rivers (No 6)* (n 3) and *WH Holding Limited v E20 Stadium LLP* [2018] EWCA Civ 2652, [2018] All ER (D) 17 (Dec) [27] that this is required. As to the inclusion of 'to aid in the conduct' of litigation see *Waugh v British Railways Board* (n 71) 544 (Lord Edmund-Davies), quoting with approval Barwick CJ in *Grant v Downs* (n 71) 677.
[79] *Re Highgrade Traders* (n 30) 174.
[80] *SFO v ENRC Ltd* (n 23) [102], [118]; *WH Holding Limited v E20 Stadium LLP* (n 78) [12]–[15], [27].
[81] *WH Holding Limited v E20 Stadium LLP* (n 78).
[82] *Waugh v British Railways Board* (n 71).
[83] ibid 544 (Lord Edmund-Davies), quoting with approval Barwick CJ in *Grant v Downs* (n 71) 677.

contacting other third parties to obtain evidence relevant to the defence case. Before a client is charged, if a prosecution is reasonably in contemplation, litigation privilege will apply, for example, to communications with the client's psychiatrist to obtain information relevant to the question of whether a prosecution is in the public interest, with the intention of using it in support of a letter of representations to the CPS seeking to persuade them not to charge the client.

1.64 A detailed review of the case law relating to the dominant purpose requirement of litigation privilege in the context of internal investigations (but also of relevance to criminal investigations more generally) can be found at paras 12.81–12.113.

4 Pre-existing Documents

1.65 As a general rule, documents created for a purpose other than obtaining/providing legal advice or conducting litigation (loosely described as 'pre-existing documents') do not become privileged simply because they are subsequently provided to a lawyer by their client, even if the purpose of providing them is to enable the lawyer to advise their client or to conduct litigation on their behalf. If, for example, a client under investigation for harassment provides their lawyer with text messages and emails exchanged with the complainant so that the lawyer can advise on whether they have committed a criminal offence, those messages and emails will not become privileged. Their existence is entirely independent of the privileged client-lawyer relationship and the use to which they may subsequently be put does not alter their character.

1.66 One exception to this rule is that, in certain circumstances, if an original non-privileged document is in the hands of a third party and a lawyer obtains a copy for the purpose of litigation, the copy will be privileged even though the original is not. This principle was established by the case of *The Palermo*[84] and was followed in *Watson v Cammell Laird & Co*,[85] although it has attracted judicial criticism[86] and some commentators have advised caution in seeking to apply it.[87]

1.67 The facts of *The Palermo* were that there had been a collision between two vessels, the Palermo and the Rivoli, and the Board of Trade had taken depositions from the master and members of the crew of the Rivoli. In proceedings brought by the owners of the Rivoli against the owners of the Palermo, the latter sought discovery of copies of the depositions that the plaintiffs' solicitors had obtained from the Board of Trade. The application was necessary because the Board of Trade had refused to provide copies to the defendants. The copies had been obtained by the plaintiffs' solicitors for the purposes of the action 'to form part of the brief' and were therefore held to be privileged. Discovery was refused.

---

[84] (1883) 9 PD 6 (CA).
[85] [1959] 1 WLR 702 (CA).
[86] See eg *Ventouris v Mountain (The Italia Express) (No 1)* (n 57) 616–17 (Bingham LJ).
[87] See eg Thanki (n 72) para 4.14.

It mattered not for what purpose the original depositions were taken or the fact that they were not privileged.

In *Watson v Cammell Laird & Co*, a case which also concerned copies of documents made by the plaintiff's solicitor for the purposes of litigation, Lord Evershed MR was not persuaded by the submission that, because the original documents would be liable to be produced at the trial in response to a subpoena served on the person in possession of them, and since the originals were not privileged, a mere verbatim copy could be in no better position. Whilst that may well have been the case, Lord Evershed MR thought that the question of privilege did not really have any significance in regard to the original. The only question the Court was concerned with was whether the copy document had come into existence by being obtained by the solicitor for the purpose of advising his client in regard to the litigation.[88] It had, and therefore it was held to be privileged.

1.68

Another exception to the general rule is that, if a selection of non-privileged third party (rather than a client's own) documents copied or assembled by a solicitor betrays the trend of the legal advice that they are providing to their client, those documents will be privileged.[89] However, this is only likely to arise in exceptional circumstances, especially in 'an age of indiscriminate photocopying', to adopt the phrase of Bingham LJ in *Ventouris v Mountain (The Italia Express) (No 1)*.[90]

1.69

5 Loss of Privilege

Despite the 'once privileged, always privileged' maxim, it is possible for privilege to be lost, intentionally or unintentionally, in a number of circumstances. Losing or waiving privilege is an extremely important issue for criminal practitioners and much of this book examines in detail the specific circumstances which can cause privilege to be lost. What follows is a general overview of the key underlying principles which are expanded upon in the course of later chapters.

1.70

There are a number of ways in which the right to assert privilege may be lost:

1.71

1. Loss of confidentiality.
2. Waiver.
3. Collateral waiver.
4. Inadvertent disclosure.
5. Implied waiver, for example by suing a legal adviser.[91]

It is only the client, as the privilege holder, who is entitled to waive privilege. A lawyer is not permitted to waive their client's privilege unless authorized to do so. However, it is possible for privilege to be lost or waived as a result of a lawyer's actions (and even the actions of a

1.72

---

[88] *Watson v Cammell Laird & Co* (n 85) 704.
[89] *Lyell v Kennedy (No 3)* (n 57), as interpreted by Bingham LJ in *Ventouris v Mountain (The Italia Express) (No 1)* (n 57) 615; *Sumitomo Corpn v Credit Lyonnais Rouse Ltd* [2001] EWCA Civ 1152, [2002] 1 WLR 479 [72].
[90] *Ventouris v Mountain (The Italia Express) (No 1)* (n 57) 621.
[91] See Leggatt J's helpful summary in *Serdar Mohammed v Ministry of Defence* [2013] EWHC 4478 [14] (QB).

third party, such as an expert witness), even if there is no intention to do so, as the question of whether privilege has been lost or waived is assessed objectively. Given this strict and objective interpretation, a lawyer's mistake can severely prejudice their client's position and have serious professional consequences.

Loss of Confidentiality

1.73 Confidentiality is an essential requirement for privilege; once it is lost, privilege can no longer apply. It has been suggested that confidentiality in this context means that the relevant document or information is 'not properly available for use'.[92] Loss of privilege as a result of confidentiality being lost is sometimes described as a 'waiver' of privilege, but this is not strictly a correct application of the term. It is more accurate to say that privilege cannot be claimed because confidentiality has been lost.[93]

1.74 Confidentiality is not a binary quality.[94] Whilst confidentiality will be lost in its entirety if a party does an act which has the effect of making a document or information public,[95] a document can cease to be confidential against a particular person or persons but remain confidential as against 'the rest of the world'. This means the right to assert privilege may only be lost against those who have seen the document.

References in open court

1.75 A privileged document may enter the public domain and thereby cease to be confidential in all respects if it is referred to or quoted in open court and sufficient publicity is given to its contents so that it can no longer be regarded as confidential. This is a question of fact and degree.[96] However, there is a distinction between the information in a document and the document itself,[97] and it is possible for confidentiality over part of its contents to be lost without losing confidentiality over the document as a whole, depending on the detail and extent of the references.[98]

1.76 Confidentiality may also be lost if references made in court, although not of themselves sufficient to destroy confidentiality according to the above, engage the principle of open justice which gives the public a right of access to the evidence placed before a court and referred to during a hearing so that the way and basis on which the matter has been decided can properly be understood.[99] Provisions relating to open justice in criminal proceedings can be found in Crim PR 5 and Crim PD 2 (and in case law). Ultimately, access through open justice is a matter within the discretion of the court and should not be applied

---

[92] *Bourns Inc v Raychem Corp* (n 72) 1041.
[93] *Serdar Mohammed v Ministry of Defence* (n 91) [14].
[94] *Jinxin Inc v Aser Media Pte Limited* [2022] EWHC 2856 (Comm), [2023] 1 WLR 1084 [45].
[95] *Serdar Mohammed v Ministry of Defence* (n 91) [14].
[96] ibid [19], as summarized by Hildyard J in *SL Claimants v Tesco Plc* [2019] EWHC 3315 (Ch), [2019] All ER (D) 30 (Dec) [37].
[97] *SL Claimants v Tesco Plc* (n 96).
[98] As was the case in *SL Claimants v Tesco Plc* (n 96).
[99] See discussion in ibid [37], referring to Leggat J's analysis in *Serdar Mohammed v Ministry of Defence* (n 91) [20].

mechanistically. It does not confer an unqualified right of access to documents that have been referred to, especially where the references have been sparing and unspecific, and/or where no specific or material reference has actually been made, although the court has considered the contents.[100]

Confidential disclosure to third parties

Disclosure of privileged material to a third party does not automatically result in a complete loss of confidentiality. It is possible for privileged material to be shared on a confidential basis with one or more third parties without destroying its overall confidential nature. Confidentiality, and therefore privilege, will usually be lost as against the third parties with whom it has been shared,[101] but privilege can continue to be asserted against the rest of the world. The following example is often cited:

1.77

> If A shows a privileged document to his six best friends, he will not be able to assert privilege if one of those friends sues him because the document is not confidential as between him and the friend. But the fact six other people have seen it does not prevent him claiming privilege as against the rest of the world.[102]

The circumstances of the disclosure must carry an obligation or expectation of confidence. This can be express or implied. In *Gotha City v Sotheby's (No 1)*,[103] for example, a dispute arose over a privileged letter of advice sent by solicitors to their client, C, which was later shared with Sotheby's, and a minute of a meeting between the solicitors, C and Sotheby's at which information was provided to the solicitors by C for the purpose of obtaining legal advice. Sotheby's were involved as they held a painting on C's behalf over which ownership was disputed. In proceedings brought against Sotheby's and C, the plaintiff, who claimed to be the owner, sought disclosure of the letter and minutes of the meeting on the basis that privilege over the letter had been lost when it was shared with Sotheby's and privilege over the instructions provided in the meeting had been lost because Sotheby's were present. Despite neither the disclosure of the privileged letter nor the meeting having been expressly stated to be confidential by the parties, the Court of Appeal was prepared to recognize an implied agreement to that effect. Staughton LJ considered this to be 'the sort of situation where, in the ordinary way, one would expect confidentiality to be assumed by all present rather than expressly agreed upon'. Furthermore, there appeared to be 'a plain inference that the communications were intended to be confidential and understood to be confidential as between [the parties]'.[104] As such, there had been no wider loss of confidentiality over the material and privilege could still be maintained as against the rest of the world, including against the plaintiff.

1.78

---

[100] *SL Claimants v Tesco Plc* (n 96) [41].
[101] Although see para 1.87 for a discussion about the possibility of a loss of confidentiality for a limited purpose only.
[102] *Gotha City v Sotheby's (No 1)* [1998] 1 WLR 114, 121 (CA); *USP Strategies Plc v London General Holdings Ltd (No 2)* (n 46) [19].
[103] *Gotha City v Sotheby's (No 1)* (n 102) 121.
[104] ibid 122.

1.79 Common examples of confidential disclosure of privileged material include dissemination of legal advice obtained by a company to individuals within the same organization who are not part of the 'client' group, a lawyer sharing their advice with a client's non-legal advisers to help with the advice they are providing on the same matter, and a client sharing legal advice with a partner or family member.

Waiver

1.80 In *Serdar Mohammed v Ministry of Defence* Leggatt J said that 'true waiver' will occur 'if one party either expressly consents to the use of privileged material by another party or chooses to disclose the information to the other party in circumstances which imply consent to its use'.[105] The distinction between waiver and loss of confidentiality is not always clear, but in general terms, waiver tends to be associated more with a voluntary decision to disclose privileged material for a particular purpose despite the right to withhold disclosure,[106] whereas loss of confidentiality has less to do with the intention or purpose of the disclosure and is more concerned with the fact that a third party has seen privileged material such that it can no longer be regarded as confidential as against them, regardless of the circumstances.

1.81 A party is entitled to waive privilege at any stage of proceedings. Waiver may be general (ie no restrictions as to use of the material are imposed on the recipient) or limited in scope.[107] However, if privilege over certain material is waived during the course of court proceedings, the waiver will extend to other material relating to the same issue through what is known as 'collateral waiver'. This is discussed further at paras 1.94–1.96.

1.82 Waiver is assessed on an objective basis. If, objectively, a party's actions cause privilege to be waived, they cannot later claim that waiver did not occur simply because they, subjectively, assert that there was no waiver.[108] A reference to legal advice or privileged information in a witness statement or correspondence accompanied by a statement to the effect that it is not to be taken as a waiver of privilege is not, therefore, determinative and will not prevent a court from finding that, as a matter of law, objectively considered, the statement does in fact give rise to a waiver.[109]

Different types of disclosure

1.83 In order to understand the principles governing waiver of privilege fully, it is helpful to distinguish between two broad types of disclosure that can cause privilege to be waived. The first is where a privileged document *in its entirety* is disclosed to a third party with express or implied consent as to its use by the recipient. Here, there can be no suggestion that privilege over the document has not been waived, albeit this may be on a limited basis only. The

---

[105] *Serdar Mohammed v Ministry of Defence* (n 91) [14].
[106] The authors of Hodge Malek (ed), *Phipson on Evidence* (20th edn, Sweet & Maxwell 2021) suggest the following helpful definition of waiver: 'Waiver of privilege properly named involves the voluntary production of documents where there would otherwise be a right to object to compulsory production' (para 26-01).
[107] *Serdar Mohammed v Ministry of Defence* (n 91) [14].
[108] *R (AL) v Serious Fraud Office* [2018] EWHC 856 (Admin), [2018] 1 WLR 4557 [118].
[109] *Digicel Ltd v Cable & Wireless Plc* [2009] EWHC 1437 (Ch), [2009] All ER (D) 44 (Jul) [31].

second type of disclosure is where privileged advice or other privileged material is partially quoted, summarized, mentioned, or referred to in some other way but is not revealed in full. This is less straightforward and is the focus of much of the discussion below.

In criminal proceedings, waiver of the second kind most often arises at trial when, in an attempt to prevent an adverse inference being drawn from their silence when interviewed by the police, a defendant discloses in evidence the content of the legal advice they received at the police station. This is discussed in more detail at paras 6.39–6.47 and in Chapter 10, Section 4. **1.84**

Limited waiver
A limited waiver will limit the use to which the material may be put by the receiving party and will maintain privilege in all other respects and against all other parties. A limited waiver may be either express or implied. If disputed, the question of whether a waiver is only limited and, if so, the parameters of the limitation is determined by reference to all the circumstances of the disclosure, in particular what was expressly or impliedly communicated between the person sending and the person receiving the documents in question and what they must or ought reasonably to have understood.[110] **1.85**

Limited waivers typically arise in criminal cases where a cooperating party, often a company, voluntarily discloses privileged material to investigators for the limited purpose of assisting with their investigation and any subsequent prosecution. This is explored in more detail in Chapter 7. **1.86**

There can be some conflict between the concept of a limited waiver and the principle that once a document ceases to be confidential as against a third party, privilege can no longer be claimed against them. The authors of *Phipson on Evidence* draw attention to several cases in which privileged material has been shared with another party on the basis of a limited waiver, and has therefore ceased to be confidential as between those parties, but the recipient has been prevented from using the privileged documents in subsequent proceedings between the same parties.[111] The authors of this work suggest that this apparent conflict can be reconciled (at least to some extent) if the loss of confidentiality as a result of the disclosure is seen as only a limited loss of confidentiality for the particular purpose for which privilege has been waived. In other words, the material disclosed remains confidential as against the third party for all purposes other than those covered by the limited waiver. Whilst this may somewhat stretch the meaning of 'confidential', it has been noted already that confidentiality is not a binary concept and can be lost in some respects whilst being retained in others.[112] **1.87**

Test for waiver
Generally speaking, the starting point for determining whether privilege has been waived is to consider whether the *content* or *substance* of the advice or document has been revealed as opposed merely to its *effect*, and whether there has been *deployment* of or *reliance* placed **1.88**

---

[110] *Berezovsky v Hine* [2011] EWCA Civ 1089, [2011] All ER (D) 61 (Oct) [29].
[111] See in particular *B v Auckland District Law Society* (n 1); *Berezovsky v Hine* (n 110); Malek (n 106) para 26–35.
[112] See para 1.74.

on the content or substance to advance the privilege holder's case rather than mere *reference* to it.[113] However, recent authorities have cautioned against applying this distinction too mechanistically, suggesting instead that a more nuanced and context-specific approach is required, focusing above all on fairness.[114]

1.89 In *Kyla Shipping Co Ltd v Freight Trading Ltd*[115] it was suggested, by reference to Elias J's observations in *Brennan v Sunderland City Council*,[116] that the focus should be on two related matters: first, the nature of what has been revealed: is it the substance, gist, content, or merely the effect of the advice? And, secondly, the circumstances in which it has been revealed: has it simply been referred to, or has it been used, deployed, or relied upon in order to advance the party's case? The fuller the information provided about the legal advice or other privileged information, the greater the risk that waiver will have occurred, but a degree of reliance is required before waiver can arise.[117]

1.90 In *PCP Capital Partners LLP v Barclays Bank plc*[118] Waksman J was of the view that, first, the reference to legal advice must be 'sufficient', and, secondly, the party said to be waiving privilege must be relying on that reference in some way to support or advance their case on an issue that the court has to decide. He considered that the content/effect distinction had to be 'viewed and made through the prism of (a) whether there is any reliance on the privileged material adverted to; (b) what the purpose of that reliance is; and (c) the particular context of the case in question'.[119]

1.91 Ultimately, the underlying principle when determining whether privilege has been waived in these circumstances is fairness. Elias J in *Brennan* expressed this in the following terms:

> The fundamental question is whether, in the light of what has been disclosed and the context in which disclosure has occurred, it would be unfair to allow the party making disclosure not to reveal the whole of the relevant information because it would risk the court and the other party only having a partial and potentially misleading understanding of the material. The court must not allow cherry picking.[120]

Elias J suggested that focusing on this principle of fairness rather than the contents/effect distinction may make it easier to discern whether there has been a waiver.[121]

1.92 Applying these principles, Waksman J in *PCP* thought that a purely narrative reference to the giving of legal advice would not constitute waiver because, on any view, there would be no reliance upon it in relation to an issue in the case. Similarly, a mere reference to the fact of legal advice along the lines of, 'My solicitor gave me detailed advice. The following

---

[113] See eg *Dunlop Slazenger International Ltd v Joe Bloggs Sports Ltd* [2003] EWCA Civ 901, [2003] All ER (D) 137 (Jun) [11].
[114] See eg Elias J's observations in *Brennan v Sunderland City Council* [2008] UKEAT/349/08, [2009] ICR 479 [62]–[67]; also note *Henderson and Jones Ltd v Ross* [2022] EWHC 2560 (Ch), [2022] All ER (D) 50 (Oct) [32], in which it was said that there may still be waiver where the effect of legal advice is referred to.
[115] [2022] EWHC 376 (Comm).
[116] *Brennan v Sunderland City Council* (n 114) [67].
[117] *Kyla Shipping Co Ltd v Freight Trading Ltd* (n 115) [41].
[118] [2020] EWHC 1393 (Comm).
[119] ibid [48], [60].
[120] *Brennan v Sunderland City Council* (n 114) [63].
[121] ibid [67].

day I entered into the contract', would not amount to waiver, whereas 'I entered into the contract as a result of that legal advice' would.[122] This highlights how careful lawyers and their clients must be whenever it is necessary to refer to legal advice or other privileged communications.

Where part of a privileged document has been disclosed or quoted and this is held to amount to a waiver, the waiver will apply to the whole document, unless the undisclosed section deals with an entirely different subject matter such that the document can in effect be divided into two (or more) separate and distinct documents, each dealing with a separate subject matter and each of which is complete.[123] **1.93**

Collateral Waiver

If privilege is waived over legal advice or a particular document during the course of court proceedings, the waiver will extend to any other privileged advice or material relating to the same issue. This is known as 'collateral waiver' and it is based on the same principle of fairness as discussed in the previous section. A party must not be allowed to 'cherry-pick' by choosing only to waive privilege over material that suits their case whilst maintaining privilege over unhelpful material. In *Nea Karteria Maritime Co Ltd v Atlantic & Great Lakes Steamship Corp (No 2)*, Mustill J explained it in the following terms: **1.94**

> Where a party is deploying in court material which would otherwise be privileged, the opposite party and the court must have an opportunity of satisfying themselves that what the party has chosen to release from privilege represents the whole of the material relevant to the issue in question. To allow an individual item to be plucked out of context would be to risk injustice through its real weight or meaning being misunderstood.[124]

The general approach is to treat the waiver as extending to all other privileged material that relates to the same issue or 'transaction'. This is a highly fact-specific question. The issue or transaction may be nothing more than what somebody said on a particular occasion rather than the subject matter of the conversation,[125] or it may extend to the advice given by counsel on a specific issue on a particular occasion.[126] In cases involving a defendant waiving privilege at trial in an attempt to prevent an adverse inference being drawn from their silence when interviewed by the police, the issue or transaction will usually be the process of receiving advice at the police station. This means that, if they disclose in evidence the reason for their solicitor's advice to answer no comment, privilege will usually be waived not only over the advice but also the factual account they provided to their solicitor on which the advice was based.[127] **1.95**

---

[122] *PCP Capital Partners LLP v Barclays Bank plc* (n 118) [49].
[123] *Great Atlantic Insurance Co v Home Insurance Co* [1981] 1 WLR 529, 536 (CA).
[124] [1981] Com LR 138, 139 (QB).
[125] Suggested by Hobhouse J in *General Accident Fire & Life Assurance Corp Ltd v Tanter (The Zephyr)* [1984] 1 WLR 100 (Com Ct) 115.
[126] Suggested by Mann J in *Fulham Leisure Holdings Limited v Nicholson Graham & Jones* [2006] EWHC 158 (Ch), [2006] 2 All ER 599 [11].
[127] See eg *R v Loizou* [2006] EWCA Crim 1719, [2006] All ER (D) 215 (Jul).

1.96 Where there is difficulty in identifying the issue or transaction, it should be borne in mind that, ultimately, what matters is fairness: what further disclosure is necessary in order to avoid unfairness or misunderstanding of what has been disclosed?[128]

When Can Waiver and Collateral Waiver Occur?

1.97 The key principle underpinning waiver and collateral waiver is fairness. This is usually expressed in terms of fairness to the opposing party and the court in the course of litigation, and the general consensus is that waiver arises only when the relevant material is deployed *at court* (either at trial or during other hearings).[129] However, the courts have not always followed this approach, and there are a number of civil cases where it has been held that waiver has taken place prior to the privileged material being deployed at court, for example at the point at which it is mentioned in a witness statement, but not before litigation commences.[130] In *Re Yurov*,[131] for example, Judge Matthew Parfitt was unwilling to wait until the substantive hearing of an application under the Insolvency Act 1986 to determine that privilege had been waived over legal advice referred to in evidence in support of the application. He considered that:

> It would be manifestly unjust and risk undermining the proper management of litigation if the party on the receiving end of an application supported by privileged material had to wait until the substantive hearing before being able to obtain sight of the remainder of the privileged material concerning the issue in question. To have to wait until that point would invite an application for an adjournment at the last minute, wasting court time and costs for both sides.[132]

The judge thought that 'the moment at which a party is taken to have deployed material in court must be earlier than that, at least if it is clear that the party will ultimately be relying on the material'.[133]

1.98 In *Howes v Hinckley and Bosworth BC*,[134] a limited reference to the content of legal advice in correspondence between the parties before litigation had begun did not constitute a waiver of privilege because it was not a case where 'reliance [was] being placed on [the advice] in legal proceedings so as to render it unfair for the privilege to be maintained'. The only issue at play was loss of confidentiality, but the reference was not sufficient to result in confidentiality over the advice being lost. However, Elias J added that, 'I would reserve the position as to whether the privilege would have been waived if the communication had been made in the context of the court proceedings themselves.'[135] Whilst this observation

---

[128] *Fulham Leisure Holdings Limited v Nicholson Graham & Jones* (n 126) [11].
[129] See eg Malek (n 106) ch 26; Thanki (n 72) ch 5.
[130] See eg *MAC Hotels Ltd v Rider Levett Bucknall UK Ltd* [2010] EWHC 767 (TCC); *Re Yurov* [2022] EWHC 2112 (Ch), [2022] BPIR 1616.
[131] *Re Yurov* (n 130).
[132] ibid [39].
[133] ibid [39]. In reaching this view, reliance was placed on *R v Secretary of State for Transport, ex p Factortame Ltd* (1997) 9 Admin LR 591, in which a similar conclusion was reached and which was 'broadly approved' by the Court of Appeal in *Dunlop Slazenger International Ltd v Joe Bloggs Sports Ltd* (n 113).
[134] [2008] UKEAT/0213/08/MAA, [2008] All ER (D) 112 (Aug).
[135] ibid [46].

was obiter and did not indicate either way whether such a finding would be made, Elias J did not seem to have any conceptual difficulty with the possibility that waiver could take place during the course of litigation but otherwise than through the deployment of evidence before the court.

1.99 This distinction is perhaps of more significance in civil proceedings, where the service of documents such as statements of case, witness statements and affidavits plays a far more integral role in the conduct of litigation than in criminal proceedings (at least as far as a criminal defendant is concerned). Pre-trial, it will often be the case in criminal proceedings that the only equivalent document a defendant will serve (other than expert reports[136]) is a defence case statement. Nevertheless, to the extent that it is necessary to refer to legal advice or other privileged material in a written document served pre-trial as part of a defendant's case in criminal proceedings, a cautious approach should be adopted, mindful of the possibility that the prosecution (or a co-defendant) might argue (successfully) that privilege has been waived.

1.100 As regards disclosure of the first kind envisaged in para 1.83 (disclosure of the whole of a privileged document), it is the authors' view that in criminal cases there can be a 'waiver' of privilege in circumstances other than the deployment of evidence before the court and even outside the context of litigation. As noted above, companies cooperating with a criminal investigation will often disclose privileged material to investigators for the express purpose of assisting with their investigation and any subsequent prosecution. Although this take places before litigation has commenced, it is usually understood by both parties to amount to a limited waiver of privilege (and is consistently referred to as such, for example in the deferred prosecution agreement cases discussed in Chapter 7, Section 3), and it would seem to fall squarely within Leggatt J's definition of 'true waiver' in *Serdar Mohammed v Ministry of Defence*, in that the disclosing party is expressly consenting to the use of privileged material by the other party. Alternatively, it can be understood as a loss of confidentiality (and therefore privilege) over the disclosed documents as against the investigating authority that has received them.

1.101 In practical terms, it may make little difference how such a disclosure is classified. Most of the issues that arise in cases concerning waiver are to do with partial disclosure of privileged advice or a document and whether the disclosure is sufficient to cause privilege over the whole of that advice or document to be waived. If the whole document has been disclosed, that question does not arise. As far as collateral waiver over other material is concerned, the case law is clear that collateral waiver has no application outside of litigation and the deployment of evidence before the court. It is defined by reference to the opposing party in litigation and the court and is designed to bring fairness to the proceedings by ensuring that the court is not left with a misleading or incomplete picture on a relevant issue when reaching its factual and legal conclusions. That consideration cannot be said to apply at the investigation stage in a criminal case.

---

[136] These require separate consideration and are discussed at paras 9.47–9.57.

1.102 Where the nature of the disclosure is of the second kind envisaged in para 1.83 (partial disclosure), there can be no suggestion that privilege over the whole of the document or advice is waived if the disclosure takes place at the investigation stage. This is for the same reason as why collateral waiver does not apply outside the context of litigation: issues of fairness between parties and ensuring the court does not have an incomplete understanding are not applicable.

1.103 However, in circumstances where waiver and/or collateral waiver do not arise, there is still a risk that what is said prior to litigation commencing, for example in an interview under caution, will be adduced in evidence at court in the event of a prosecution, thereby engaging the fairness principles discussed above and potentially resulting in a waiver at that point. This is discussed at paras 6.45–6.46. There is also the separate issue of loss of confidentiality, which exists irrespective of whether or not litigation is in progress.[137] The authors of *Phipson on Evidence* suggest, by way of an example, that referring to privileged documents such as counsel's advice in open correspondence may cause confidentiality over the document to be lost, thereby precluding a subsequent claim to privilege, although the loss of confidentiality will be limited to the section that is quoted or summarized rather than the whole document, unless there is nothing of substance remaining in the undisclosed parts of the document, and collateral waiver does not result from loss of confidentiality.[138]

Inadvertent Disclosure

1.104 In criminal cases, if privileged material is inadvertently disclosed to investigating or prosecuting authorities, privilege will be lost as against those authorities and it will not be possible to prevent them from making use of the material in connection with their investigation or prosecution.[139] Once they have possession of the material, they are free to do with it as they wish, regardless of the fact that the privilege holder would otherwise have been entitled to resist disclosure on the grounds of privilege. This is markedly different from the approach taken in civil proceedings.

1.105 The courts have justified this approach on the basis that, first, there is a strong public interest in the state being able to apprehend and prosecute criminals without being denied access to relevant evidence; and, secondly, privilege is concerned with disclosure rather than admissibility.[140] According to Waksman J in *Eurasian Natural Resources Corp Ltd v Dechert LLP*, the recognition of privilege as a fundamental right does not affect the question of admissibility in criminal proceedings if the material has already been obtained.[141]

---

[137] These two issues are suggested in the context of inter-solicitor correspondence in Thanki (n 72) para 5.79.
[138] Malek (n 106) paras 26-01, 26-03.
[139] *Butler v Board of Trade* [1971] Ch 680 (Ch), approved by the Court of Appeal in *R v Tompkins* (1978) 67 Cr App R 181 (CA), *R v Cottrill* [1997] Crim LR 56 (CA), and *R v K (A)* [2009] EWCA Crim 1640, [2010] QB 343, and more recently by the High Court in *Eurasian Natural Resources Corp Ltd v Dechert LLP* [2022] EWHC 1138 (Comm).
[140] See eg *Butler v Board of Trade* (n 139) 690–91; *R v K (A)* (n 139) [69].
[141] *Eurasian Natural Resources Corp Ltd v Dechert LLP* (n 139) [1734].

Accordingly, once the material is in the hands of the prosecution, privilege cannot then be relied upon as a basis, in and of itself, for excluding the material if relevant. Whilst a defendant in criminal proceedings could make an application to exclude the evidence under the Police and Criminal Evidence Act 1984 (PACE 1984), section 78, the mere fact that a document is privileged would not automatically mean the application would succeed; the judge would need to be satisfied that the admission of the evidence would render the trial unfair.[142]

1.106

By way of an example, in *R v Tompkins*[143] a privileged handwritten note the defendant had passed to counsel during his trial was found on the floor of the court by a member of the prosecution team and was passed to prosecution counsel, who used it to cross-examine the defendant. Absent the inadvertent disclosure, the prosecution would not have been entitled to see the document. However, the Court of Appeal held that once the document was in the hands of the prosecution, notwithstanding the circumstances in which it had been obtained, privilege was lost and the document was admissible in evidence. *Tompkins* is discussed further at paras 10.18–10.20.

1.107

This line of authority has its limits. It does not, for example, override the various provisions discussed in Chapter 3, Section 4, which prohibit the seizure or compelled production of privileged material. In *Tompkins*, the Court made clear the distinction between production of a document and admissibility.[144] The same is true as regards the obligations under the Criminal Justice and Police Act 2001 (CJPA 2001) requiring investigators to return or isolate seized privileged material (see Chapter 3, Section 7). *Tompkins* would not permit the prosecution to rely on seized privileged material in contravention of the CJPA 2001 as it would not lawfully be in possession of the material. A judge would be bound to exclude the evidence under PACE 1984, section 78, otherwise the entire purpose of these statutory protections would be undermined. The key factor in *Tompkins* (and other cases which have followed the same approach) is that the prosecution came into possession of the material lawfully. Once that was established, the only question was whether the material was admissible in the proceedings.

1.108

The authors agree with the observation in *The Law of Privilege*[145] that, given the focus on fairness when considering collateral waiver, inadvertent disclosure of privileged material is unlikely to result in collateral waiver over other material.

1.109

Implied Waiver: Suing Legal Advisers

A client who sues a former legal adviser for negligence waives privilege over any communications between them so far as is necessary for the claim to be determined fairly.[146] This is often referred to as 'implied waiver'.

1.110

---

[142] As acknowledged by Moore-Bick LJ in *R v K (A)* (n 139) [73].
[143] *R v Tompkins* (n 139).
[144] ibid 184.
[145] Thanki (n 72) para 5.38.
[146] *Paragon Finance v Freshfields* [1999] 1 WLR 1183, 1188 (CA).

1.111 The extent to which a similar principle applies in criminal appeals where previous legal advisers are criticized is discussed at paras 11.32–11.37.

6 Joint Interest Privilege and Common Interest Privilege

1.112 Joint interest privilege and common interest privilege are concepts that apply to particular types of relationship between two or more parties where those parties share a joint or common interest in the subject matter of a privileged communication or litigation. In broad terms, they allow the parties to benefit from the same privilege by extending one party's right to claim privilege (legal advice privilege or litigation privilege) to the other party/parties to the joint/common interest. The material must already be covered by legal advice privilege or litigation privilege. It is beyond the scope of this book to review these concepts in any great detail, and they are of only limited relevance as far as criminal proceedings are concerned.

1.113 Although often referred to interchangeably by practitioners, they are not identical. It has helpfully been suggested by one commentator that the difference between a joint and common interest is that a joint interest is one in which the parties share in the *same* right or interest, such as beneficiaries of the same trust, whereas a common interest is one in which the parties have identical or very similar interests but they are *distinct in law*, such as identical tenancy rights in separate flats in the same property.[147]

1.114 Joint interest privilege can arise in two circumstances: (1) when two or more legal persons jointly retain the same lawyer; or (2) when, even though there is no joint retainer, the parties have a joint interest in the subject matter of the communication in issue at the time that it comes into existence.[148] Where joint interest privilege applies, the parties to the joint interest cannot claim privilege against each other in respect of material relating to the joint interest, but they can assert it against the rest of the world. The privilege can only be waived jointly by consent.[149] The rationale behind joint interest privilege is that there is no distinction between the interests of the two parties; advice obtained for the benefit of one is advice obtained for the benefit of the other.[150]

1.115 In criminal cases, a joint interest may exist between a company as a legal entity and its directors and/or senior employees in relation to legal advice provided to the corporate concerning its potential criminal liability. A company can only attract criminal liability through the acts and omissions of its officers and employees, and so advice on whether the corporate has committed an offence may include advice on whether individuals within the company have committed an offence.[151]

---

[147] Passmore (n 51) para 6-005.
[148] *R (Ford) v Financial Services Authority* [2011] EWHC 2583 (Admin), [2012] 1 All ER 1238 [16], adopting the summaries set out in Thanki (n 72) and Malek (n 106).
[149] *Hellenic Mutual War Risks Association (Bermuda) Ltd v Harrison (The Sagheera)* [1997] 1 Lloyd's Rep 160 (QB), cited with approval in *R (Ford) v Financial Services Authority* (n 148) [17].
[150] *R (Ford) v Financial Services Authority* (n 148) [18].
[151] See eg ibid [39].

Common interest privilege allows a party to share their privileged communications/advice **1.116** with another party who has a common interest in the subject matter of the communication/ advice or litigation to which it relates without there being a wider loss of privilege as against the rest of the world. It also gives the receiving party their own right to assert privilege over the communications against third parties, which would otherwise not be possible.[152] Although initially envisaged as arising only in respect of anticipated litigation,[153] its scope has since broadened so as also to encompass legal advice provided in non-contentious situations.[154] In criminal proceedings a common interest may exist between co-defendants,[155] although the question of whether a common interest arises will be fact-specific.

As far as sharing privileged material is concerned, which is where common interest privilege most often arises in criminal cases, it has been noted by a number of other commentators that the ability to share privileged material with third parties on a confidential basis without having to establish a common interest (as discussed at paras 1.77–1.79) means that it will rarely be necessary to rely on common interest privilege to protect privileged material that is shared with another party.[156] **1.117**

---

[152] See eg *Winterthur Swiss Insurance Co v AG (Manchester) Ltd (In Liquidation)* [2006] EWHC 839 (Comm), [2006] All ER (D) 196 (Apr) [78].
[153] *Buttes Gas & Oil Co v Hammer (No 3)* [1981] QB 223, 243 (CA).
[154] See eg *Svenska Handelsbanken v Sun Alliance and London Insurance plc* [1995] 2 Lloyd's Rep 84 (Com Ct) 88.
[155] See ch 10, s 4.
[156] See eg Malek (n 106) para 24-09; Passmore (n 51) para 6-080; Thanki (n 72) para 6.24.

2
The Crime-Fraud Exception

1 Introduction

Communications that are made in furtherance of a criminal or fraudulent purpose will not be protected by privilege. This is known as the crime-fraud or iniquity exception.[1] Although it is described as an exception to the rule of privilege, the principle in fact means that no privilege ever attaches to communications of this nature in the first place. The rationale for the exception is that a legal adviser consulted in order to pursue a criminal or fraudulent purpose is not acting within the scope of their ordinary professional engagement, and it is therefore not in the interests of justice to protect such communications.

2.01

The risk in criminal proceedings is that by invoking the exception, the very issue to be determined at trial may be examined prematurely. The crime-fraud exception therefore requires extremely cautious application when considered in the context of criminal proceedings. Where it is suggested that it arises, it is imperative that all parties thoroughly consider the basis on which it is asserted and ensure that the strict evidential requirements are satisfied so that it does not lead to actions being taken that cause prejudice to the proceedings.

2.02

This chapter begins by considering the general principles underpinning the crime-fraud exception before looking at its application in criminal proceedings.

2.03

2 General Principles

In Which Cases Can the Crime-Fraud Exception Apply?

The crime-fraud exception applies equally to legal advice privilege and litigation privilege and can arise in both criminal and civil cases.[2]

2.04

What Conduct Will Engage the Crime-Fraud Exception?

The crime-fraud exception was first developed in the case of *R v Cox and Railton*.[3] It is helpful to consider the facts of this case before examining how the scope of the exception has broadened since then.

2.05

---

[1] 'Crime-fraud exception' is adopted in this work as this is how it has traditionally been expressed, but 'iniquity' and 'iniquitous' are used at certain points to refer to the conduct giving rise to the exception to reflect the fact that its scope has extended beyond criminal and fraudulent conduct in more recent times
[2] *Kuwait Airways Corp v Iraqi Airways Co* [2005] EWCA Civ 286, [2005] 1 WLR 2734 [25], [31].
[3] (1884) 14 QBD 153 (Crown Cases Reserved).

R v Cox and Railton

2.06 Cox and Railton, who were business partners, were prosecuted for conspiracy to defraud. It was alleged that they had conspired to defraud M after he had successfully brought a civil action allowing him to take possession of goods belonging to Railton. When seizure of goods in execution of the judgment was attempted, Cox claimed the goods belonged to him and produced a bill of sale in his favour, signed by Railton, which was dated after the judgment in the civil action. The validity of the bill of sale was challenged, in response to which Cox produced the deed of partnership between him and Railton bearing an endorsement purporting to show that they had dissolved their partnership before the civil action brought by M had commenced. This led to Cox and Railton being prosecuted for conspiracy to defraud, the prosecution's case being that the memorandum of dissolution of the partnership had in fact been endorsed on the partnership deed after the date of the judgment in the civil action but falsely backdated and that the bill of sale was a fraudulent bill of sale of the partnership assets, entered into between Railton and Cox when they were partners. The prosecution alleged that their intention had been to deprive M of the assets to which he was entitled in execution of the judgment.

2.07 During the criminal trial, the prosecution relied upon evidence from a solicitor from whom Cox and Railton had sought advice about how they might go about defeating the judgment handed down in favour of M, and particularly whether a bill of sale could legally be executed by Railton after the judgment. The solicitor had advised that a bill of sale in favour of Cox could not be executed because of the partnership agreement which was in place. The partnership dissolution document was not prepared by the solicitor, but his evidence was relevant to the defendants' intention. The defendants were found guilty at trial. On appeal, they objected to the introduction of the evidence from the solicitor on the basis that their communications were subject to privilege. The Court rejected their argument, holding that privilege could not apply to communications where advice was being sought in order to further a criminal purpose. The evidence, therefore, was admissible. Stephen J held that:

> The reason on which the [privilege] rule is said to rest cannot include the case of communications, criminal in themselves, or intended to further any criminal purpose, for the protection of such communications cannot possibly be otherwise than injurious to the interests of justice and to those of the administration of justice. Nor do such communications fall within the terms of the rule. A communication in furtherance of a criminal purpose does not 'come into the ordinary scope of professional employment'.[4]

Expanded scope of the exception

2.08 Subsequent authorities have confirmed that the crime-fraud exception is not confined only to cases involving a criminal purpose. It also covers 'fraud or other equivalent underhand conduct which is in breach of a duty of good faith or contrary to public policy or the interests of justice'.[5] Reviewing the various authorities on non-criminal conduct sufficient to engage the exception, Norris J in *BBGP Managing General Partner Ltd v Babcock & Brown Global Partners* provided this summary:

---

[4] ibid 167.
[5] *JSC BTA Bank v Ablyazov* [2014] EWHC 2788 (Comm), [2014] 2 CLC 263 [68].

The enumeration of examples is useful only in so far as it enables some underlying theme or connectedness to be identified. In each of these cases the wrongdoer has gone beyond conduct which merely amounts to a civil wrong; he has indulged in sharp practice, something of an underhand nature where the circumstances require good faith, something which commercial men would say was a fraud or which the law treats as entirely contrary to public policy.[6]

The key feature of the iniquitous conduct is that it must take the advice or assistance that is being sought from the legal adviser outside the ordinary scope of their professional engagement. In *JSC BTA Bank v Ablyazov* Popplewell J explained it in the following terms:

I would conclude, therefore, that the touchstone is whether the communication is made for the purposes of giving or receiving legal advice, or for the purposes of the conduct of actual or contemplated litigation, which is advice or conduct in which the solicitor is acting in the ordinary course of the professional engagement of a solicitor. If the iniquity puts the advice or conduct outside the normal scope of such professional engagement, or renders it an abuse of the relationship which properly falls within the ordinary course of such an engagement, a communication for such purpose cannot attract legal professional privilege.[7]

2.09 A more extreme (and questionable) example of the expanded scope of the crime-fraud exception is *R v Brown*.[8] The Court of Appeal held that based on the highly unusual facts of the case, it was justifiable to extend the application of the crime-fraud exception to prevent a privileged consultation taking place when the privileged consultation itself (as opposed to the advice being sought) was intended to be used in furtherance of a criminal purpose, in this case the infliction of unlawful violence against the solicitor. The case is discussed in detail at paras 6.29–6.34 in the context of consultations which take place in the presence of a third party. It will be noted from that discussion that care should be taken in the application of *Brown* as it is the view of the authors that the appellant was not, as a matter of law, actually denied a privileged consultation. As has been suggested elsewhere, the case does, however, remain authority for the proposition that there may be rare and specific circumstances under which the courts will consider extending the crime-fraud exception for public policy reasons.[9]

Whose Conduct Will Engage the Crime-Fraud Exception?

2.10 It is usually the client whose conduct or purpose engages the crime-fraud exception. However, the exception can apply even if the iniquitous purpose is that of a third party and the lawyer and/or the client is/are unaware that they are being used as an innocent dupe in furtherance of that purpose.[10]

---

[6] [2010] EWHC 2176 (Ch), [2011] Ch 296 [62].
[7] *JSC BTA Bank v Ablyazov* (n 5) [93].
[8] [2015] EWCA Crim 1328, [2016] 1 WLR 1141.
[9] Bankim Thanki (ed), *The Law of Privilege* (3rd edn, OUP 2018) para 4.55.
[10] *R v Central Criminal Court, ex p Francis & Francis* [1989] AC 346, 396 (HL); *Banque Keyser Ullman SA v Skandia (UK) Insurance Company Limited* [1986] 1 Lloyd's Rep 336, 337 (CA).

2.11 In *R v Central Criminal Court ex p Francis & Francis*[11] a production order was sought to obtain a solicitor's file in relation to a client's property transaction. It was alleged that the transaction was being carried out for the purpose of laundering the proceeds of crime on behalf of a third party. The House of Lords considered whether the criminal intention of the third party was sufficient to engage the crime-fraud exception in circumstances where it was not alleged that either the solicitor or their client had the intention of furthering a criminal purpose. Lloyd LJ made the following observations:

> I am fortified by [the] concession that 'a criminal purpose' in section 10(2) [Police and Criminal Evidence Act 1984][12] must mean 'any criminal purpose'. If so, then the logic of the argument which I have accepted so far, leads to the conclusion that the criminal purpose may be the purpose of a third party as well as the client, at any rate if the client is the innocent instrument or beneficiary of the third party's criminal purpose. That is indeed the position in the present case on the facts alleged by the police.[13]

2.12 If the iniquitous conduct is carried out by an agent on behalf of a principal who is the beneficiary of the privilege, the exception will still be engaged. In *Gerrard v Eurasian Natural Resources Corp Ltd*[14] it was held that no litigation privilege attached to communications regarding the instruction of surveillance agents by the defendants, as the actions of the surveillance agents amounted to the offence of harassment of the claimant and therefore engaged the exception.

Standard of Proof

2.13 The burden is on the party who seeks the relevant material to establish that the exception applies. Although expressed in different formulations in the authorities, Popplewell LJ concluded in the case of *Al Sadeq v Dechert LLP* that, save in exceptional cases, the merits threshold for the exception is a balance of probabilities test: the existence of the iniquity must be more likely than not on the material available to the decision-maker. This is what cases speaking of a 'prima facie case' have in mind.[15]

2.14 The case of *C v C (Privilege)*[16] helpfully demonstrates what will not be sufficient. A wife suspected that her husband was attempting to dispose of assets whilst their divorce proceedings were pending in order to prejudice her position. She requested disclosure of a conveyancing file relating to the sale of a property, on the basis that the crime-fraud exception was engaged and therefore privilege did not apply. The Court held that the disclosure was being sought in an attempt to discover what the husband was doing, and whilst the wife had much reason to be suspicious, even 'gravely suspicious', this amounted to nothing more than 'suspicion and assumption' and 'surmise and conjecture, some of it founded on mere rumour', and she had made no 'clear and definite allegation'. This was not sufficient to satisfy

---

[11] *R v Central Criminal Court, ex p Francis & Francis* (n 10).
[12] See ch 3.
[13] *R v Central Criminal Court, ex p Francis & Francis* (n 10) 355.
[14] [2020] EWHC 3241 (QB), [2021] EMLR 8.
[15] *Al Sadeq v Dechert LLP* [2024] EWCA Civ 28 [63].
[16] [2006] EWHC 336 (Fam), [2008] 1 FLR 115.

the heavy burden which rests upon anyone who seeks to go behind privilege on the grounds of fraud or iniquity.[17] The application for disclosure was therefore refused on the grounds that the documents were privileged and the exception was not engaged.

3 Application in Criminal Cases

The 'Ordinary Run' of Criminal Cases

2.15 If communications in furtherance of a criminal or fraudulent purpose are not privileged, how is privilege to be claimed when defending a client in criminal proceedings, where the issue to be determined is whether or not the defendant has committed a crime? The authorities have consistently distinguished between what has come to be known as the 'ordinary run' of criminal cases, in which the exception does not apply, and cases involving conduct that falls outside that, where the exception will be engaged. But what is meant by the 'ordinary run' of criminal cases?

2.16 Advice on an intended course of action in order to understand whether or not it is lawful, or, having been accused of a criminal offence, advice on how best to deal with the allegation, fall squarely within the 'ordinary run' of criminal cases.[18] In *R v Cox and Railton* (see paras 2.06–2.07), the defendants had sought advice from their solicitor for the fraudulent purpose of illegitimately defeating the civil judgment and putting assets out of reach of M. That was not capable of attracting privilege. However, there was no suggestion that when Cox and Railton communicated with the lawyers representing them in the criminal proceedings, those communications were not privileged.

2.17 The fact that a client is guilty of the offence in respect of which they are seeking legal advice will not engage the principle, and it will not arise merely because a lawyer is engaged to defend a client in proceedings by putting forward an account which the client (but not the lawyer) knows is untrue and which therefore involves a deliberate strategy by the client to mislead the court and to commit perjury.[19]

2.18 In *JSC BTA Bank v Ablyazov*[20] Popplewell J held that if a solicitor is engaged to advance a false case for their client supported by false evidence, it will be a question of fact and degree whether it involves an abuse of the ordinary professional engagement of a solicitor in the circumstances in question such that the exception applies. He stated:

> In the 'ordinary run' of criminal cases the solicitor will be acting in the ordinary course of professional engagement, and the client doing no more than using him to provide the services inherent in the proper fulfilment of such engagement, even where in denying the crime the defendant puts forward what the jury finds to be a bogus defence. But where in

---

[17] ibid [60], [62].
[18] *O'Rourke v Darbishire* [1920] AC 581, 613 (HL).
[19] *JSC BTA Bank v Ablyazov* (n 5) [71], in reference to *R v Central Criminal Court, ex p Francis & Francis* (n 10) 397 and *R v Snaresbrook Crown Court, ex p DPP* [1988] QB 532, 537–38 (QB).
[20] *JSC BTA Bank v Ablyazov* (n 5).

civil proceedings there is deception of the solicitors in order to use them as an instrument to perpetrate a substantial fraud on the other party and the court, that may well be indicative of a lack of confidentiality which is the essential prerequisite for the attachment of legal professional privilege. The deception of the solicitors, and therefore the abuse of the normal solicitor/client relationship, will often be the hallmark of iniquity which negates the privilege.[21]

Similarly, in *O'Rourke v Darbishire*[22] it was held that cases where a fraud has been concocted between a solicitor and a client, or where a solicitor's advice enables the client to carry out a fraudulent transaction, should be distinguished from cases in which, after the commission of a crime, a client consults a solicitor in their professional capacity to obtain the benefit of confidential advice and assistance. The crime-fraud exception would apply in the former examples as it is not part of the professional duty of a solicitor either to take part in the concoction of fraud or to advise their client on how to carry out a fraud.[23]

Overlap between Iniquitous Conduct and Issues to Be Determined at Trial

2.19 In criminal cases, there is a risk that in determining whether the crime-fraud exception applies, the court would be required to pass judgment on substantive issues which are to be determined at trial. In *Kuwait Airways Corporation v Iraqi Airways Co* Longmore LJ gave as examples of these types of issues a denial of having committed a crime, an assertion of an alibi and telling a lie to a solicitor about a key factual issue.[24] The authorities urge caution in this area and suggest that issues in the case should not be determined prematurely in this way.[25] It is only if there is free-standing and independent evidence of the iniquitous conduct that the court may be in a position to assess whether the exception applies before the substantive case has been determined.

2.20 *R (Hallinan Blackburn Gittings and Nott) v Middlesex Guildhall Crown Court*[26] demonstrates how this distinction is applied in practice.[27] The claimants were a firm of solicitors who had been made subject to a production order which sought witness statements and other documents in respect of their client, P. The firm brought a claim for judicial review of the decision to issue the production order on the basis that the judge who granted it had erred in law by finding that the crime-fraud exception as set out in the Police and Criminal Evidence Act 1984, s 10(2)[28] applied to the material. The firm acted for their client, P, in

---

[21] *JSC BTA Bank v Ablyazov* (n 5) [93].
[22] *O'Rourke v Darbishire* (n 18).
[23] ibid 621–22.
[24] *Kuwait Airways Corp v Iraqi Airways Co* (n 2) [29].
[25] Although it was suggested by Longmore LJ in *Kuwait Airways Corp v Iraqi Airways Co* (n 2) [40] that it is not necessarily a precondition that the fraud which is said to give rise to the crime-fraud exception must not relate to the issues to be tried; just that it is easier to evaluate the facts justifying the exception if the fraud does not relate to the very issue which is to be tried. Also note Popplewell LJ's comments in *Al Sadeq v Dechert LLP* (n 15) [101], [102], [104]–[106], [108] doubting that there is a distinction between cases in which the iniquity is one of the issues in the proceedings and those where it is not.
[26] [2004] EWHC 2726 (Admin), [2005] 1 WLR 766.
[27] Although note Popplewell LJ's discussion of this case in *Al Sadeq v Dechert LLP* (n 15) [99]–[101], [104]–[106].
[28] See para 3.27.

respect of allegations of possession of cocaine with intent to supply, possession of a stun gun and driving offences. The police received evidence that P, along with two others, M and K, were engaged in a conspiracy to pervert the course of justice by colluding to provide statements to P's solicitors in support of P's defence which contained false information. The evidence the police had found included information that, whilst K was proposing to say that she had been present at P's arrest, she was in fact at her place of work on that date. There was also material supporting a clear inference that she had made a false diary entry at her place of work in relation to her whereabouts that day. The police had also obtained correspondence between K and M which appeared to show that K had been guided by M in respect of her witness statement and that M knew that what K was saying was false, including the line, 'How do you know the coppers won't know you weren't there?'

2.21 The police and the CPS were clear that the solicitors were innocent of any wrongdoing and had effectively been used by P, M, and K in furtherance of their criminal purpose. The police originally sought disclosure of the material by requesting that the solicitors provide it to them, but the solicitors refused on the grounds of privilege. The police then obtained the production order which was the subject of the judicial review. The issue for the Divisional Court to determine was the extent to which the crime-fraud exception could be applied in circumstances where the conduct said to give rise to the exception went to the question of guilt in relation to an allegation of perverting the course of justice, rather than in relation to the issues to be determined in respect of the drugs, firearms, and driving offences giving rise to the original privilege. It was held that in circumstances where there was free-standing evidence of a conspiracy to pervert the course of justice, the crime-fraud exception was engaged. These cases could be distinguished from those where the prosecution simply suspects that the defence being advanced is not true. Rose LJ stated:

> It is a truism that whether material is legally privileged depends on the circumstances of the particular case. In order to defeat a claim to legal professional privilege, it will not be appropriate, for example in a case where an alibi has been raised, to seek to analyse the issues which are likely to arise in the criminal investigation or trial which gives rise to the initial privilege. To do so, as it seems to me, would be to put the cart, in the form of analysis of the issues, before the horse, that is the trial. Where, however, there is evidence of specific agreement to pervert the course of justice, which is freestanding and independent, in the sense that it does not require any judgment to be reached in relation to the issues to be tried, the court may well be in a position to evaluate whether what has occurred falls within or outwith the protection of legal professional privilege as explained in *R v Cox and Railton*.[29]

2.22 The same approach was taken in *R v Minchin, Dwyer and Healey*,[30] a case which concerned the provision of an allegedly false alibi put forward by Minchin in support of Healey in respect of an allegation of attempted murder. Healey's solicitor contacted the police and gave them details of Healey's alibi: he had on the day in question been with a friend, Kimpton, at the home address of a customer, Small. When the police spoke to Small she gave a statement consistent with that account, that two men she had never met before came to her house in

---

[29] *R (Hallinan Blackburn Gittings and Nott) v Middlesex Guildhall Crown Court* (n 26) [25].
[30] [2013] EWCA Crim 2412.

response to her enquiry about double glazing for a conservatory, the description of the men corresponding to Kimpton and Healey. She said that she had not had any contact with the men since then. She later retracted her statement, and, on the same day, it was discovered that she was the sister of Kimpton's partner. She and Kimpton were arrested and items were seized from her home which were described by the prosecution as documents giving instructions for the alibi, including a note saying: 'We visited you on the 11th June for a quote for a conservatory. We came again today 3/11/10 Wednesday and said do you remember us only we have to make ourselves accountable for the 11th June. So you may get a visit from the police to confirm that you saw us on 11th June between 1–1.30pm and on 3/11 in the morning.'

2.23 The police obtained a production order for all documents held by Healey's solicitors, Guney Clark and Ryan (GCR), relating to Healey's alibi. As in *Hallinan*, the judge held that there was free-standing and independent evidence of a specific agreement to pervert the course of justice such that the material sought by the police engaged the crime-fraud exception and was not privileged. The material included two attendance notes and a draft section 9 witness statement. It was relied upon at trial and Minchin and Healey were both convicted of conspiracy to pervert the course of justice. Healey was also convicted of causing grievous bodily harm with intent.

2.24 Minchin and Healey appealed against their convictions for conspiracy to pervert the course of justice, with counsel for both arguing that the material produced from the GCR files should not have been put before the jury because it was privileged and the judge had not applied the test in *Hallinan* sufficiently strictly. It was submitted that the evidence was not free-standing and independent in the sense that it did not require any judgment to be reached in relation to the issues to be tried. The Court rejected the appellants' argument, holding that there was plainly free-standing and independent evidence that the alibi was false. There was evidence of the lies told by Small, of the concealed relationship between Small and Kimpton, of the instructions for the alibi, and of Small's retraction of the alibi. The evidence of a conspiracy to concoct a false alibi was already there and the judge granting the production order was properly able to determine the existence of the conspiracy by looking at the evidence in isolation from the case as a whole. The test in *Hallinan* had been applied correctly and the judge was right to have determined that the crime-fraud exception applied.[31]

2.25 The facts in both *Hallinan* and *Minchin* demonstrate the strict evidential requirements for establishing that the crime-fraud exception applies in criminal cases. In both cases, the police were in possession of documentary evidence which demonstrated a clear plan to put forward false evidence which was sufficient to found a separate charge of perverting the course of justice. In considering this evidence, the judges granting the production orders did not need to assess issues that were to be determined at trial; the evidence already available was sufficient to cross the necessary threshold for establishing the crime-fraud exception.

---

[31] ibid [32] and see [18] for the judge's reasoning when granting the production order.

4 Practical Considerations

When Will the Crime-Fraud Exception Arise in Practice?

2.26 The crime-fraud exception can arise at any point during the life of a case. However, in criminal cases, it is most likely to be asserted in connection with the exercise of powers of search and seizure and compulsion by investigating authorities, as in *Hallinan* and *Minchin*. It will either be relied upon when a search warrant or production order is applied for, or it will be determined by independent counsel when reviewing seized material believed to be covered by privilege on behalf of an investigating authority. This is explored in more detail at paras 3.50–3.56.

Establishing whether the Exception Applies

2.27 Lawyers must be alive to the risks of readily accepting an assertion by the police or other investigating agency that the crime-fraud exception applies to material sought. It is not the role of an investigator or prosecutor unilaterally to decide that the exception applies, and defence practitioners must carefully scrutinize the evidential and legal basis for the assertion. Where a production order has been obtained *ex parte*, it may not be possible to establish from the production order itself that the principles have been considered and applied correctly. Where this is the case, the defence should try to obtain a copy of the application for the production order so that this can be assessed. The most appropriate method of challenging a production order that has been incorrectly issued is through judicial review.

2.28 The same level of scrutiny should be applied to any suggestion by independent counsel who is reviewing seized material on the instruction of an investigating agency that the crime-fraud exception applies. As per the guidance outlined at paras 4.31–4.35, there ought to be a direct line of communication between the defence and independent counsel, and this should allow disagreements over the application of the exception to be discussed.

Professional Obligations

2.29 A lawyer who discovers during the course of their instruction that they have unwittingly become part of a criminal, fraudulent, or iniquitous scheme must carefully consider their professional obligations and whether they are able to continue to act for their client. The normal rules of professional ethics apply and it may be necessary to seek advice from either the Law Society or Bar Council. However, even if the lawyer believes that the material they hold is subject to the crime-fraud exception, it does not automatically follow that it can voluntarily be provided to the authorities. The material is very likely to be confidential and therefore subject to the lawyer's professional obligations in respect of confidential client information, notwithstanding the crime-fraud exception applying. In almost all cases, this will constitute special procedure material (see paras 3.50–3.56) and will require a production order compelling its disclosure, with the obligation being on the applicant investigator to satisfy the judge that the crime-fraud exception applies.

3
Search and Seizure, Compulsion, Surveillance, and Interception

1 Introduction

One of the most important areas in which privilege issues arise in criminal cases is the exercise of statutory powers of search and seizure and compulsion by investigating authorities. The ubiquity of mobile phones, computers and other electronic devices with huge data storage capabilities means that investigators and prosecutors now come into possession of more data than ever before, and the likelihood of privileged material being seized, whether intentionally or not, is significantly increased. These powers must therefore be exercised with great care and in full compliance with the strict conditions imposed by the statutes that govern them. There must also be meaningful defence engagement and scrutiny to ensure the integrity of the process. **3.01**

It is beyond the scope of this book to review in detail the plethora of statutory provisions conferring powers of search and seizure and compulsion on law enforcement agencies. Instead, this chapter focuses on the treatment of privilege under the most commonly invoked powers and the key principles that apply at each stage of the process when investigators wish to obtain material that may include privileged items. This chapter also briefly examines covert surveillance and interception of privileged communications by law enforcement agencies. **3.02**

2 Search and Seizure and Compulsion: Main Powers

Police and Criminal Evidence Act 1984

The Police and Criminal Evidence Act 1984 (PACE 1984) contains the main powers of search and seizure for the police in criminal investigations. The powers are also conferred on HMRC officers and, if designated by the Director General of the NCA, NCA officers. **3.03**

Under PACE 1984, section 8 a justice of the peace (JP) can issue a warrant authorizing a constable to enter and search premises and seize material. This does not extend to certain categories of confidential material known as 'excluded material' and 'special procedure material'. Excluded material includes, inter alia, medical records and journalistic material held in confidence. Special procedure material is broader and includes, inter alia, confidential business records, but not items subject to privilege. If the police wish to obtain excluded material or special procedure material, they must apply to the Crown Court for a production order or a search and seizure warrant under PACE 1984, section 9 and schedule 1. **3.04**

3.05 PACE 1984 contains several other powers that authorize search and/or seizure without a warrant. These include section 18 (search of premises and seizure following arrest), section 19 (seizure whilst lawfully on premises), section 32 (search of person and premises and seizure following arrest other than at a police station), and section 54 (search of person and seizure at a police station).

Criminal Justice Act 1987, section 2

3.06 The Criminal Justice Act 1987 (CJA 1987), section 2 confers powers of compulsion on the Director of the SFO in relation to its investigations. The Director may issue a notice under section 2(3) requiring a person to produce documents which are relevant to an investigation. If a person fails to comply with a notice or it is not practicable or appropriate to issue one, an application can be made to a JP under section 2(4) to issue a warrant authorizing a constable to enter and search premises and seize material.

Proceeds of Crime Act 2002

3.07 The Proceeds of Crime Act 2002 (POCA 2002) contains a number of powers available in money laundering investigations and a range of other proceeds of crime investigations. A Crown Court judge can make a production order under section 345 or a disclosure order under section 357, or issue a search and seizure warrant under section 352. The type of investigation determines who can make the application.[1] In money laundering investigations, for example, an application can be made by a constable, an SFO officer, a HMRC officer, an accredited financial investigator, or an immigration officer.

3.08 POCA 2002 also contains a number of powers available in civil recovery investigations. Although they operate in a criminal context, they are not examined in this chapter.

Serious Organised Crime and Police Act 2005

3.09 The Serious Organised Crime and Police Act 2005 (SOCPA 2005) confers certain powers on the Director of Public Prosecutions (DPP) or, by delegation, a Crown Prosecutor, in connection with investigations into a number of serious offences, including lifestyle offences under POCA 2002, terrorist financing, tax offences, false accounting, cheating the public revenue, and bribery. A disclosure notice can be issued under section 62 requiring a person to answer questions, provide information, or produce documents. This can be issued by the DPP/Crown Prosecutor or, if authorized, a constable, NCA officer, or HMRC officer. Under section 66, an application can be made to a JP for a warrant authorizing a constable, NCA officer or HMRC officer to, inter alia, enter and search premises and seize documents.

---

[1] POCA 2002, s 378.

Financial Services and Markets Act 2000

The Financial Services and Markets Act 2000 (FSMA 2000) contains a number of powers exercisable in FCA investigations. These include, under sections 171 to 173 and 175, powers to compel the production of information or documents from a person depending on the type of investigation being carried out. Under section 176, an application can be made to a JP for a warrant authorizing a constable to enter and search premises and seize material. The FCA also has a general power under section 165 to issue a notice to an authorized person/firm requiring them to provide information or documents in connection with the exercise of the FCA's statutory functions under FSMA 2000. **3.10**

Witness Summons

Once a prosecution is underway, an application can be made to the court for a witness summons requiring a person to attend before the court at a specified time and produce any document likely to be material evidence for the purpose of the proceedings. The power to issue a witness summons is provided by the Criminal Procedure (Attendance of Witnesses) Act 1965, section 2 (for Crown Court proceedings) and the Magistrates' Court Act 1980, section 97 (for magistrates' court proceedings). **3.11**

Mutual Legal Assistance

Through mutual legal assistance (MLA), some powers of compulsion and search and seizure can be exercised on behalf of overseas authorities to obtain evidence located in the UK for their own investigations. By virtue of the Crime (International Co-operation) Act 2003, sections 16 and 17, the police, HMRC or the NCA can apply for a search warrant under PACE 1984, section 8 or a search warrant or production order under PACE 1984, schedule 1 if directed to do so by the Secretary of State after receiving a request for MLA. If the request appears to relate to an offence involving serious or complex fraud, the Secretary of State may refer it to the Director of the SFO,[2] who will then use powers of compulsion under the CJA 1987, section 2. Under FSMA 2000, section 169 the FCA may exercise the power conferred by section 165 at the request of an overseas regulator. **3.12**

Seizure of Privileged Material

As discussed in Section 4 below, none of these powers authorizes the seizure or compelled production of privileged documents or information. **3.13**

---

[2] Crime (International Co-operation) Act 2003, s 15(2).

3 Additional Powers of Seizure: Criminal Justice and Police Act 2001

Introduction

3.14 The powers of search and seizure referred to above are limited to specific items or categories of material specified on the warrant. This can present difficulties where material on the premises is voluminous and/or stored on computers or other electronic devices. It would not be practicable to require investigators to review the material on-site to determine what could lawfully be seized under the warrant or to separate the seizable property from that which there is no authority to seize.

3.15 This problem is addressed by additional powers of seizure under the Criminal Justice and Police Act 2001 (CJPA 2001), sections 50 and 51, which allow material to be seized and then, at a later stage, either: (1) reviewed to determine whether it is or contains something that the investigator is entitled to seize; or (2) to enable the seizable material to be separated from that in which it is comprised and which there is no power to seize. The powers, which are often referred to as 'seize and sift' powers, are wide-reaching and can be exercised in conjunction with all of the powers of seizure described above (and others).[3]

3.16 References in the CJPA 2001 to 'seizable' property and property that an investigator 'would be' entitled to seize are references to the power to seize property pursuant to the warrant issued under the relevant non-CJPA 2001 provision.

3.17 The CJPA 2001 is of particular importance as far as privilege is concerned as the additional powers of seizure provide a lawful route by which investigators may knowingly come into possession of privileged material, albeit subject to strict requirements. It also contains important provisions for how privileged material must be handled if seized pursuant to a non-CJPA 2001 power without relying on the CJPA 2001, sections 50 or 51. Given its importance to privilege, this chapter will review the relevant provisions in some detail and attempt to make sense of the Act's rather labyrinthine drafting.[4]

CJPA 2001, sections 50 and 51

3.18 Section 50 relates to searches of premises and section 51 relates to searches of the person.

3.19 Section 50(1) provides that, where:

- a person lawfully on premises finds something that they have reasonable grounds for believing may be or may contain something for which they are authorized to search;

---

[3] CJPA 2001, sch 1, pts 1 and 2.
[4] As such, the provisions discussed in this chapter are not direct quotes from the CJPA 2001.

- a power of seizure to which section 50 applies (all of the non-CJPA 2001 powers described earlier in this chapter, and others[5]) would entitle them, if they found it, to seize whatever it is that they have grounds for believing that thing to be or to contain; and
- in all the circumstances, it is not reasonably practicable for it to be determined, on those premises:
  o whether what they have found is something that they are entitled to seize, or
  o the extent to which what they have found contains something that they are entitled to seize,

that person's powers of seizure shall include the power to seize so much of what they have found as it is necessary to remove from the premises to enable that to be determined.

Section 50(2) provides that, where:

- a person lawfully on any premises finds something which they would be entitled to seize but for its being comprised in something else that they have no power to seize;
- the power under which they would have power to seize the seizable property is a power to which section 50 applies (the same powers as for section 50(1) above); and
- in all the circumstances, it is not reasonably practicable for the seizable property to be separated, on those premises, from that in which it is comprised,

that person's powers of seizure shall include the power to seize both the seizable property and that from which it is not reasonably practicable to separate it.

3.20 Section 51(1) and (2) provide equivalent powers in respect of lawful searches of the person.

3.21 When considering whether or not it is reasonably practicable on the premises or at the time and place of a search of a person for something to be determined, or for something to be separated from something else, factors to be taken into account include:

- how long it would take to carry out the determination or separation on those premises or at the time and place of the search of the person;
- the number of persons that would be required to carry out that determination or separation on those premises or at the time and place of the search of the person within a reasonable period;
- whether the determination or separation would involve damage to property;
- the apparatus or equipment that it would be necessary or appropriate to use for carrying out the determination or separation; and
- in the case of separation, whether the separation would be likely to prejudice the use of some or all of the separated seizable property for a purpose for which something seized under the power in question is capable of being used.[6]

3.22 An example of when it might be appropriate to exercise these powers is when a warrant under PACE 1984, section 9 and schedule 1 is executed at a business premises in connection

---

[5] CJPA 2001, sch 1, pt 1.
[6] ibid ss 50(3), 51(3).

with a police investigation into suspected fraud and one of the categories of documents specified on the warrant is supplier invoices covering a particular date period. These are likely to be held in electronic form on computers or other devices. The warrant alone would not authorize seizure of the devices, but by exercising the power under section 50(1), they could lawfully be seized. The police would have reasonable grounds for believing that the computers may contain something for which they are authorized to search (the supplier invoices), the power of seizure under the warrant would entitle the police to seize the supplier invoices, and it would not reasonably be practicable to determine on the premises the extent to which the computers contain those records as that would most likely involve searching through the contents of every computer. The computers could therefore be seized and taken away to allow the determination to take place.

3.23 Alternatively, using the same example, it may be that section 50(2) would be more appropriate. This would be the case if the police *knew* the computers contain the relevant documents, for example if somebody on the premises had told them, rather than having reasonable grounds for believing this to be the case. The documents stored on the computers would be 'comprised in something else that [the officer] has ... no power to seize' (the computers themselves) and it would not reasonably be practicable for the documents to be 'separated' on the premises.

4 Seizure and Compelled Production of Privileged Material

Non-CJPA 2001 Provisions

Express statutory exclusions

3.24 None of the powers described above, excluding the CJPA 2001, sections 50 and 51, authorizes the seizure or compelled production of material subject to legal professional privilege, and each of the statutory provisions (save for those relating to witness summonses; as to which, see para 3.31) contains an express exclusion to this effect.

3.25 PACE 1984, section 19(6) contains a general exclusion that applies to all powers of seizure conferred on a constable: 'No power of seizure conferred on a constable under any enactment (including an enactment contained in an Act passed after this Act) is to be taken to authorise the seizure of an item which the constable exercising the power has reasonable grounds for believing to be subject to legal privilege.'

3.26 Section 10(1) defines 'items subject to legal privilege' under PACE 1984 as:

  (a) communications between a professional legal adviser and his client or any person representing his client made in connection with the giving of legal advice to the client;
  (b) communications between a professional legal adviser and his client or any person representing his client or between such an adviser or his client or any such representative and any other person made in connection with or in contemplation of legal proceedings and for the purposes of such proceedings; and

(c) items enclosed with or referred to in such communications and made—
  (i) in connection with the giving of legal advice; or
  (ii) in connection with or in contemplation of legal proceedings and for the purposes of such proceedings,

when they are in the possession of a person who is entitled to possession of them.

3.27 Under section 10(2), 'Items held with the intention of furthering a criminal purpose are not items subject to legal privilege.'

3.28 Section 10 essentially mirrors the common law definition of legal professional privilege and the crime-fraud exception.[7]

3.29 Similar exclusions can be found in the other statutes. For example, the CJA 1987, section 2(9) states that:

> A person shall not under this section be required to disclose any information or produce any document which he would be entitled to refuse to disclose or produce on grounds of legal professional privilege in proceedings in the High Court, except that a lawyer may be required to furnish the name and address of his client.

Note that this does not adopt the same definition of privilege as under PACE 1984, section 10. Whilst there is little, if any, practical difference,[8] section 2(9) more obviously reflects the common law definition since one would be 'entitled to refuse to disclose or produce' a document or information in proceedings in the High Court if it were privileged according to the common law.[9]

3.30 POCA 2002 and SOCPA 2005 adopt the same definition of legal privilege as the CJA 1987, section 2 and contain similar exclusions on compelling privileged information.[10] FSMA 2000 excludes the production or disclosure of 'protected items' rather than privileged items, but the definition of 'protected items' under section 413 is very similar to the definition of 'legal privilege' under PACE 1984, section 10, and the FSMA 2000 powers are subject to the same exception regarding a lawyer being required to furnish the name and address of their client as under the CJA 1987.[11]

---

[7] In *R v Central Criminal Court, ex p Francis & Francis* [1989] AC 346 (HL), Lord Goff (at 382) and Lord Griffiths (at 384–85) both considered s 10 to reflect the common law. Lord Griffiths stated: 'I am convinced that Parliament was not seeking to enact a special code of legal privilege of different import to the common law position. I believe the draftsman was seeking to spell out the common law position for the benefit of those unacquainted with it.' The House of Lords' confirmation of this principle was referenced with apparent approval by the Court of Appeal in *The Director of the Serious Fraud Office v Eurasian Natural Resources Corp Ltd (SFO v ENRC Ltd)* [2018] EWCA Civ 2006, [2019] 1 WLR 791 [62].

[8] Especially in light of the comments of Lord Goff and Lord Griffiths in *R v Central Criminal Court, ex p Francis & Francis* (n 7) 382, 384-85.

[9] Although note that, in certain exceptional cases, a client's name and/or address have been held to be covered by privilege. See eg *SRJ v Persons Unknown* [2014] EWHC 2293 (QB), [2014] All ER (D) 129 (Jul).

[10] See POCA 2002, ss 348, 354, and 361(1) for exclusions relating to POCA 2002, ss 345, 352, and 357, respectively; see SOCPA 2005, ss 64(1) and 66(9) for exclusions relating to SOCPA 2005, ss 62 and 66, respectively.

[11] FSMA 2000, s 175(4).

Witness summons

3.31 Neither the Criminal Procedure (Attendance of Witnesses) Act 1965, section 2 nor the Magistrates' Court Act 1980, section 97 contains an express exclusion for privileged documents. However, in *R v Derby Magistrates' Court, ex p B* the House of Lords confirmed that a witness summons under section 97 of the 1980 Act cannot compel the production of privileged documents,[12] and the same is true for section 2 of the 1965 Act.

Mutual legal assistance

3.32 Just as these powers do not authorize the seizure or compelled production of privileged material in domestic investigations, the same is true when they are being exercised on behalf of an overseas authority through MLA.

Other provisions

3.33 If, like the above-mentioned provisions concerning witness summonses, a statute is silent (or ambiguous) on whether a power of search, seizure or compelled production/disclosure or a similar power enables investigators, prosecutors, or the court to obtain privileged documents or information, the principles governing statutory abrogation of privilege discussed at paras 1.09–1.10 will be determinative of the issue. In the absence of express words, a statutory provision will only be interpreted as overriding privilege if this appears by 'necessary implication' from the wording.[13] This is exceptional.

Electronic devices

3.34 Notwithstanding the above provisions, a mobile phone, computer or other electronic device as a single object (as opposed to specific items it contains) can lawfully be the subject of a warrant issued under a non-CJPA 2001 provision even if it may contain privileged material, provided the wording of the warrant clearly excludes privileged material from that which can be sought or seized.[14] The principles concerning express exclusion of privileged material are discussed in more detail at paras 3.57–3.60. In these circumstances, there is no need to rely upon the additional powers of seizure conferred by the CJPA 2001, section 50. It is not a case of those executing the warrant finding something that *may contain* something for which they are authorized to search; the warrant will already expressly authorize seizure of the whole device.[15]

Sections 50 and 51 CJPA 2001

3.35 The CJPA 2001, sections 50(4) and 51(4) expressly disapply PACE 1984, section 19(6) to the CJPA 2001, sections 50(2) and 51(2), respectively. As a consequence, investigators exercising these powers may lawfully seize material that they have reasonable grounds

---

[12] [1996] AC 487 (HL).
[13] *R (Morgan Grenfell & Co Ltd) v Special Commissioners of Income Tax* [2002] UKHL 21, [2003] 1 AC 563.
[14] *R (A) v Central Criminal Court* [2017] EWHC 70 (Admin), [2017] 1 WLR 3567 [43]; *R (Glenn & Co (Essex) Ltd) v HM Commissioners for Revenue and Customs* [2011] EWHC 2998 (Admin), [2012] 1 CR App R 22 [57].
[15] See Fulford LJ's discussion of this point in *R (Cabot Global Ltd) v Barkingside Magistrates' Court* [2015] EWHC 1458 (Admin), [2015] 2 Cr App R 26 [46].

Inadvertent Seizure

3.36 It is also possible for privileged material to be seized inadvertently, where the fact is only discovered at a later stage. This, in and of itself, will not render the seizure unlawful. Under PACE 1984, section 19(6) it is the knowledge available to the officer at the time of the seizure that is relevant, and the seizure will only be unlawful if the officer's knowledge at that time constituted reasonable grounds for believing the item in question to be in fact subject to privilege; it is not sufficient if it only raises that possibility.[16]

Obligations after Seizure

3.37 Regardless of the route by which investigators may seize privileged material, whether that be as a result of one of the additional powers of seizure conferred by the CJPA 2001 or a non-CJPA 2001 power, the CJPA 2001 imposes strict obligations concerning its return, retention, and use. These are discussed at Section 7 below.

5 Applying for a Search Warrant

3.38 Although search warrants cannot authorize the seizure of privileged material, the mere fact that it is anticipated at the time of the application for the warrant that on the premises to be searched there will or may be items subject to privilege does not mean that a warrant for the search of those premises is unlawful.[17] However, as the cases discussed below demonstrate, deficiencies in the information provided when applying for a warrant or in how the warrant is worded can render it unlawful.

PACE 1984 Section 8 Warrants

3.39 One of the requirements for a PACE 1984, section 8 warrant is that the JP must have reasonable grounds for believing that the material which is the subject of the application does not consist of or include items subject to legal privilege (or excluded material or special procedure material) (section 8(1)(d)).

3.40 However, in *R (Sharer) v City of London Magistrates' Court*[18] the Divisional Court upheld the lawfulness of section 8 warrants even though a substantial amount of privileged material was found on the premises and seized under the CJPA 2001, section 50. For the

---

[16] *R v Chesterfield Justices, ex p Bramley* [2000] QB 576, 585 (QB).
[17] *Gittins v Central Criminal Court* [2011] EWHC 131 (Admin), [2011] Lloyd's Rep FC 219 [36].
[18] [2016] EWHC 1412 (Admin), (2017) 181 JP 48.

purposes of section 8(1)(d), what had to be assessed was, at the time the applications were being considered by the JP, whether the JP could properly be satisfied that there were reasonable grounds for believing that the material for which the search was to be made did not include privileged material or special procedure material. That ultimately was a matter of evaluation for the JP. In this case, the claimant was not a solicitor or accountant but a property developer and professional landlord. There was no reason to think that such material would be found on the premises. What was being sought was material concerning 'transactional matters' such as sales and purchases, prices, and rental receipts. Privileged and special procedure material would have been irrelevant to this. As such, when the warrants were applied for, there were no reasonable grounds for believing that privileged documents would be included in the material to be sought. The fact that the warrants were directed at, among other things, 'computers and communication devices' did not materially alter the position. There was no greater reason in this case to think that computer devices would contain privileged or special procedure material compared to ordinary physical files.[19]

3.41 In *Bates v Chief Constable of Avon and Somerset*,[20] however, a warrant issued under section 8 to search the property of a discredited expert in computer forensics who had acted as an expert witness in civil and criminal cases over many years was held to be unlawful as the police officer applying for the warrant and the JPs who granted it knew about the claimant's role as an expert witness and could not therefore have been satisfied that there were reasonable grounds for believing that his computers would not contain material subject to privilege (or special procedure material). The question had clearly not been addressed. Had it been, they would have come to the conclusion that the claimant's computers might contain such material and, in those circumstances, there was a means by which the police could have examined the computers for material relevant to their investigation, namely by exercising powers of seizure under the CJPA 2001.[21]

Duty to Make Full and Frank Disclosure

3.42 As a matter of general principle whenever an application for a search warrant is made without notice, the applicant is under an obligation to make full and frank disclosure of all matters that may be relevant to the decision whether to issue the warrant.[22] This is of particular importance where there may be privileged material on the premises. In *R (S) v Chief Constable of the British Transport Police*,[23] warrants were issued under PACE 1984, section 9 and schedule 1 for the search of a solicitor's (S) home and his and another firm's office

---

[19] ibid [24]–[30].
[20] [2009] EWHC 942 (Admin), [2009] All ER (D) 59 (May).
[21] ibid [28].
[22] In *R (S) v Chief Constable of the British Transport Police* [2013] EWHC 2189 (Admin), [2014] 1 WLR 1647 [45], this obligation was expressed in the following terms: '[The Information] must make full and frank disclosure. This means, in the words of Hughes LJ in *Re Stanford International Limited* [2010] 3 WLR 941 at [191] that "in effect a prosecution seeking an ex parte order must put on his defence hat and ask himself what, if he was representing the defendant or a third party with the relevant interest, he would be saying to the judge, and, having answered that question, that is precisely what he must tell". This is a heavy burden but a vital safeguard. Full details must be given. It is a useful reminder to the person laying the Information to state expressly which information is given pursuant to the duty of full and frank disclosure.'
[23] *R (S) v Chief Constable of the British Transport Police* (n 22).

premises. The warrant covering S' office premises was limited to his custody notebook/ solicitor's pad that was used when representing a client, MS, at the police station on a particular date, and 'any directly associated documentation relating to [MS]'. However, when executing the warrant, the police provided the occupier with a document specifying the items sought which included not only what was specified on the warrant but also 'the case file and associated documents relating to your client [MS]'. By its very nature, this would (and did in fact) contain material that was subject to privilege. Granting the application to quash the warrant, the Court was of the view that this additional material fell outside the terms of the warrant and the true purpose of the warrant was to go far beyond what was expressly stated on it. The police were, in fact, seeking all documents held by the firm that related to MS. If the police wanted to have access to the client file, the judge should have been explicitly told this so that he could fulfil his statutory duty when considering the application. The police had failed to give full, complete, and frank disclosure and the warrant was therefore unlawful.[24]

3.43 It was further noted by the Court in *S* that the information supporting an application for a search warrant under PACE 1984, section 9 and schedule 1 must state whether, despite there being reasonable grounds for the constable believing that the material sought consists of or contains special procedure material or excluded material, there might be a claim for privilege in respect of any communications sought and, if so, how and why that would arise together with precise details of the arrangements which are to be taken to ensure that there will be an independent supervising lawyer present at the time of the search.[25]

3.44 In the later case of *R (B) v Huddersfield Magistrates' Court*,[26] Stuart-Smith J did not consider *S* to establish 'a general and binding principle that full detail must be given of any possibility that legally privileged, excluded or special procedure materials might be encountered in a search where such material[s] are neither the intended target of the search nor intrinsically likely to be a significant element of what will probably be encountered'. It was also not accepted that it is always necessary to disclose that an occupant of premises to be searched is a solicitor. However, in the present case, the failure to disclose the fact that the occupants of the residential premises in respect of which a PACE 1984, section 8 warrant was being sought were solicitors amounted to a breach of the duty of full and frank disclosure, since it was highly likely that the terms of the warrant as drafted would include significant quantities of material that was legally privileged. Rejecting an argument that it could not be assumed that these particular solicitors would take home their work computers or would have legally privileged materials on their personal phones, the Court noted that, even if a solicitor were rigorous in maintaining separate phones and computers for home and work, there would be every likelihood that they would take their work-based devices home. This was particularly true for these solicitors as they were criminal defence duty solicitors and needed to be readily contactable and to have ready access to work contacts and content at short notice. Their work-based devices would therefore be kept close at hand. Furthermore,

---

[24] ibid [72]–[80].
[25] ibid [45]. See also *R v Southampton Crown Court, ex p J* [1993] Crim LR 962 (QB) for guidance on the information about potentially privileged material that should be provided to a judge when applying for a search warrant.
[26] [2014] EWHC 1089 (Admin), [2015] 1 WLR 4737.

it was said to be common knowledge that solicitors practising in this field might keep both work and home content on one device rather than maintain separate devices.[27]

Applications Are Not Mere Formalities

3.45 The Administrative Court's approach to one of the other warrants successfully challenged in *S* helpfully demonstrates the strict obligations imposed on investigators and judges when dealing with applications for search warrants. The warrant in question authorized a search of S' home address for his phone and laptop. The Court noted that the police were not interested in these items as items in and of themselves, but rather the material stored on them, such as emails, documents, and text messages, and this would have included material acquired in the course of S' occupation as a solicitor. Such material would, at the very least, amount to special procedure material and could also possibly comprise excluded material. Furthermore, it was highly likely that material stored on the devices would include items subject to privilege.[28] Rather than address these matters in their application, the police simply set out verbatim the wording of the requirements in PACE 1984, schedule 1 with no application to the facts or any elaboration.

3.46 As to the requirement that other methods of obtaining the material had been tried without success or had not been tried because they were bound to fail (PACE 1984, schedule 1, paragraph 2(b)), the information laid in support of the application merely recited this statutory obligation and asserted, without giving reasons, that there were reasonable grounds for believing that both requirements were satisfied. In his witness statement in the judicial review proceedings, the officer who applied for the warrant said that other methods of obtaining the material had not been tried 'since evidence might be destroyed or concealed and S was put on notice of our intention. The offence involved allegations of corruption by a solicitor'. The Court considered this to be a 'surprising assertion' considering an earlier request for S to provide his client's phone to the police had been complied with (albeit after some hesitation) and he was a practising solicitor against whom no allegation of dishonesty had previously been made and who would in the ordinary course of events be expected to comply with a request from the police to hand over a document or at least not destroy it. In any event, if there was to be an assertion that the police contemplated that if the search warrant was not issued then the material sought might have been destroyed or concealed, it should have been included in the information and the assessment should have been drawn to the attention of the judge. As there was no reference in the information to any basis on which the assertion was made, the judge could not possibly have satisfied himself of the requirement.[29]

3.47 The information also did not address whether it was in the public interest, 'having regard (i) to the benefit likely to accrue to the investigation if the material is obtained; and (ii) to the circumstances under which the person in possession of the material holds it, that the

---

[27] ibid [17]–[20].
[28] *R (S) v Chief Constable of the British Transport Police* (n 22) [57]–[58].
[29] ibid [62]–[64].

material should be produced or that access should be given' (PACE 1984, schedule 1, paragraph 2(c)). The Court stated:

> This provision requires a balancing exercise to be carried out which appraises, on the one hand, the benefit to the investigation of obtaining the information against, on the other hand, the seizure of a computer with the possibility that it would contain in it a mass of 'excluded material' and/or material subject to LPP, which was not concerned with the investigation and the seizure of which might well cause considerable professional disruption. The Judge's attention should have been drawn to this point with an explanation as to why this balancing exercise should be resolved in favour of the police.[30]

Instead, the information merely repeated the statutory wording with no such explanation or elaboration.

3.48 Another defect was that, according to the transcript of the hearing at which the application was made, it appeared that it had only taken two or three minutes before the judge reached his decision. From this, the Court concluded that: 'it does not appear as if he gave the required careful scrutiny to this application for a warrant to search the home of a solicitor for his "mobile phones and laptops" which might well contain "excluded material" or material subject to LPP'. In addition, the judge should have given reasons and explained, at least briefly, why he was satisfied that the various statutory requirements under PACE 1984, schedule 1 were fulfilled.[31]

3.49 These issues all highlight how the application for a search warrant should not be treated by either the applicant investigator or the judge as a mere formality or 'rubber-stamping' exercise. All statutory requirements must properly be addressed and the judge must apply careful scrutiny to the information presented by the applicant.

Crime-Fraud Exception and Overlap with Special Procedure Material

3.50 All material held by a solicitor that relates to their client but is not privileged is very likely to constitute special procedure material. This may include material which, by reason of the crime-fraud exception, is not privileged but is still held subject to an obligation of confidentiality. Where the crime-fraud exception does apply (see Chapter 2), a warrant under PACE 1984, section 8 will not be available, as it cannot be used to seize special procedure material, and the police will instead have to apply for a warrant under PACE 1984, section 9 and schedule 1.

3.51 In *R v Guildhall Magistrates' Court, ex p Primlaks Holdings Co (Panama) Inc*[32] the police obtained warrants under section 8 to search the premises of two firms of solicitors. Among the items seized was material over which the solicitors asserted privilege but which the police considered to be subject to the crime-fraud exception in section 10(2). Granting the application for judicial review to quash the warrants, the Divisional Court rejected the police's

---

[30] ibid [66].
[31] ibid [68].
[32] [1990] 1 QB 261 (QB).

argument that if, prima facie, privilege is lost by virtue of section 10(2), the result is that no express or implied undertaking to hold the material in confidence can exist. The Court held that a solicitor's correspondence with their client will, if not privileged, fall squarely within the definition of special procedure material. There was no basis on which the JP who issued the warrant could have had reasonable grounds for believing that section 8(1)(d) was satisfied. The warrants were unlawful and should have been sought under section 9 and schedule 1.[33]

3.52 Rather at odds with this decision is the case of *Fitzpatrick v Commissioner of Police of the Metropolis*,[34] which involved a claim for damages against the police arising from the arrest of two solicitors on suspicion of money laundering and the execution of a search warrant at their firm's premises. The police arrested one of the solicitors immediately after a prison legal visit with a client and seized conveyancing documents that the client had just signed. The police also obtained a section 8 warrant to enter and search the firm's premises. The material sought was limited to correspondence and computer records relating to conveyancing transactions concerning two of their clients. At the start of the search when the warrant was executed, one of the solicitors was asked by the police whether everything in the office was not privileged because it related to conveyancing. The solicitor replied that he thought that would be the case but he could not be sure. A large amount of documentation was then seized, invoking the CJPA 2001, section 50 powers because it was deemed impracticable to examine everything at the scene and because some of the material may have included privileged material.

3.53 One of the issues the Court had to consider when determining the claim for damages was whether the police executing the warrant had a defence under the Constables Protection Act 1750, section 6, which provides that a constable has a defence if acting in 'obedience' to a warrant wrongly granted. The claimants argued that the defence did not apply because there was a formal defect on the face of the warrant sufficiently grave to invalidate it, namely that the warrant related to material which was covered by privilege, in which case there was an absolute bar to it being covered by a search warrant, or, if the crime-fraud exception applied, it constituted special procedure material which necessitated an application under PACE 1984, section 9 and schedule 1. The warrant, it was submitted, therefore failed to satisfy PACE 1984, section 8(1)(d).

3.54 Rejecting this argument, the Court held that, in the circumstances of the case, there was no defect on the face of the warrant that raised a clear doubt as to whether an application had been lawfully made to, and granted by, the district judge in the exercise of his jurisdiction. Although not entirely clear from the judgment, the Court appears to have reached this conclusion on the basis of the police's submissions, which included the police placing reliance on the fact that the solicitor at the start of the search of the firm's premises had indicated that he thought files in the office would not be privileged. The police also argued that the crime-fraud exception applied to any material that may have been privileged and it could not be assumed that documents within the conveyancing files would have been held in confidence and would have amounted to special procedure

---

[33] ibid 270–72.
[34] [2012] EWHC 12 (Admin), [2012] Lloyd's Rep FC 361.

material. Furthermore, the police submitted that, even if it could be assumed that there would be special procedure material, the warrant was not void on its face because it was apparent that the application to the district judge related to the office of a firm of solicitors and the district judge would have been well aware of the nature of the material that was being sought.

3.55 This is a surprising decision. Considering the relevant test under section 8(1)(d) is whether there are reasonable grounds for believing that the material includes items subject to privilege or special procedure material at the time of the *application*, it is difficult to see how the solicitor's indication when the warrant was executed could have been of any relevance. Furthermore, if the crime-fraud exception did apply, it should have been obvious that the material would constitute special procedure material, as the Court in *Primlaks Holdings* had clearly held.

3.56 It perhaps mattered less to find that the warrant had wrongly been granted as this was a claim for damages and a relevant consideration was whether an application under section 9 and schedule 1 would have succeeded in respect of any special procedure material (the Court thought it would have). Less therefore seems to have turned on the question of whether the warrant was lawfully issued. *Fitzpatrick* can therefore probably be distinguished from *Primlaks* on the basis of its specific facts and considering the context of a civil claim for damages rather than judicial review.

Exclusion of Privileged Material in Wording of Warrant

3.57 Since no warrant can authorize the seizure of items subject to privilege, the wording of the warrant must clearly exclude any such material from that which can be sought or seized. Such exclusion need not necessarily be in express terms,[35] and a warrant that does not expressly exclude a search for privileged material does not automatically impliedly permit it, particularly in light of PACE 1984, section 19(6).[36] Nevertheless, in *R (F) v Blackfriars Crown Court*,[37] Elias LJ understood the authorities that suggested a warrant need not contain an express exclusion to have been so decided only because, in those cases, the terms of the warrant would not reasonably have been taken to extend to privileged material; 'Once the warrant does on its face extend to [privileged material], then it seems to us that on the authorities, it would be necessary expressly to exclude [it]'.[38]

3.58 In *F*, therefore, the absence of an express exclusion for privileged material rendered a warrant under PACE 1984, section 9 and schedule 1 unlawful. The warrant authorized a search of the premises of a company that provided services to firms of solicitors, including a cost drafting service, and which was suspected of submitting fraudulent claims for reimbursement of legal costs to HMCTS. The material identified on the warrant included, 'All

---

[35] *R (A) v Central Criminal Court* (n 14) [46]; *Gittins v Central Criminal Court* (n 17) [36].
[36] *R (Goode) v Nottingham Crown Court* [2013] EWHC 1726 (Admin), [2013] All ER (D) 281 (Jun).
[37] [2014] EWHC 1541 (Admin).
[38] ibid [50].

correspondence, documents, case files, fee notes and invoices relating to cases in the name of [four case names]', 'any other Defence Costs Order case' and 'Any computer hard-drive or other information storage device capable of storing [this information]'. The application acknowledged that privileged material might be encountered and that independent counsel would accompany officers when executing the warrant to ensure the police did not come into possession of privileged material. However, the Court held that, in this particular case, it was not enough for the police to have implemented a very careful procedure to ensure there was no abuse of any of the principles designed to protect privileged material; an express exclusion was required. Elias LJ noted that:

> [T]he rationale for requiring these exclusions on the face of the warrant is, as has often been said, to make sure both that the officers who carry out the search know precisely what they are entitled to do, and to enable the occupier of the premises where the search is being carried out to understand the proper limits of the power of the officers.[39]

3.59 Similarly, in *S* (discussed above), the Court was unable to confidently conclude that the warrant on its true interpretation did not extend to privileged material, since the terms of the warrant simply referred to a mobile phone and a computer said to be in the possession of a solicitor or firm of solicitors.[40]

3.60 As *F* demonstrates, if, on its true construction, a warrant extends to privileged material, it cannot be saved by precautions governing its execution on the day, such as the instruction of independent counsel.[41]

6 Executing a Search Warrant

3.61 Just as the application for and issuing of a search warrant requires great care where there may be privileged material on the premises, so too does the execution of the warrant itself.

Independent Counsel

3.62 The police and other investigating agencies will sometimes instruct independent counsel to attend the execution of a search warrant if it is anticipated that there may be privileged material on the premises, especially if that material is in hard copy and can be reviewed on the premises without the need for invoking the CJPA 2001, section 50. Their role during the search is to review potentially privileged documents before seizure and make a determination as to whether they are in fact covered by privilege, in which case they will not (and cannot) be seized (unless the CJPA 2001, section 50 is used). It is an important safeguard that has been recognized by the courts on a number of occasions. In *R (Rawlinson & Hunter Trustees) v Central Criminal Court*, for example, the Court stated that: 'The execution of a

---

[39] ibid [52].
[40] As understood by Parker J in *R (F) v Blackfriars Crown Court* (ibid) [64].
[41] *Gittins v Central Criminal Court* (n 17) [36].

warrant requires the presence of independent lawyers where there is the prospect of privileged documentation. This expense has to be resourced.'[42]

3.63 Independent counsel are also routinely instructed by investigating authorities to conduct privilege reviews after material has been seized. This arises most often in respect of material seized under the CJPA 2001, sections 50 and 51. The use of independent counsel to carry out privilege reviews after seizure is discussed in Chapter 4.

3.64 The Bar Council has issued guidance for independent counsel instructed to advise on privilege in relation to seized material.[43] In addition to points that are applicable to both privilege reviews conducted after seizure and those carried out on the premises,[44] the guidance includes the following points that specifically relate to independent counsel attending the execution of a search warrant:

- The fact counsel is instructed to enter the premises being searched should expressly be stated in their instructions and confirmation should be provided that the warrant specifically authorizes them to enter. If it does not, written permission to enter will need to be obtained from the owner or occupier of the premises.
- There is no restriction on counsel being informed by the person making a claim to privilege their reasons for making such a claim. If the person claiming privilege does not accept counsel's opinion, counsel can expect the disputed items to be 'blue bagged'[45] for later determination, whether by agreement or by the court under the CJPA 2001, section 59 (see paras 4.31–4.35 for more guidance on disputes).
- Counsel will be expected to give an oral opinion to those conducting the search. Counsel should keep a careful written record of all documents provided to them or seen by them and the opinion they have given. That opinion should then be reduced into writing and provided to those instructing counsel as soon as practicable thereafter.

3.65 In some cases, the instruction of independent counsel may indicate that, at the time the application for the search warrant was made, the police did have reasonable grounds for believing that the material sought would include privileged items. In respect of the warrant to search the firm's premises in *S*, the Court considered independent counsel's presence when the warrant was executed and his decision to take away the client file in order to review it for privileged material to be evidence that the police must have appreciated all along the likelihood that the material sought would include items subject to privilege.[46] However, in *R*

---

[42] [2012] EWHC 2254 (Admin), [2013] 1 WLR 1634 [293]; see also Gross LJ in *Gittins v Central Criminal Court* (n 17) [36]: '[g]ood practice will no doubt involve the taking of suitable precautions such as the engagement of independent counsel to deal with contingencies arising in the course of the search'; *R v Customs and Excise Commissioners, ex p Popely* [2000] Crim LR 388, 389 (QB); *R v Middlesex Guildhall Crown Court, ex p Tamosius & Partners* [2000] 1 WLR 453, 463 (QB); *R (McKenzie) v Director of the Serious Fraud Office* [2016] EWHC 102 (Admin), [2016] 1 WLR 1308 [40].

[43] The Bar Council, 'Barristers instructed as "Independent Counsel" to advise upon legal professional privilege in relation to seized material' (2010, reviewed September 2021) https://www.barcouncilethics.co.uk/wp-content/uploads/2017/10/LPP-Independent-Counsel-in-relation-to-seized-material-sept-2021.pdf (accessed 10 June 2023).

[44] As to which, see paras 4.29–4.30.

[45] Where privileged or potentially privileged material is encountered when executing a search warrant or reviewing seized material, the term 'blue bagged' is used to refer to the process by which the material is isolated from investigators either permanently or until independent counsel has reviewed it to determine if it is in fact privileged.

[46] *R (S) v Chief Constable of the British Transport Police* (n 22) [88].

(B) v Huddersfield Magistrates' Court,[47] the Court did not accept the claimants' submission that the fact the police instructed independent counsel to attend the execution of a section 8 warrant demonstrated that PACE 1984, section 8(1)(d) was not satisfied when the warrant was issued. Stuart-Smith J considered the instruction of independent counsel in this case to be 'entirely consistent' with a belief that material sought did not include privileged material, 'while prudently recognising the possibility of that belief proving to be wrong when the search was conducted'.[48]

Attendance of Lawyers

3.66 Since applications for search warrants are made *ex parte*, the owner or occupier of the premises will have little or no advance warning that the warrant is to be executed. As such, it may not be possible for their lawyers to attend the premises whilst the search is taking place, or at least not for the entirety of the search. Where they are able to attend, lawyers can play a valuable role in ensuring the protection of items subject to privilege, drawing investigators' attention to any such material and ensuring that it is handled correctly. If independent counsel has been instructed to attend, representations about specific documents can be made directly to them.

Obligations when Exercising CJPA 2001 Powers

3.67 An investigator exercising a power under the CJPA 2001, section 50 must give the occupier of the premises a written notice specifying, inter alia, what has been seized in reliance on the power and the grounds on which the power has been exercised.[49] There is a similar requirement when exercising a power under the CJPA 2001, section 51; the notice must be given to the person from whom the seizure is made.[50] Where it appears to the person exercising a power under section 50 that the occupier of the premises is not present but there is some other person on the premises who is in charge of the premises, the notice must be left with them.[51] Where it appears that there is no one present on the premises to whom a notice can be given, it must be attached to a prominent place on the premises.[52]

3.68 As with the other powers of seizure discussed in this chapter, the exercise of powers under sections 50 and 51 should not be treated as routine or trivial with little thought as to whether the necessary conditions are fulfilled. For example, in *S* (discussed above), independent counsel attended the search of S's firm's premises and took away a client file to review it for privilege at another location. This was done without the police relying on section 50 or 51 and the removal was therefore deemed unlawful. However, it seems from the Court's observations that even if the police had exercised these powers to allow the file to be removed, the

---

[47] *R (B) v Huddersfield Magistrates' Court* (n 26).
[48] ibid [15].
[49] CJPA 2001, s 52(1).
[50] ibid s 52(4).
[51] ibid s 52(2).
[52] ibid s 52(3).

conditions under section 50 would not have been satisfied. The evidence suggested that the client file was very slim and there seemed no reason why it could not be examined and sifted on the premises. It was 'particularly unfortunate' that the sifting process did not take place on the premises with a representative of the firm invited to be present. Referring to Kennedy LJ's remark in *R v Chesterfield Justices, ex p Bramley* that 'the owner of the material or his representative should have a right to be present when the sorting takes place',[53] the Court commented that this seemed 'particularly apposite when a solicitor's premises were being searched for material relating to his work and clients'.[54]

PACE 1984 Code B offers important guidance for officers seeking to rely on powers under the CJPA 2001: **3.69**

> The removal of large volumes of material, much of which may not ultimately be retainable, may have serious implications for the owners, particularly when they are involved in business or activities such as journalism or the provision of medical services. Officers must carefully consider if removing copies or images of relevant material or data would be a satisfactory alternative to removing originals. When originals are taken, officers must be prepared to facilitate the provision of copies or images for the owners when reasonably practicable.[55]

7 After Seizure

As well as creating additional powers of seizure, the CJPA 2001 also governs the procedure to be followed after seizure and imposes important obligations for how the material should be handled. With the exception of the obligations under section 53, the provisions discussed below apply equally to material seized under the CJPA 2001, sections 50 and 51 as to the other, non-CJPA 2001 statutory powers of seizure discussed earlier in this chapter (all of which are listed in the CJPA 2001, schedule 1, parts 1 and 2). **3.70**

Examination and Return of Property Seized under CJPA 2001, sections 50 and 51

An initial examination of property seized under sections 50 and 51 must be carried out as soon as reasonably practicable after seizure (section 53(2)(a)). Under section 53(2)(b), this initial examination must be confined to whatever is necessary for determining how much of the property falls within any of the categories specified in section 53(3): **3.71**

- property for which the person seizing it had power to search (in accordance with the warrant) when making the seizure and which is not property that must be returned by virtue of section 54 (relating to privileged material; see paras 3.75–3.78) (section 53(3)(a));

---

[53] *R v Chesterfield Justices, ex p Bramley* (n 16) 586.
[54] *R (S) v Chief Constable of the British Transport Police* (n 22) [88]–[89].
[55] PACE 1984 Code of Practice B, para 7.7.

- property the retention of which is authorized by section 56 (property obtained in consequence of the commission of an offence or which is evidence in relation to an offence) (section 53(3)(b)); or
- property which, in all the circumstances, it will not be reasonably practicable, following the examination, to separate from property falling within either of the above two categories (section 53(3)(c)).

3.72 Material falling into the last category is known as 'inextricably linked' material. PACE 1984 Code B provides, as an example, a computer disk whose separate items of data cannot be separated without damaging their evidential integrity.[56] Section 53(3)(c) is determined by reference to whether or not it is reasonably practicable to separate the property without prejudicing the lawful use of the property (or part of it) that falls into either of the first two categories.[57]

3.73 In determining the earliest practicable time for carrying out the initial examination, due regard should be given to the desirability of allowing the person from whom the property was seized, or a person with an interest in the property, an opportunity of being present or represented at the examination.[58]

3.74 Anything which is found on the initial examination not to fall within any of the categories under section 53(3) must be separated from the rest of the seized property and returned as soon as reasonably practicable after the initial examination of all the seized property has been completed (section 53(2)(c)). Until the initial examination of all seized property has been completed and anything which does not fall within section 53(3) has been returned, the seized property must be kept separate from anything seized under any other (non-CJPA 2001) power (section 53(2)(d)).

Obligation to Return Privileged Material

3.75 The CJPA 2001, section 54 imposes an obligation on investigators to return seized material that is subject to legal privilege. For the purposes of the CJPA 2001, 'legal privilege' has the same meaning as under PACE 1984, section 10 save in respect of property seized under POCA 2002, section 352(4), for which the definition of 'any material which a person would be entitled to refuse to produce on grounds of legal professional privilege in proceedings in the High Court' is adopted.[59]

3.76 Under section 54, if, at any time after seizure of anything in exercise of powers under the CJPA 2001, sections 50 or 51 or the various other non-CJPA 2001 powers of seizure specified in CJPA 2001, schedule 1, parts 1 and 2, it appears that the property is an item subject to legal privilege or has such an item comprised in it, it must be returned as soon as reasonably practicable after the seizure.

---

[56] ibid para 7H.
[57] CJPA 2001, s 53(5).
[58] ibid s 53(4).
[59] ibid s 65.

However, where the item subject to privilege is comprised in something else which has been lawfully seized, the obligation to return the privileged item does not arise if: **3.77**

- the whole or a part of the rest of the property is:
  - property for which the person seizing it had power to search when making the seizure and is not property which is required to be returned under sections 54 or 55 (section 55 relates to excluded material and special procedure material); or
  - property the retention of which is authorized by section 56 (property obtained in consequence of the commission of an offence or which is evidence in relation to an offence); and
- in all the circumstances, it is not reasonably practicable for the privileged item to be separated from the rest of that property (or, as the case may be, from that part of it) without prejudicing the use of the rest of that property, or that part of it, for purposes for which (disregarding the privileged item) its use, if retained, would be lawful.[60]

This means there is no requirement to return privileged material which is 'inextricably linked' to other material that is not privileged and that does not itself have to be returned. However, it is subject to restrictions on its use under section 62, as discussed below. **3.78**

Use of Inextricably Linked Property

The CJPA 2001, section 62 contains important provisions regarding the use that can be made of inextricably linked property seized under any power conferred by sections 50 or 51 or specified in schedule 1, parts 1 or 2. For the purposes of this section, property is 'inextricably linked' property if it falls into any of the following categories: **3.79**

- it has been seized under a power conferred by sections 50 or 51 and, but for section 53(3)(c), its return would be required by section 53(2)(c) (see paras 3.71–3.74);
- it has been seized under a power to which section 54 applies and, but for the exemption under that section for inextricably linked material, its return would be required by section 54 (see paras 3.75–3.78); or
- it has been seized under a power of seizure to which section 55 (relating to excluded material and special procedure material) applies and, but for the exemption under that section for inextricably linked material, its return would be required by section 55.[61]

Under section 62, the person in possession of the seized inextricably linked property must ensure that arrangements are in force which secure that that property (without being returned) is not at any time examined, copied or put to any other use, except with the consent of the person from whom it was seized.[62] However, such arrangements need not prevent inextricably linked property from being put to any use which is necessary for facilitating the **3.80**

---

[60] ibid ss 54(1)(b), 54(2), 54(3).
[61] ibid s 62(5)–(8).
[62] ibid s 62(2).

use, in any investigation or proceedings, of property in which the inextricably linked property is comprised.[63] PACE 1984 Code B expressly limits this by stating that: 'Inextricably linked material must not be examined, imaged, copied or used for any purpose other than for proving the source and/or integrity of the linked material.'[64]

Handling Privileged Material

3.81 Where computers or other electronic devices are seized under the CJPA 2001, sections 50 or 51 or a non-CJPA 2001 power and they contain privileged material, investigators will usually ensure compliance with the CJPA 2001 provisions discussed above by using keyword searches or other filters to isolate files that are relevant to the investigation and blocking access to everything else. If the material has been seized under the CJPA 2001, sections 50 or 51, keyword searches or filters for relevant material should return results which, unless privileged, are likely to be covered by the warrant and will therefore be 'property for which the person seizing it had power to search when making the seizure' (section 53(3)(a)), and they may also or alternatively be evidence in relation to an offence (section 53(3)(b)). Those results can then have privilege search terms run across them and any positive results either sent to independent counsel to review to determine if they are in fact privileged or isolated immediately without further review on the assumption that they are privileged. This should leave investigators only with relevant files that are not privileged and which may be retained under section 53. Everything else, whether privileged or not, will be inextricably linked to these items (by virtue of the fact that they are all saved on the same drive or device so cannot be separated) and will not need to be returned (in accordance with section 53(2)(c)). The requirement under section 62 to ensure that inextricably linked property is not examined, copied, or put to any other use is usually satisfied by members of the investigation team not having access to this material on whatever document review platform or system they are using.

3.82 If the electronic devices have been seized under a non-CJPA 2001 provision and it appears that they contain privileged material, although there is no requirement for an initial examination under section 53, the same steps as outlined above will ensure that any privileged material is isolated and access to it blocked, in accordance with section 62.

3.83 If the seized material is in hard copy, the keyword searches will have to be replaced by a manual review, unless the material can be scanned and have text recognition applied, allowing keyword searches to be run. Where hard copy documents that potentially contain privileged items do have to be reviewed manually, the exercise should be carried out by independent counsel.

3.84 The process of identifying and reviewing potentially privileged material, regardless of the power under which it has been seized or compelled, is examined in more detail in Chapter 4.

---

[63] ibid s 62(3)–(4).
[64] PACE 1984 Code of Practice B, para 7H.

Application for Return of Material

3.85 The CJPA 2001, section 59 provides a route for applying for the return of material seized in exercise, or purported exercise, of a power of seizure under sections 50 or 51 or specified in schedule 1, parts 1 or 2. An application can be made to a Crown Court judge by any person with a relevant interest in the seized property on one or more of several grounds, including that the seized property is or contains an item subject to privilege that is not caught by the inextricably linked exception under section 54.[65] A person has a relevant interest in seized property if they are the person from whom it was seized, they have an interest in the property (which includes, as far as privileged material is concerned, the person in whose favour the privilege is conferred) or they had custody or control of the property immediately before its seizure.[66]

3.86 On an application under section 59, the judge can order the return of the whole or a part of the seized property to which the application relates, dismiss the application or give such directions as they think fit as to the examination, retention, separation or return of the whole or any part of the seized property.[67] In addition, the judge can authorize the retention of any property which has been seized in exercise, or purported exercise, of the above-mentioned powers and would otherwise fall to be returned, if they are satisfied that the retention of the property is justified because, if the property were to be returned, it would immediately become appropriate to issue (on an application) a warrant for its lawful seizure (under any provision) or a production order under PACE 1984, schedule 1, paragraph 4 for it to be delivered up or produced.[68]

3.87 If an application is made under section 59 for the return of property seized under sections 50 or 51 on the grounds that the seized property is or contains an item subject to privilege that is not caught by the inextricably linked exception under section 54, a duty to secure the seized property arises under section 61 on the part of the person who has possession of the property in consequence of its seizure.[69] The duty requires that person to secure that arrangements are in place to ensure that the seized property (without being returned) is not, at any time after the giving of the notice of the section 59 application, either examined or copied or put to any use to which its seizure would entitle it to be put, except with the consent of the applicant or in accordance with the directions of the judge.[70]

8 Asserting Privilege in Response to Powers of Compulsion

3.88 As discussed above, investigators cannot compel the production or disclosure of privileged material or information. However, asserting that material is privileged in response to a production order or some other power of compulsion may not be accepted by the agency that has issued it (or on whose behalf it has been issued). For example, the privilege dispute

---

[65] CJPA 2001, s 59(3)(b).
[66] ibid s 59(11)–(12).
[67] ibid s 59(4)–(5).
[68] ibid s 59(6)–(7).
[69] ibid s 60(1)–(2).
[70] ibid s 61(1).

in *The Director of the Serious Fraud Office v Eurasian Natural Resources Corp Ltd*[71] began with the SFO issuing notices under the CJA 1987, section 2(3) requiring the production of documents relevant to its investigation, in response to which ENRC asserted privilege over certain of the documents and refused to provide them. The SFO challenged this by issuing a claim under part 8 of the Civil Procedure Rules for a declaration that documents in four specific categories were not 'information or … any document which ENRC would be entitled to refuse to disclose or produce on grounds of legal professional privilege in proceedings in the High Court' (in accordance with the CJA 1987, section 2(9)). The claim was then determined at a trial before the High Court at which oral evidence was called, resulting in Andrews J's judgment (later overturned by the Court of Appeal).

3.89 In other circumstances, the investigating authority may try to obtain a search warrant in respect of the disputed material, but this is unlikely to offer a complete solution to the problem as a search warrant cannot authorize the seizure of privileged material. Such an approach is suggested by the CPS in its guidance on the exercise of powers under SOCPA 2005, which includes the following points:

> Prosecutors may be faced with assertions - possibly blanket assertions - that material is subject to legal professional privilege. This does not have to be taken at face value.
>
> Such assertions are not necessarily made with the intention of frustrating the investigation. Some recipients of disclosure notices may simply be uncertain about what constitutes material that is subject to legal professional privilege and consider that they are preserving their position by claiming privilege. In such cases it may be possible to resolve issues by negotiation.
>
> Where it is not possible to do so, then an independent lawyer should be appointed, if the recipient agrees, to arbitrate, on the understanding that both sides will abide by his/her views. The recipient should be able to instruct the lawyer as to his/her views.
>
> If the recipient is not prepared to agree to negotiation then it may be necessary to obtain a warrant to obtain the disputed material. In such circumstances the material should be sealed and the opinion of an independent lawyer sought.[72]

In the authors' view, this does not reflect the most appropriate procedure. First, it would appear to be encouraging prosecutors to assume that privilege claims made in response to SOCPA 2005 notices are not legitimate. Secondly, where the recipient of a notice withholds material on the grounds of privilege and does not agree to an independent lawyer reviewing it to make a determination, whilst that may be unhelpful, it does not diminish the validity of the privilege claim, and, if the document is in fact privileged, it cannot be seized under a warrant. If a warrant is issued, independent counsel should attend its execution and determine whether the material is privileged at the time of the search if practicable. Only if it is not practicable to make that determination or to separate privileged items from non-privileged items at the time of the search may the material be taken away, but only by exercising powers under the CJPA 2001, section 50.

---

[71] *SFO v ENRC Ltd* (n 7).
[72] CPS, 'Director's Investigatory Powers: Legal Guidance' https://www.cps.gov.uk/legal-guidance/directors-investigatory-powers (accessed 10 June 2023).

3.90 The guidance also states that 'transactions conducted by a solicitor in a conveyancing matter, are very unlikely to be covered by legal professional privilege in High Court proceedings and will be obtainable. In the experience of the SFO they are frequently the subject of a disclosure notice'. This is, with respect, not an accurate reflection of the law. There is nothing unique about a conveyancing matter conducted by a solicitor that means that legal advice relating to it will fall outside the scope of privilege.

3.91 Once a prosecution is underway, if a third party holds material over which privilege is claimed but the prosecution disputes this, and it is likely to be material evidence in the proceedings, the witness summons provisions outlined at para 3.11 can be used to bring the issue before the court so that it can determine whether the material is privileged. This approach was endorsed by the Divisional Court in *R (AL) v Serious Fraud Office*.[73]

9 Impact of Seizure on Fair Trial

3.92 In *R v Kular*[74] an unsuccessful attempt was made to stay the case as an abuse of process after the police seized and read privileged documents. The appellant had been charged with murder and, whilst in custody awaiting trial, his prison cell was searched by the police for information relating to a suspected conspiracy to pervert the course of justice. During the search, the police seized a number of privileged documents relating to the murder case, including the appellant's instructions on the conduct of the trial and instructions regarding prosecution witnesses. The documents were read by the police and prosecution. Once the prosecution realized that this material was privileged, it was returned to the defence and the prosecution gave assurances that it had not copied any of the documents and that they played no part whatsoever in the case to be presented at trial.

3.93 The trial judge's refusal to stay the case as an abuse of process was upheld by the Court of Appeal. There was no suggestion of bad faith on the part of the police or prosecution in respect of seizure of the material. The trial judge had rightly concluded that the fact that, without bad faith, privileged material had been seen did not mean that an irremediable injustice had been caused. It was particularly significant that the material had been returned and formed no part of the prosecution case.

3.94 The Court of Appeal also held that the trial judge had rightly rejected an additional submission that the prosecution, having had sight of the material, had an unfair advantage if the appellant decided to give evidence, and that that knowledge would be a source of unfair pressure on the appellant in deciding whether to give evidence. The Court rejected the suggestion that the appellant had a legitimate fear that material might be used improperly and adversely against him if he gave evidence. The reality of the case was that there was an overwhelming body of evidence against the appellant, and there was accordingly no reason whatsoever for regarding his conviction as unsafe.

---

[73] *R (AL) v Serious Fraud Office* [2018] EWHC 856 (Admin), [2018] 1 WLR 4557 [69]–[71].
[74] CA (18 April 2000).

3.95 In *R (on the application of Her Majesty's Commissioners of Customs & Excise) v Nottingham Magistrates' Court*[75] Kennedy LJ set out guidance regarding the approach a court should take if a prosecutor comes into possession of material which the defence justifiably claims is subject to legal professional privilege (and that claim is either conceded or upheld) and the defence contends that the way in which the material came into the possession of the prosecutor needs to be investigated and/or that the disclosure of that material has so prejudiced the conduct of the defence that the case should not proceed. He stated the following:

> If such a contention is raised, there is then a duty on the prosecutor [to] explain to the court, so far as he is able to do so, either by calling evidence or by means of uncontested statements of fact, how he came into possession of the material, and what, if any, use he has made of it, failing which the court may infer—
>
> (a) that he has obtained it by improper means, and/or
> (b) that his use of it will unfairly prejudice the defendant in his conduct of the proceedings.
>
> ...
>
> In the light of the explanation given by the prosecution, the defence may want to call evidence directed to—
>
> (a) the way in which the prosecutor obtained possession of the material;
> (b) the extent to which its contents have been disclosed; and/or
> (c) any resultant prejudice or potential prejudice to the conduct of the defence. The solicitor acting for the defendant may be able to help as to that.
>
> ...
>
> The court will then be in a proper position to decide what has happened and what needs to be done to ensure that the defendant receives a fair trial. The nature of the inquiry, as set out above, is such that it will probably be convenient to start with the prosecution, but that is a matter for the judge. What he must never lose sight of is the overall object of the criminal proceedings, namely to investigate the alleged criminality of the defendant by means of a fair trial, without allowing the process to be derailed by technical problems which can be overcome. In most circumstances there would seem to be no obvious reason why he should not see the particular critical material, at least if it has been looked at by anyone acting for the prosecution.[76]

3.96 Although not concerned with seizure of privileged material, the Court of Appeal in *R v Grant*[77] held that deliberate, unlawful eavesdropping and tape recording of privileged conversations by the police (not in pursuance of powers authorizing covert surveillance or interception of communications discussed at Section 10 below) amounted to an abuse of process. The conduct in this case was so egregious that there was no reasonable prospect of the proceedings being allowed to continue. *Grant* is discussed in more detail at paras 6.13–6.14.

---

[75] [2004] EWHC 1922 (Admin), [2004] All ER (D) 241 (Jul).
[76] ibid [60]–[62].
[77] [2005] EWCA Crim 1089, [2006] QB 60.

10 Covert Surveillance and Interception of Communications

The Regulation of Investigatory Powers Act 2000 (RIPA 2000) and the Investigatory Powers Act 2016 (IPA 2016) allow, in certain exceptional circumstances, for investigating agencies and other public authorities to have access to privileged communications by way of covert surveillance (RIPA 2000) or through interception (IPA 2016). Despite the circumstances in which such powers are likely to be used being rare and extreme, these powers represent a concerning erosion of the fundamental and inviolable rights that legal professional privilege exists to protect, particularly because it is unlikely ever to become clear if the powers have been used in a particular case as they will yield information which will be used for intelligence purposes only. The practical implication is that if a legal adviser has reason to believe that surveillance or interception has been or will be authorized, the client should be made aware, and this is likely to have an impact on the way the client communicates with their legal adviser. In any event, whether or not surveillance or interception actually takes place, the knowledge that the legislation exists undermines the right to communicate freely and confidentially with a legal adviser.

3.97

Covert Surveillance: RIPA 2000

The RIPA 2000, Part II allows for the authorization of two types of covert surveillance: 'directed' surveillance (section 28) and 'intrusive surveillance' (section 32). Directed surveillance is that which is carried out for the purposes of a specific investigation or operation in such a manner as is likely to result in the obtaining of private information about a person, but it does not include surveillance by way of an immediate response to events or circumstances the nature of which is such that it would not be reasonably practicable for an authorization to be sought.[78] Intrusive surveillance is that which is carried out in relation to anything taking place on residential premises or in a private vehicle and which involves the presence of an individual on the premises or in the vehicle or is carried out by means of a surveillance device.[79] It is assumed that intrusive surveillance will always be likely to result in the obtaining of private information.[80]

3.98

The public authorities who can apply for authorization for directed surveillance are listed in the RIPA 2000, schedule 1, parts A1, I, and II. They include, inter alia, the police, NCA, SFO, HMRC, FCA, CMA, and the intelligence services. Intrusive surveillance applications can only be made by public authorities whose 'senior authorising officer' is listed in section 32(6) or by public authorities listed in or designated under section 41(1).[81] They include,

3.99

---

[78] RIPA 2000, s 26(2).
[79] ibid s 26(3).
[80] 'Covert Surveillance and Property Interference: Revised Code of Practice' (August 2018) (RIPA 2000 Code) para 3.21 https://www.gov.uk/government/publications/covert-surveillance-and-covert-human-intelligence-sources-codes-of-practice (accessed 10 June 2023).
[81] ibid para 2.10.

inter alia, the police, NCA, HMRC, CMA and the intelligence services. Directed surveillance can be authorized by persons within the public authority who have been designated by order of the Secretary of State, whereas intrusive surveillance can only be authorized by 'senior authorising officers' within the relevant public authority or by the Secretary of State.

3.100 Under section 27, covert surveillance is lawful 'for all purposes' if authorized. There is no express provision for privileged communications in the Act itself, but in *McE v Prison Service of Northern Ireland*[82] the House of Lords confirmed that the RIPA 2000 permits covert surveillance of privileged communications, provided that the surveillance is carried out in accordance with the Act and the Code of Practice issued under section 71 and does not violate the European Convention on Human Rights (ECHR). The words 'for all purposes' in section 27 were considered a clear indication of Parliament's intention to include privileged communications with those which could be covertly surveilled. The Code of Practice made detailed provision for obtaining authorization for monitoring consultations covered by privilege and Parliament had not objected to the inclusion of those provisions. The RIPA 2000 was therefore capable of permitting covert surveillance of privileged communications. However, the Court held that directed surveillance carried out under section 28 and the Code of Practice in place at the time (since revised) infringed the rights of the privilege holder under the ECHR, art 8 and was therefore unlawful. Enhanced authorization such as that pursuant to the intrusive surveillance provisions of the RIPA 2000, section 32 was required in order for it to be compliant.

3.101 In light of the House of Lords' decision in *McE*, the Regulation of Investigatory Powers (Extension of Authorisation Provisions: Legal Consultations) Order 2010[83] was passed. This provides that surveillance in places used for the purpose of legal consultations shall be treated for the purposes of the RIPA 2000, part II as intrusive surveillance, thereby requiring enhanced authorization and ensuring compliance with the ECHR, in accordance with *McE*. The list of premises includes prisons, police stations, lawyers' offices, and courts.

3.102 The current version of the RIPA 2000 Code of Practice[84] (RIPA 2000 Code) envisages three different circumstances in which privileged material may be acquired through covert surveillance:

1. where privileged material is intentionally sought;
2. where privileged material is likely to be obtained; and
3. where the purpose, or one of the purposes, of the surveillance is to obtain items that, if they were not generated or held with the intention of furthering a criminal purpose, would be subject to privilege (the crime-fraud exception).[85]

---

[82] [2009] UKHL 15, [2009] 1 AC 908.
[83] SI 2010/461.
[84] 'Covert Surveillance and Property Interference: Revised Code of Practice' (August 2018) https://www.gov.uk/government/publications/covert-surveillance-and-covert-human-intelligence-sources-codes-of-practice (accessed 10 June 2023).
[85] RIPA 2000 Code, para 9.50.

Interception of Communications: IPA 2016

Under the IPA 2016, communications can be lawfully intercepted if authorized by a warrant issued under pt 2 or ch 1 of pt 6 of the Act. A 'targeted interception warrant' authorizes or requires the person to whom it is addressed to secure the interception of and/or the obtaining of secondary data from communications described in the warrant.[86] A 'targeted examination warrant' authorizes the person to whom it is addressed to select for examination intercepted content obtained under a 'bulk interception warrant'.[87] A 'bulk interception warrant' is a warrant which has as its main purpose the interception of overseas-related communications and/or the obtaining of secondary data from such communications. It authorizes or requires the person to whom it is addressed to do one or more of the following: to intercept communications described in the warrant, to obtain secondary data from such communications, to select for examination the intercepted content or secondary data, or the disclosure of anything obtained under the warrant.[88] Applications for warrants under the IPA 2016 can be made by only a limited number of public authorities. In the case of targeted interception warrants, they include, inter alia, the NCA, the Metropolitan Police, HMRC and the intelligence services,[89] and in the case of a targeted examination or bulk interception warrant, only the intelligence services can apply.[90] Warrants are issued by the Secretary of State and must be approved by a 'Judicial Commissioner'.[91]

3.103

Unlike the RIPA 2000, the IPA 2016 expressly authorizes the interception and examination of privileged communications. This includes warrants where privileged material is intentionally sought or selected for examination or is likely to be obtained or selected for examination, as well as warrants that seek the interception or selection for examination of material that would be privileged but for the crime-fraud exception.

3.104

Safeguards: RIPA 2000 and IPA 2016

Although the RIPA 2000 and the IPA 2016 allow public authorities access to privileged communications, there are important requirements that must be satisfied when applying for and exercising these powers to ensure that the impact on privilege is limited only to what is necessary. These safeguards can be found in the RIPA 2000 Code in the case of covert surveillance and in the terms of the IPA 2016 itself and the corresponding Code of Practice[92]

3.105

---

[86] IPA 2016, s 15(2).
[87] ibid s 15(3); and see explanation in the 'Interception of Communications Code of Practice' (December 2022) (IPA 2016 Code), para 4.5 https://assets.publishing.service.gov.uk/government/uploads/system/uploads/attachment_data/file/1123773/revised_Interception_of_Communications_Code_of_Practice_Dec_2022.pdf (accessed 10 June 2023).
[88] IPA 2016, s 136; and see explanation in IPA 2016 Code, paras 6.1–6.2.
[89] IPA 2016, ss 18(1) and 19.
[90] ibid ss 19(2) and 138.
[91] ibid ss 19 and 23.
[92] 'Interception of Communications Code of Practice' (December 2022) https://assets.publishing.service.gov.uk/government/uploads/system/uploads/attachment_data/file/1123773/revised_Interception_of_Communications_Code_of_Practice_Dec_2022.pdf (accessed 10 June 2023).

(IPA 2016 Code) in respect of interception.[93] The safeguards for both the RIPA 2000 and the IPA 2016 are broadly similar as far as privilege is concerned and can therefore be addressed together in the brief overview that follows.

3.106 Where the relevant conduct is intended to acquire privileged information, authorization/a warrant can only be granted/issued if there are 'exceptional and compelling circumstances' that make it necessary.[94] 'Exceptional and compelling circumstances' can only arise where: (1) there is a threat to life or limb or it is in the interests of national security; (2) the public interest in obtaining the information outweighs the public interest in maintaining its confidentiality; and (3) there are no other reasonable means of obtaining the information.[95] The surveillance/interception must reasonably be regarded as likely to yield the intelligence necessary to counter the threat,[96] and the proposed conduct must be proportionate to what is sought to be achieved.[97] The RIPA 2000 and the IPA 2016 Codes make it clear that this test will only be met in exceptional cases.[98] Both Codes give as an example a public authority monitoring or targeting privileged communications where the legal consultation might yield intelligence that could prevent harm to a potential victim or victims. If they have intelligence to suggest that an individual is about to carry out a terrorist attack and the consultation may reveal information that could assist in averting the attack (such as by revealing details about the location and movements of the individual), the public authority may seek to rely on these powers to target/monitor the legally privileged communications.[99]

3.107 Where the relevant conduct is likely to result in the acquisition of privileged information (as opposed to this being the intention), the application for authorization/a warrant must be clear that the acquisition of such information is likely and should include an assessment of how likely it is that privileged information will be acquired.[100] Specific requirements for the acquisition of material believed to be covered by the crime-fraud exception can be found at paragraphs 9.55–9.57 of the RIPA 2000 Code and the IPA 2016, section 27(11)–(13).

3.108 There are also important provisions for the handling, retention, deletion, and dissemination of privileged material. For example, where it is discovered that privileged material has been obtained inadvertently, an early assessment must be made of whether it is necessary and proportionate to retain it for one or more of the authorized purposes under the RIPA 2000 Code or the IPA 2016, section 53(3). If it does not meet this test, the material should not be retained, other than for the purpose of its destruction.[101] A public authority cannot act on or further disseminate privileged items unless it has first informed the Investigatory Powers

---

[93] In *R (National Council for Civil Liberties) v Secretary of State for the Home Department* [2023] EWCA Civ 926 [200], the Court of Appeal held that the relevant parts of the IPA 2016 provide adequate safeguards for the protection of legally privileged material and are compatible with the ECHR, art 8.
[94] RIPA 2000 Code, para 9.51; IPA 2016, s 27(4)(a).
[95] RIPA 2000 Code, para 9.51; IPA 2016, s 27(6).
[96] RIPA 2000 Code, para 9.51; IPA 2016 Code, para 9.54.
[97] RIPA 2000 Code, para 9.52; IPA 2016 Code, para 9.55.
[98] RIPA 2000 Code, para 9.51; IPA 2016 Code, para 9.54.
[99] RIPA 2000 Code, para 9.51; IPA 2016 Code, para 9.54.
[100] RIPA 2000 Code, para 9.54; IPA 2016, s 27(8).
[101] RIPA 2000 Code, para 9.74; IPA 2016, s 55; IPA 2016 Code, para 9.67.

Commissioner that the items have been obtained/selected for examination, except in urgent circumstances.[102] Furthermore, dissemination of privileged material:

> [S]hould be safeguarded by taking reasonable steps to remove the risk of it becoming available, or its contents becoming known, to any person whose possession of it might prejudice any criminal or civil proceedings to which the information relates, including law enforcement authorities. In this regard civil proceedings includes all legal proceedings before courts and tribunals that are not criminal in nature. Neither the Crown Prosecution Service lawyer nor any other prosecuting authority lawyer with conduct of a prosecution should have sight of any legally privileged material, held by the relevant public authority, with any possible connection to the proceedings. In respect of civil proceedings, there can be no circumstances under which it is proper for any public authority to have sight of or seek to rely on legally privileged material in order to gain a litigation advantage over another party in legal proceedings.[103]

---

[102] RIPA 2000 Code, para 9.80; IPA 2016 Code, para 9.72.
[103] RIPA 2000 Code, para 9.81 (an almost identical version is in IPA 2016 Code, para 9.73).

4
Privilege Reviews

1 Introduction

Chapter 3 examines the routes through which investigating authorities may legitimately come into possession of privileged material and the strict requirements concerning its retention, examination, and use. In the first part of this chapter, we look in more detail at the procedure to be followed for reviewing the material after seizure/compelled production and how to navigate the issues that may arise. The guidance will be of assistance to all parties involved in the process, including defence lawyers, independent counsel, investigators, and prosecutors.

4.01

The second part of the chapter examines the privilege review process in other circumstances, where the material has not been seized and the review is carried out by lawyers in private practice. Such circumstances might include a review of material to remove privileged items prior to voluntary disclosure to the authorities or in response to a production order, or a review in the course of an internal investigation.

4.02

In the final part of the chapter, we consider particular categories of documents and the practical issues that are often encountered in all types of privilege review, regardless of who is conducting the review and for what purpose.

4.03

The term 'privilege review' is used to refer to any review of electronic files or physical documents to determine whether they are covered by privilege.

4.04

2 Privilege Reviews: Seized/Compelled Material

Procedure

As explained in Chapter 3, Section 7, the Criminal Justice and Police Act 2001 (CJPA 2001) imposes important obligations on investigators for how seized material that is or may be privileged must be handled after seizure. Where material has been seized pursuant to the additional powers of seizure under the CJPA 2001, sections 50 and 51 (allowing the determination of whether there is an entitlement to seize the material or the separation of seizable material from that in which it is comprised to take place at a later stage), an initial examination must take place as soon as reasonably practicable to determine how much of the seized property can lawfully be retained according to the categories in section 53 (see para 3.71). For material seized under section 50 or section 51 or any other (non-CJPA 2001) power, section 54 requires any privileged items to be returned as soon as reasonably practicable after seizure, unless they are 'inextricably linked' to other material which

4.05

is not privileged and which does not itself have to be returned, in which case arrangements must be put in place to secure that the privileged material is not examined, copied, or put to any other use (section 62) (see paras 3.75–3.80). In the case of electronic devices, on which all material will be inextricably linked, the implication of the CJPA 2001 provisions is that investigating authorities must find a way of blocking investigators' access to privileged items.

4.06 Regardless of the power under which material has been seized or its production compelled, the following procedure should be followed whenever investigators and/or prosecutors are alerted to the possibility that privileged material is among that which has been seized (or produced/disclosed subject to powers of compulsion). It reflects best practice and will ensure compliance with the CJPA 2001.

1. Before any material is reviewed, search terms should be run across electronic devices and any other electronic data to locate files that may be privileged (see suggested search terms at paras 4.15–4.19). Where possible, these searches should be applied to files that have already been identified as potentially relevant to the investigation (and for which there is a lawful basis for retaining and examining, for example because they are items for which there was a power to search when making the seizure) through the application of other search terms or filters. Running searches in this order should reduce the volume of potentially privileged material that will need to be reviewed.
2. All files responsive to the privilege search terms and any other potentially privileged material that has been seized/compelled (for example, hard copy documents) should be sent to independent counsel to be reviewed and for determinations to be made as to whether they are in fact privileged. No member of the investigation or prosecution team should have access to any of these files unless and until they are deemed not to be privileged. Investigators can of course accept that these items are privileged and block access to them without asking independent counsel to review them, but this is not the approach that is usually taken in practice.
3. Before concluding their review, independent counsel should share their proposed determinations with the defence and invite representations on any areas of disagreement.
4. Once finalized, independent counsel will inform the investigating agency which files (and/or hard copy documents) are privileged and they will be permanently isolated from the investigation and/or prosecution team dealing with the case (or returned if not inextricably linked, for example hard copy documents).

4.07 Steps 1 and 2 should be undertaken by somebody who is not part of the investigation or prosecution team, such as in-house technical staff.

4.08 Steps 2 to 4 should also be followed if privileged or potentially privileged items are encountered unexpectedly by investigators or prosecutors when reviewing material. In some cases, this might identify the need for additional privilege search terms if the documents indicate that other privileged items may potentially have been missed.

4.09 It is possible that the investigating agency will not agree to follow step 3, on the basis that it is not considered a proportionate step. Whilst it is not explicitly stated in the guidance discussed below, it is an entirely reasonable request for the defence to make and is consistent with the notion of defence engagement envisaged in the guidance.

4.10 The procedure outlined above reflects the relevant guidance issued to investigators and prosecutors. The Attorney General's Guidelines on Disclosure, which apply to all investigators and prosecutors, include the following:

> Where LPP material or material suspected of containing LPP is seized, it must be isolated from the other material which has been seized in the investigation. Where suspected LPP material is discovered when reviewing material, and it was not anticipated that this material existed, again it must be isolated from the other material and the steps outlined below taken. The prosecution will need to decide on a case by case basis if the material is LPP material or not—[the] defence may be able to assist with this.
>
> Where material has been identified as potentially containing LPP it must be reviewed by a lawyer independent of the prosecuting authority. No member of the investigative or prosecution team involved in either the current investigation or, if the LPP material relates to other criminal proceedings, in those proceedings should have sight of or access to the LPP material.
>
> If the material is voluminous, search terms or other filters may have to be used to identify the LPP material. If so this will also have to be done by someone independent and not connected with the investigation.
>
> It is essential that anyone dealing with LPP material maintains proper records showing the way in which the material has been handled and those who have had access to it, as well as decisions taken in relation to that material.[1]

4.11 The CPS has very similar guidance which essentially adopts the Attorney General's Guidelines:

> If [privileged] material is seized, where it could not be separated or where it was seized inadvertently and discovered on review, the investigator must arrange for it to be isolated from other seized material and any other investigation material in the possession of the investigating authority. Consideration should be given to having independent counsel present during a search.
>
> Where material has been identified as potentially containing LPP it must be reviewed by a lawyer independent of the prosecuting authority. No member of the investigative or prosecution team involved in the current investigation should have sight of or access to the LPP material.
>
> If the material is voluminous, search terms or other filters may have to be used to identify the LPP material. If so, this will also have to be done by someone independent and not connected with the investigation.
>
> The defence should be invited to engage to assist in the process.[2]

---

[1] Attorney General's Office, 'Attorney General's Guidelines on Disclosure' (26 May 2022) Annex A, paras 28–31 https://assets.publishing.service.govuk/media/628ce5efd3bf7f1f3b19efa7/AG_Guidelines_2022_Revision_Publication_Copy.pdf (accessed 14 October 2023).

[2] CPS, 'Disclosure Manual: Chapter 30: Digital Material' (14 July 2022) https://www.cps.gov.uk/legal-guidance/disclosure-manual-chapter-30-digital-material (accessed 10 June 2023).

4.12 The Serious Fraud Office (SFO) Operational Handbook[3] sets out the following policy for handling privileged material:

> When the SFO requires the production of material, or seizes material pursuant to its statutory powers, all material which is potentially protected by LPP must be treated with great care to:
>
> - Minimise the risk that LPP material is seen or seized by an SFO investigator or a lawyer involved in the investigation
> - Ensure that any LPP material which is seized is properly isolated and promptly returned to the owner without having been seen by an SFO investigator or a lawyer involved in the investigation
> - Ensure that any dispute relating to LPP is resolved in advance of the material being seen by an SFO investigator or a lawyer involved in the investigation
> - Ensure that where an SFO investigator or a lawyer involved in the investigation inadvertently sees LPP material, measures are in place to ensure that the investigation and any subsequent prosecution is not adversely affected as a result. Care must always be taken that LPP material is not viewed by the SFO staff involved in the investigation.

As for handling digital material potentially containing privileged items, the Handbook[4] advises the following:

> Digital material which potentially contains LPP material, such as the contents of a laptop will be processed and loaded onto the Digital Review System ('DRS'), but isolated from the case team's access.
>
> The case controller should contact the owner or his or her legal representative to seek search terms to be applied to identify potential LPP material embedded in the digital material. Those search terms will be applied by a member of the Digital Review System team, who is independent of the case team. The results of the search terms applied will be confined in a separate folder to which the case team and case controller do not have access. The material will then be reviewed by an independent LPP lawyer.
>
> Following the review, any material which is identified as LPP will be extracted from the non-LPP material. Only the non-LPP material (hard and digital) will be made available to the investigation team.

4.13 As indicated in the guidance, organizations such as the SFO will make use of their own in-house technical staff to run the search terms to identify specific files which may be privileged and which will then be sent to independent counsel to be reviewed. The lawfulness of this practice was upheld by the Divisional Court in the case of *R (McKenzie) v Director of the Serious Fraud Office*.[5] The Court interpreted 'someone independent and not connected to the investigation' in the Attorney General's guidelines not to be

---

[3] As understood from passages quoted in *R (McKenzie) v Director of the Serious Fraud Office* [2016] EWHC 102 (Admin), [2016] 1 WLR 1308 [8]–[9].
[4] As understood from passages quoted in ibid [8]–[9].
[5] ibid.

someone independent in the sense of not being employed by the investigating authority, but someone who could be in-house but functionally independent of the investigation. However, the Court emphasized the positive duty the law imposes upon a seizing authority to guard against the risk that an investigator will read a document protected by privilege.[6] Burnett LJ stated that:

> [A] seizing authority has a duty to devise and operate a system to isolate potential LPP material from bulk material lawfully in its possession, which can reasonably be expected to ensure that such material will not be read by members of the investigative team before it has been reviewed by an independent lawyer to establish whether privilege exists. That approach to LPP material imports the necessary rigour required by the law for its protection in this context.
>
> ...
>
> [T]here should also be clear guidance in place meaning that, if an investigator does by mischance read material subject to LPP, that fact is recorded and reported, the potential conflict recognised, and steps taken to prevent information which is subject to privilege being deployed in the investigation. There may be cases where it is necessary to remove the relevant investigator from the case.[7]

4.14 For completeness, it is worth noting that there is no reason why investigators or prosecutors cannot accept a claim to privilege over a document at face value and return or isolate it without instructing independent counsel to review it. This might be the case if, for example, the defence draws attention to a specific document or file. However, it is very likely that investigators will want to have the document reviewed by independent counsel to ensure that the privilege claim is valid so that they are not deprived of potentially relevant evidence that they would otherwise be entitled to see.

Search Terms

4.15 As is clear from the guidance above, an important preliminary step that will usually be required before a privilege review can begin is for keyword searches to be run across electronic devices and any other electronic data. The purpose is to identify privileged communications between a client and their lawyer, communications with third parties that are covered by litigation privilege and any other privileged communications and documents. It is important to devise appropriate search terms that will have the greatest chance of identifying privileged items. Although they may not capture everything, they are a very good starting point. Set out below are suggested search terms that should be relevant in the vast majority of cases, along with the fields/filters to which they should be applied. They are divided into two categories: 'generic' and 'specific' search terms. The latter are related to the specific circumstances of the case and material that has been seized and will vary from case to case, whereas generic search terms are unrelated and require no adaptation from one case to the next.

---

[6] ibid [16], [33].
[7] ibid [34], [36].

Generic search terms

> Search terms:
>
> - 'Privilege'
> - 'Privileged' (may not be needed if 'Privilege' is not limited to 'whole word only')
> - 'LPP' (whole word only, to avoid words or text that include these letters consecutively)
>
> Fields:
>
> - File name
> - Email subject
> - Body of email
> - Body of document

> Search terms:
>
> - 'Solicitors Regulation Authority'
> - 'Bar Standards Board'
>
> Fields:
>
> - Body of email
> - Body of document

The standard footer used by many law firms and barristers' chambers in emails and sometimes letters includes a reference to the fact that they are regulated by the Solicitors Regulation Authority or Bar Standards Board. Running these searches can therefore be an effective way of identifying correspondence from lawyers that might otherwise be missed.

4.16 In some cases it may be appropriate also to search for 'Private' and/or 'Confidential', but often these will result in a disproportionate number of results, many of which will not be privileged.

4.17 Other generic search terms that are sometimes used where the technology allows it, and where the number of results is not disproportionate, are combinations such as 'advice'/'advise' within ten words of 'legal'/'law', or variations thereof, applied across the body of emails and documents. These sorts of search terms can be an effective way of identifying evidence of privileged communications as opposed to the original communications themselves, such as where legal advice is shared confidentially with a third party.

Specific search terms

4.18 The starting point for most 'specific' search terms will be to identify as far as is possible all lawyers who have or may have provided legal advice to the owner of the device(s) or to any other person whose privileged communications may be stored on them. This includes identifying their names, firms or chambers, email addresses, and phone numbers.

Search terms:

- Lawyer's name (whether first name or surname or both is preferable may depend on how common the name is)
- Name of law firm

Fields:

- Email sender
- Email recipient (including CC and BCC)
- Text message (or similar) sender (if device is a phone)
- Text message (or similar) recipient (if device is a phone)
- File name
- Email subject
- Body of email
- Body of document
- Body of text message (or similar) (if device is a phone)

Search terms:

- Lawyer's full email address
- Law firm's (or chambers') email domain, eg '@nameoflawfirm.co.uk' (not limited to 'whole word only')

Fields:

- Email sender
- Email recipient (including CC and BCC)
- Body of email

Search terms:

- Lawyer's phone number (if device is a phone)

Fields:

- Text message (or similar) sender
- Text message (or similar) recipient

There may be additional specific search terms that are appropriate for the case. For example, there may be communications with experts or other third parties which are covered by litigation privilege, in which case their names and contact details should be included in the searches. If the material includes documents and communications generated in the course of an internal investigation, a project name may have been assigned and its use in email subjects may indicate privileged material. Similarly, there may be a specific issue on which

4.19

Devices belonging to a lawyer

4.20 The search terms suggested above will not be appropriate if the device to be searched belongs to a lawyer and is used for business purposes or the entire contents of a lawyer's work email inbox (excluding privileged items) is to be reviewed. Similar search terms could be adopted using clients' details, but considering the likelihood that a significant proportion of the content on the devices or in the mailbox will be privileged, it will usually be more appropriate to apply search terms to identify potentially relevant material and then review all of the results for privilege.

Refining search terms

4.21 In some cases, search terms may need to be refined if they yield a significant number of results. Investigating agencies in particular will be keen to reduce the number of documents that have to be reviewed if possible, and it is legitimate for them to do so if it is proportionate and necessary. However, the mere fact that the number of results is large should not be the basis, in and of itself, for narrowing or removing search terms. Often a significant number of devices will have been seized and there will inevitably be a significant amount of data to review as a result. It may be appropriate to refine search terms where there is a high likelihood that a large proportion of the results are items that are not privileged. In these circumstances, investigators should explain the basis for refining the search terms and provide the number of results for the relevant search terms to the defence, who should be invited to make representations.

4.22 This is most likely to arise with generic search terms. For example, many organizations include words to the effect of 'This email and its contents are confidential and may be privileged' in the standard footer of their emails. This often results in a large number of false positives where 'privilege' or 'privileged' is used as a search term. It may therefore be appropriate to remove the offending search term or to narrow it, for example by limiting 'privilege' or 'privileged' to email subjects and file names only, rather than the body of emails.

The Defence's Role

4.23 As is clear from the guidance above and the legal provisions discussed in Chapter 3, where investigating authorities come into possession of material that is or may be privileged, responsibility for ensuring that privileged items are identified and returned or isolated is theirs and theirs alone. The defence bears no legal responsibility. However, this does not mean that the defence should play no active role in the process. Defence engagement from the outset is key to ensuring the integrity of the process and to reduce the chance that investigators or prosecutors will inadvertently see privileged material. This means drawing privileged material to the attention of investigators at the point of seizure or as soon as possible thereafter and proposing appropriate search terms to help identify privileged material on electronic devices.

4.24 Agencies such as the SFO and HMRC, who routinely seize vast quantities of material in their investigations, will in most cases follow the approach suggested at para 4.06

without prompting. However, in the authors' experience, the police are often less familiar with the provisions of the CJPA 2001 and the practical arrangements for dealing with privileged material, and may therefore require more proactive engagement from the defence to ensure that the correct procedure is followed. For example, it will often not occur to the police that a mobile phone they have seized from a suspect following arrest may contain communications with a solicitor assisting them in relation to the current investigation or with an unrelated matter.

In any event, regardless of which investigating authority has obtained the material, the defence should ask for confirmation at the outset that the procedure suggested above will be followed. **4.25**

In some cases, particularly when dealing with a police investigation or a privately funded matter, the defence may volunteer to take on some of the responsibility for the review process by identifying specific files on a seized device over which privilege is asserted. The investigating agency will then send these specific files to independent counsel to be reviewed rather than sending them all files responsive to search terms which *may* be privileged. This might be considered appropriate if, for example, there are concerns about the thoroughness or integrity of the review process if left solely in the hands of the investigating authority. **4.26**

However, this approach is not without its risks and should only be adopted in exceptional cases. Consider, as an example, a case in which the police provide a copy of a hard drive from a seized computer to the defence at their request so that the defence can carry out a privilege review. The defence would run search terms across the contents of the device, review the results and provide a list of file paths of privileged documents to the police. The police's technical team would then locate those files on the device and send them to independent counsel to be reviewed. Once independent counsel had finished their review, the items agreed as being covered by privilege would be permanently isolated from the investigation team. On its face, this may seem like an appropriate approach to take. However, problems are likely to arise if the police (or other investigating authority) and the defence are using different systems with different search parameters, which is entirely likely. The defence may use an unsophisticated (but fairly standard) method of running search terms only against 'live' files on the hard drive, which will not include deleted files that may still be accessible or all sectors of the hard drive. The police, on the other hand, may use a far more comprehensive and sophisticated tool that searches everything on the hard drive, including deleted files. As a consequence, the defence's searches may fail to capture some privileged items, such as deleted emails that are still accessible, which will not be identified to the police or reviewed by independent counsel and will therefore be among the material that is released to the investigation team after independent counsel's review. **4.27**

It is suggested, therefore, that wherever possible the defence should leave the investigating authority to manage the review process but ensure close scrutiny and engagement in the way suggested in this chapter. **4.28**

Independent Counsel

4.29 Privilege reviews on behalf of investigating authorities should always be carried out by independent counsel. Independent counsel will usually be a self-employed barrister in chambers who is instructed by the authority in possession of the material for the sole task of reviewing it for privilege. Although instructed to advise the investigating authority, rather than the privilege holder, they are expected to make an independent, objective assessment. They will be kept apart from the investigation team and information will be limited only to what is necessary for them to carry out their review. As the Bar Council's guidance for independent counsel notes, 'Independent counsel's role is to assist the investigating authority in *maintaining the proper protections of privilege*'.[8]

4.30 The Bar Council's guidance includes several other important points:

- Clear written instructions should be provided from the investigating authority, containing sufficient information to allow counsel to make an informed assessment of the content of the material provided. Counsel's ability to provide an opinion is dependent upon the amount and quality of information provided. If counsel is unsure of the status of the material inspected or unable to provide the advice sought, they are entitled to ask for further information from those instructing.
- Instructions should set out in clear terms the test that the law enforcement agency is asking counsel to apply in relation to the existence of privilege, and should identify the statutory provisions under which the search will be, or has been, carried out.
- Counsel should ensure that they are instructed on the basis that they would not be permitted to divulge to the investigators any information which is seen by counsel or disclosed to them in the course of their duties that is subject to the privilege of someone other than the investigating agency.
- In providing an opinion and in the course of communications with the investigators, counsel must be careful not to disclose the content of any privilege material that they have seen.
- Counsel should ensure that their instructions address the issue of communications made to them on behalf of someone asserting privilege, including whether counsel is permitted to receive communications and how to deal with them.
- Counsel may be asked to advise on whether the crime-fraud exception applies to any of the material. Even if not expressly instructed in relation to this issue, the point may arise and counsel must be familiar with the relevant principles and have it mind when carrying out the review. If counsel does not have the information necessary in order to be able to advise on the issue, they should say so, and if the necessary information is not provided or insufficient information is available, counsel should either refuse to give such advice or should qualify their advice (as appropriate).

---

[8] The Bar Council, 'Barristers Instructed as "Independent Counsel" to Advise upon Legal Professional Privilege in Relation to Seized Material' (2010, reviewed September 2021) https://www.barcouncilethics.co.uk/wp-content/uploads/2017/10/LPP-Independent-Counsel-in-relation-to-seized-material-sept-2021.pdf (accessed 10 June 2023) (emphasis added).

Disagreement between Independent Counsel and the Defence

It is in the defence's best interests for there to be a collaborative and constructive relationship with independent counsel. The defence and independent counsel are not adverse parties. As explained above, best practice is that before independent counsel provides their determinations to the investigating authority, the defence is invited to review them and make representations on any areas of disagreement. This is an important part of the process as the defence can often provide vital background or contextual information to support a privilege claim. **4.31**

Contact between independent counsel and the defence should be direct to avoid investigators or prosecutors being privy to privileged information. If this is not possible, contact should be facilitated by somebody who is not involved in the investigation, such as a member of the investigating authority's in-house technical team. **4.32**

Occasionally, there may be disagreements between independent counsel and the defence over what is privileged, despite the defence's representations. If the disagreement cannot be resolved, and the investigating authority will follow independent counsel's advice notwithstanding the dispute (as is likely), the most appropriate course of action will depend on the form in which the material is held. As explained at paras 3.85–3.87, any person with a relevant interest in seized property may apply to the Crown Court for its return under the CJPA 2001, section 59, on the grounds that the property is or contains an item subject to privilege that is not caught by the inextricably linked exception under the CJPA 2001, section 54. If the document over which there is a dispute is not inextricably linked material, an application under section 59 will likely be the most appropriate route for settling a dispute with independent counsel. The application will seek a ruling from the judge that the item is in fact privileged and must therefore be returned under section 54. The judge may wish to examine the document in order to make a determination. **4.33**

Where the item is inextricably linked, however, a section 59 application is not possible, and there is no other mechanism under the CJPA 2001 that allows a judge to order an investigating authority to treat an inextricably linked item as privileged and therefore comply with the requirements under section 62 for isolating the material. Instead, the best option is likely to be an application under part 8 of the Civil Procedure Rules for a declaration that the document is privileged. If successful, the investigating authority would then have to comply with the requirements for handling inextricably linked privileged material under the CJPA 2001, section 62 (see paras 3.79–3.80). As noted in Chapter 3, Section 8, a part 8 claim was the route used by the SFO in *Director of the Serious Fraud Office v Eurasian Natural Resources Corp Ltd*[9] for resolving a dispute over whether certain categories of documents were privileged and could therefore be withheld from disclosure in response to a production order. As an alternative, a claim for judicial review might be possible, but the cost and complexity compared to a part 8 claim will probably mean that it is not a viable option. **4.34**

---

[9] [2018] EWCA Civ 2006, [2019] 1 WLR 791.

4.35 If there has been no engagement from the defence, or they have not been consulted, and independent counsel has wrongly determined a document not to be privileged, thereby releasing it to the investigation team, this does not strip the document of its privileged status. The defence's non-engagement will not amount to a waiver (see discussion about waiver principles generally in Chapter 1, Section 5) and the investigating authority will have a continuing obligation to return the item if it discovers that it is privileged (CJPA 2001, section 54) or, if it is inextricably linked, to isolate it (CJPA 2001, section 62). If investigators do not realize that the document is privileged and it is relied upon in a subsequent prosecution, the defence should apply for its exclusion under PACE 1984, s 78.[10]

The Use of Artificial Intelligence

4.36 Although still in its relative infancy, the use of artificial intelligence (AI) for privilege reviews and other types of document reviews is becoming more common, and its use will only increase over the coming years. It is beyond the scope of this book to explain in detail how AI operates in the context of privilege reviews, but, in very broad terms, it essentially involves the review exercise being carried out by an automated computer system that uses complex algorithms and other tools to identify patterns and attributes across a selection of data and to predict items that are likely to be privileged.

4.37 The form of AI used in privilege reviews is commonly referred to as 'machine learning', and there are two main types: supervised and unsupervised. Supervised machine learning, which is the more common type, involves human reviewers 'training' the machine to identify privileged documents. The process will usually begin with a human reviewing a batch of documents, perhaps 1,000 or 2,000, and recording their privilege determinations. These documents and the determinations will then be analysed by the system to identify patterns and common traits between documents falling into the various categories (privileged, not privileged etc.). The system will then analyse the rest of the material (which will be larger in size than the initial batch) and make its own determinations based on what it has learnt from the initial human review. Throughout this stage of the process, there will usually be quality control dip-sampling of the machine's determinations by the human, perhaps in small batches. Any errors that are identified and corrected will be fed back into the system and result in further 'learning' by the machine, thereby improving overall accuracy.

4.38 With supervised machine learning, the accuracy and effectiveness of the system are dependent upon the level of human interaction and training. This means that it is only likely to be appropriate in cases involving a significant number of documents. Unsupervised machine learning does not involve human training. Instead, the system analyses a batch of documents and tries to identify categories and patterns itself without any direction from human reviewers. This is often used as a means of sorting and categorizing a large number

---

[10] See also the discussion about abuse of process arguments in ch 3, s 9.

of documents to understand what they contain, perhaps at the start of an internal investigation. It is less effective for privilege reviews.

4.39 It is very likely that investigating agencies will adopt AI technology for privilege reviews over the next few years, especially as the volume of seized electronic data continues to grow and it becomes increasingly difficult for humans alone to carry out the review. The SFO made use of the technology in its investigation into Rolls Royce, where the system was used to analyse an estimated 30 million documents to identify material potentially covered by privilege. According to the SFO, the system was able to scan documents at speeds 2,000 times faster than a human lawyer.[11] It is not clear whether the SFO has adopted the same technology in any other cases.[12] It has not been used by HMRC, the FCA, or the CMA.[13]

4.40 As the new technology becomes more common in criminal investigations, it will, inevitably, change the procedure for privilege reviews of seized/compelled material. For the time being, however, the procedure outlined at para 4.06 will continue to be the most appropriate.

3 Privilege Reviews: Other Cases

4.41 Criminal defence lawyers, lawyers carrying out internal investigations, and other legal professionals in private practice will sometimes be required to carry out a privilege review of material that is in their possession. For example, a client may have been served with a production order under the Proceeds of Crime Act 2002, section 345 or a notice under the Criminal Justice Act 1987, section 2(3), or they might be providing material to the authorities voluntarily as part of a self-reporting process, perhaps following an internal investigation. The purpose of the review in these cases, assuming there is no intention to waive privilege, is to identify privileged items and remove them from the material that is to be provided to the investigating authority or another third party.

Document Review Platforms

4.42 In the vast majority of cases, the material to be reviewed will be in an electronic form rather than in hard copy. Where there is hard copy material, it may be appropriate to scan it to

---

[11] SFO News Release, 'AI Powered "Robo-Lawyer" Helps Step Up the SFO's Fight against Economic Crime' (10 April 2018) www.sfo.gov.uk/2018/04/10/ai-powered-robo-lawyer-helps-step-up-the-sfos-fight-against-economic-crime/ (accessed 10 June 2023).

[12] In response to a Freedom of Information request submitted by the authors to the SFO in March 2022, the SFO confirmed that AI/machine learning tools had not been used for privilege reviews in any other cases. The SFO declined to confirm whether this was still the position when a further request was submitted in April 2023, stating that the information was exempt from disclosure.

[13] Information obtained in response to Freedom of Information requests submitted by the authors to HMRC, the CMA, and the FCA in April 2023.

create a digital copy to be reviewed, especially if there is also electronic material. This helps ensure consistency and that there is a clear audit trail. Scanning hard copy documents also potentially allows for text recognition to be applied so that the content of the documents can be searched in the same way as other electronic files.

4.43 If the number of items to be reviewed is small and the process is unlikely to take a significant amount of time, reviewing documents on standard applications such as Adobe Acrobat (for pdfs) and recording determinations on a schedule may suffice. However, large-scale privilege reviews involving hundreds or thousands of documents and more than one reviewer should be conducted on a document review platform. There are many different platforms available, some of which are common to a number of different e-discovery companies, whilst others are bespoke products offered exclusively by one provider. They provide a quick and easy way to view and categorize a large number of documents whilst leaving a full audit trail.

4.44 Regardless of which document review platform is used, e-discovery companies will usually take the raw data and process it so that it can be searched for potentially privileged documents. The guidance on search terms set out at paras 4.15–4.22 is equally applicable in these circumstances. Material that is responsive to the search terms will be uploaded onto the platform and made available for review. If necessary, further searches and filters can be applied. If there are multiple reviewers, batches of documents can be created and allocated, and, if necessary, user access can be restricted.

4.45 Documents can be viewed individually either by using the viewer tool on the platform itself or downloading the 'native' file and viewing it offline. For example, Excel spreadsheets are often difficult to read if using the platform's viewer tool and so may need to be downloaded to be opened up in Excel on the reviewer's computer.

4.46 When a reviewer looks at a document, they will have a number of options to select to record their determinations. In some cases these options can be customized by the review team themselves rather than the e-discovery company. In any case, it will usually be appropriate to include the following options for reviewers to select for each document:

- Privileged
- Not privileged
- Partly privileged
- Query
- Technical issue

There should also be a 'free text' comments box in which reviewers can record comments, such as identifying which parts of a document are privileged (if partly privileged) or recording a query if unsure about whether a document is privileged.

4.47 If the review is to be divided into different stages, such as first-tier and second-tier reviews (see para 4.50), the document review platform can usually be set up accordingly so that reviewers are able to select which review they are conducting when recording their determinations.

Managing a Privilege Review

4.48 In large cases, it will often be necessary to set up a small team of reviewers to carry out the exercise. In these cases, it is important that the privilege review is carefully managed from the outset to preserve the integrity of the process and ensure that a consistent approach is taken. Large-scale reviews involving lots of reviewers can often lead to undesirable results, such as reviewers reaching different conclusions on duplicate versions of the same document or taking an inconsistent approach to redactions in partly privileged documents. Privilege is a complex area of law and differences of opinion as to whether or not a document is privileged are inevitable. This makes the need for careful oversight and consistency all the more important.

4.49 Ideally, one lawyer should have overall responsibility for the review, resolving any queries or issues that arise as the review progresses. That lawyer should make sure all reviewers are fully briefed at the outset to ensure they understand the background to the case and the context to individual documents and are able to identify privileged items. The briefing should include names of lawyers and law firms whose communications are likely to be encountered, issues on which legal advice has been provided, claims/disputes potentially giving rise to litigation privilege and on which legal advice may have been given, and the names of third parties whose communications may be covered by litigation privilege. Guidance should also be given on how to approach particular categories of documents and how to deal with the sorts of practical issues discussed in Section 4 below. As the review progresses and queries inevitably arise, this guidance should be updated to ensure that the team takes a consistent approach.

4.50 Depending on the volume of material, it will often be most effective to have a two-tier structure to the review. A number of reviewers will carry out an initial, first-tier review of everything, erring on the side of caution in their determinations. This group may comprise paralegals, trainee solicitors, or more junior lawyers, depending on their familiarity with the law of privilege. A smaller number of lawyers (the smaller the better) will then carry out a second-tier review of everything flagged as potentially privileged by the first-tier reviewers to determine whether the documents are in fact privileged. The second-tier review may also involve reviewing a sample of documents determined not to be privileged by the first-tier reviewers, to ensure there are no obvious problems with the approach that has been taken, for example if certain issues or categories of documents have been misunderstood. Finally, it may be prudent for the lawyer with overall responsibility to review a sample of the second-tier reviewers' determinations to check that there are no issues.

4.51 In appropriate cases, lawyers may wish to utilize AI/machine learning to carry out the review (see paras 4.36–4.38).

4 Document Types and Practical Issues

4.52 In this section, we look at some of the practical issues that can arise with particular types of documents in privilege reviews. The guidance is equally applicable to all legal professionals who are involved in privilege reviews, including independent counsel reviewing seized material and criminal defence lawyers and others in private practice conducting their own reviews.

4.53 In this section, 'document' is used for convenience to refer also to emails.

How to Approach Individual Documents

4.54 The starting point when reviewing any document is to treat it as a single item and consider whether, taken as a whole, it satisfies the test for privilege. For example, an email from a client to their lawyer requesting legal advice is a single confidential communication made for the dominant purpose of seeking legal advice and is therefore covered by legal advice privilege in its entirety. It would not be correct to carry out a line-by-line analysis of the content of the email and treat only those specific sentences or paragraphs expressly containing instructions or legal advice as privileged. If the whole document satisfies the test for privilege, then the whole item should be marked as privileged and withheld from disclosure or production (as the case may be).

4.55 Treating the whole document as privileged means that, as far as emails are concerned, email headers (details of the sender, recipient, date and time, and subject) and footers (details about the sender or their organization, contact details, confidentiality warnings etc.) are treated as part of the privileged communication and will not be disclosed.

4.56 If, on the other hand, the document as a whole is not privileged, reviewers should consider whether part of the document is privileged. There are two bases on which a particular section of a document might be privileged:

1. If that section amounts to a separate communication in and of itself that meets the test for privilege. For example, a client might send one email to several professional advisers, including their lawyer, with questions for each (as in the example at para 4.64). The email itself will not be covered by legal advice privilege as it will fail to satisfy the dominant purpose test,[14] but the section that is clearly directed at the lawyer only will be.
2. If it evidences or reveals the content of a separate communication that is privileged, for example an internal email within a company that summarizes legal advice provided by the company's lawyers.

Unlike with documents that are privileged in their entirety, this approach does require a line-by-line analysis, and only the specific sentences or paragraphs that fall within either of the above two categories can be treated as privileged.

---

[14] See para 1.31.

Redactions and Partly Privileged Documents

The correct approach when dealing with documents that are only partly privileged is to redact the privileged sections but keep the rest of the document visible. If the documents are then disclosed to an investigating authority or another third party, the redacted versions can be provided to them. This will not result in any waiver of privilege over the redacted information,[15] and it is not a requirement that the part of the document redacted on the grounds of privilege must be severable from the unredacted parts or deal with an entirely different subject matter.[16]

4.57

Note, however, that in *Al Sadeq v Dechert LLP* Murray J endorsed a passage from *The Law of Privilege*[17] suggesting that, if privileged and non-privileged information are so intertwined in a document that redacting the privileged parts becomes 'impracticable or unfeasible', 'the balance will have to fall in favour of withholding the entire document on the basis of privilege'.[18]

4.58

Some document review platforms allow redactions to be applied directly to documents. Otherwise, the free text 'comments' box should be used to record clear instructions for the person who will apply the redactions at the end of the process, for example, 'Redact from "Our lawyers have advised us..." to "... good prospects of success"'.

4.59

Email Chains

Most document review platforms will display email chains as single documents with all earlier emails in the chain included below the most recent. However, when reviewing email chains for privilege, each email in the chain should be treated as a separate and distinct communication. Each email will have been sent as a separate communication and it would be artificial to consider a chain to be a single communication merely because the act of replying has caused earlier emails to be included underneath the reply.

4.60

This means that some emails in the chain might be privileged while others will not be, and redactions will therefore need to be applied. As at para 4.59, if the document review platform does not allow for redactions to be applied directly, reviewers should use the comments box to record clear instructions of precisely what needs to be redacted, for example,

4.61

---

[15] *GE Capital Corporate Finance Group v Bankers Trust Co* [1995] 1 WLR 172 (CA), although concerned with discovery in civil proceedings, confirmed the general principle that disclosure of the unprivileged parts of a document does not waive privilege over the redacted parts. Hoffmann LJ stated, at 175, that: 'I think that Saville J. was right in *Bank of Nova Scotia v. Hellenic Mutual War Risks Association (Bermuda) Ltd. (Note) (No. 2)* [1992] 2 Lloyd's Rep. 540 when he held that disclosure of the unprivileged part of a document was not a waiver of privilege for the rest, even though both dealt with the same subject matter; likewise Gatehouse J. in *British and Commonwealth Holdings v. Quadrex* (unreported), 4 July 1990.'

[16] In *GE Capital Corporate Finance Group v Bankers Trust Co* (n 15), Hoffmann LJ stated, at 175, that: 'The test for whether part [of a document] can be withheld on grounds of privilege is simply whether that part is privileged. There is no additional requirement that the part must deal with an entirely different subject matter from the rest.' See also *Al Sadeq v Dechert LLP* [2023] EWHC 795 (KB) [224].

[17] Bankim Thanki (ed), *The Law of Privilege* (3rd edn, OUP 2018) para 4.06.

[18] *Al Sadeq v Dechert LLP* (n 16) [224].

'First three emails in chain are privileged'. It is important that all reviewers adopt the same language when referring to email chains in the comments box, so that, for example, 'first email in chain' is understood to mean the earliest in time and 'last email in chain' the most recent.

4.62 If dealing with an email chain in which some of the emails are privileged and others are not, reviewers will need to ensure a consistent approach to redacting email headers and footers. With the possible exception of the email subject,[19] this information is not privileged. It is automatically generated and does not reveal anything about the content of the email. The mere fact that a lawyer has emailed their client on a particular day is not privileged. Technically, therefore, there is no issue with redacting only the body of a privileged email in a mixed chain and keeping the header and footer unredacted (assuming the subject is not privileged[20]). However, the authors suggest that a more appropriate approach is to redact everything in the privileged email, including the header and footer, as this is consistent with the approach taken to single emails that are privileged in their entirety (see para 4.55). It is very unlikely that investigating authorities will take exception to this approach.

Multi-addressee Emails

4.63 As noted at para 1.33, the dominant purpose test for legal advice privilege presents particular difficulties for multi-addressee emails between a client and their lawyer and one or more other, non-legal professional advisers. It is likely that emails of this nature will be encountered in a privilege review. If the seeking or provision of legal advice is not the dominant purpose of the email, it will not be privileged. However, in some cases, if a multi-addressee email fails to satisfy the dominant purpose test as a whole, it may be possible to separate it into two or more communications to the different advisers and treat as privileged only the parts of the email that are directed at the lawyer. As was noted by Hickinbottom LJ in *R (Jet2.com Ltd) v Civil Aviation Authority*:

> Where there is no such intermingling [of the legal and non-legal parts of a document], and the legal and non-legal can be identified, then the document or communication can be severed: the parts covered by [legal advice privilege] will be non-disclosable (and redactable), and the rest will be disclosable.[21]

4.64 Avoiding such 'intermingling' is likely to require a clear separation within the body of the email between a message intended for the lawyer and a message intended for the other, non-legal adviser(s). For example, a client might email their lawyer and PR adviser in the following terms:

---

[19] Also note that the identity of a witness is capable of attracting litigation privilege unless and until it is disclosed in proceedings, so the recipient's/sender's name and/or email address may need to be redacted if they are a witness and if inclusion of these details would reveal this fact. See para 9.25.
[20] And assuming n 19 above does not apply.
[21] [2020] EWCA Civ 35, [2020] QB 1027 [69].

> Hi both,
>
> I have a couple of questions arising from the recent developments.
>
> [Lawyer], do you think this is going to increase the pressure on the CPS to bring charges against us or will they be unmoved by what's being reported?
>
> [PR adviser], I think it would be good to generate some helpful publicity on everything that has happened this week, in a way that projects our company in the most favourable light. What do you think?
>
> Kind regards

Although sent as one email, the legal and non-legal questions are clearly separated and are essentially two distinct communications. The client may simply have combined the requests for advice into one email in order to save time or to keep the advisers informed of what the other was being asked. Since privilege is primarily concerned with communications, and considering Hickinbottom LJ's comments above, the most accurate way of reviewing an email of this nature would be to treat it as two separate communications and redact the paragraph addressed to the lawyer.

4.65 It is no different to, say, minutes of a board meeting at which the company's lawyer provides legal advice on a particular issue but the remainder of the meeting deals with non-legal, commercial matters that do not concern the lawyer. The correct approach here would be to treat as privileged the passage in the minutes recording the legal advice and to redact it, rather than consider whether the dominant purpose of the whole meeting was to seek or provide legal advice. Indeed, this very point was made by Hickinbottom LJ in *Jet2*:

> If the dominant purpose of the discussions [at a meeting] is commercial or otherwise non-legal, then the meeting and its contents will not generally be privileged; although any legal advice sought or given within the meeting may be. It is likely that, where not inextricably intermingled, the non-privileged part will be severable (and, on disclosure, redactable[22]).[23]

Email Attachments

4.66 As discussed in Chapter 1, Section 4, a document does not become privileged simply because a client provides it to their lawyer for the purpose of seeking legal advice. This same principle applies to email attachments, which must be considered as separate documents to the email to which they are attached. A non-privileged document does not become privileged simply because it is attached to a privileged email.

---

[22] This is presumably an error. It is the privileged part that will be redactable, not the non-privileged part.
[23] *R (Jet2.com Ltd) v Civil Aviation Authority* (n 21) [100].

5
Compelled Interviews

1 Introduction

5.01 In addition to powers to compel the production of documents, discussed in Chapter 3, Section 2, investigators also have powers to compel a person to attend an interview to answer questions or otherwise to provide information. Compelled interviews are not covered by the Police and Criminal Evidence Act 1984 (PACE 1984) and so interviewees do not have the same rights and protections as suspects interviewed under caution. Most importantly, there is no right to silence in a compelled interview, and a failure without reasonable excuse to comply with a requirement to answer questions is a criminal offence. These powers are, however, subject to important limitations preventing the information obtained from being used in evidence against the person, save in certain limited circumstances, such as in connection with a prosecution for making false or misleading statements in purported compliance with the requirement to answer questions. As such, compelled interviews are usually used to obtain evidence from potential witnesses rather than suspects in criminal investigations.

2 Compelled Interviews: Main Powers

5.02 One of the most common types of compelled interview used in criminal investigations is an interview conducted by the SFO under the Criminal Justice Act 1987 (CJA 1987), section 2(2). This confers powers on the Director of the SFO to require, by written notice, a person under investigation, or any other person whom they have reason to believe has relevant information, to answer questions or otherwise furnish information with respect to any matter relevant to the investigation.

5.03 Under the Serious Organised Crime and Policing Act 2005 (SOCPA 2005), section 62 the DPP, or, by delegation, a Crown Prosecutor, may issue, or authorize a constable, NCA officer or HMRC officer to issue, a disclosure notice requiring a person to answer questions in connection with investigations into certain serious offences, such as lifestyle offences under the Proceeds of Crime Act 2002 (POCA 2002), terrorist financing, tax offences, false accounting, cheating the public revenue and bribery.

5.04 The FCA has similar powers under the Financial Services and Markets Act 2000 (FSMA 2000), sections 171 to 173 to compel a person to answer questions in connection with an FCA investigation.

5.05 There are a range of other statutory provisions that confer similar powers on other criminal enforcement agencies, such as the CMA (Enterprise Act 2002, section 193) and the HSE

(Health and Safety at Work Act 1974, section 20). In addition, once a prosecution is underway, an application can be made to the court for a witness summons requiring a person to attend before the court at a specified time and give evidence likely to be material evidence for the purpose of the proceedings. The power to issue a witness summons is provided by the Criminal Procedure (Attendance of Witnesses) Act 1965, section 2 (for Crown Court proceedings) and the Magistrates' Court Act 1980, section 97 (for magistrates' court proceedings).

3 Exclusion of Privileged Information

5.06   None of the powers mentioned above permit investigators to compel the disclosure of privileged information, and all contain an express exclusion to this effect (or, in the case of witness summonses, have been held as such by the courts[1]).

5.07   In the case of SFO interviews conducted under the CJA 1987, section 2(2), privileged information is excluded by virtue of section 2(9), which states that:

> A person shall not under this section be required to disclose any information or produce any document which he would be entitled to refuse to disclose or produce on grounds of legal professional privilege in proceedings in the High Court, except that a lawyer may be required to furnish the name and address of his client.

This is the same exclusion that applies to the SFO's power to compel the production of documents, discussed at para 3.29.

5.08   Similarly, SOCPA 2005, section 64 states that a person may not be required by a disclosure notice under section 62 to answer any privileged question or provide any privileged information. This is subject to the same proviso that 'a lawyer may be required to provide the name and address of a client of his'. Privilege is defined by reference to proceedings in the High Court, as with the CJA 1987, section 2(9).

5.09   For interviews conducted by the FCA under FSMA 2000, the exclusion is found in section 413. Although the Act refers to 'protected items' rather than privileged items, the definition of 'protected items' under section 413 is very similar to the definition of 'legal privilege' under PACE 1984, section 10 (see para 3.26) and can therefore be considered a reflection of the common law definition of privilege.[2]

5.10   Other statutory provisions that confer powers to compel information on criminal enforcement agencies, such as those mentioned in Section 2 above in respect of the CMA and the HSE, contain similar express exclusions for privileged information.

---

[1] *R v Derby Magistrates' Court, ex p B* [1996] AC 487 (HL); see discussion at para 3.31.
[2] In *R v Central Criminal Court, ex p Francis & Francis* [1989] AC 346 (HL), Lord Goff (at 382) and Lord Griffiths (at 384–85) both considered s 10 to reflect the common law. Lord Griffiths stated: 'I am convinced that Parliament was not seeking to enact a special code of legal privilege of different import to the common law position. I believe the draftsman was seeking to spell out the common law position for the benefit of those unacquainted with it.' The House of Lords' confirmation of this principle was referenced with apparent approval by the Court of Appeal in *The Director of the Serious Fraud Office v Eurasian Natural Resources Corp Ltd* [2018] EWCA Civ 2006, [2019] 1 WLR 791 [62].

4 Failing to Comply without Reasonable Excuse

A failure, without reasonable excuse, to comply with a requirement imposed under the CJA 1987, section 2 or SOCPA 2005, section 62 is a criminal offence.[3] Similarly, if a court is satisfied that a person has failed, without reasonable excuse, to comply with a requirement imposed under FSMA 2000, sections 171, 172, or 173, it may deal with the person as if they were in contempt.[4] Similar offences exist in respect of other powers of compulsion.

5.11

Whilst 'reasonable excuse' does not have a clear definition and will be fact-specific, it is the authors' view that withholding information on the grounds of privilege would amount to a reasonable excuse.[5] One could even argue that withholding privileged information would not engage the offence at all, since the powers cannot be used to compel privileged information, so there would be no failure to comply with any requirement.

5.12

5 During the Interview

There is no automatic right for a witness interviewed by the SFO under the CJA 1987, section 2 to have a lawyer present.[6] The SFO's guidance on legal advisers attending section 2 interviews says that it will be allowed only if the case controller believes it is likely to assist the purpose of the interview and/or investigation or if the lawyer will provide essential assistance to the interviewee by way of legal advice or pastoral support.[7] In practice, the SFO will usually allow a lawyer to attend, albeit by prior agreement and subject to the lawyer providing various confidentiality undertakings. The SFO's guidance is clear that lawyers must not disrupt the flow of information in the interview, although it acknowledges that they may be required to deal with privilege issues that might arise:

5.13

> If a particular lawyer is allowed to attend the interview, it will be on the agreed understanding that certain ground rules apply. They may, if they are able to, advise the interviewee in the event that any matter of legal professional privilege (LPP) arises. Otherwise, they must not do anything to undermine the free flow of information which the interviewee, by

---

[3] CJA 1987, s 2 and SOCPA 2005, s 67(1).
[4] FSMA 2000, s 177(2).
[5] Although in a different context, a defence is available to the principal money laundering offences under POCA 2002 if a person intended to make an authorized disclosure but had a reasonable excuse for not doing so. In its guidance on AML for the legal sector, the Legal Sector Affinity Group suggests that lawyers will have a reasonable excuse for not making an authorized disclosure if their knowledge or suspicion is based on privileged information. See Legal Sector Affinity Group, 'Anti-Money Laundering Guidance for the Legal Sector 2023' (28 March 2023) para 16.4.3 https://www.lawsociety.org.uk/topics/anti-money-laundering/anti-money-laundering-guidance (accessed 10 June 2023).
[6] *R (Lord) v Director of the Serious Fraud Office* [2015] EWHC 865 (Admin), [2015] 2 Cr App R.
[7] SFO, 'Presence of interviewee's legal adviser at a section 2 interview' https://www.sfo.gov.uk/download/sfo-operational-guidance-presence-interviewees-legal-adviser-section-2-interview-internal-guidance/ (accessed 10 June 2023).

law, is required to give. It is the duty of the interviewer to ensure that this rule is observed. In the event of any perceived infraction, or obstruction of the interview process generally, the lawyer will be excluded from the interview.

5.14 The Law Society has published guidance on this issue reflecting its concerns about the SFO's policy.[8] The guidance reminds solicitors that the SFO's policy does not override their professional obligations and they must ensure that any agreements entered into with the SFO do not compromise their ability to comply with their obligations. The guidance acknowledges the fact that there is no automatic entitlement to legal representation during a section 2 interview, but it warns that: 'It does not follow from this position that the SFO can dictate how that practitioner should conduct themself [sic] in the performance of their professional role as their client's legal adviser and representative as a condition to permitting a practitioner to attend a section 2 interview.' The guidance continues that in considering whether a solicitor can agree to act within the SFO's parameters without compromising their duty to act in the best interests of their client, they should bear in mind the sorts of issues on which they may be required to advise during the interview, including ensuring that 'questions do not risk breaching legal professional privilege, whether belonging to the client or to another party, such as the client's employer'.

5.15 The FCA's position on interviews generally is that it will allow a person to be accompanied by a legal adviser, if they wish.[9]

5.16 Lawyers must not assume that investigators carrying out compelled interviews will always understand the limits of what they can ask, and should have in mind that questioning may stray into areas covered by privilege. There may be occasions where the lawyer has to intervene. If the lawyer believes the answer to a question will disclose privileged information, they should intervene before their client answers the question and tell the interviewer(s) that the information they are seeking is privileged and their client cannot provide it. Investigators should not require the lawyer to explain why the information is privileged as this will risk disclosing the very information that is protected.

5.17 Lawyers should intervene regardless of whether the privilege belongs to their client or a third party. If necessary, the lawyer can specify whose privilege it is. Compelled interviews will often be conducted with employees of a company that is under investigation and the interviewee may have information that is subject to the company's privilege, for example if they attended a meeting with the company's lawyers or exchanged correspondence with them in the course of their employment. This is particularly likely if they hold/held a senior position and can be considered part of the 'client' group for the purposes of legal advice privilege (in accordance with *Three Rivers District Council v Governor and Co of the Bank of England*[10]). The position will be the same regardless of whether or not the interviewee still works for the company. As discussed at para 6.51 in the context of interviews under caution, an interviewee is not entitled to waive a third party's privilege,

---

[8] The Law Society, 'Representing Clients at Section 2 CJA Interviews' (20 May 2020) https://www.lawsociety.org.uk/topics/criminal-justice/representing-clients-at-section-2-cja-interviews (accessed 10 June 2023).
[9] FCA Handbook, Enforcement Guide, 4.11.4.
[10] [2003] EWCA Civ 474, [2003] QB 1556. See para 1.20.

even if it is in their interests to do so, and investigators are not permitted to ask questions that would require the interviewee to provide information that is subject to a third party's privilege.

Ideally, the lawyer will have informed the investigators prior to the interview about topics of questioning that are likely to stray into privileged areas. These might be general topics or more specific matters, such as particular meetings where legal advice was provided/discussed or issues about which the interviewee communicated with external lawyers. Flagging these issues in advance should reduce the likelihood of problematic questions being asked. Where the privilege belongs to the interviewee's employer, it may be appropriate to agree with the company a form of words to use in response to certain questions, for example to indicate the existence of legal advice having been given but not to disclose what the advice was. 5.18

In some cases, the interviewee's corporate employer may have agreed a limited waiver of privilege with the investigating authority. Before the interview, the lawyer should check if there has been a waiver and, if so, on what terms. It may, for example, be limited to advice relating to a particular issue or covering a specified date range. The lawyer should discuss the waiver with their client and ensure they understand the limits as they apply to the information the client will likely be providing in the interview. 5.19

6 Interviews with Lawyers

Investigating authorities such as the SFO may sometimes use compelled powers to interview a lawyer, usually an in-house lawyer working for the company that is under investigation. This is permissible, but extreme care is needed to ensure the interviewee does not disclose any information that is privileged. Lawyers are under an obligation to protect their clients' privilege, and this remains the case even when they are being interviewed in these circumstances. If an in-house lawyer is interviewed, the privilege will belong to the company, and unless a waiver has been agreed by the company, the lawyer will not be permitted to disclose any privileged information. Their actions can, however, result in privilege being lost inadvertently, even if the company has not agreed a waiver.[11] 5.20

Information that is confidential but not privileged can be provided to investigators in a compelled interview. This is because the obligation to protect a client's confidentiality is qualified and disclosure is permitted if required by law, such as when answering questions in a compelled interview.[12] 5.21

All of the guidance in Section 5 above is equally applicable to interviews with lawyers, and it is particularly important that all participants in the interview understand the limits to what 5.22

---

[11] See also para 6.51 regarding this issue in the context of an interview under caution, and see ch 1, s 5 for waiver and loss of privilege more generally.
[12] See the Law Society's guidance on this topic: 'Responding to a financial crime investigation' (24 January 2022) s 8.1 https://www.lawsociety.org.uk/topics/anti-money-laundering/responding-to-a-financial-crime-investigation (accessed 10 June 2023).

can be discussed. It may be advisable for either the interviewee or their legal adviser to read a statement at the start of the interview that addresses the following points (as applicable):

- Given the witness's role, it is very likely that topics of questioning will touch on areas that are covered by privilege.
- If a waiver has been agreed by the company, privileged information can be provided if it falls within the terms of the waiver. The provision of such information will be on the same basis as the waiver that the company has agreed. (Explicit reference should be made to the terms of the waiver and/or the witness' understanding of what it covers.)
- The witness cannot answer questions relating to areas where privilege has not been waived. (It may be helpful to specify these areas or provide examples.)

5.23 The need for caution in interviews of this nature is demonstrated by an issue that arose in *Eurasian Natural Resources Corp Ltd v Dechert LLP*.[13] One of the claims made by ENRC against the SFO was that one of its investigators (a case manager in the Proceeds of Crime Unit who was not a lawyer) had induced ENRC's Global Head of Compliance to disclose privileged information and/or failed to stop him from doing so during a section 2 compelled interview. The interviewee was a dual-qualified US/English lawyer, and whilst Waksman J did not think he was 'strictly, even an in-house lawyer', his advice was capable of being privileged if he was advising ENRC about legislation, whether ENRC was complying with it or what ENRC must do in order to comply with it.[14] Privileged matters were indeed discussed during the interview and included the scope of Neil Gerrard's (the partner at Dechert dealing with the case) retainer, information about what or was not brought to Gerrard's attention, information that a lawyer instructed to advise ENRC had reservations about the matter, advice the Head of Compliance had given about non-compliance with various laws, and information about the nature of internal investigation policies advised or contributed to by Gerrard. Waksman J held that, whilst these items were privileged, the interviewer did not appreciate it at the time. A distinction was drawn between what would be obvious to a lawyer and what would be obvious to a non-lawyer such as the SFO interviewer:

> To a lawyer, the details of a lawyer's instructions to advise may be regarded as fairly obvious examples of privileged information since it is ancillary to the task of giving the advice, itself privileged. But to someone in the position of Mr Thompson [the interviewer] it may very well not be ... But here, for the purposes of assessing his state of mind, the distinction between what is plainly or obviously privileged and what is less obviously privileged is an important one.[15]

Privilege of the kind at issue in the context of this interview was not 'of the most obvious kind'. As such, Waksman J considered the interviewer to have been 'thoughtless (and negligent) but not reckless'. He found no instance where the interviewer knowingly or recklessly received (and then recorded) privileged information which he should have stopped the interviewee from communicating to him, or knowingly solicited it.[16]

---

[13] [2022] EWHC 1138 (Comm).
[14] ibid [671].
[15] ibid [690].
[16] ibid [703], [719], [720].

5.24 This is an important decision as far as compelled interviews with lawyers are concerned. Whilst the circumstances would undoubtedly have been different if the interviewee had had a solicitor present (notwithstanding the fact that he was a qualified lawyer in his own right), the judge's distinction between what would have been obvious to a lawyer compared to a non-lawyer highlights a potential problem area. Competent interviewers will be aware of privilege generally and will have at least a basic grasp of its key principles, but they may not have a detailed understanding of the more nuanced aspects such as those which arose in this case. There is a risk that their questioning will stray into areas covered by privilege without being aware of it. Solicitors advising clients who are lawyers (or indeed any type of client) in compelled interviews must therefore be alive to this risk and be ready to intervene before privileged information is provided. They cannot rely solely on the interviewer (or interviewee, as was the case in *ENRC v Dechert*) to be aware of the appropriate boundaries.

5.25 This is particularly important considering how the law treats inadvertent disclosure of privileged information to investigators/prosecutors in criminal cases, as discussed at paras 1.104–1.109. Indeed, this very issue arose in *ENRC v Dechert*. ENRC sought a declaration that the SFO was not entitled to publish, disclose, divulge, or otherwise make use of any confidential and privileged material which was disclosed to the SFO by Dechert and/or Gerrard in breach of duty. Refusing to grant the declaration, Waksman J was bound to follow the line of authority established by *Butler v Board of Trade*,[17] which clearly held that if evidence of a privileged communication has fallen into the hands of the prosecution, the prosecution cannot be prevented from relying upon it. It was therefore not open to the Court to grant such a declaration.[18]

---

[17] [1971] 1 Ch 680 (Ch).
[18] *Eurasian Natural Resources Corp Ltd v Dechert LLP* (n 13) [1731].

6
The Police Station and Interviews under Caution

1 Introduction

6.01 In the vast majority of criminal cases, the earliest stage at which a suspect will be required to engage with the investigating authorities will be during an interview under caution. An interview under caution is the means by which an investigator asks questions of a suspect, the answers to which will be admissible in any subsequent criminal proceedings. The caution refers to the provisions set out in the Police and Criminal Evidence Act 1984 (PACE 1984) which determine the conditions which must be present before anything said in an interview can assume evidential significance in any subsequent prosecution. It is therefore an extremely important stage of the investigative process, and decisions made by suspects at this stage (with or without legal advice) can change the course of the investigation. This chapter focuses on the interaction between privilege and the practice and procedure of providing advice regarding an interview under caution.

6.02 Interviews under caution are most commonly conducted by the police, but they are also conducted by a wide range of other bodies with investigative powers, such as the Serious Fraud Office (SFO) and the Financial Conduct Authority (FCA). The principles set out in this chapter apply equally to interviews under caution carried out by any investigating agency and in any location. An interview under caution may take place after a suspect has been arrested and detained at a police station or following a request to attend to be interviewed as a volunteer.

6.03 When conducted by the police, interviews most commonly take place at a police station, although not necessarily in the custody suite if the suspect is attending as a volunteer. Interviews can also take place at locations other than police stations, such as the suspect's home address or a solicitor's office. The location of the interview in itself is unlikely to significantly alter the advice or the privilege issues to be considered. However, there will be some additional practical considerations when an interview under caution takes place following a suspect's arrest, as opposed to following a voluntary attendance. These issues are considered in further detail below.

6.04 Some investigating authorities have powers to compel a person to attend an interview to answer questions. Compelled interviews are not covered by PACE 1984 and there is no right to silence. These types of interview are dealt with separately in Chapter 5.

6.05 In some circumstances, an individual may be required to attend an interview by or on behalf of their current or former employer, sometimes in connection with an internal investigation that may involve allegations of criminal wrongdoing. Whilst interviews of this nature may be a precursor to a criminal investigation or run in parallel to it, they are not typically PACE 1984-compliant and therefore the admissibility of answers provided in interviews of this nature in any subsequent criminal proceedings is subject to different considerations. Chapter 12 considers the privilege issues which may arise in respect of internal investigation interviews.

2 Initial Engagement and Instruction

Contact from the Police Station

6.06 Being instructed by a client who has been arrested and is in police custody will mean that their initial communication with the solicitor may be via telephone from a place which is not private. Confidentiality is an essential component of privilege, such that communications with legal advisers which do not take place in confidential circumstances cannot be privileged.

6.07 Whilst there is no English authority which directly addresses the issue in the context of a police station, where a communication between a client and a lawyer takes place knowingly in the presence or hearing of an adverse party, such as a police officer, a claim to privilege will almost certainly fail. This is because the communication must be made in circumstances which carry an obligation or expectation of confidentiality in order to be privileged, and this will not be the case if the conversation takes place in the presence or hearing of an adversary. The point was considered in the Australian case of *R v Braham and Mason*,[1] in which a suspect who had been held at the police station telephoned his solicitor in the presence of a police officer and sought advice about whether to sign a statement. During the course of the consultation he made admissions as to his involvement in criminality. At trial he was not permitted to claim privilege over the communication with his solicitor. Lush J stated:

> The fact of the presence of a third party should be examined to see whether that presence indicates that the communication was not intended to be confidential, or whether the presence of the third party was caused by some necessity or some circumstances which did not affect the primary nature of the communication as confidential.[2]

6.08 Given the busy and public nature of most custody suite telephones, it is unlikely that communication from the custody suite between a suspect and their legal adviser will be deemed to be sufficiently confidential to be privileged.

6.09 To what extent can a distinction be drawn between situations in which a client knowingly engages in communication with their legal adviser in the presence of an adversary and those cases where the client may, unbeknownst to them, be overheard by a third party who may be an adversary? In the former case, according to *Braham*, this will almost certainly be interpreted as the client not intending or expecting the communication to be confidential, and therefore the communication will not be privileged. In the latter scenario, the position

---

[1] [1976] VR 547 (SC Victoria).
[2] ibid 552.

is less clear. It was held in the New Zealand case of *R v Uljee*[3] that the presence of an 'eavesdropper' did not cause the client to lose privilege. In *Uljee* a client's consultation with his solicitor was overheard by a police officer who was guarding the premises and did not intend to eavesdrop. Richardson J stated:

> Solicitor and client should be able to act in the belief that what they legitimately discuss in the interview is confidential. If they cannot do so because of the possibility that an eavesdropper may retell in evidence what passed between them then this must have an inhibiting effect on 'that free and confidential communication between solicitor and client which lies at the foundation of the use and service of the solicitor to the client': *Pearce v Foster* (1885) 15 QBD 114 at 119–129 ... The exclusion of overheard communications is ... a logical extension of the privilege as it applies to solicitors and clients.[4]

6.10 *Uljee* does not sit comfortably alongside the English authorities on inadvertent disclosure of privileged material in criminal cases more generally, such as *R v Tompkins*.[5] In *Tompkins* the defendant had passed a note containing privileged instructions to his solicitor during the course of his trial. At the end of the court day the note was found on the floor of the courtroom by a legal assistant for the prosecution who passed it to prosecution counsel. The following day, prosecution counsel put the note to the defendant in cross-examination. It was held that this was permissible, as privilege exempts material from compelled disclosure but does not determine admissibility once the material is in the hands of the prosecution.[6]

6.11 Arguably, there are distinctions between the positions in *Uljee* and *Tompkins* which may explain the difference in approach. In *Uljee* the inadvertent eavesdropping was carried out by a police officer, and admission of evidence obtained in this manner would probably undermine confidence in a client's ability to consult freely with their legal representative if there was a chance that their discussion might, unbeknownst to them, be overheard and therefore not attract privilege to begin with. In *Tompkins*, however, the inadvertently disclosed note had originally been privileged and would have remained so but for the defendant's or his lawyer's carelessness. A finding of inadvertent waiver in these circumstances would not necessarily inhibit a client's ability to communicate freely with their legal representatives.

6.12 However, in *Eurasian Natural Resources Corp Ltd v Dechert LLP*[7] Waksman J effectively dismissed *Uljee* as having any application in English law on the basis that it is inconsistent with *Tompkins*. He said that *Tompkins* would have led to a different result in *Uljee*, and therefore the New Zealand court must have declined to follow it. He noted that the court in *Uljee* made reference to various other jurisdictions to support its decision.[8] It seems, therefore, that were the facts in *Uljee* to arise in a case in this jurisdiction, the court would find that privilege had been lost, unless the *Tompkins* line of authority could be distinguished in the way suggested above.

---

[3] [1982] 1 NZLR 561 (CA NZ).
[4] ibid 572.
[5] (1978) 67 Cr App R 181 (CA).
[6] *Tompkins* is discussed further at paras 1.18–1.20.
[7] [2022] EWHC 1138 (Comm).
[8] ibid [1735].

6.13 It was noted in *Tompkins* that the privileged note had come into the hands of the prosecution 'fortuitously' and no impropriety was raised.[9] This can clearly be distinguished from cases in which the police or other agencies deliberately listen in on privileged communications or listen in on communications being reckless as to whether those communications may be privileged, without reliance on powers authorizing covert surveillance or interception of communications.[10] In *R v Grant*[11] the Court of Appeal considered whether deliberate, unlawful eavesdropping and tape recording of privileged conversations by the police amounted to an abuse of process. The Court heard that the police had installed listening devices in the exercise yard of a police station, purporting to attempt to capture conversations between suspects. The police did, in fact, record privileged conversations between solicitors and their clients, although it was maintained by the police that this happened inadvertently. The Court emphasized that acts carried out by the police with a view to eavesdropping on privileged communications are unlawful and are at the very least capable of amounting to an abuse of the court's process. Laws LJ held that:

> We have concluded that this is a mistaken approach. True it is that nothing gained from the interception of solicitors' communications was used as, or (however indirectly) gave rise to evidence relied on by the Crown at the trial. Nor, as we understand it, did the intercepts yield any material which the Crown might deploy to undermine the defence case. But we are in no doubt but that in general unlawful acts of the kind done in this case, amounting to a deliberate violation of a suspected person's right to legal professional privilege, are so great an affront to the integrity of the justice system, and therefore the rule of law, that the associated prosecution is rendered abusive and ought not to be countenanced by the court.[12]

Laws LJ also stated that:

> Acts done by the police, in the course of an investigation which leads in due course to the institution of criminal proceedings, with a view to eavesdropping upon communications of suspected persons which are subject to legal professional privilege are categorically unlawful and at the very least capable of infecting the proceedings as abusive of the court's process. So much seems to us to be plain and obvious and no authority is needed to make it good.[13]

6.14 There was no attempt by the prosecution to rely on the content of any privileged communications, so the issue for the Court in *Grant* was whether the effect of the conduct was that the overall proceedings amounted to an abuse of process. What was not addressed was the question of admissibility of privileged information obtained as a result of unlawful or improper conduct by the police. Had there been any attempt in *Grant* to rely on the content of the privileged communications, the abuse of process argument could still have been made and would almost certainly have led to the same outcome. However, whilst the conduct in *Grant* was so egregious as to defy any reasonable prospect of the proceedings being allowed

---

[9] (1978) 67 Cr App R 181, 184 (CA).
[10] See ch 3, s 10.
[11] [2005] EWCA Crim 1089, [2006] QB 60.
[12] [2005] EWCA Crim 1089, [2006] QB 60 [54].
[13] ibid [52].

to continue, it is possible to envisage a situation which falls somewhere between the factual circumstances of *Uljee* and *Grant*, where the conduct in question is improper but not to the extent that it crosses the threshold for an abuse of process.[14] Once privileged material is in the hands of the prosecution, the test is admissibility, and its once privileged status does not render the material inadmissible. Its relevance, as well as the circumstances in which it came into the prosecution's hands, will determine its admissibility. The authors' view is that, if the prosecution has obtained or is in possession of privileged material unlawfully, but the conduct does not amount to an abuse of process, the trial judge must exclude the evidence under PACE 1984, section 78. To hold otherwise would effectively endorse unlawful conduct by investigators or prosecutors and render statutory protections of privilege meaningless.[15]

Third Party Instructions

The position generally

6.15 When a suspect is held at a police station in order to be interviewed under caution, the initial instruction requesting advice may not come from the suspect themselves, but from a third party such as a friend or family member who seeks to instruct a legal adviser on the suspect's behalf.[16] To what extent are communications with a third party on the client's behalf privileged and/or confidential? Legal advice privilege does not cover communications with third parties, and the conditions for litigation privilege may not be met at the investigation stage.

6.16 Communications with a third party to update on the progress of the investigation or for the purposes of facilitating the instruction are therefore unlikely to be privileged. It does not, however, follow that the sharing of privileged information with a third party on a confidential basis causes privilege to be lost. The confidentiality in the information is lost as against that third party, such that privilege cannot be asserted against them, but the information remains confidential and privileged as against the rest of the world.[17]

Availability of litigation privilege

6.17 Confidential communications with third parties can be privileged in circumstances where litigation is in progress or reasonably in contemplation and the sole or dominant purpose of the communication is the conduct of that litigation.[18]

---

[14] In *R (on the application of Her Majesty's Commissioners of Customs & Excise) v Nottingham Magistrates' Court* [2004] EWHC 1922 (Admin), [2004] All ER (D) 241 (Jul), Kennedy LJ provided guidance on the approach a court should take if a prosecutor comes into possession of material which the defence justifiably claims is subject to legal professional privilege (and that claim is either conceded or upheld) and the defence contends that the way in which the material came into the possession of the prosecutor needs to be investigated and/or that the disclosure of that material has so prejudiced the conduct of the defence that the case should not proceed. This is discussed in ch 3, s 9.

[15] See para 1.108 for a discussion of this point in relation to seizure of privileged material.

[16] *R v Sally Jones* [1984] Crim LR 357 (CA); and see PACE 1984 Code C and PACE 1984 Code H, Annex B, para 4.

[17] See further discussion at paras 1.77–1.79 and in *Gotha City v Sotheby's (No 1)* [1998] 1 WLR 114, 121 (CA).

[18] *Three Rivers District Council v Governor and Company of the Bank of England* [2004] UKHL 48, [2005] 1 AC 610 [102]. See ch 1, s 3.

6.18 A criminal investigation does not amount to litigation for the purposes of litigation privilege. However, to what extent can it be said that when an interview under caution is planned, or has taken place, litigation is reasonably in contemplation? The case of *United States of America v Philip Morris Inc*[19] makes clear that, for litigation to reasonably be in contemplation, there must be more than a 'mere possibility' or 'general apprehension' of litigation. What is not required, however, is a greater than 50 per cent chance of litigation.[20]

6.19 The authorities are clear that the question of whether litigation is reasonably in contemplation will be an issue to be determined on the facts, having regard to the nature of the allegations made, the available evidence and defence(s) and the assessment of the client's prospects by their legal advisers.[21] In *R v Jukes*[22] the Court of Appeal considered whether a witness statement given by the appellant in the early stages of a health and safety investigation was admissible evidence in his subsequent criminal trial or whether it was covered by litigation privilege. The dispute centred on the issue of whether litigation was reasonably in contemplation at the time the statement was provided (to his employer's solicitors during an internal investigation). The defendant was not interviewed by the Health and Safety Executive until sixteen months after he had provided the statement. The Court of Appeal held that the statement was not privileged as, at the time it was given, litigation was not reasonably in contemplation. Although the case concerned a witness statement rather than an interview under caution, it helpfully demonstrates the difficulties that can be faced at the early stages of an investigation when an interview under caution may be carried out. Flaux LJ stated:

> The difficulty with [the appellant's] argument that the statement attracts litigation privilege is that there is no evidence from the company or from [the co-defendant], let alone from the appellant, that at the time that these investigations by the company were taking place in February 2011, any of them had enough knowledge as to what the investigation would unearth or had unearthed when the Health and Safety Executive concluded its investigations, that it could be said that they appreciated that it was realistic to expect the Health and Safety Executive to be satisfied that it had enough material to stand a good chance of securing convictions.[23]

6.20 The decision in *Jukes* turns on its own facts, as any assessment of this issue is likely to. *Jukes* was referred to by the Court of Appeal in *The Director of the Serious Fraud Office v Eurasian Natural Resources Corp Ltd (SFO v ENRC Ltd)*,[24] in which the issue of whether criminal litigation was reasonably in contemplation was also considered. In *SFO v ENRC Ltd* it was the Court of Appeal's view that a criminal prosecution was not reasonably in contemplation simply because there was reasonable contemplation of an SFO investigation. However, the Court concluded that the documents and evidence available pointed clearly to the contemplation of a prosecution in circumstances where ENRC was engaging in a self-reporting

---

[19] [2004] EWCA Civ 330, [2004] 1 CLC 811.
[20] ibid [68]. See para 1.56.
[21] A detailed review of the case law relating to reasonable contemplation of litigation in the context of internal investigations, but also of relevance to criminal investigations more generally, can be found at paras 12.38–12.80.
[22] [2018] EWCA Crim 176, [2018] 2 Cr App R 9.
[23] ibid [24].
[24] [2018] EWCA Civ 2006, [2019] 1 WLR 791.

process with a view to avoiding prosecution but may not have succeeded in doing so. A full discussion of *SFO v ENRC Ltd* and *Jukes* is set out at paras 12.43–12.54.

The agency principle

6.21 The agency principle is likely to be applicable in circumstances where a third party is doing no more than facilitating communication between the client and their legal adviser. The principle of agency means that privilege can still apply even if communications between a client and their legal adviser are made indirectly via an agent acting on behalf of the client or the lawyer, or both. It is therefore not a requirement of privilege that communication between the client and the legal adviser is made directly, as long as the agent through whom the communication is passed is simply a means of communication.[25] This may be the case if a third party instructing a solicitor on behalf of a suspect in custody passes on their instructions.

3 Consultation with the Client

Consultation with the Client in the Presence of Third Parties

6.22 When attending a police station to advise a client regarding an interview under caution, the meeting will, save in exceptional circumstances, take place in conditions where confidentiality can be expected. There are various circumstances under which consultation with the client may be in the presence of a third party, and it is therefore necessary to consider the effect of the third party's presence on confidentiality and privilege.

6.23 As set out above at para 6.16, it is permissible to share privileged information with a third party on a confidential basis without losing privilege more generally, so the presence of a third party during consultation does not have the effect of destroying privilege if there is an obligation or expectation of confidentiality. There are, however, nuances to the position which are important to consider.

Interpreters

6.24 Authority for the principle that privileged communication through an interpreter remains confidential and therefore privileged is well established, dating back to the case of *Du Barre v Livette*,[26] in which it was held to be impermissible to call the client's interpreter to give evidence of the admissions made by the defendant to his legal representative in the presence of the interpreter. The issue was further considered in *R (Bozkurt) v Thames Magistrates' Court*,[27] which concerned the circumstances under which an interpreter could be called by the prosecution to give factual evidence about a drink driving procedure carried out at the police station at which the interpreter was present to assist the defendant. It was held that the interpreter could be called to give factual evidence but could not give evidence regarding any matters which were covered by the defendant's privilege.

---

[25] *Anderson v Bank of British Columbia* (1876) 2 Ch D 644 (CA).
[26] 170 ER 96.
[27] [2001] EWHC Admin 400, [2002] RTR 15.

6.25 The role of an interpreter falls squarely within the definition of an agent for the purposes of privilege as they are merely a means of communication between the client and their legal adviser. It is not necessary for the client to require an agent to facilitate communication in order to render the communication privileged; the fact that the client could have communicated directly, rather than through an agent, does not mean the communication is not privileged.[28] Therefore, communications through and in the presence of an interpreter will be privileged regardless of whether an interpreter was required to facilitate communication or not.

Appropriate Adults

6.26 Whilst the role of an appropriate adult, unlike an interpreter, is wider than a mere conduit of information, the appropriate adult's role does involve facilitating the giving of instructions and the receiving of advice, and, as such, the agency principle is likely to apply to communications between the client and their lawyer that pass via the appropriate adult. Furthermore, the presence of an appropriate adult during a privileged consultation does not destroy privilege. Privileged information can be shared with the appropriate adult on a confidential basis without losing the right to assert privilege against the rest of the world.[29] An appropriate adult is not entitled to waive the client's privilege.

6.27 In *A Local Authority v B*[30] a fifteen-year-old boy, B, was arrested and interviewed under caution regarding allegations that he had sexually assaulted his eight-year-old half-sister. As it was not appropriate in the circumstances for either of B's parents to act as an appropriate adult, a social worker was invited to do so. The solicitor requested that consultation with B took place in the presence of the appropriate adult, during which B made a partial admission. The solicitor advised B to answer no comment to the questions put to him in interview and B followed this advice. Following the interview, returning to her role as a social worker, the appropriate adult relayed to her supervisor what she had come to know about B's conduct towards his half-sister from the consultation. The supervisor stopped the conversation and asked the appropriate adult to note her recollections in a password protected document and not to make any further disclosures. Social Services then sought the assistance of the High Court (Family Division) as to their competing obligations to respect the confidentiality and privilege of B and their duty to safeguard the welfare of children.

6.28 Hedley J identified that the issue was of general importance and considered the applicable principles, noting that B's conversation with his solicitor was privileged and that the presence of the appropriate adult did not destroy that privilege. It was not therefore open to the appropriate adult to waive that privilege. This did not, however, prevent another social worker interviewing B about his half-sister's complaints in the course of child protection procedures.

---

[28] *Carpmael v Powis* (1846) 1 Ph 687, 693.
[29] *Gotha City v Sotheby's (No 1)* (n 17) 121.
[30] [2008] EWHC 1017 (Fam), [2009] 1 FLR 289.

Consultation in the presence of other third parties

6.29 An interview under caution may exceptionally be required to take place in circumstances which render a private consultation impossible or impractical. How does this affect the client's privilege? The case of *R v Brown*[31] concerned the extent to which the court could prohibit a client from consulting privately with his legal adviser in circumstances where the client was being tried for attempted murder and had indicated a desire to kill his solicitor and/or harm himself. Whilst the consultations in this case were for the purpose of giving instructions during the course of a trial, the principle will be equally applicable should a similar requirement be imposed at the interview stage.

6.30 The defendant, Brown, appealed against his conviction on the basis that he was prevented from consulting privately with his lawyers because the judge had ordered that he must be handcuffed to two nurses during the consultations to prevent him harming his lawyers and/or himself. The extreme nature of the defendant's determination to fashion and conceal weapons and use them to harm himself and others was noted in the judgment as an indication of the unusual nature of this case. It was argued on Brown's behalf that the presence of the nurses, and the intervention of one nurse during a conference with counsel (discussed below), inhibited his ability to communicate freely with his lawyers. On appeal, the Court of Appeal identified that the issue for the court was whether it should prevent privileged consultations being used to enable individuals to inflict violence on themselves or others, and whether it was justified to extend the crime-fraud exception, which precludes privilege from attaching to communications in furtherance of a criminal purpose,[32] in a limited way in order to do so.

6.31 The case, to an extent, turns on its own facts, and particular reliance was placed upon the fact that during a conference with counsel, one of the nurses sought to intervene when counsel was advising whether or not Brown should give evidence. It was noted that the nurse said: 'one of the things he stated yesterday was how he was feeling generally leading up to this incident. That's what you said the other day. You told us you would ... you remember? You said ...', before the nurse was interrupted by counsel. This intervention led to counsel telling the judge that Brown's instructions were being given under apparent pressure because of the presence of the nurses. On appeal it was argued that the presence of, and alleged pressure from, the nurses contributed to Brown's decision to instruct his counsel not to cross-examine certain witnesses, thereby affecting the safety of his conviction.

6.32 The Court approached the issue from the starting point that privilege is absolute and inviolable, which followed from consideration of the numerous authorities on this point, including *R v Derby Magistrates' Court ex p B*.[33] The Court considered the applicability of the crime-fraud exception to the facts and noted that this was not a case in which the privilege itself was being abused to facilitate the commission of a crime, but that there was a different improper purpose for which the privileged meeting was being used which warranted intervention, namely the infliction of unlawful violence. The Court held that the crime-fraud

---

[31] [2015] EWCA Crim 1328, [2016] 1 WLR 1141.
[32] See ch 2.
[33] [1996] AC 487 (HL).

exception did apply in this case, acknowledging that this involved a limited but significant extension to the exception which was justified in these particular circumstances.

6.33 It was asserted that Brown had been denied the ability to consult confidentially with his legal advisers due to the presence of the nurses and, separately, that the presence of the nurses had inhibited his ability to consult freely. As a matter of fact, given the interventions of one of the nurses, the latter point may have been correct. But as a matter of law, the presence of one or more third parties does not destroy the confidential nature of the communications between a client and their lawyer. Notwithstanding the unwelcome contribution of one of the nurses, there was no suggestion that there had been onward disclosure of confidential information, nor that the confidential nature of the consultation had otherwise been destroyed by their presence. The consultation, therefore, remained privileged. There is no distinction in the authorities between the position of a third party who is present during a privileged consultation at the client's behest and one who is present as a result of some other requirement. The situation in *Brown* is broadly analogous to the presence of the appropriate adult in *A Local Authority v B*, in which the appropriate adult was required by the solicitor, rather than the client, to be present during the consultation (see paras 6.27–6.28). In that case, the consultation was held to have remained privileged. It was therefore open to the Court in *Brown* to interpret the facts in such a way that, as a matter of law, privilege had not been breached, before considering whether the circumstances in fact did not allow him to consult freely with his lawyer, and whether that impacted the safety of his conviction.

6.34 Given the very narrow issue in *Brown*, it is perhaps best to interpret the case as the authors of *The Law of Privilege* suggest: it is authority for the principle that there are rare and distinct exceptions to the inviolable nature of privilege which will arise infrequently.[34]

Statutory surveillance of privileged consultation

6.35 The Regulation of Investigatory Powers Act 2000 allows, in certain exceptional circumstances, for covert surveillance to take place with the intention of acquiring knowledge of matters subject to privilege. Chapter 3, Section 10 looks at these powers in further detail. Most pertinent for the purpose of this discussion is that, in certain limited circumstances, it is possible for authorized surveillance of legal consultations at various locations, including police stations, prisons, and lawyers' offices, to take place.

6.36 Surveillance to acquire knowledge of matters subject to privilege should only be authorized for use where there are exceptional and compelling circumstances that make the authorization necessary, and the proposed conduct is proportionate.[35] Considering these requirements, it may be argued that covert surveillance will be carried out rarely. However, it is unlikely that the extent of its use will ever be publicly known, given that it will yield information which will be used for intelligence purposes only, and will not be admissible in court proceedings.

---

[34] Bankim Thanki (ed), *The Law of Privilege* (3rd edn, OUP 2018) para 4.55.
[35] 'Covert Surveillance and Property Interference: Revised Code of Practice' (August 2018) paras 9.51–9.52 https://www.gov.uk/government/publications/covert-surveillance-and-covert-human-intelligence-sources-codes-of-practice (accessed 10 June 2023).

4 During the Interview

Communications during the Interview

6.37 Instructions taken at the police station remain privileged unless and until they form part of any account put forward to the investigator. Communications between a suspect and an interviewer are not privileged, and communications which take place between the legal adviser and the suspect in the presence of the investigator will not be confidential or privileged. Deciding what, if any, account to put forward in interview will almost certainly be based on a balance between the risk of self-incrimination and the possibility of an adverse inference from silence being drawn at any subsequent trial.

6.38 As information provided in the interview is not confidential, it follows that any record of the interview in the form of an attendance note which merely records what was said will not be a privileged document.[36] A note of advice given to the client outside the interview will, however, be privileged, as it records a privileged conversation.

References to the Reasons for Advice Given

6.39 In order to pre-empt an adverse inference being drawn in respect of a failure to provide an account in interview, suspects and/or legal advisers will sometimes state during the interview why a suspect is not answering questions. The extent to which this may lead to a loss or waiver of privilege requires careful consideration. The implications of a no comment interview, and any justification provided for it, are also considered at paras 10.27–10.34 from the perspective of comments made during questioning at court. This section will focus on how, at any subsequent trial, privilege might be deemed to have been waived as a result of comments made during the interview.

6.40 It is not necessary to assert in an interview, or at all, that a suspect is giving a no comment interview based on legal advice. However, doing so will not amount to a waiver of privilege. In *R v Condron*[37] the Court of Appeal considered the extent to which giving evidence at trial about the reasons for the advice given at the police station not to answer questions in interview could amount to a waiver of privilege. The Court distinguished between referring to the fact that advice had been given and disclosing the substance of that advice. The Court held that where a suspect or their legal adviser goes beyond the mere fact of the advice and relays the reasons for or basis upon which the advice was given, this will amount to a waiver of privilege. The effect of the waiver is that questioning will be permitted on the details of both the instructions given to the legal adviser and the precise nature of the advice provided in response. It will not be possible to rely upon privilege to resist answering questions on these matters at court.

---

[36] *Parry v News Group Newspapers* [1990] NLJR 1719 (CA).
[37] [1997] 1 WLR 827 (CA).

6.41 The principle will apply similarly if the reasons for the advice given at the police station are disclosed during the interview under caution. Privilege belongs to the client and only the client is permitted to waive it. However, if the solicitor makes a statement in interview which discloses the substance of their advice, this will have the effect of waiving the client's privilege, regardless of whether this was the client's intention. The rationale for this is that legal representatives are assumed to have their clients' authority in the steps they take when conducting cases on their behalf and this includes the disclosure of privileged information. It does not require the client to authorize the waiver expressly. It will therefore not be open to the client effectively to reverse a waiver of privilege caused by disclosure from their legal adviser.[38]

6.42 *R v Bowden*[39] considered the issue of waiver based on comments made by a solicitor during an interview under caution. The defendant was convicted of robbery and appealed against his conviction on the grounds that he had not waived privilege over the advice given by his solicitor at the police station and, as such, the prosecution ought not to have been permitted to question him at trial about the instructions provided to his solicitor at that time.

6.43 The case against Bowden was based on identification evidence by a police officer who had been shown still photographs taken from video footage of the robbery and recognized Bowden, identification by an off-duty officer who happened to be present at the time of the robbery and identified Bowden in an identification parade, and evidence that Bowden had gone on holiday to the Canary Islands four days after the robbery, allegedly funded with the proceeds from the robbery. When Bowden was interviewed, he was shown the video footage. He declined to answer questions, saying that he did so on legal advice. In the third, and final, interview of the day his solicitor made a statement in the following terms:

> Yes, more of a statement really in terms of the advice that I have given to Mr. Bowden during the course of this evening and particularly prior to the first interview. You have been good enough to show me the video on a total of three occasions, two of which, of course, were during the course of that first interview, if I am not mistaken. The view that I take is that the video is not poor in quality, though I have seen better on occasions and, of course, I have made mention of various things as the video was being shown. But obviously reference to that can be made again in due course with regard to the person to which, or to whom you referred in the video. I am not satisfied in my own mind that the video in itself shows that person to be Mr. Bowden and as a consequence of that having regard to the fact that the remaining evidence that you have presented is entirely circumstantial, I am of the view that at this point any charge of robbery brought against Mr. Bowden cannot in the long term be sustained, and that is the reason why at this point I have rendered the advice to him that I have, and which he has followed, of course, by saying 'no comment' during the course of the three interviews. Of course, and it is something we have discussed during the course of this evening's sessions, it may well be that you arrange for identification parades, and it may well be as a consequence of the outcome of those parades that my advice to Mr.

---

[38] *Causton v Mann Egerton (Johnsons) Ltd* [1974] 1 WLR 162 (CA).
[39] [1999] 1 WLR 823 (CA).

Bowden would change, but obviously that is a matter for the future not a matter for this evening.[40]

The statement clearly set out the basis for his advice to Bowden to give a no comment interview. At trial, the prosecution deliberately did not put the solicitor's statement before the jury, but counsel for the defendant, in an attempt to demonstrate that no adverse inferences should be drawn from Bowden's silence in interview, adduced the statement through the police officer who gave evidence of the interviews. The prosecution submitted that by doing so the defendant had waived privilege over the police station advice and as such it was permissible for him to be questioned about the instructions he had provided to his solicitor at the police station. The judge allowed this and the defendant was asked by prosecution counsel whether he had given his solicitor the facts he now relied upon in his defence at the time of the interview. He said that he could not remember. The judge correctly directed the jury regarding their ability to draw an adverse inference from Bowden's silence in interview. On appeal it was held that this was the correct approach and the conviction was safe.

6.44

It is clear, therefore, that if a client or their legal adviser discloses the substance of or basis for the legal advice during an interview under caution, this will amount to a waiver of privilege and may lead to the client being questioned at any subsequent trial about the instructions they provided to their legal representative at the police station. Although it makes little difference to the approach that should be taken at the interview stage, it is the view of the authors that the precise point at which waiver occurs is when evidence of what was said in interview is adduced at trial. This is because, as discussed at paras 1.88–1.96, the underlying principle of waiver of privilege is to ensure fairness between parties in litigation and to prevent the court from having only a partial and potentially misleading understanding of relevant issues. It is unfair for a jury, when determining whether to draw an adverse inference from a defendant's silence in interview or deciding whether or not the defendant is guilty, to have before it only those aspects of the legal advice that suit the defendant's case rather than the complete picture. These same considerations cannot be said to apply at the investigation stage. There is no equivalent unfairness to the police. On this basis, therefore, it would not be possible for an investigating authority to compel disclosure of privileged material at the investigation stage on the basis that privilege had been waived as a result of comments made in interview.

6.45

Notwithstanding the above, for practical purposes lawyers should consider the point of waiver as the interview itself because, once the privileged information has been disclosed, there is nothing to prevent the prosecution from adducing evidence of the interview at trial, thereby bringing about a waiver of privilege. Thus, in *R v Hall-Chung*,[41] the Court of Appeal, relying on comments made by Lord Bingham CJ in *Bowden* that the prosecution in that case would have been entitled to adduce evidence of the solicitor's statement had it so wished,[42] rejected the appellant's submission that privilege had not been waived because it was the prosecution, not the defence, who had sought to adduce evidence of comments made by the appellant's solicitor in the course of the interview explaining the basis for their advice to

6.46

---

[40] ibid 825.
[41] [2007] EWCA Crim 3429, [2007] All ER (D) 429 (Jul).
[42] *Bowden* (n 39) 829.

answer no comment. The Court stated that it made no difference whether the prosecution or defence adduced the evidence: 'The essential question is whether legal professional privilege was waived, not at what stage it was waived.'[43]

6.47 It should be noted, however, that confidentiality will be lost at the point at which the advice is disclosed in the interview, but this will be limited only to what has been disclosed rather than any additional advice or communications.

Prepared Statements

6.48 A prepared statement may take the form of a written document which is read out by or on behalf of the suspect during an interview under caution, or it may simply be an oral statement made by the suspect or their legal adviser during the interview. Once the information has been communicated to the interviewer, it is no longer confidential, and any privilege that may previously have attached to the information is lost.

6.49 It is, however, important to distinguish between the statement being made by or on behalf of the suspect and the physical document from which it may have been read. The words which are spoken are not privileged. However, if the statement is being read from a physical document, it does not automatically follow that the document itself is no longer privileged. The legal adviser must consider whether the document remains privileged or contains privileged information before agreeing to provide a copy to the investigator. A document which has visible amendments may contain privileged information, for example if sections or words have been struck through but remain legible. In these circumstances the document is a draft document and is distinct from the oral statement that has been read. Draft documents remain privileged unless they are served,[44] and as such a draft prepared statement is a privileged document.

6.50 In many cases, it will be the intention of the suspect and the legal adviser to provide a physical copy of the statement to the investigator after reading it. However, if a suspect declines to provide a physical copy, an investigator may not compel the suspect or legal adviser to do so. It is not open to an investigator to compel production of any document if it is asserted that it is a privileged document or that it contains privileged information. Additionally, the Association of Chief Police Officers' (ACPO) guidance on dealing with prepared statements acknowledges that there is no requirement or power to physically seize a prepared statement (whether or not privileged) if the legal adviser or suspect declines to provide a copy.[45] The guidance states that a prepared statement is not privileged once it has been read out,

---

[43] *Hall-Chung* (n 41) [16]–[18]. Although the Court also said that: '[w]here a solicitor states in the presence of his client that his client will not answer questions and gives reasons or grounds why that advice is given, then legal professional privilege has been waived by that client through the mouth of his agent acting within the scope of his authority', it is clear from the overall reasoning of the decision that this should be understood as an explanation about whether, not when, privilege is waived.

[44] *USP Strategies Plc v London General Holdings Ltd (No 2)* [2004] EWHC 373 (Ch), [2004] All ER (D) 132 (Mar) [48], referring to *Three Rivers District Council v Governor and Company of the Bank of England* [2003] EWCA Civ 474, [2003] QB 1556 [29]. See para 1.38.

[45] National Investigative Interviewing Strategic Steering Group (NIISSG), 'ACPO Position Statement: Dealing with Prepared Statements in Investigative Interviews with Suspects' https://library.college.police.uk/docs/APP REF/ACPO-Position-Statement-Prepared-Statements.pdf (accessed 10 June 2023).

which is accurate only to the extent that the document from which the statement has been read contains only the words which have been read aloud. If, for the reasons set out above, the document itself is a draft, it will be privileged. Regardless of its privileged status, the guidance makes clear that an investigator cannot compel disclosure of a prepared statement and instead should take steps to transcribe the statement before continuing with the interview.

Privilege Belonging to Another Party

Only the privilege holder is entitled to waive privilege, and a suspect cannot be compelled to provide information which is privileged. If the person being interviewed is asked questions, the answers to which would involve breaching the privilege of a third party, the suspect cannot disclose the information without the express consent of the privilege holder. In practice, this may mean that the suspect is deprived of the opportunity to put forward an exculpatory account. This may arise in circumstances where a solicitor or barrister is interviewed in respect of matters relating to the affairs of their client. In *R v Devani*[46] a solicitor was accused of conspiring with her client to pervert the course of justice by participating in a scheme designed to fabricate evidence to assist the client's defence to a charge of attempted murder. The case is discussed in detail at paras 10.47–10.60 as it illustrates the complexities privilege issues can present at trial and the difficulties that even experienced practitioners face in navigating them. Whilst the approach to privilege taken by the investigators and the court in *Devani* was somewhat inconsistent with the established principles, and regardless of the fact that Devani did in fact waive her client's privilege in interview, it was made clear that the privilege was the client's alone to waive. Devani's conviction was upheld despite her complaint that she was unable to cross-examine her client at trial about the contents of their consultation due to his reliance on privilege.

6.51

---

[46] [2007] EWCA Crim 1926, [2008] 1 Cr App R 4.

7
Waiver and Cooperation

1 Introduction

Whilst investigators and prosecutors cannot gain access to privileged material through powers of search and seizure and compulsion (as discussed in Chapter 3), it is open to a party during the course of an investigation or prosecution to waive privilege over their own material and disclose it voluntarily to investigating or prosecuting authorities. This will often be a company that is cooperating with an investigation or prosecution. This has become increasingly more common since the Crime and Courts Act 2013, section 45 and schedule 17 introduced deferred prosecution agreements (DPAs) for the SFO and CPS in February 2014. Corporate cooperation is an important consideration when deciding whether to offer and enter into a DPA, and, as will be seen from the discussion that follows, the SFO considers a waiver of privilege over relevant material to be a strong indication of cooperation. **7.01**

As a consequence, there is now a greater incentive for companies voluntarily to provide relevant privileged material to the SFO (and, to a lesser extent, other authorities). However, this is not without its risks, and there are important issues companies and their advisers must consider before handing over privileged documents to the authorities. **7.02**

This chapter examines these issues in detail before reviewing the relevant guidance and case law surrounding DPAs and cooperation with other authorities. **7.03**

2 Waiving Privilege through Voluntary Disclosure

Summary of Main Principles

A party is entitled to waive privilege at any stage of proceedings. Waiver may be general or limited in scope. A limited waiver will limit the use to which the material may be put by the receiving party, and often the material will be confined to a particular issue or category of documents, but privilege will be maintained in all other respects. It can be either express or implied, although, if disputed, the question of whether a waiver is limited and, if so, the parameters of the limitation will be assessed on an objective basis. Whilst waiver is generally understood to be a concept that applies to the deployment of material at court, there can also be a waiver of privilege at the investigation stage in criminal cases where documents are provided to the authorities. The law concerning waiver of privilege is examined in detail in Chapter 1, Section 5. **7.04**

Limited Waiver to Assist with Investigation/Prosecution

7.05 In most cases, a party that discloses privileged material to an investigator or prosecutor will do so on the basis of a limited waiver of privilege rather than a general waiver. The terms of the limited waiver should be expressly stated in writing and the investigator/prosecutor should be asked to confirm in writing that they accept the terms of the waiver before any material is disclosed. However, even if there is no express agreement in place, it is likely that an implied limited waiver will exist, the extent of which will depend on the circumstances of the disclosure, in particular what was communicated between the parties and what they must or ought reasonably to have understood.[1]

7.06 An express limited waiver in these circumstances will usually state that the investigating/prosecuting authority may only use the material for the purpose of its investigation and/or prosecution of one or more third parties, including compliance with statutory duties of disclosure, and possibly also for the purpose of sharing intelligence with law enforcement partners, but that privilege is maintained in all other respects. This is also likely to be the scope of an implied limited waiver. This has the effect of limiting what the authority receiving the material can do with it and also preserving privilege over the material as against third parties. This includes subsequent proceedings between the party whose privilege it is and one or more of the suspects or defendants in the criminal proceedings, even if the material has been disclosed to them by the prosecution in the course of the criminal proceedings,[2] as long as the material has not lost its confidentiality by being referred to in open court (see paras 7.25–7.32). Not only will the terms of the limited waiver prevent use of the privileged material in the subsequent proceedings, but the party who has received it as unused material in the criminal proceedings will be prevented from using it for a collateral purpose without the court's permission, by virtue of the Criminal Procedure and Investigations Act 1996 (CPIA 1996), section 17.

7.07 In addition to imposing restrictions on what the authorities can do with the material, the disclosing party will often limit the waiver to particular categories of documents, such as those relating to a particular issue or covering a certain date range, or types of documents, the most common being records of internal investigation witness interviews. They may provide parts of documents only, redacting other content that falls outside the scope of the waiver.

7.08 That privilege can be waived on a limited basis even where the material is disclosed to the police or other authorities to assist with a criminal investigation or prosecution is a well-established principle. In *British Coal Corp v Dennis Rye (No 2)*[3] the plaintiff suspected that it had been overcharged for work carried out by the defendant and instructed quantity surveyors to investigate. Documents generated during the course of the investigation were accepted as being covered by litigation privilege, the relevant litigation being anticipated civil proceedings against the defendant. The documents were provided to the police, and the defendant and others were subsequently charged with

---

[1] *Berezovsky v Hine & Ors* [2011] EWCA Civ 1089, [2011] All ER (D) 61 (Oct) [29].
[2] As in *British Coal Corp v Dennis Rye (No 2)* [1988] 1 WLR 1113 (CA).
[3] ibid.

criminal offences relating to the work carried out for the plaintiff. In the course of the criminal proceedings that followed, the privileged documents were disclosed by the prosecution to the defendants in that case. In subsequent civil proceedings against one of the criminal defendants, the plaintiff applied for the return of the documents. The Court of Appeal held that the plaintiff had made the documents available to the police for a limited purpose only, namely to assist in the conduct, first, of a criminal investigation, and then a criminal trial (albeit this was an implied purpose rather than anything expressly agreed). This did not constitute a waiver of the privilege to which the plaintiff was entitled in the civil proceedings. The voluntary disclosure to the police was 'in accordance with [the plaintiff's] duty to assist in the conduct of the criminal proceedings', and it would be 'contrary to public policy if the plaintiff's action in making the documents available in the criminal proceedings had the effect of automatically removing the cloak of privilege which would otherwise be available to it in the civil litigation for which the cloak was designed'.[4]

7.09 A similar approach has been taken in a number of other cases. In *Property Alliance Group Ltd v Royal Bank of Scotland Plc*[5] RBS had voluntarily shown and/or disclosed a number of privileged documents to US regulators/authorities (the Commodity Futures Trading Commission, the Securities and Exchange Commission, and the Department of Justice, and Attorneys General of various US states) on the basis of express confidential 'non-waiver' agreements. The agreements explicitly stated that the documents were being provided on the basis that confidentiality and privilege would be preserved as against third parties, although they also contained 'carve-outs' which allowed the regulators to share the documents with other third parties, such as other governmental or regulatory agencies, and/or to make the material public or to disclose it further. In the proceedings between PAG and RBS, the claimant challenged RBS' contention that it was entitled to withhold inspection of the documents on the grounds of privilege. PAG argued that privilege had been waived as a result of RBS' disclosure to the regulators and because of the carve-outs which did not completely prohibit further disclosure of the documents by the regulators. It was claimed that the effect of these agreements was that RBS had relinquished control of the documents.

7.10 This argument was rejected by Birss J, who held that the existence of the carve-outs did not undermine the express provision in the agreements that privilege and confidence were maintained. RBS had provided the documents to the regulators on a limited basis for the purpose of the ongoing investigations. They were entitled to maintain the claim to privilege notwithstanding the existence of legal rights or duties on the part of the regulators to use, act on, or even publish the documents pursuant to their regulatory powers. The fact that the carve-outs recognized the regulators' rights and obligations to take a step which could ultimately lead to privilege being lost (see discussion at para 7.32) made no difference if that had not yet happened.[6]

7.11 In reaching this conclusion, Birss J made reference to authorities from other jurisdictions in which limited waivers had been upheld despite the presence of equivalent

---

[4] ibid 1121–22.
[5] [2015] EWHC 1557 (Ch), [2016] 1 WLR 361.
[6] ibid [113].

carve-outs.⁷ *Fyffes v DCC*⁸ was a decision of the Supreme Court of Ireland in which a company, DCC, was under investigation by the DPP for suspected insider trading. This followed a report made to the DPP by the Irish Stock Exchange, which had a statutory duty to report if it appeared that an offence had been committed. In the hope of persuading the Stock Exchange to try to influence the DPP against prosecution, DCC disclosed privileged documents to the Stock Exchange and asked that they be transmitted to the DPP, which was done in due course. Notwithstanding this request, the documents were otherwise covered by an express agreement that the Stock Exchange would keep the documents confidential and would not share them with any third party unless obliged by law or court order or with DCC's prior written consent. Rejecting the claimant's argument in subsequent civil proceedings that privilege over the documents had been waived, the Supreme Court followed the reasoning in *British Coal* and held that DCC could maintain its claim to privilege over the material as against the claimant in those proceedings.

7.12 Birss J in *Property Alliance Group* also relied on *Citic Pacific Ltd v Secretary for Justice*,⁹ a decision of the Hong Kong Court of Appeal. The case concerned six privileged documents that were voluntarily disclosed to the Hong Kong Securities and Futures Commission (SFC) by Citic in connection with the SFC's (regulatory) investigation into why Citic had delayed publication of a profit warning. The documents were provided with no express statement as to the limited basis on which they were disclosed, but Citic later asserted that privilege was waived only to the extent necessary to enable the SFC to conduct its investigation and for no other purpose. Following disclosure, Citic learned that the SFC had shared the documents with the Hong Kong Department of Justice for the purpose of seeking legal advice. The police subsequently launched their own (criminal) investigation and Citic learned that the police also wished to have sight of the documents to advance their investigation. Citic initiated proceedings seeking the return of the documents from the Secretary of Justice on the basis that the limited waiver of privilege did not allow the SFC to share the documents with the Secretary. Alternatively, Citic sought a declaration that, if the Secretary of Justice was in lawful possession of the documents, it was for the purpose only of giving legal advice to the SFC and the Secretary was not entitled to disclose the documents to any third party.

7.13 The Court held that the documents were indeed disclosed on a limited waiver of privilege but that the limited purpose must also have included enabling the SFC to take legal advice, as this was integral to the conduct of the investigation, and therefore the disclosure to the Department of Justice was permitted. This was the extent of the limited waiver, however, and privilege was maintained in all other respects, including as against the police. The Court noted that, at the time the documents were provided to the SFC, Citic understood the investigation to be focused on regulatory and not criminal issues. The evidence indicated that Citic was prepared to waive privilege for the only purpose then known, namely the SFC

---

⁷ ibid [109]–[112].
⁸ [2005] IESC 3.
⁹ [2012] HKCA 153.

investigation, but it would have adopted a very different approach if faced with the prospect of a criminal investigation.[10]

Further authority, if needed, for the principle that a limited waiver of privilege in these circumstances is possible can be found in the DPAs agreed with the SFO that are discussed later in this chapter at paras 7.61–7.75. As will be seen, the vast majority involved a limited waiver of privilege of some kind, and the judges who approved the DPAs had no conceptual difficulty with this. 7.14

Furthermore, the FCA expressly recognizes the concept in its Enforcement Guide, noting that 'the FCA considers that English law does permit such "limited waiver" and that legal privilege could still be asserted against third parties notwithstanding disclosure of [an internal investigation report] to the FCA'.[11] 7.15

Risks with Limited Waivers

Use of the material against the privilege holder

In most cases, if the party that has disclosed the privileged material is prosecuted in relation to the same matter with which they have sought to assist by agreeing the limited waiver, they will not be able to prevent the prosecution from relying on the privileged material in support of its case against them, should they be prosecuted. The limited waiver will be taken to include use of the material for this purpose, unless it is expressly excluded in the terms of the waiver, but it is unlikely that an investigator or prosecutor would agree to such an exclusion. 7.16

There is more scope for arguing that a limited waiver prevents a prosecutor from relying on the material if the prosecution is for a separate, unrelated matter which was not anticipated when the limited waiver was agreed. The fact that the prosecutor has seen the material and has access to it does not mean that confidentiality as against the prosecutor has been lost in all respects so that privilege can no longer apply. As noted at para 1.87, there are a number of cases where the courts have prevented a party who has received privileged material subject to a limited waiver from using it in subsequent proceedings against the privilege holder. The most appropriate recourse for a defendant in criminal proceedings would be an application under PACE 1984, section 78 to exclude the evidence. The prosecution might seek to rely on the line of authority concerning inadvertent disclosure of privileged material to the prosecution (see paras 1.104–1.109) to argue that it is free to make use of the material however it wishes once the material is in its possession. 7.17

Waiver more extensive than intended

Because the extent of any waiver will be determined on an objective basis rather than purely by reference to the assertions and understanding of the parties involved (although these are relevant factors), a limited waiver can result in a loss of privilege that is more extensive 7.18

---

[10] ibid [71]–[73], [108].
[11] FCA Handbook, Enforcement Guide, 3.29.

than intended. This was the case in *Citic Pacific Ltd*, discussed at paras 7.12–7.13, where the Court disagreed with one of Citic's arguments that the limited waiver did not extend to allowing the SFC to share the documents with the Department of Justice.

7.19 The point is also helpfully demonstrated by *R v Ungvari*.[12] The appellant was suspected (and later convicted) of being involved in a conspiracy to evade duty on the import of cigarettes into the UK. He instructed a solicitor to advise him regarding the affairs of a company he owned, and, after Customs became involved, he informed his solicitor that he (his solicitor) could talk freely with Customs about what passed between him and the appellant. The solicitor proceeded to give Customs a nine-page statement, which he expanded upon in an interview on the same date. He also provided them with full access to his client file. In the criminal prosecution that followed, some of the material from the client file was disclosed by Customs to the appellant and his co-defendants, and counsel for one of the co-defendants cross-examined the appellant about it. In light of the appellant's denials about certain facts contained in one of the privileged documents, the co-defendant's counsel sought to call the appellant's solicitor to deal with the same subject matter. The appellant objected on the grounds that the content of his communications with his solicitor was privileged, and he withdrew any waiver, whether express or implied, which might have been given to permit the co-defendant to adduce the evidence. The trial judge ruled that the documents were not subject to privilege as there had been a waiver and no valid withdrawal of that waiver.

7.20 On appeal, the appellant argued that the waiver could not have been wide enough to permit the solicitor effectively to give evidence against the appellant as part of a cut-throat defence advanced by his co-defendant. In the alternative, he contended that he was entitled to withdraw the waiver, which he had done through his counsel at trial. The Court of Appeal rejected the appellant's arguments, holding that the limited waiver was for the purpose of assisting in the conduct of the criminal investigation and subsequent trial, as in *British Coal*. The appellant's solicitor was made available to Customs for precisely that purpose and it was therefore open to Customs and the co-defendant to call him to give evidence. The appellant could not later withdraw the waiver. The material provided to Customs was relevant unused material which Customs owed a duty to disclose to each defendant, and it was not received by Customs subject to any relevant condition which might prevent them from discharging their duty. Once disclosed, any other defendant was entitled to deploy it in evidence as the waiver necessarily extended to proper use of the material for the purposes of the criminal trial.[13]

7.21 *R (AL) v Serious Fraud Office*[14] is a case in which, surprisingly, there seems to have been no intention to waive privilege, but it nevertheless demonstrates the objective basis on which waiver is assessed, as well as highlighting a number of other important points that will be discussed later in this chapter. After becoming aware of suspected bribes paid by some of its executives to secure business, XYZ Ltd (later revealed to be Sarclad Ltd) instructed a law firm, ABC LLP, to investigate. ABC interviewed four employees of Sarclad with the

---

[12] [2003] EWCA Crim 2346, [2003] All ER (D) 335 (Jul).
[13] ibid [58]–[68].
[14] [2018] EWHC 856 (Admin), [2018] 1 WLR 4557.

purpose of deciding whether or not to self-report to the SFO. No verbatim transcript of the interviews was taken, but the lawyers conducting the interviews took detailed notes. Sarclad decided to self-report to the SFO and a criminal investigation was commenced. The SFO requested the lawyers' notes of the employee interviews, but ABC declined to provide them on the basis that they were covered by legal advice privilege and/or litigation privilege. ABC did, however, agree to engage in 'proffer sessions', which involved a partner of ABC providing an oral summary of the interviews which the SFO was able to record and transcribe. Proffer sessions are an established process for discussions between lawyers and authorities in US investigations, but not in the UK. The lawyer from ABC began the proffer sessions by stating that: 'The provision of these facts is not to be taken as a waiver by [Sarclad] of its lawyer/client privilege either (a) specifically with regard to the matters being investigated by the SFO or (b) generally regarding any other proceedings arising from these matters.' Sarclad eventually entered into a DPA with the SFO, a condition of which was for the company to cooperate on an ongoing basis with the SFO, including a duty to disclose all relevant information and material not protected by a valid claim of privilege.

7.22 One of the interview summaries related to AL, who was subsequently charged with bribery and corruption offences. The summary of his interview ran to only five pages. During the course of the prosecution, AL made a request for prosecution disclosure which was sufficiently broad to encompass full records and notes of the interviews which had been summarized in the proffer sessions. The SFO disclosed the summaries to AL and his co-defendants and made further requests to Sarclad for disclosure of the underlying interview notes, but Sarclad persistently refused on the grounds of privilege. The SFO chose not to make use of its powers of compulsion to obtain the documents. In light of the SFO's position, AL made an application to the Crown Court for disclosure under the CPIA 1996, section 8. The judge concluded that, since the SFO was not in possession of the documents, there was no obligation to disclose the interview notes under the CPIA 1996. The judge did, however, express misgivings about the position taken by the SFO. In light of this ruling, the SFO wrote to ABC and explained that, since the acceptance of the proffers, there had been significant developments in the law of privilege, in particular *The RBS Rights Issue Litigation*[15] and the first instance decision in *The Director of the SFO v Eurasian Natural Resources Corp Ltd* (*SFO v ENRC Ltd*).[16] In light of this case law, any claim for privilege was now 'unlikely to succeed'. The SFO, in referring to the terms of the DPA and Sarclad's disclosure obligation under it, asked ABC to reconsider the claim for privilege and provide the interview notes. In their response, ABC stated that the issue had been reconsidered but their view concerning privilege remained unchanged. ABC disagreed with the SFO's reliance on recent case law, pointing out that *SFO v ENRC Ltd* was under appeal and that the present case could be distinguished from the facts of that case and *The RBS Rights Issue Litigation*. In light of this response, the SFO decided not to pursue the request for disclosure and confirmed this in writing to AL.

7.23 AL instigated judicial review proceedings against the SFO, challenging its decision not to compel Sarclad, in compliance with its duty of cooperation under the DPA, to produce the

---

[15] [2016] EWHC 3161 (Ch), [2017] 1 WLR 1991.
[16] [2017] EWHC 1017 (QB), [2017] 1 WLR 4205.

full interview notes. The SFO submitted that, inter alia, whilst it did not accept Sarclad's privilege arguments, privilege was still asserted and the arguments were 'not obviously wrong', and the SFO had formed a view, on the basis of a review of the material already in its possession, that there was no material in the full interview notes which was not adequately encapsulated in the oral proffer summaries.

7.24 The Divisional Court was bound to refuse the application for judicial review on the basis that the Crown Court was the most appropriate forum for resolving the dispute. However, it noted that had the Court not been so bound, it would have quashed the decision of the SFO and remitted it for reconsideration. Green J examined in detail the SFO's position and expressed serious concerns (obiter) about the approach taken. On the question of waiver, he observed that by proffering summaries which contained material over which Sarclad asserted privilege (since Sarclad claimed privilege over the entire contents of the interviews), privilege had been waived and, prima facie, this opened the door to disclosure of the underlying interview notes. As to whether it could be argued that the waiver had only been on a limited basis, the only argument the Court could envisage was that privilege had been waived for the exclusive use of the SFO only. However, there was no evidence that the SFO ever addressed the question of waiver, and this argument was not raised by the SFO. Even if it had been raised, the Court would have had difficulties with it because, at the time the oral proffers were made, Sarclad knew or must have known that there was a real likelihood that the SFO's summaries would be provided by way of disclosure to the defendants in the event of a prosecution (which itself was a very real possibility) and that the proffers were of material over which Sarclad was asserting privilege. Even if the Court accepted that waiver was on a limited basis only, 'we do not see how that limited purpose would not have included transmission of the underlying documents to the Defendants since this was squarely in contemplation and was an integral part of the process being undertaken.' The lawyers' assertion at the start of the proffer sessions that the provision of the facts was not to be taken as a waiver was rejected without hesitation by the Court, noting that the test for waiver is not subjective.[17]

Disclosure to defendants in criminal proceedings and reference in open court

7.25 Another important issue with a limited waiver is the potential loss of privilege that can result in the event there is a prosecution against one or more third parties and the authority with whom the material has been shared is required to disclose it to the defendant(s) in compliance with its statutory disclosure obligations. The disclosure test will be met if the material might reasonably be considered capable of undermining the prosecution case or assisting the defence.

7.26 Once a document has been disclosed to the defence, even if it was provided to the investigating/prosecuting authority subject to a limited waiver of privilege, a defendant is entitled to make such use of it as they wish in the course of the criminal proceedings in which it has been disclosed, including reading it in open court and relying on it to advance their case. Alternatively, the prosecution may rely on it during the course of the trial if it supports the prosecution case. As discussed at paras 1.75–1.76, reading a privileged

---

[17] *R (AL) v Serious Fraud Office* (n 14) [116]–[118].

document in open court can have the effect of attracting sufficient publicity to its contents that it can no longer be regarded as confidential, with the result that privilege over the document is lost in its entirety. Confidentiality may also be lost if references to a document in open court engage the principle of open justice, which gives the public a right of access to the evidence placed before a court and referred to during a hearing.[18] As Passmore notes in his discussion of this issue, the problem for the privilege holder is that, in disclosing the documents to the authorities, they have effectively lost control over them.[19] It is up to the prosecutor to decide whether the documents meet the disclosure test (and/or whether to serve them as part of the prosecution's case), and the extent to which they are relied upon in open court is a matter entirely for the parties to those proceedings, not the privilege holder.

7.27 This issue is demonstrated by *PCP Capital Partners LLP v Barclays Bank Plc*.[20] In the course of the SFO's investigation into Barclays and several of its senior executives, Barclays agreed to provide privileged documents to the SFO under a limited waiver of privilege. The terms of the waiver were expressed in a letter from Barclays' solicitors to the SFO:

> You have agreed to accept these documents on the basis that they are being provided to the SFO for the sole purpose of your criminal investigation and pursuant to a limited waiver of privilege for this limited purpose. The SFO will of course be able to use the documents for the purpose of its investigation, prosecution and SFO related criminal proceedings and to disclose them to a third party in accordance with its statutory functions, including under the Criminal Justice Act 1987.

The SFO subsequently charged several defendants and made use of a number of the documents during the criminal proceedings, including referring to them in open court at trial and cross-examining one of the defendants about them. As a result, it was common ground between the parties in the subsequent civil proceedings that the documents referred to at trial in this way had ceased to be confidential and therefore had lost the privilege previously attaching to them.[21]

7.28 The case is also notable for the fact that Barclays' reliance on the documents in the civil proceedings with PCP was held to engage the collateral waiver principles (see paras 1.94–1.96). This was despite the fact that the documents had already ceased to be privileged in the course of the criminal proceedings and it had been the SFO, not Barclays, who had deployed them in those proceedings. Barclays was therefore not relying on privileged documents to advance its case. However, Waksman J said that:

> As to who deployed it, it is of course correct that the SFO deployed them but the privilege belonged to Barclays and as set out in its solicitors' letter ... Barclays gave a limited waiver in the full knowledge that some or all would see the light of day at trial. So it can hardly be said that Barclays had nothing to do with the deployment of the [privileged documents]. In

---

[18] See discussion in *Serdar Mohammed v Ministry of Defence* [2013] EWHC 4478 (QB) [18]–[20]; *SL Claimants v Tesco Plc* [2019] EWHC 3315 (Ch), [2019] All ER (D) 30 (Dec) [37].
[19] Colin Passmore, *Privilege* (4th edn, Sweet & Maxwell 2020) para 7-087.
[20] [2020] EWHC 1393 (Comm), [2020] Lloyd's Rep FC 460.
[21] ibid [11].

the circumstances of what happened, its original disclosure under the limited waiver was the starting point for what follows.[22]

As a result, it was held that privilege had been waived over all documents relating to the relevant 'transaction' through collateral waiver. As has been noted elsewhere,[23] this is a highly questionable application of the concept of collateral waiver.

7.29 *SL Claimants v Tesco PLC*[24] provides further support for the notion that privileged material provided under a limited waiver can cease to be confidential through disclosure to defendants in criminal proceedings and reference in open court. Among other matters, the High Court had to determine an application by the claimants for production of a privileged document held by Tesco. The document in question was a nine-page note of an interview between a senior in-house lawyer at Tesco and the company's external lawyers. Tesco had provided it to the SFO on the basis of a limited waiver of privilege and it was then disclosed by the SFO to the defendants in criminal proceedings that followed. In the course of pre-trial legal argument, counsel for two of the defendants referred the judge to the note, quoted a paragraph of it and invited the judge to read the first three pages to himself, which he did. Counsel then described or summarized, without quoting, what the note recorded Tesco's in-house lawyer as having said about certain matters, drawing the judge's attention to the first three pages and a particular paragraph. Counsel for Tesco was also in attendance at the hearing and referred to and read small extracts from the first three pages.

7.30 In subsequent civil proceedings against Tesco, the claimants argued that this had the effect of the document having lost confidentiality by being deployed in open court and, as a result, privilege could no longer be maintained in the civil proceedings. Rejecting this argument, Hildyard J held that there is a distinction between the information in a document and the document itself. Whether references are such as in fact to constitute such an exposure of the document to the public that confidentiality in it is lost is a matter of degree. In this case, the references did not, either in terms of their detail or extent, amount to a loss of confidentiality in the document itself. Furthermore, the principle of open justice did not require disclosure of the document to enable the public to understand the court's approach to the procedural decision before it. Confidentiality in the document had therefore not been lost and privilege was maintained.[25]

7.31 Despite Hildyard J's conclusion, for the purpose of this discussion it is notable that he had no conceptual difficulty with the principle that, notwithstanding the limited waiver pursuant to which the document had been provided to the SFO, which could not have been intended to allow use by third parties in civil litigation against Tesco, reference to a privileged document in open court could nevertheless result in a complete loss of confidentiality and privilege over the whole document if the extent of the reference was sufficient. In other words, it mattered not that Tesco had expressly sought to limit the use to which the document could be put when providing it to the SFO. The defendants in the criminal proceedings were free

---

[22] ibid [106].
[23] Tamara Oppenheimer KC, Rebecca Loveridge, and Samuel Rabinowitz, 'Privilege: The UK Perspective' in Judith Seddon and others (eds), *The Practitioner's Guide to Global Investigations* (7th edn, Law Business Research Ltd 2023) vol 1 s 18.8.1.
[24] [2019] EWHC 3315 (Ch), [2019] All ER (D) 30 (Dec).
[25] ibid [42].

to deploy the document as they wished, and, had more extensive reference been made to the content of the document in open court during the criminal proceedings, privilege may well have been lost, thereby allowing the claimants in the civil proceedings to have access to it. As Hildyard J noted: '[i]f in the course of the trial the [document] is deployed or referred to the matter will have to be re-assessed at that time'.[26]

Finally, it is worth noting one of the observations of Birss J in *Property Alliance Group Ltd v Royal Bank of Scotland Plc* (discussed at paras 7.09–7.10). Birss J had no difficulty with upholding a limited waiver despite the 'carve-outs' allowing regulators to potentially go as far as publishing the information in the documents, but he implied that were such a step to be taken, that could result in a complete loss of privilege: **7.32**

> The fact that the carve outs recognise the regulator's rights and obligations to take a step, which might go as far as even publishing the information in the document, makes no difference if that has not happened. *Until they do*, I fail to see why the confidentiality and privilege would not be preserved.[27]

Lawyers advising corporate clients who are considering a limited waiver may try to mitigate this risk by expressly excluding disclosure to third parties for any purpose when setting out the terms of the limited waiver. However, this is not a viable solution. In the unlikely event that an investigator agreed to such a restriction (as to which, see para 7.35), it would almost certainly not be upheld if tested before a court. If, for example, a defendant in a subsequent prosecution made an application to the court under the CPIA 1996, section 8 for disclosure of the material because the prosecution had refused to disclose it on the basis that the terms of the limited waiver prevented it from doing so, a judge would surely rule against the prosecution and deem the restriction intended by the limited waiver to be invalid. It would be open to the judge to disregard the express terms of the waiver since, as has been mentioned, the extent of any waiver is determined on an objective basis rather than purely by reference to the terms agreed between the parties. As statutory obligations of disclosure impose mandatory requirements on the prosecution and are fundamental to ensuring a fair trial, it is inconceivable that a judge would uphold the terms of a waiver which purportedly prevented a prosecutor from complying with them. As Passmore submits, even if the authority was to agree to such a limitation, the statutory disclosure obligations under the CPIA 1996 and the importance of ensuring a fair trial would surely trump the privilege of the privilege holder.[28] This would not be a case of the CPIA 1996 abrogating the privilege of the party that had agreed the limited waiver;[29] rather, it would be a matter of determining, objectively, the extent of the limited waiver at the point at which the material was provided by the privilege holder. It would be the voluntary provision of the material to the authority concerned that caused privilege to be waived as regards defendants in the subsequent prosecution, not the disclosure under the CPIA 1996. **7.33**

---

[26] ibid [43].
[27] [2015] EWHC 1557 (Ch), [2016] 1 WLR 361 [113] (emphasis added).
[28] Passmore (n 19) para 7-099.
[29] See discussion about abrogation of privilege at paras 1.09–1.10, and, in relation to the prosecution's own privilege, paras 8.23–8.27.

7.34 The Divisional Court's position on the question of waiver in *R (AL) v Serious Fraud Office* (see paras 7.21–7.24) indicates the likely approach a court would take if it was suggested that the terms of a waiver prohibited compliance with statutory disclosure obligations. As noted above, the Court was of the view that, even if it accepted that waiver to the SFO was only on a limited basis, it would have included disclosure of the interview notes to the defendants since this was 'squarely in contemplation' and 'an integral part of the process being undertaken'.[30]

7.35 These points are essentially academic as it is extremely unlikely that an investigator or prosecutor would agree to a limited waiver that purported to prevent compliance with statutory disclosure obligations, for the very reason that it would not be upheld if tested before a court. Indeed, the FCA acknowledges this point in its Enforcement Guide in the context of voluntary disclosure of internal investigation reports by regulated firms. Whilst noting that English law does allow for a limited waiver that would mean privilege could still be asserted against third parties:

> [T]he FCA cannot accept any condition or stipulation which would purport to restrict its ability to use the information in the exercise of the FCA's statutory functions. In this sense, the FCA cannot 'close its eyes' to information received or accept that information should, say, be used only for the purposes of supervision but not for enforcement.[31]

Onward disclosure to authorities in other jurisdictions

7.36 A further issue related to the above when considering voluntary disclosure of privileged material to the authorities is the possibility that the documents will be passed on to law enforcement in other jurisdictions.[32] This is particularly important to consider when advising multinational corporate clients who may be subject to criminal or regulatory investigations in more than one country. This potentially creates the same problem in the other jurisdictions as with voluntary disclosure in this jurisdiction, in that the overseas authorities may be required to disclose the material to defendants in criminal proceedings, thereby potentially resulting in the material entering the public domain and privilege being lost. This is particularly problematic considering the different scope of the law of privilege in different jurisdictions, such that privilege may be lost more easily in one country compared to the situation in this jurisdiction.

7.37 Unlike with disclosure to defendants by a prosecutor, it may be possible to expressly prohibit the UK authority from sharing the documents with other authorities, so long as this would not be in conflict with any statutory or other legal obligation. Whether an investigator or prosecutor would agree to such a restriction is a different matter, however, as it may be a matter of policy that there should be close collaboration between the two agencies. If the terms of the waiver are silent on this point, it may be possible in certain circumstances to argue that such a restriction is included implicitly. Although it concerned two agencies within the same jurisdiction, it is of note that the Hong Kong Court of Appeal in *Citic Pacific Ltd* (discussed at paras 7.12–7.13) interpreted the waiver in that case as not extending

---

[30] *AL* (n 14) [117].
[31] FCA Handbook, Enforcement Guide, 3.29.
[32] For example, the SFO may share information with authorities in other jurisdictions under the Criminal Justice Act 1987, s 3(5).

to allow the SFC to share documents with the police. This was based on the fact that, at the time the material was shared with the SFC, Citic understood the investigation to be focused on regulatory and not criminal issues, and it would have taken a very different approach if faced with a criminal investigation. Absent any legal obligation to share material with other agencies, it is possible that an English court would take the same approach if the circumstances were such that the disclosing party had no reasonable expectation that the material would be shared with authorities in other jurisdictions or that other authorities were potentially investigating them.

Advising Clients on Limited Waivers

7.38 To summarize the issues discussed above, privilege can be waived on a limited basis when providing material to investigators and prosecutors. So long as the material does not enter the public domain as a result of being disclosed to defendants in a prosecution and referred to in open court to such an extent that confidentiality is lost, privilege in all other respects will be maintained. There are, however, clear and significant risks associated with a limited waiver in these circumstances, and whether privilege is ultimately lost will be dependent upon the actions of parties other than the privilege holder.

7.39 It is important, therefore, when advising a client on the possibility of a limited waiver, to ensure they are fully aware of the risks associated with it, namely:

- A limited waiver cannot prevent compliance with statutory obligations of disclosure by a prosecutor.
- Privileged material disclosed on the basis of a limited waiver may, therefore, be disclosed to defendants in the event of a prosecution.
- Once the material has been disclosed, a defendant will be entitled to rely upon and deploy it during the course of the proceedings and this may include reading it in open court.
- If the material is read in open court, this is very likely to result in confidentiality, and therefore privilege, being lost in its entirety. The client will lose the right to assert privilege over that material in all other proceedings.

7.40 That there is a clear duty to advise a client on the consequences for privilege more generally when engaging with the SFO (or indeed any other authority) was confirmed in *Eurasian Natural Resources Corp Ltd v Dechert LLP*.[33] Waksman J expressed it in the following terms:

> There can be no doubt that a solicitor, when dealing with the SFO on behalf of a client which involves the voluntary submission of information and perhaps documents has a duty, as part of the Core Duty, to advise as to how privilege may be lost or how it may be protected. It is a fundamental point which arises where there is engagement with an authority like the SFO.[34]

---

[33] [2022] EWHC 1138 (Comm).
[34] ibid [1354].

7.41 In that case, ENRC's solicitor, Neil Gerrard of Dechert, was found to have breached that duty by failing to give ENRC proper advice about the possibility of protecting privilege in connection with the company's engagement with the SFO at an early stage and having not considered possible approaches to the SFO and some form of agreement going forward. The only step he had taken was that, when writing to the SFO asking for confirmation that ENRC was still considered to be part of the corporate self-reporting process prior to submitting a draft internal investigation report, he stated that any report provided to the SFO would be 'submitted under a limited waiver of legal professional privilege for the purposes of the corporate self-report only'. The letter also asked the SFO to confirm that, should an equitable settlement not be reached between the SFO and ENRC, the report would not be used by the SFO as evidence of any wrongdoing or in any criminal proceedings against ENRC, a subsidiary of ENRC or any employee or director of ENRC or its subsidiaries.

7.42 Waksman J did not consider Gerrard's claim that the client was fully aware that privilege was always likely to be lost as an adequate answer to the issue, especially as his own view was not quite so categorical, as demonstrated by the fact that he had sought agreement from the SFO on the question of privilege in the above-mentioned letter. In the end, the SFO took a much stronger line against ENRC in relation to privilege, refusing to give any assurances as to whether it would accept that reports were covered by privilege or what use the SFO would make of any report disclosed to it, but Waksman J did not think that it could be said that such a stance was inevitable so that there was no point in trying. Moreover:

> Mr Gerrard should have advised as to, and at least considered, making a more general approach to the SFO at the outset on the status of the privileged information which might be communicated. Or at least he should have considered this in the course of the extant discussions with the SFO. The need for this was heightened by the fact that this was not a 'usual' [self-reporting] process where an initial report was given showing criminality, and there then followed a further investigation which might—or might not—be able to be safeguarded on questions of privilege.[35]

Waksman J believed that, 'had it been possible to agree some early and clear protection on privilege to cover all the communications with the SFO', that might have at least reduced the scope for the arguments around privilege which later arose between ENRC and the SFO and which were litigated, ultimately resulting in the Court of Appeal's ruling in *SFO v ENRC Ltd*.[36] As such, the notion of early engagement on the question of privilege was 'not necessarily pointless' or of no benefit. Furthermore, Waksman J thought Dechert's argument that any attempt to engage with the SFO on privilege could be taken by the SFO as ENRC not cooperating was 'hopeless'.[37]

---

[35] ibid [1364].
[36] [2018] EWCA Civ 2006, [2019] 1 WLR 791.
[37] [2022] EWHC 1138 (Comm) [1359]–[1367].

3 Deferred Prosecution Agreements and Cooperation with the SFO

Introduction

Limited waivers to the SFO warrant special attention as it is in this area that limited waivers in criminal cases have had the most prominence in recent years. This is because of the emergence of DPAs (deferred prosecution agreements), brought into force by the Crime and Courts Act 2013, section 45 and schedule 17. A DPA is an agreement between a designated prosecutor (the Director of the SFO or the DPP) and an organization to the effect that prosecution will be suspended if the organization agrees to comply with certain conditions, usually including, inter alia, payment of a substantial fine, disgorgement of any profits made from the alleged offence(s), changes to the organization's compliance programme and cooperation in any investigation relating to the offence(s). If, after a specified period of time, the conditions have been complied with, proceedings are discontinued and the organization is not prosecuted. **7.43**

At the time of writing, the SFO has entered into twelve DPAs, making this more than a merely hypothetical outcome for lawyers advising corporate clients. The avoidance of prosecution and/or the prospect of a reduced sanction means that there is a significant incentive for companies to self-report potential criminality to the SFO and to cooperate fully with any subsequent investigation and prosecution. Cooperation is listed as one of the public interest factors tending against prosecution in the DPA Code of Practice.[38] An important aspect of cooperation is the provision of relevant material, which may include privileged items. **7.44**

Waiving Privilege: What Does the SFO Expect?

The SFO's Corporate Cooperation Guidance[39] provides more detail about what the SFO considers may constitute true cooperation by a company. Much of the focus is on the provision of relevant material to the SFO, including witness accounts and other material gathered during an internal investigation. The guidance specifically addresses privileged material in a section headed 'Witness Accounts and Waiving Privilege'. This includes the following points: **7.45**

- 'Organisations seeking credit for co-operation by providing witness accounts should additionally provide any recording, notes and/or transcripts of the interview and identify a witness competent to speak to the contents of each interview.'
- 'When an organisation elects not to waive privilege, the SFO nonetheless has obligations to prospective individual defendants with respect to disclosable materials.'

---

[38] SFO & CPS, 'Deferred Prosecution Agreements Code of Practice' (DPA Code of Practice) para 2.8.2(i) https://www.sfo.gov.uk/download/deferred-prosecution-agreements-code-practice/?ind=1564739655028&filename=1564739654wpdm_DPA%20final%20CoP.pdf&wpdmdl=1447&refresh=62d2c6d9abc061657980633 (accessed 10 June 2023).

[39] SFO, 'Corporate Co-operation Guidance' (August 2019) https://www.sfo.gov.uk/publications/guidance-policy-and-protocols/guidance-for-corporates/corporate-co-operation-guidance/ (accessed 10 June 2023).

- 'The existence of a valid privilege claim must be properly established.'
- 'During the investigation, if the organisation claims privilege, it will be expected to provide certification by independent counsel that the material in question is privileged.'
- 'If privilege is not waived and a trial proceeds, where appropriate, the SFO will apply for a witness summons under section 2 Criminal Procedure (Attendance of Witnesses) Act 1965.'[40]
- 'An organisation that does not waive privilege and provide witness accounts does not attain the corresponding factor against prosecution that is found in the DPA Code … but will not be penalised by the SFO.' This is expanded upon in a footnote: 'The Court of Appeal has not ruled out a court's consideration of the effect of an organisation's non-waiver over witness accounts as it determines whether a proposed DPA is in the interests of justice: *SFO v ENRC Ltd* [2018] EWCA Civ 2006 at [117].'

7.46 Another indicator of cooperation as far as privilege is concerned is if an organization 'Promptly provide[s] a schedule of documents withheld on the basis of privilege, including the basis for asserting privilege'. This is supplemented by a note that states, 'If an organization decides to assert legal privilege over relevant material (such as first accounts, internal investigation interviews or other documents), the SFO may challenge that assertion where it considers it necessary or appropriate to do so'.

7.47 Whilst the DPA Code of Practice does not make explicit reference to waiving privilege, it says the following about internal investigation material and witness accounts:

> Co-operation will include identifying relevant witnesses, disclosing their accounts and the documents shown to them. Where practicable it will involve making the witnesses available for interview when requested. It will further include providing a report in respect of any internal investigation including source documents.[41]

The Code of Practice also states that:

> It must be remembered that when [an organization] self-reports it will have been incriminated by the actions of individuals. It will ordinarily be appropriate that those individuals be investigated and where appropriate prosecuted. [The organization] must ensure in its provision of material as part of the self-report that it does not withhold material that would jeopardise an effective investigation and where appropriate prosecution of those individuals. To do so would be a strong factor in favour of prosecution.[42]

7.48 Further indication of the SFO's expectations concerning waiver of privilege can be found in various public speeches made by senior SFO officials. For example, in a March 2016 speech by the then General Counsel of the SFO, it was emphasized that the SFO's interest essentially lies in factual internal investigation material, not legal advice:

> Let me be clear. We have no interest in communications between client and lawyer on questions of liability or rights. We are focused on the underlying facts, including the accounts of witnesses spoken to in corporate investigations. We do not regard ourselves as constrained from asking for them even if they are privileged and, as with our colleagues

---

[40] See discussion about this provision at para 3.11.
[41] DPA Code of Practice, para 2.8.2(i).
[42] ibid para 2.9.1.

in US DoJ who do operate under that constraint, our experience is that at least some corporates are not themselves constrained from letting us know what their investigators were told. As the saying goes, there are more solutions than problems.[43]

These comments were echoed in a later speech by the then Head of Fraud at the SFO in November 2018:

We do not, and never have, required the waiver of privilege, but if you want to waive privilege that will be viewed as a positive feature. We are very disinterested in privileged material that is the proper legal advice you are receiving from your solicitors. We have obviously more interest in internal investigation material and specifically interviews with witnesses, but that issue has now been clarified by the Court of Appeal. But even in light of that, do not expect engagement with us to be a civil negotiation about what a corporate can and cannot produce. We have powers to compel the production of documents and we'll use them if we need to. We are going to ask a lot of companies who self-report to us.[44]

7.49 In an April 2019 speech, the then Director of the SFO made the following observations about corporate cooperation:

[I]n carrying out their own investigation, we need to see the ultimate objective of co-operating with law enforcement by preserving vital evidence such as first-hand accounts and witness testimony. This is different from when a company calls in a team of lawyers and then throws the blanket of Legal Professional Privilege over all the material they have gathered—especially material that we in law enforcement need to assess individual culpability, which is the very same material that individuals may need to defend themselves. That is not co-operation: courts do not like it, it does not help law enforcement, it does not make the job of dispensing justice fairly any easier.

…

[W]aiving privilege over that initial investigative material will be a strong indicator of co-operation and an important factor that I will take into account when considering whether to invite a company to enter into DPA negotiations; it also highlights whether a DPA is in the public interest in that case.[45]

It should be noted that these comments were made prior to publication of the revised Corporate Cooperation Guidance in August 2019, but the sentiments expressed in these speeches are very much reflected in the guidance.

7.50 There has also been some judicial commentary on this issue, which, considering DPAs must be approved by the court, should be borne in mind. In *SFO v ENRC Ltd*, when commenting on waiver of privilege in the context of negotiating a DPA, Sir Brian Leveson P said:

---

[43] Alun Milford, SFO General Counsel, 'Speech to Compliance Professionals' European Compliance and Ethics Institute, Prague (29 March 2016) https://www.sfo.gov.uk/2016/03/29/speech-compliance-professionals/ (accessed 10 June 2023).

[44] Hannah von Dadelszen, SFO Head of Fraud, 'Engage Now or Hide Behind Smoke and Mirrors at Your Peril' Pinsent Masons Business Crime and Compliance Conference (9 November 2018) https://www.sfo.gov.uk/2018/11/09/engage-now-or-hide-behind-smoke-and-mirrors--your-peril/ (accessed 10 June 2023).

[45] Lisa Osofsky, SFO Director, 'Fighting Fraud and Corruption in a Shrinking World' Speech at the Royal United Services Institute in London (3 April 2019) https://www.sfo.gov.uk/2019/04/03/fighting-fraud-and-corruption-in-a-shrinking-world/ (accessed 10 June 2023).

[T]o determine whether a DPA is in the interests of justice, and whether the terms of the particular DPA are fair, reasonable and proportionate, the court must examine the company's conduct and the extent to which it co-operated with the SFO. Such an examination will consider whether the company was willing to waive any privilege attaching to documents produced during internal investigations, so that it could share those documents with the SFO.[46]

As far as the case before him was concerned, Sir Brian Leveson P thought that: 'Had the court been asked to approve a DPA between ENRC and the SFO, the company's failure to make good on its promises to be full and frank would undoubtedly have counted against it.' This was a reference to the fact that, despite giving repeated indications to the SFO that it intended to make full and frank disclosure of relevant information and material, ENRC never actually did so, and then 'retreated to the position that everything was covered by legal professional privilege'.[47]

7.51 Reflecting on these comments in 2019, the then Director of the SFO warned corporates and their advisers that 'The President of the Queen's Bench has spoken. Especially in a jurisdiction where the judge plays such a critical role in determining whether to accept a DPA, it behoves us all to listen—and to take heed.'[48]

7.52 In *R (AL) v Serious Fraud Office*, Green J considered there to be 'evidence that the SFO does treat waiver (in so far as it exists) as relevant to the duty of disclosure under a DPA'.[49] Counsel for one of the interested parties drew the Court's attention to various public statements made by senior officials within the SFO which 'highlighted the crucial importance of the SFO obtaining first interview accounts and to concerns within the SFO that spurious claims for privilege were made by lawyers acting for companies being investigated'.[50] These included the 2016 speech by the then General Counsel of the SFO mentioned above in which he also made the following points:

1. We will view as unco-operative false or exaggerated claims of privilege, and we are prepared to litigate over them: to do otherwise would be to fail in our duty to investigate crime.
2. If a company's assertion of privilege is well-made out, then we will not hold that against the company: to do otherwise would be inconsistent with the substantive protection privilege offers. We will simply judge the question of cooperation in our normal way against our published criteria.
3. By the same token if, notwithstanding the existence of a well-made-out claim to privilege, a company gives up the witness accounts we seek, then we will view that as a significant mark of cooperation: here again, to do otherwise would be inconsistent with the substantive protection privilege offers.

---

[46] *SFO v ENRC Ltd* (n 36) [117].
[47] ibid [137].
[48] Osofsky (n 45).
[49] *AL* (n 14) [120].
[50] ibid [121].

4. For the same reason, we will view as a significant mark of cooperation a company's decision to structure its investigation in such a way as not to attract privilege claims over interviews of witnesses.[51]

7.53 As to the form in which internal investigation witness accounts are provided to the SFO, it seemed for a while that summaries, even oral summaries, might be acceptable to the SFO. We have seen already that oral 'proffers' were provided by Sarclad Ltd,[52] and it is understood that the SFO also accepted summary witness accounts from Rolls-Royce and Standard Bank in its respective investigations into those companies.[53] In the Standard Bank investigation, it was reported that the summary of the account of at least one witness was provided to the SFO orally.[54] All three investigations concluded with DPAs.

7.54 It now seems unlikely, however, that the SFO will agree to receive summaries only, whether written or oral, rather than transcripts, recordings or notes of interviews (where such items exist). This is partly in light of the heavy criticism levelled against the SFO in *R (AL) v Serious Fraud Office*,[55] where Sarclad's questionable claims to privilege and refusal to provide interview notes were barely challenged by the SFO. We have noted already the swift (and correct) conclusion reached by the Court on the question of waiver of privilege over the underlying notes (see paras 7.21–7.24). As to the SFO's conclusion that there was nothing in the full interview notes which was not adequately encapsulated in the oral proffer summaries, the Court had 'real difficulties' in understanding what sort of testing could have been undertaken which would have come up with any sort of a reliable answer on this point, considering the SFO did not have sight of the notes. The Court was also concerned by the reliance the SFO placed on Sarclad's privilege argument being 'not obviously wrong'. Such 'cursory tests of obviousness' could not form the basis of regulatory decision-making. Furthermore, the law as it stood then was settled and clear: notes of interviews with witnesses in these circumstances were not covered by privilege.[56] Green J concluded the judgment with the following comments:

> In summary: (i) in the decision letter of 13th October 2013 the SFO simply accepted the assertion of privilege made by ABC LLP even though it is the SFO's own case that privilege does not apply and the SFO's position is supported by current case law; (ii) the SFO never addressed itself to the issue of waiver of privilege (either as a matter of law or as part of the company's duty to co-operate) arising as a result of the oral proffers; (iii) The SFO adopted a test of 'not obviously invalid' and in so doing it erred since its duty is to assess claims for privilege properly and not cursorily and superficially; (iv) but in any event the SFO has not (even now) provided any sort of reasoning for its conclusion that the points advanced by

---

[51] Milford (n 43).
[52] See discussion of *AL* (n 14) at paras 7.21–7.24.
[53] Confirmed in a speech by Alun Milford, SFO General Counsel, *GIR Live* (London, 27 April 2017), reported by Michael Griffiths, 'Milford: Cooperation Means More than "Going through the Motions"' *Global Investigations Review* (27 April 2017) https://globalinvestigationsreview.com/article/milford-co-operation-means-more-going-through-the-motions (accessed 10 June 2023).
[54] Rahul Rose, 'Standard Bank DPA: Interview Transcripts Not Required' *Global Investigations Review* (26 April 2016) https://globalinvestigationsreview.com/article/standard-bank-dpa-interview-transcripts-not-required (accessed 10 June 2023).
[55] *AL* (n 14).
[56] ibid [96]–[112].

ABC LLP in its letter of 19th September 2017 were 'not obviously wrong'; and (v) if and in so far as the SFO adopted an approach whereby it declined to reassess its disclosure obligations in the light of 'developments' in the law because of 'finality' reasons, then it erred since that is tantamount to an argument that the SFO can ignore the law and its duty to keep its disclosure obligation under review.[57]

7.55 Not only will the SFO be keen to avoid another humiliating decision such as this in future cases, but the current Corporate Cooperation Guidance is clear in stating that 'Organisations seeking credit for co-operation by providing witness accounts should additionally provide any recording, notes and/or transcripts of the interview'. This would appear to leave no room for summaries only if more comprehensive documents exist.

Waiving Privilege: What Does this Mean for Companies?

7.56 Whilst the SFO cannot demand or require that privilege be waived, there can be no doubt from the above that companies who become aware of suspected fraud, bribery or corruption, and who may themselves attract corporate criminal liability for those offences, will feel significant pressure to waive privilege in the hope of avoiding prosecution and/or attracting a less severe sanction. The same pressure might be felt even where the company is a victim and does not think it will attract corporate criminal liability, for example if the company is the victim of the fraud that has been uncovered. The pressure to waive privilege is likely to concern material generated as part of any internal investigation, particularly witness accounts/interviews, but there may also be privileged material from before the wrongdoing was discovered that is highly relevant to the SFO's investigation.

7.57 It is unclear how much cooperation credit, if any, a company will lose if it does not waive privilege over witness accounts and interview notes and transcripts. There are many other ways a company can be cooperative, and the SFO claims that companies 'will not be penalised' if they do not waive privilege. However, it is not clear exactly what this means in practice. Whilst it is still possible for a DPA to be offered in the absence of a waiver (see para 7.74), it is less likely than if witness accounts and similar material are provided voluntarily. The Law Society has expressed concern on this issue, emphasising that any form of pressure to waive privilege is improper and undermines the absolute nature of the protection. It considers that in the context of criminal and regulatory investigations, pressure to waive privilege could take the form of suggesting that if the privilege holder does not waive privilege, they will not be regarded as cooperative. Whilst the Law Society acknowledges that it is for a regulator to decide whether any waiver of privilege should in some way be credited, 'no client should be criticised, let alone treated detrimentally, for asserting their LPP rights, however helpful a waiver might be to the regulator or investigator'.[58] The SFO, however, takes the view that a DPA is a pragmatic device and that in exchange for helping the SFO significantly by providing material that it would otherwise not be able to obtain,

---

[57] ibid [124].
[58] The Law Society, 'Legal Professional Privilege' Practice Note (12 August 2021) pts 11.3–11.4 https://www.lawsociety.org.uk/topics/client-care/legal-professional-privilege#sub-menu-dy21 (accessed 9 June 2023).

prosecution can be avoided. A company will not be able to avoid prosecution if it does not help the SFO significantly, even if the company's conduct in the investigation has been entirely proper.

If a company decides not to waive privilege over witness accounts or other internal investigation material, the basis for asserting privilege may be challenged. At the very least, the SFO will expect to see certification by independent counsel that the material in question is privileged (as per the Corporate Cooperation Guidance). The SFO is unambiguous in emphasising the importance of witness accounts to its investigations. The fact that, as a matter of law, it can often be difficult to establish a compelling claim to privilege over internal investigation witness interviews (as discussed in Chapter 12) means that there is greater scope for challenge by the SFO. Furthermore, the SFO will no doubt be keen to avoid the sort of criticism levelled against it for its failure to challenge the dubious claim to privilege in *R (AL) v Serious Fraud Office* (see para 7.54). 7.58

Lawyers advising corporate clients wishing to avoid prosecution must therefore ensure that their clients are aware of the more favourable treatment they are likely to receive if they waive privilege and that a decision not to waive privilege over relevant material is likely to be challenged and will require certification by independent counsel. Where it is proposed that privilege will be waived, lawyers must ensure that their clients understand the potential risks resulting from a limited waiver (as discussed at paras 7.16–7.37). 7.59

It should be noted that the question of waiver of privilege will not necessarily arise in every case. There may have been no internal investigation carried out or at least no witness interviews conducted, or the corporate and its legal advisers may not consider there to be an arguable claim to privilege in any event. 7.60

Waiving Privilege: What Happens in Practice?

The best indicator of the extent to which companies feel under pressure to waive privilege comes from the details of the DPAs that have been agreed since their introduction. Of the 12 DPAs that have so far been entered into, we know that at least eight involved an intentional waiver of privilege. 7.61

The SFO's investigation into offences of conspiracy to corrupt, false accounting and failure to prevent bribery allegedly committed by Rolls-Royce Plc concluded with a DPA that was approved by Sir Brian Leveson P in January 2017.[59] Pursuant to its cooperation with the SFO, Rolls-Royce disclosed 'all interview memoranda' in respect of its internal investigation on a limited waiver basis, 'despite Rolls-Royce's belief that the material was capable of resisting an order for disclosure, on the basis that it was privileged'.[60] Privilege was not waived over everything, but the SFO was allowed access to 'complete digital repositories or email containers where available of in excess of 100 key employees or former employees, without filtering the material for potential privilege, but, instead, permitting issues of privilege to be 7.62

---

[59] *Serious Fraud Office v Rolls-Royce Plc* [2017] Lloyd's Rep FC 249 (Southwark CC, 17 January 2017).
[60] ibid [20].

resolved by independent counsel'.[61] Rolls-Royce also agreed to the use of artificial intelligence to carry out some of the privilege review.[62] In approving the DPA, Sir Brian Leveson P commended Rolls-Royce for demonstrating 'extraordinary co-operation', which included 'voluntary disclosure of internal investigations, with limited waiver of privilege over internal investigation memoranda and certain defence aerospace and civil aerospace material', 'providing un-reviewed digital material to the SFO and cooperating with independent counsel in the resolution of privilege claims' and 'agreeing to the use of digital methods to identify privilege issues'.[63] Taking into account Rolls-Royce's extraordinary cooperation, the financial penalty was reduced by 50 per cent.

7.63 2017 also saw the conclusion of a DPA with Tesco Stores Limited in respect of false accounting offences.[64] Tesco agreed a limited waiver of privilege over 'relevant material which pre-dated the profit statement' that was at the centre of the case. Tesco also provided 'mailbox accounts of its employees and former employees, without first filtering their contents for any privileged items which fell outside the limited waiver, agreeing that any issues of privilege that might arise as a result could be resolved by independent counsel'.[65] The company avoided any issue with privilege over witness accounts by not conducting any interviews of its own with witnesses or potential witnesses in the criminal investigation. In approving the DPA, Sir Brian Leveson P noted that Tesco had provided 'the very fullest co-operation' with the SFO's investigation,[66] and a total discount of 50 per cent was applied to the penalty.

7.64 In July 2019, a DPA between the SFO and Serco Geografix Ltd was approved by Davis J.[67] This related to offences of fraud and false accounting connected with Serco's contract with the Ministry of Justice to provide electronic monitoring services. Serco 'cooperated fully and substantially with the SFO's investigation', which included a limited waiver of privilege over certain forensic accounting and first account material. In a similar vein to Rolls-Royce and Tesco, the company also provided 'access to mailbox accounts of its employees and former employees and other data without first filtering their contents for privileged items other than by reference to narrowly defined search terms', and agreed 'that any issues of privilege that might arise as a result could be resolved by independent counsel'.[68] Serco's financial penalty was reduced by 50 per cent.

7.65 January 2020 saw the approval of a DPA between the SFO and Airbus SE in connection with offences of failure to prevent bribery.[69] Airbus agreed to disclose material including internal

---

[61] ibid [19].
[62] Ben Morgan, Joint Head of Bribery and Corruption at the SFO, 'The Future of Deferred Prosecution Agreements after Rolls-Royce' Speech at a seminar at Norton Rose Fulbright LLP (7 March 2017) https://www.sfo.gov.uk/2017/03/08/the-future-of-deferred-prosecution-agreements-after-rolls-royce/ (accessed 10 June 2023). See also the discussion about the use of artificial intelligence in privilege reviews more generally at paras 4.36–4.40.
[63] *Serious Fraud Office v Rolls-Royce Plc* (n 59) [121].
[64] *Serious Fraud Office v Tesco Stores Ltd* [2019] Lloyd's Rep FC 283 (Southwark CC, 10 April 2017).
[65] ibid [38].
[66] ibid [37].
[67] *Serious Fraud Office v Serco Geografix Limited* [2020] Crim LR 66 (Southwark CC, 4 July 2019).
[68] *Serious Fraud Office v Serco Geografix Limited* Statement of Facts (20 June 2019) [11] https://www.sfo.gov.uk/download/deferred-prosecution-agreement-serco-geografix-ltd-sfo/?ind=1619599318440&filename=Serco%20DPA%20SOF%20for%20publication.pdf&wpdmdl=23813&refresh=6484be91cea161686421137 (accessed 10 June 2023).
[69] *Director of the Serious Fraud Office v Airbus SE* [2021] Lloyd's Rep FC 159 (Southwark CC, 31 January 2020).

investigation interview transcripts and memoranda under a limited waiver of privilege for the purposes of the joint investigation conducted by the SFO and the French Parquet National Financier. Airbus also provided a schedule of contemporaneous documents withheld on the basis of privilege, including the reasons for asserting privilege, which were verified by the SFO.[70] In the judgment approving the DPA, Airbus was noted to have 'adopted a co-operative position in respect of privilege', and Dame Victoria Sharp P considered Airbus' overall cooperation to have been 'exemplary'.[71] It too received a 50 per cent discount to the financial penalty imposed.

7.66 In July 2020, the SFO's DPA with G4S Care & Justice Services (UK) Ltd was approved.[72] This concerned three offences of fraud against the Ministry of Justice in connection with G4S' provision of electronic monitoring services. G4S' cooperation with the SFO included providing 'access to all interviews conducted by its solicitors and accountants' on a limited waiver of privilege.[73] Davis J applied a 40 per cent reduction to the penalty imposed against the company, reflecting the fact that there were aspects of the company's cooperation which were less than full at the outset and full cooperation with the SFO investigation came relatively late in the day.[74]

7.67 2020 also saw the approval of the SFO's DPA with Airline Services Limited (ASL) for offences of failure to prevent bribery.[75] ASL agreed a limited waiver of privilege over its own investigations into two relevant issues. This was cited by counsel for the SFO as an example of the 'very high degree of co-operation' by ASL.[76] As with most of the other DPAs, the overall penalty imposed against the company was reduced by 50 per cent.

7.68 In July 2021, a DPA was agreed between the SFO and Amec Foster Wheeler Energy Limited, relating to ten offences of corruption.[77] The company 'co-operated extensively' with the SFO's investigation, including 'Agreeing to a limited waiver of legal professional privilege for the purposes of the SFO investigation over advice received by the Foster Wheeler Group during the period of the alleged offending with respect to FWEL's dealings with agents, and public and quasi-public officials in the oil and gas sector'.[78] A 50 per cent reduction to reflect the company's cooperation was applied when calculating the financial penalty.

---

[70] *R v Airbus SE* Statement of Facts (undated) [42] https://www.sfo.gov.uk/download/airbus-se-deferred-prosecution-agreement-statement-of-facts/?ind=1583153569888&filename=R%20v%20Airbus%20-%20Statement%20of%20Facts%20amended.pdf&wpdmdl=25653&refresh=6484bf6994f7f1686421353 (accessed 10 June 2023); *Director of the Serious Fraud Office v Airbus SE* (n 69) [74].

[71] *Director of the Serious Fraud Office v Airbus SE* (n 69) [74], [87].

[72] *Serious Fraud Office v G4S Care and Justice Services (UK) Ltd* [2021] Crim LR 138 (Southwark CC, 17 July 2020).

[73] ibid [23].

[74] ibid [40].

[75] *Director of the Serious Fraud Office v Airline Services Ltd* [2021] Lloyd's Rep FC 42 (Southwark CC, 30 October 2020).

[76] ibid [72].

[77] *Serious Fraud Office v Amec Foster Wheeler Energy Ltd* [2021] Lloyd's Rep FC 353 (Southwark CC, 1 July 2021).

[78] *Serious Fraud Office v Amec Foster Wheeler Energy Limited* Statement of Facts (undated) [16] https://www.sfo.gov.uk/wp-content/uploads/2022/02/Statement-of-Facts-AFWEL.pdf (accessed 10 June 2023).

7.69 Two other DPAs were also approved in July 2021, both with subsidiaries of the real estate company Jones Lang LaSalle: Bluu Solutions Limited (BSL) and Tetris Projects Limited (TPL).[79] The companies provided a limited waiver of privilege over 'a significant amount of material, including pre-acquisition due diligence reports, lawyer's notes on the interviews of witnesses during the internal investigation, some internal correspondence and external legal advice', and they engaged 'constructively and pragmatically' with independent counsel instructed by the SFO to identify privileged documents.[80] The judgment suggests that the notes of the witness interviews were summaries rather than full transcripts,[81] but it seems that whatever form they were provided in was the most comprehensive available as the SFO was 'satisfied that all relevant material [had] been disclosed to it'.[82] In recognition of the significant cooperation provided, a reduction of 50 per cent was applied to the financial penalty.

7.70 As for the other DPAs, the judgments and case documents do not expressly confirm whether there was a waiver of privilege. The very first DPA, which was agreed with Standard Bank Plc in 2015 in relation to failure to prevent bribery,[83] may have involved a waiver. The full judgment confirming the DPA notes that, 'Of particular significance was the promptness of the self-report, the fully disclosed internal investigation and co-operation of Standard Bank'.[84] The preliminary judgment also notes that 'a summary of first accounts of interviewees' was provided by Standard Bank, which was an example of how it had 'fully co-operated with the SFO from the earliest possible date'.[85] If privilege had been claimed over any of the internal investigation material, one would expect to see explicit reference to this in the judgment, considering the significance attached to waiving privilege. Perhaps, therefore, privilege was not claimed over the material and therefore the question of waiver did not arise.

7.71 The financial penalty imposed against Standard Bank was reduced by only one-third, but this seems to have been because Sir Brian Leveson P based the reduction purely on the equivalent that would have been applied for an early guilty plea in the event of a conviction for the same offence.[86] The practice of applying the maximum discount of 50 per cent did not emerge until the second DPA (Sarclad Ltd).

7.72 The DPA with Sarclad Ltd in 2016[87] did not involve an intentional waiver of privilege, but we have seen from the discussion about *R (AL) v Serious Fraud Office* at paras 7.21–7.24 that the oral 'proffer' sessions did in fact result in privilege being waived over the underlying notes of the internal investigation interviews. The preliminary judgment noted that 'Sarclad provided oral summaries of first accounts of interviewees, facilitated the interview of current employees, and provided timely and complete responses to requests for information and material, save for those subject to a proper claim of legal professional privilege.' Despite

---

[79] *Director of the Serious Fraud Office v AB Limited and CD Limited* (Southwark CC, 19 July 2021).
[80] ibid [74(12)–(13)].
[81] ibid [74(4)], [83(6)].
[82] ibid [83(6)].
[83] *Serious Fraud Office v Standard Bank PLC* [2016] Lloyd's Rep FC 102 (Southwark CC, 30 November 2015).
[84] ibid [14].
[85] ibid [30].
[86] ibid [57].
[87] *Serious Fraud Office v Sarclad Limited* (Southwark CC, 8 July 2016).

the decision not to (intentionally) waive privilege, Sir Brian Leveson P thought that Sarclad had nevertheless shown 'full and genuine co-operation' which militated very much in favour of finding that a DPA was likely to be in the interests of justice.[88] The full 50 per cent discount was applied to the financial penalty and the company appears not to have been treated any less favourably than if it had agreed to waive privilege.[89]

7.73 Finally, the SFO's DPA with Güralp Systems Ltd (GSL) in 2019[90] seems not to have involved any waiver of privilege. Although the DPA documents do not mention privilege, one of the terms of the DPA indicates that it was not waived, at least as far as the internal investigation was concerned. The company's continued cooperation with the SFO was to 'include the retention, until such investigations and prosecutions are concluded, of all material gathered as part of GSL's internal investigation leading to this Agreement'.[91] The fact that this refers to *retention* as opposed to *disclosure* would suggest privilege was not waived. Unusually in this case, GSL was not ordered to pay any financial penalty as the SFO was satisfied that it could not sensibly meet any penalty over and above the disgorgement of profits sum.

7.74 Drawing together the details of these 12 cases, it is not possible to say whether those that did involve a waiver of privilege would still have resulted in a DPA if privilege had not been waived. It is, however, of some significance that the vast majority did involve a waiver, and the more DPAs that are entered into following a waiver of privilege, the greater the pressure will be on companies under investigation voluntarily to provide privileged material to the SFO, and the more the SFO will expect to see a waiver when considering whether to enter into a DPA. That being said, there is some comfort to be taken from the fact that the DPAs with Sarclad and GSL appear not to have involved any waiver of privilege but the companies seemingly were not treated any less favourably as a result.

7.75 Finally, it is worth considering an SFO investigation that did not result in a DPA. During the course of the SFO's investigation into Glencore Energy UK Ltd, the company agreed a limited waiver of privilege with the SFO in respect of certain internal investigation interviews.[92] Despite cooperating fully with the investigation, the company was unable to avoid prosecution and was charged with two counts of bribery and five counts of failure to prevent bribery. The company pleaded guilty at the first available opportunity and received a substantial fine and orders for costs and confiscation. The case demonstrates that a waiver of privilege, although strongly encouraged by the SFO, does not guarantee that a prosecution will be avoided.

---

[88] ibid [39].
[89] Ultimately, the financial penalty was set at a figure far below that which was arrived at after applying the 50% discount, as the company could not realistically afford to pay that amount.
[90] *Serious Fraud Office v Guralp Systems Ltd* [2020] Lloyd's Rep FC 90 (Southwark CC, 22 October 2019).
[91] *Serious Fraud Office v Guralp Systems Limited* Deferred Prosecution Agreement (22 October 2019) [9] https://www.sfo.gov.uk/download/deferred-prosecution-agreement-statement-of-facts-approved-judgment-sfo-v-guralp-systems-ltd/?ind=1576839933055&filename=1576839932wpdm_Deferred%20Prosecution%20Agreement.pdf&wpdmdl=25160&refresh=6484cd5269cfc1686424914 (accessed 10 June 2023).
[92] *Serious Fraud Office v Glencore Energy UK Ltd* (Southwark CC, 3 November 2022) (sentencing remarks of Fraser J) [34].

4 Cooperation with Other Authorities

7.76 This section briefly considers the approach authorities other than the SFO take to waiver of privilege in the context of their own investigations and prosecutions.

Agreements under SOCPA 2005 and Sentencing Act 2020

7.77 The Serious Organised Crime and Police Act 2005 (SOCPA 2005), sections 71 and 72 allow prosecutors to offer a person immunity from prosecution or an undertaking that information will not be used against them in criminal proceedings. These powers can be used as a means of encouraging offenders to provide intelligence or evidence to assist with an investigation or prosecution. The powers are available to, inter alia, the DPP, the Director of the SFO, the FCA, and a prosecutor designated by any of the above-mentioned. In addition, the Sentencing Act 2020, sections 74 and 388 contain provisions for reduction or review of sentences for offenders who provide assistance to investigators or prosecutors.

7.78 The CPS has issued guidance for how prosecutors may use these powers.[93] The guidance suggests that it may be appropriate to consider asking the offender/potential witness whether they are prepared to waive privilege 'in order to support the process of "cleansing"', and that information received following a waiver may be of assistance in assessing their overall credibility and their suitability for a written agreement under SOCPA 2005 or the Sentencing Act. It also states that:

> Decisions on whether or not to request a waiver of LPP will be taken on a case-by-case basis. If it is considered that requesting such a waiver is appropriate as part of the cleansing process and the potential witness refuses such a request, the prosecutor must assess the issues that are likely to arise in connection with the witness's credibility and consider whether it remains appropriate to enter into an assistance agreement. The refusal by a potential witness to waive LPP will not necessarily mean however that they cannot be considered for a written agreement.

Competition and Markets Authority

7.79 The Competition and Markets Authority (CMA) operates a 'leniency policy' under which businesses and individuals who provide evidence of cartel activity and cooperate with the CMA's investigation may obtain immunity from prosecution or a reduction in or immunity from financial penalties.

7.80 The CMA has adopted earlier guidance issued by the Office of Fair Trading (the CMA's predecessor) on applications for leniency and no-action in cartel cases.[94] The guidance states

---

[93] CPS, 'Assisting Offenders (Immunity, Undertakings and Agreements)' (2 August 2022) https://www.cps.gov.uk/legal-guidance/assisting-offenders-immunity-undertakings-and-agreements (accessed 10 June 2023).
[94] Office of Fair Trading, 'Applications for Leniency and No-action in Cartel Cases' (July 2013) (CMA Leniency Guidance) https://assets.publishing.service.gov.uk/government/uploads/system/uploads/attachment_data/file/284417/OFT1495.pdf (accessed 10 June 2023) (confirmed as applicable to CMA investigations at https://www.gov.uk/government/publications/leniency-and-no-action-applications-in-cartel-cases).

that the CMA will not require a waiver of privilege as a condition of leniency, but it may inquire as to whether a leniency applicant may be prepared to waive privilege over certain material during the course of a possible criminal cartel prosecution. '[A]ny refusal to waive LPP will not have any adverse consequences for the leniency application' and 'granting such a waiver will not yield any additional leniency discount or any other advantage to the leniency applicant'. The purpose of inquiring as to the possibility of a waiver will be 'for the purposes of clarity in a possible criminal cartel prosecution, so that the defence and the court can know as early as possible the leniency applicant's position with respect to LPP material'.[95]

7.81 Notwithstanding this position, which is notably softer than the SFO's, the CMA will 'ordinarily require a review of any relevant information in respect of which LPP is claimed, by an independent counsel (IC) selected, instructed and funded on a case by case basis by the [CMA]', save for where 'the position is uncontroversial and clear to the [CMA]'s satisfaction'. A refusal to provide the relevant information to independent counsel 'could result in the withdrawal of the leniency marker or revocation of the leniency agreement (as the case may be), on the grounds of noncompliance with the duty of complete and continuous cooperation'. If independent counsel forms the view that the relevant information is not privileged, the CMA will expect the leniency applicant to provide it as a condition of leniency. Failure to provide the relevant information to independent counsel or the CMA (having been reviewed and determined not to be privileged by independent counsel) may result in withdrawal of the leniency marker or revocation of the leniency agreement 'on the grounds of noncompliance with the obligation to provide all relevant information'.[96]

7.82 When considering whether the leniency applicant has discharged their duty of complete and continuous cooperation in respect of the process of independent counsel reviewing potentially privileged material, the CMA may consider whether the applicant made 'what, on any objective view, were manifestly baseless claims to LPP', whether a blanket claim was made in respect of a large number of documents without sufficient specificity and whether the applicant 'appeared to be motivated by a desire to delay or otherwise prejudice the [CMA] investigation'.[97]

7.83 Independent counsel's opinion will ordinarily be regarded as determinative. However, if a claim to privilege over any material is disputed, the CMA will expect the applicant to make the material available 'for review by the court, if required, … in order that the court can conclusively determine whether LPP is properly claimed'.[98] The guidance does not indicate under what legal provision such a dispute would be heard by the court.

Financial Conduct Authority

7.84 The FCA's Enforcement Guide[99] addresses privilege in the context of regulated firms that conduct their own investigations in anticipation of FCA enforcement action. The guidance

---

[95] ibid para 3.15 and fn 30.
[96] ibid paras 3.16–3.21.
[97] ibid para 3.22.
[98] ibid para 3.23.
[99] FCA Handbook, Enforcement Guide.

notes that an internal investigation report may be useful to the FCA where there is an issue of regulatory concern. Firms are not under an obligation to share the content of privileged reports, and it is for the firm to decide whether to provide it to the FCA, 'but a firm's willingness to volunteer the results of its own investigation, whether protected by legal privilege or otherwise, is welcomed by the FCA and is something the FCA may take into account when deciding what action to take, if any'.[100]

7.85 The guidance notes that arguments about whether certain documents are privileged 'tend to be time-consuming and delay the progress of an investigation'. If a firm decides to disclose the report, the FCA considers that 'the greatest mutual benefit is most likely to flow from disclosure of the report itself and any supporting papers'. A reluctance to disclose the supporting documents 'will, in the FCA's opinion, devalue the usefulness of the report and may require the FCA to undertake additional enquiries'.[101]

---

[100] ibid 3.18.
[101] ibid 3.27.

8
Prosecution Privilege

1 Introduction

This chapter considers the availability of privilege for the police, other criminal investigation authorities, and prosecutors[1] in respect of their own communications and documents and how this operates alongside a prosecutor's statutory disclosure obligations.

8.01

2 Availability of Privilege

Legal professional privilege can be claimed by prosecutors, the police, and other investigators over communications and documents that are sent or created in connection with a criminal investigation or prosecution. The requirements that must be satisfied in order for either legal advice privilege or litigation privilege to apply are exactly the same as with a claim to privilege made by a suspect or defendant.[2]

8.02

Legal advice privilege is capable of applying to communications between the police and a prosecutor where the police are seeking legal advice in relation to a criminal investigation. In these circumstances, the police are the client of the prosecution lawyer. Litigation privilege ought to apply to communications between the police and potential witnesses if a prosecution is reasonably in contemplation and the dominant purpose of the communication is to obtain information or advice in connection with the conduct of the prosecution. Although a prosecutor rather than the police will have conduct of any prosecution that is brought, the police and prosecution are both representatives of the Crown and effectively form the same party to the proceedings such that both can benefit from litigation privilege when communicating with third parties. Alternatively, the police can be considered to be acting as agents of the prosecutor for the purposes of privilege.

8.03

Once a prosecution is underway, the prosecutor effectively becomes their own client, since it is they who bring the proceedings against the defendant. If the prosecutor instructs external counsel, legal advice privilege will apply to their communications in exactly the same way as with a defence solicitor instructing counsel. Most communications between the prosecutor and police will be privileged either on the basis that they are a continuation of the lawyer–client relationship that existed before charge and are therefore covered by legal advice privilege or because they are for the dominant purpose of the conduct of litigation and are therefore covered by litigation privilege. Communications between the police and third parties such as witnesses in order to obtain evidence or information in connection

8.04

---

[1] For ease, many of the references in this chapter are to the police and the Crown Prosecution Service (CPS), but the points apply equally to other investigation and prosecution bodies.
[2] See ch 1, ss 2 and 3.

with the conduct of the prosecution also ought to be covered by litigation privilege on the same basis as above.

8.05 A number of cases have considered the existence of privilege for the police and prosecutors and have consistently held that it is capable of applying. In *Auten v Rayner (No 2)*,[3] a subpoena was served on the Director of Public Prosecutions (DPP) requiring him to produce all documents in his possession relevant to the issues in the civil action. In response, the DPP claimed privilege over notes of conferences, briefs and instructions to prosecuting counsel, counsel's opinions, proofs of witnesses, and all other material accompanying the briefs to counsel. Upholding the claim to privilege, Glyn-Jones J considered that the rules of public policy underpinning privilege applied with equal, if not greater, force to the position of the DPP.[4]

8.06 In *Al-Fayed v Commissioner of Police of the Metropolis*[5] two written advices from prosecution counsel to the CPS were disclosed by mistake in a civil claim. It was not in dispute that the advices were covered by privilege; the issue for the Court of Appeal was whether that privilege had been waived. In addition to counsel's advice, reference was made in the judgment to one of the volumes of bundles of material disclosed in the civil proceedings, which included correspondence between the police and CPS. The Court noted that this material 'would no doubt originally have been subject to LPP' in the same way.[6]

8.07 In *Goodridge v Chief Constable of Hampshire*[7] the question arose of whether privilege applied to reports submitted to the DPP by a police officer investigating a murder. Moore-Bick J held as follows:

> In view of the fact that one of the functions of the Director of Public Prosecutions is to give advice to the police when they consider it appropriate to ask for it, I should be unwilling to say, on the basis of the material before me, that the relationship of client and lawyer cannot arise between the police and the Director of Public Prosecutions in an appropriate case. It seems to me that the statutory provisions which govern the relationship between them are such as might make it appropriate for the police to seek the advice of the Director of Public Prosecutions on matters with which they are concerned, in such circumstances as would make it appropriate for the request for advice, and any advice given in response to that request, to attract the protection of legal professional privilege.[8]

However, on the facts of this particular case, Moore-Bick J rejected the privilege claim. It seemed that the police officer had provided the DPP with the reports in circumstances where the officer thought there was a prima facie case for proceeding and therefore had a statutory obligation to report to the DPP. The Prosecution of Offences Regulations 1978,[9] regulation 6(1) provided that: 'The chief officer of police of every police area ... shall give to the Director of Public Prosecutions information with respect to any of the following

---

[3] [1960] 1 QB 669 (QB).
[4] ibid 680–81.
[5] [2002] EWCA Civ 780, [2002] All ER (D) 450 (May).
[6] ibid [66].
[7] [1999] 1 WLR 1558 (QB).
[8] [1999] 1 WLR 1558, 1564 (QB).
[9] SI 1978/1357.

offences where it appears to him that there is a prima facie case for proceedings.' Homicide was one such offence. Therefore, there was:

> [N]o evidence which suggests that this was a case in which the police were seeking legal advice for their own benefit of a kind or in circumstances which would be analogous to a client approaching his solicitor for legal advice. In those circumstances, although, as I have said, I would not rule out the possibility of legal professional privilege attaching to communications between the police and the Director of Public Prosecutions in an appropriate case, I do not think that the evidence before me bears out that case here.[10]

The CPS' guidance on disclosure of privileged material to third parties (not including defendants in criminal proceedings) suggests that a completed form MG3 (the form used by the police to refer cases to the CPS for charging advice and decisions and on which the CPS lawyer records their advice and decisions) will always be covered by privilege, on the basis that: 'The MG3 is in substance a request by the police for legal advice on whether there is sufficient evidence to charge a suspect.'[11] However, it is the authors' view that the approach taken in *Goodridge* reflects the correct application of legal advice privilege to certain communications between the police and CPS in cases where the charging decision must be made by the CPS rather than by the police. In such cases, the police refer the case to the CPS because they are required to do so by virtue of their statutory obligations.[12] It is a request for the CPS to make a decision required by law, not a request for legal advice. The CPS must then communicate its decision to the police by giving 'notice'[13] so that the police can either inform the suspect that they are not to be prosecuted[14] or caution or charge them in accordance with the CPS' decision.[15] In these circumstances, the submission of the case to the CPS and the CPS' notification of the decision to the police fall outside the scope of legal advice privilege. To the extent that an MG3 records these matters only, it would not be privileged. However, privilege is capable of applying to other communications between the police and the CPS in relation to the same cases, for example if the CPS is asked to provide 'early advice' before a charging decision is made (see section 3 below).

8.08

In an extradition context, it was held in one case (at first instance) that privilege did not apply to communications between the CPS and the requesting state. In *R (United States) v Bow Street Magistrates' Court*[16] the Divisional Court was concerned with the question of whether the extradition judge was able to order disclosure in relation to allegations of abuse of process made by the requested persons. Among the documents sought by the requested persons in connection with their abuse of process argument was correspondence between

8.09

---

[10] [1999] 1 WLR 1558, 1565 (QB).
[11] CPS, 'Disclosure of Material to Third Parties' (2 August 2022) https://www.cps.gov.uk/legal-guidance/disclosure-material-third-parties (accessed 10 June 2023).
[12] DPP, 'Director's Guidance on Charging: Sixth edition' (31 December 2020) https://www.cps.gov.uk/legal-guidance/charging-directors-guidance-sixth-edition-december-2020-incorporating-national-file (accessed 10 June 2023). Custody officers must have regard to this guidance under the Police and Criminal Evidence Act (PACE) 1984, s 37A(3).
[13] PACE 1984, s 37B(4).
[14] ibid s 37B(5).
[15] ibid s 37B(6).
[16] [2006] EWHC 2256 (Admin), [2007] 1 WLR 1157.

the CPS and the US government, over which the CPS claimed privilege (and public interest immunity (PII)). At first instance, the senior district judge (SDJ) was satisfied that there was 'an argument for saying that the relationship between the Crown Prosecution Service and the Government [of the requesting state] is one of a Solicitor and Client', and so there may well be documents which are privileged on this basis. However, in this particular case, the SDJ had concluded that privilege did not apply. Summarizing the SDJ's reasoning, Lord Phillips CJ in the Divisional Court said:

> As to the meetings and e-mail exchanges between the CPS and the Assistant District Attorney, it was necessary to establish the nature and the role of the responsibility of the CPS in relation to extradition proceedings. If the US Government instructed a private firm of solicitors to act, then the relationship of solicitor and client would be established. However, the position of the CPS was significantly different; [the SDJ] concluded that the CPS was 'effectively acting for the United Kingdom authorities in relation to this country's treaty obligations'. The CPS did not act in a solicitor and client relationship with the requesting state that gave rise to a claim of legal professional privilege. [The SDJ] made it clear that the decision he had made was in respect of an abuse of process argument and did not touch upon the law relating to disclosure in extradition proceedings in general.[17]

In the judicial review proceedings before the Divisional Court, although reference was made to the SDJ's reasoning, the question of whether the documents were subject to privilege did not require determination, so the Court did not opine on this particular issue.

8.10 It is the authors' view that the SDJ's reasoning was incorrect. In extradition proceedings, the CPS acts on behalf of the requesting state, not the UK government. The UK's treaty obligations enable the CPS to conduct the proceedings, but it does not follow that the UK government is the CPS' client. As the SDJ acknowledged, the requesting state can instruct a private firm of solicitors to act on its behalf instead of the CPS.[18] If the relationship of solicitor and client would be established in those circumstances, as the SDJ accepted, there should be no difference where the CPS is performing the same function. Even if the SDJ was correct that the UK government is the CPS' client in extradition proceedings, the communications between the CPS and the requesting state would surely be covered by litigation privilege, with the requesting state as the third party. The dominant purpose of the communications would almost certainly be to obtain information for the conduct of litigation, that litigation being the extradition proceedings.[19]

---

[17] ibid [48].
[18] As was the case in *Government of Ukraine v Kononko* [2014] EWHC 1420 (Admin).
[19] Note that Lord Phillips CJ stated at [85] that: 'Neither the rules governing disclosure in a civil action, nor those governing disclosure in a criminal trial can be applied to an extradition hearing. Furthermore, those rules form part of an adversarial process which differs from extradition proceedings. Where an order for disclosure is made, it requires one party to disclose documents to the other, not to the court. But where extradition is sought, the court is under a duty to satisfy itself that all the requirements for making the order are satisfied and that none of the bars to making the order exists.' These comments were made in relation to the question of disclosure in extradition proceedings, not the application of privilege. While they may be correct as far as disclosure is concerned, it cannot be the case that extradition proceedings are not sufficiently adversarial in order to constitute 'litigation' for the purposes of litigation privilege.

3 Examples of Privileged Material

8.11 Whether or not privilege applies to any particular communication or document sent or created by an investigator or prosecutor will ultimately depend on the requirements for legal advice privilege or litigation privilege explained in Chapter 1 being established. However, it is suggested that the following items (not an exhaustive list) will be covered by privilege in most cases:

- 'Early advice' provided by the CPS to the police before a charging decision is made, for example advice on further lines of enquiry, evidence required to satisfy the evidential test, or potential offences that may have been committed.[20] This will be the case regardless of whether it is the CPS rather than the police that is required to make the charging decision (but see section 2 above regarding the decision itself).
- Communications between the police and potential witnesses, if the dominant purpose is:
   o to obtain information or evidence that will be used to decide whether to charge a suspect in circumstances where a prosecution is in reasonable contemplation; and/or
   o to obtain information or evidence to be used in or in connection with a prosecution that is in progress or reasonably contemplated.
- Witness statements provided to the police in circumstances described above (before they are disclosed to the defence) and draft statements of witnesses whose final statements have been disclosed.
- Communications between a prosecutor and prosecution counsel that are made for the dominant purpose of giving or obtaining legal advice, including the advice itself.
- Communications between a prosecutor and a prosecution expert witness, including their reports (before they are disclosed to the defence).

4 Privilege and Disclosure Obligations

8.12 It is clear from the above discussion that prosecutors and investigators benefit from privilege in the same way as suspects and defendants. There is, however, an apparent conflict between the absolute nature of privilege and a prosecutor's statutory disclosure obligations. The Criminal Procedure and Investigations Act 1996 (CPIA 1996) requires the prosecution to disclose to the defence any prosecution material which might reasonably be considered capable of undermining the prosecution case or assisting the defence case. But what if material that meets this test is covered by privilege in the hands of the prosecutor? Can it legitimately be withheld from disclosure in a way that is compliant with the CPIA 1996?

---

[20] For more guidance on when early advice may be appropriate see DPP, 'Director's Guidance on Charging: Sixth edition' (31 December 2020) https://www.cps.gov.uk/legal-guidance/charging-directors-guidance-sixth-edition-december-2020-incorporating-national-file (accessed 10 June 2023).

What Approach Is Taken in Practice?

8.13 The question of whether privileged material can be withheld from disclosure on the grounds of privilege is, in many respects, largely academic because, in practice, prosecutors disclose privileged material if it meets the disclosure test under the CPIA 1996. Prosecutors have an overriding duty to act fairly in the interests of justice and not solely for the purpose of obtaining a conviction. A fundamental aspect of this duty is to ensure that a defendant has a fair trial. Prosecutors are bound by this obligation in all decisions they make, including disclosure decisions. If disclosure of privileged material is required to ensure a fair trial, the prosecution will usually disclose it. This is an entirely appropriate approach that is so well established and routine that many prosecutors and defence lawyers may not even realize that privilege is being waived.

8.14 The CPS Disclosure Manual reflects this general approach, stating that: 'Prosecutors should resolve any doubt they may have in favour of disclosure unless the material is sensitive and falls properly to be placed before the court in a PII application.'[21] There is no reference anywhere in the Disclosure Manual to withholding disclosable material on the ground that it is covered by privilege. It is clear that the CPS considers the only basis for withholding material that meets the disclosure test to be PII, which for the reasons discussed at para 8.25 is distinct from privilege. Even with PII material, the Disclosure Manual advises prosecutors that: 'Fairness ordinarily requires that material which weakens the prosecution case or strengthens that of the defence should be disclosed. There should only be derogation from this golden rule in exceptional circumstances.'[22]

8.15 Accordingly, the prosecution will usually disclose privileged material that meets the disclosure test, such as unused expert reports, unused witness statements, draft statements of witnesses on whom the prosecution relies, and instructions to experts. Where privileged material is withheld from disclosure, it will usually be on the basis that it is either not relevant (and therefore will not be recorded on the sensitive or non-sensitive unused material schedules) or it is relevant but does not meet the test for disclosure. In most cases, privileged material such as advice from the CPS to the police or advice from prosecution counsel to the CPS will not be considered relevant.[23] This is reflected in the CPS Disclosure Manual, which says:

> As a general rule, pure opinion or speculation, for example theories of police officers about who committed the crime, is not unused material.
>
> ...
>
> Reports, advices and other communications between the CPS and investigators in themselves will usually be of an administrative nature, generally having no bearing on the issues in the case, and thus not relevant. However, there may be instances where this material may

---

[21] CPS, 'Disclosure Manual: Chapter 12' (21 October 2021) https://www.cps.gov.uk/legal-guidance/disclosure-manual-chapter-12-applying-disclosure-test (accessed 10 June 2023).
[22] CPS, 'Disclosure Manual: Chapter 13' (21 October 2021) https://www.cps.gov.uk/legal-guidance/disclosure-manual-chapter-13-making-pii-application (accessed 10 June 2023).
[23] It is also very unlikely to be admissible.

become relevant, for example, if it could support an application by the defendant such as for abuse of process relating to delay or the conduct of the investigation. If the content of any such document is relevant and not recorded elsewhere, then the material should be described on the appropriate schedule and considered in the normal way.[24]

8.16 In exceptional cases where privileged material of this nature is considered relevant and disclosable, the CPS may limit disclosure to extracts of relevant sections or admissions rather than entire documents.[25]

8.17 Note also the guidance of the Health and Safety Executive (HSE) on preparing unused material schedules in its own criminal investigations: '[T]he investigation/prosecution report may not be relevant if it simply repeats information about evidence which is already in the prosecution evidence bundle, together with the view of the inspector as to the weight of that evidence.'[26] The HSE's guidance also states that: 'If material is legally privileged it falls outside CPIA and therefore should not be scheduled.'[27] This is presumably a reference to the fact that legal advice will usually not be relevant and therefore should not be scheduled, but it is an oversimplification of the position to suggest that *all* privileged material would fall into this category.

What Are the Consequences of Privileged Material Being Disclosed?

8.18 As explained at paras 1.94–1.96, the general approach to waiver of privilege is to treat the waiver as extending to any other privileged material relating to the same issue or 'transaction', through what is known as collateral waiver. This is based on fairness and the principle that a party should not be allowed to 'cherry-pick' the material over which they waive privilege in order to advance their own case.

8.19 These principles have less application to the disclosure of unused material by the prosecution. The material is disclosed for the benefit of the defendant, not the prosecution, and no unfairness can result from allowing the prosecution to waive privilege for this purpose. It is very unlikely to result in the court or the defendant having an incomplete or misleading impression of a particular issue because, if there is other material on the same point, it too will probably meet the disclosure test and be provided to the defendant. The authors therefore consider that the ordinary principles of collateral waiver do not apply to disclosure of unused material.

---

[24] CPS, 'Disclosure Manual: Chapter 4' (14 July 2022) https://www.cps.gov.uk/legal-guidance/disclosure-manual-chapter-4-relevance-recording-and-retention (accessed 10 June 2023).

[25] See eg CPS, 'Disclosure of Material to Third Parties' (2 August 2022) https://www.cps.gov.uk/legal-guidance/disclosure-material-third-parties (accessed 10 June 2023): 'Disclosure obligations or principles of information sharing can be met by providing extracts from police reports, MG3s or Victim Liaison Unit (VLU) letters rather than disclosing the entire MG3 document, or making appropriate admissions ... This course of action is the preferred approach when information about charging decisions is requested by third parties or defendants and/or their legal representatives.'

[26] HSE Enforcement Guide, 'Preparing the Schedules' https://www.hse.gov.uk/enforce/enforcementguide/pretrial/after-preparing.htm (accessed 10 June 2023).

[27] Although, confusingly, the guidance also states that: 'Some privileged material, for example confidential complaints, must also be included on the schedule of sensitive material.'

8.20 In practice, this too is largely academic considering that the prosecution will usually waive privilege over material that meets the disclosure test, so it is very unlikely that there will ever be a situation where collateral waiver arguments are being deployed by the defence in order to obtain further disclosure; the issue will be whether the additional material meets the disclosure test, not whether privilege over it has been waived.

Can Privileged Material Be Withheld from Disclosure?

8.21 As stated above, the question of whether the prosecution can lawfully withhold privileged material that meets the disclosure test on the basis of privilege alone is largely academic as it is not the approach taken in practice. However, there may be exceptional cases where the prosecution does (rightly or wrongly) decide to withhold privileged material that otherwise meets the test for disclosure under the CPIA 1996. It is therefore worth considering whether there would be a lawful basis for this.

8.22 The relevant provisions of the CPIA 1996 are sections 3 (initial duty of disclosure), 7A (continuing duty of disclosure), and 8 (defence applications for prosecution disclosure). All three provisions adopt the same wording for what must be disclosed: 'any prosecution material which has not previously been disclosed to the accused and which might reasonably be considered capable of undermining the case for the prosecution against the accused or of assisting the case for the accused'. None of these provisions contains an express exception for privileged material. The only exceptions to be found in sections 3, 7A, and 8 are for material which 'the court, on an application by the prosecutor, concludes ... is not in the public interest to disclose ... and orders accordingly'[28] (material subject to PII) and interception-related material.[29]

8.23 On its face, this suggests that there is no lawful basis for withholding privileged material from disclosure purely on the grounds that it is covered by privilege. Were this to be the case, however, the provisions of the CPIA 1996 would amount to an abrogation of privilege. As explained at paras 1.09–1.10, privilege can only be abrogated by statute through express words or 'necessary implication'.[30] Lord Hobhouse defined 'necessary implication' in *R (Morgan Grenfell & Co Ltd) v Special Commissioners of Income Tax* in the following terms:

> A necessary implication is not the same as a reasonable implication ... A necessary implication is one which necessarily follows from the express provisions of the statute construed in their context. It distinguishes between what it would have been sensible or reasonable for Parliament to have included or what Parliament would, if it had thought about it, probably have included and what it is clear that the express language of the statute shows that the statute must have included. A necessary implication is a matter of express language and logic not interpretation.[31]

---

[28] CPIA 1996, ss 3(6), 7A(8), 8(5).
[29] ibid ss 3(7), 7A(9), 8(6).
[30] *R (Morgan Grenfell & Co Ltd) v Special Commissioners of Income Tax* [2002] UKHL 21, [2003] 1 AC 563.
[31] ibid [45].

A persuasive argument could be made that Parliament must have intended that privileged material would not be protected from disclosure under the CPIA 1996. The disclosure test is expressed in very broad terms—'*any* prosecution material ... which might reasonably be considered capable of ...'[32]—and it is not as if exemptions have been overlooked: PII and interception-related material are expressly excluded. The purpose of the CPIA 1996 is to guarantee the defendant a fair trial, and this could be impeded if material that otherwise meets the test for disclosure cannot be disclosed because it is privileged. It could be said that the public interest in ensuring a defendant has a fair trial is more important than the public interest in maintaining privilege over prosecution material. On this basis, the PII exception could be used to protect privileged material where there are genuine concerns about the damage to the public interest if the material were to be disclosed.

8.24

However, this is not how privilege operates. It has repeatedly been emphasized by the courts that privilege does not involve a balancing exercise of competing public interests.[33] It is absolute and will apply no matter what the public interest in favour of disclosure. Reliance on the PII exception under the CPIA 1996, which requires the court to weigh up competing public interests, would not be appropriate. Indeed, it was said in *R v Derby Magistrates' Court ex p B* that:

8.25

> Legal professional privilege and public interest immunity are as different in their origin as they are in their scope. Putting it another way, if a balancing exercise was ever required in the case of legal professional privilege, it was performed once and for all in the 16th century, and since then has applied across the board in every case, irrespective of the client's individual merits.[34]

Furthermore, it is clear from Lord Hobhouse's definition of 'necessary implication' above that the points that could be made in favour of an argument that Parliament did not intend privileged material to be protected from disclosure under the CPIA 1996 fall short of the very high test for abrogation. It cannot be said that it is 'clear that the express language of the statute shows that the statute must have included' a requirement for privileged material to be disclosed. Such a reading of the CPIA 1996 would amount to nothing more than an *interpretation* rather than 'a matter of express language and logic'.

8.26

It is therefore the view of the authors that the provisions of the CPIA 1996 that impose disclosure obligations on the prosecution do not abrogate privilege. Privileged material can, in theory, be withheld from disclosure.[35]

8.27

---

[32] Emphasis added.
[33] See eg *R v Derby Magistrates' Court, ex p B* [1996] AC 487 (HL).
[34] ibid 508.
[35] It is of interest to note the approach taken by the Supreme Court of South Australia in *R v Bunting & Others* [2002] SASC 412. Martin J rejected the notion of any sort of balancing exercise between competing public interests and held instead that, in initiating or maintaining a prosecution, there is an imputed waiver of privilege as the DPP does so in the knowledge that the prosecution carries with it a duty of disclosure to the defendant, and the duty of disclosure is inconsistent with the maintenance of confidentiality over the material. For the reasons explained in this chapter, the authors do not agree that this is the correct approach, at least as far as the law of England and Wales is concerned.

What Are the Consequences of Withholding Disclosure on the Grounds of Privilege?

8.28 Although the CPIA 1996 does not abrogate privilege, in the event that a prosecutor did decide to withhold otherwise disclosable material on the grounds of privilege alone, the view of the authors is that this would amount to a failure to comply with the prosecutor's professional duties to act fairly in the interests of justice, which, as noted at para 8.13, is an overriding duty that applies to all decisions made by the prosecutor. The most appropriate remedy for the defendant would be an application to stay proceedings as an abuse of process on the basis that the defendant could not receive a fair trial if deprived of relevant and disclosable material that was being withheld in contravention of the prosecutor's professional obligations. An application for disclosure under the CPIA 1996, section 8 would not be appropriate because, as explained at paras 8.21–8.27, the prosecutor's refusal to disclose the material would not technically be a breach of the disclosure obligations under the CPIA 1996.

5 Private Prosecutions

8.29 The points discussed in this chapter apply equally to private prosecutions. The individual or entity who brings the prosecution is the client for the purposes of privilege and they will usually instruct solicitors and counsel to conduct the prosecution on their behalf. Legal advice privilege will apply to communications between the client and their lawyers that are made for the dominant purpose of giving or obtaining legal advice, and litigation privilege will attach to communications with third parties that are made for the dominant purpose of conducting the prosecution. A private prosecutor has the same disclosure obligations under the CPIA 1996 as public prosecutors and is bound by the same overriding duty to ensure the defendant receives a fair trial.[36] The relationship between privilege and disclosure obligations discussed at section 4 above is therefore equally applicable to private prosecutions.

---

[36] See eg *R (Kay) v Leeds Magistrates' Court* [2018] EWHC 1233 (Admin), [2018] 4 WLR 91 [23].

9
Evidence Gathering and Preparing for Court

1 Introduction

The charge, summons, or postal requisition marks the end of the investigation stage and begins the process of litigation in the form of a prosecution. This may mean preparation for a trial, a Newton hearing, or sentencing, with various administrative hearings in between. Litigation does not have to be a contested trial; it simply means that the matter is now before the court as an adversarial process. 9.01

Litigation privilege may be engaged at an earlier stage if litigation is reasonably in contemplation. However, once litigation has commenced, arguments about reasonable contemplation are redundant, and, as a criminal prosecution is always adversarial, it will constitute litigation for the purposes of privilege. When a criminal matter is before the court, as long as communications are confidential and for the dominant purpose of conducting the litigation, they will be subject to litigation privilege. It is therefore important to understand the limits and operation of litigation privilege, particularly when dealing with third parties in respect of any matters in preparation for litigation, including third-party funders, witnesses, and other parties in the case. 9.02

Preparing for court will also necessarily involve communication with the prosecution in respect of disclosure of material. The extent to which privilege issues can impact on the disclosure process is therefore an important aspect of case preparation. 9.03

Legal advice privilege continues to be available to the defendant once litigation is in progress, which means that certain communications will be covered by both legal advice privilege and litigation privilege. If both are engaged, the distinction is of no practical difference. The distinction becomes relevant when communicating with third parties, as legal advice privilege cannot apply. The extent to which communications with third parties are privileged, either due to litigation privilege or because of the rules permitting confidential sharing of privileged information, is a significant focus of this chapter. 9.04

2 Engaging with Third Parties

Engaging with Third Parties Generally

The principles of litigation privilege are set out fully in Chapter 1, Section 3. The authoritative definition of litigation privilege can be found in *Three Rivers District Council v Governor and Co of the Bank of England (Three Rivers (No 6))*: 9.05

Communications between parties or their solicitors and third parties for the purpose of obtaining information or advice in connection with existing or contemplated litigation are privileged, but only when the following conditions are satisfied: (a) litigation must be in progress or in contemplation; (b) the communications must have been made for the sole or dominant purpose of conducting that litigation; (c) the litigation must be adversarial, not investigative or inquisitorial.[1]

9.06 In practice this means that, post-charge, communications between a defendant or their lawyer and a third party made for the sole or dominant purpose of conducting litigation in respect of the charges will attract litigation privilege. These communications are therefore exempt from compelled disclosure.

9.07 There is a distinction between situations where litigation privilege attaches to communications and where information which may be subject to legal advice privilege and/or litigation privilege is shared with a third party on a confidential basis. The circumstances under which confidential sharing of privileged information is possible without losing or waiving privilege more widely are explained in paras 1.77–1.79. Where privileged information is shared confidentially with a third party for a purpose other than the conduct of litigation, such as sharing legal advice with a family member of the defendant, the communication itself will not be privileged, but the content, insofar as it reproduces or reveals the legal advice or a separate privileged communication, will be. However, in either case, the result will be the same: the right to assert privilege over the relevant material will usually be lost as against that third party, as the information is no longer confidential, but it will not be lost as against the rest of the world. This means that privilege could not be relied upon against the third party if they became a party to the proceedings or were involved in separate proceedings against the defendant,[2] unless the privilege holder could establish that privilege had only been lost or waived for the limited purpose for which the information was shared in the criminal proceedings but maintained in all other respects. This does not mean, however, that the third party would be free to do as they wished with the privileged information. For example, in the case of an expert witness, they will probably be bound by obligations of confidentiality, whether contractual or professional, or both, and there may be consequences if they breach the instructing party's privilege.

9.08 Preparing for trial will necessarily involve communicating with a number of third parties for a range of purposes. The most commonly encountered scenarios are considered in turn below.

Communications with the Court and Case Management Forms

9.09 An essential element of privilege is confidentiality. A communication cannot be privileged if it has lost confidentiality or never was confidential to begin with.

---

[1] [2004] UKHL 48, [2005] AC 610 [102].
[2] *Gotha City v Sotheby's (No 1)* [1998] 1 WLR 114 (CA).

9.10 Communications with the court will not have the requisite degree of confidentiality for the purposes of privilege, particularly as they are likely to be shared with the prosecution. Sharing privileged information with the court in respect of criminal proceedings will almost certainly cause the information to lose confidentiality and therefore privilege and/or amount to a waiver of privilege. Communications made in the presence or hearing of an opponent will not be deemed confidential. In the Australian case of *R v Braham and Mason*[3] a client sought legal advice from his solicitor over the telephone from a police station whilst in the presence of a police officer. It was held that the conversation was not privileged as there could have been no intention for it to have been a confidential communication. The principle will similarly apply to discussions between a client and their lawyer in open court or in the presence of court staff.

9.11 Court forms often require the parties to provide information which is based on privileged instructions or advice. For example, at the Plea and Trial Preparation Hearing (PTPH), the parties must complete a pre-hearing information form which requires the defendant to provide information about various aspects of case management and what they identify as being the issues in the case. Additionally, the form requires the defence advocate to confirm that they have explained the allegation and given advice on credit for a guilty plea. This raises two separate issues relating to privilege: the first being the extent to which information provided about the issues in the case is privileged, and secondly, whether providing that information and confirming that the allegations have been explained and advice has been given about pleas waives privilege.

9.12 The case of *R (Firth) v Epping Magistrates' Court*[4] considered the use that can be made of information provided on a case management form. The defendant, Firth, had been charged with assault by beating. At her first appearance in the magistrates' court, she pleaded not guilty and was required to complete a case progression form which, in accordance with Crim PR 3.2, required the parties to identify the issues in the case. The defendant's representative completed the form on her behalf and identified that the issue in the case was one of self-defence. Later, the prosecution reviewed the case and decided to amend the charge to one of assault occasioning actual bodily harm. The defendant was required to attend a further hearing in order to enter a plea to this charge and for mode of trial to be determined. The court declined jurisdiction and the defendant's representatives asked for a full committal hearing as it was their submission that the case served did not disclose a prima facie case. At the committal hearing it was argued on the defendant's behalf that the committal bundle did not contain evidence identifying the defendant as the person who committed the assault. However, the prosecution sought to adduce the case progression form completed at the magistrates' court into evidence. The prosecution argued that as the defendant had identified on the form that the issue in the case was self-defence, she had admitted presence. The court agreed and the case was committed to the Crown Court for trial. The defendant sought a judicial review of the decision to admit the case progression form as evidence. The arguments did not focus on privilege, but the application was refused in any

---

[3] [1976] VR 547 (SC Victoria).
[4] [2011] EWHC 388 (Admin), [2011] 1 WLR 1818.

event, with the Divisional Court noting that once the information was disclosed on the case progression form, it was no longer privileged:

> [I]nsofar as the information imparted by counsel was, until that moment, privileged (as any prior discussions between Miss Firth and her counsel undoubtedly were), thereafter by reason of the open disclosure that she made, pursuant to the rules, there can no longer be claimed to be any privilege in that information.[5]

In setting out the issues on the case progression form, the information was no longer confidential and could not therefore be privileged. There being no privilege in the information, it was deemed relevant and admissible evidence and it was open to the prosecution to adduce it in support of its case.

9.13 As regards the requirement on case management forms to confirm that advice has been given regarding aspects of the defence case, including credit for a guilty plea, confirming the fact that advice has been given on a particular matter does not waive privilege as it does not involve the defendant relying on the content or substance of the advice to advance their case. However, should the disclosure go beyond mere confirmation of the fact of advice and disclose the content or substance of the advice, this may amount to a waiver of privilege on the client's behalf depending on the nature and extent of the disclosure and its purpose. See further discussion at paras 10.27–10.34 and 10.42.

Defence statements

9.14 The Criminal Procedure and Investigations Act 1996 (CPIA 1996), section 5 requires the defendant in a trial on indictment to serve a defence statement on the court and the prosecutor. The information communicated by a defendant in a defence statement is neither confidential nor privileged and can therefore be adduced as evidence by the prosecution at trial.

9.15 The CPIA 1996, section 6A specifies the requirements of a defence statement, which include setting out the nature of the accused's defence, the defence(s) on which they will rely and matters of fact with which they take issue. In complying with sections 5 and 6A a defendant is therefore required to disclose information to the court and the prosecutor which may, until disclosure, be privileged. *R v Rochford*[6] considered the extent to which section 6A offends against a defendant's legal professional privilege and privilege against self-incrimination. It was held that the requirements do not undermine a defendant's privilege; nothing in the CPIA 1996 requires a defendant to waive privilege. The facts relied upon by a defendant in defence to the charges they face will no longer be privileged once they are communicated to the opposing party, but in order to assert and establish a positive defence it will be necessary to communicate these facts to the opposing party and the court in any event. It is effectively the *timing* of this disclosure which the CPIA 1996 seeks to regulate, to avoid a 'trial by ambush' where the facts relied upon by the defence are not disclosed

---

[5] ibid [24].
[6] [2010] EWCA Crim 1928, [2011] 1 WLR 534.

until the trial, or very shortly beforehand. If a defendant does not seek to assert a positive defence, *Rochford* makes clear that the CPIA 1996 does not require them to make an admission of guilt or explain a refusal to provide instructions. The case suggests that in those circumstances it would be permissible for a defence statement to say that the defendant does not admit the offence, that the Crown is put to proof and that the defendant advances no positive case.

Disclosing facts relied upon as part of the defendant's case does not waive privilege over any undisclosed information, such as the advice given in respect of the facts relied upon. It is, however, possible for such a waiver to occur, intentionally or unintentionally, as a result of other information included in a defence statement. For example, should a defendant set out in a defence statement the reasons for giving a no comment interview at the police station which make reference to the advice given by their legal representative and the reasons for that advice, that is very likely to amount to a waiver of privilege. If the defendant repeats the disclosure in evidence at trial or the defence statement is adduced in evidence, the prosecution will be permitted to cross-examine the defendant about instructions given and advice received at the police station.[7] The topic of waiver of privilege over police station advice is set out in more detail at paras 6.39–6.47 and 10.27–10.34. **9.16**

Communication Regarding Funding

In cases where the defendant is not directly funding their legal costs, it may be necessary to communicate with a third party in respect of the work completed on the client's behalf, which may involve sharing privileged information. It is unlikely that a communication with a third party regarding the funding of a case will be for the dominant purpose of conducting the litigation, so communications of this nature are unlikely to attract litigation privilege. However, the sharing of privileged information with a third party on a confidential basis does not destroy privilege, so it is possible to communicate with a third party in respect of costs without losing privilege as against the rest of the world. **9.17**

Invoices and fee notes

The extent to which invoices and fee notes are in themselves privileged documents is not entirely clear, with some authorities lending support for the proposition that such documents are privileged in their entirety,[8] whilst others suggest that they are only privileged to the extent that sections of the document contain evidence of privileged communications.[9] It is difficult to sustain an argument that fee notes and invoices are privileged in their entirety, especially in light of the Court of Appeal's confirmation that a dominant purpose **9.18**

---

[7] It may not even be necessary for the prosecution to adduce the defence statement in evidence if it can be established that the waiver occurred at the point at which the defence statement was served. Whilst waiver is typically understood as arising when evidence is deployed before the court, there are authorities from civil proceedings suggesting that waiver can occur sooner. See paras 1.97–1.99.

[8] *IBM v Phoenix International (Computers) Ltd* [1995] 1 All ER 413 (Ch) [424]; *Oceanic Finance Corp Ltd v Norton Rose* (QB, 26 March 1997); *Dickinson v Rushmer* [2002] 1 Costs LR 128 (Ch).

[9] *Ainsworth v Wilding (No 2)* [1900] 2 Ch 315 (Ch); *Kupe Group v Seamar Holdings* [1993] 3 NZLR 209.

test applies to legal advice privilege in *R (Jet2.com Ltd) v Civil Aviation Authority*.[10] Where bills are issued to a client, they are not communications made for the dominant purpose of seeking or providing legal advice, and where they are issued to a third party funder, despite their confidential nature, they are not communications made for the sole or dominant purpose of conducting the litigation to which they refer. Treating invoices and fee notes as documents which may contain evidence of privileged communications and are therefore capable of being partly privileged is the approach which appears the most consistent with the established principles.

Corresponding with the Legal Aid Agency

9.19 In order to make a successful application for legal aid, it will be necessary to provide confidential information which may include reference to privileged information such as the client's defence and potential witness enquiries.

9.20 *R v Snaresbrook Crown Court, ex P DPP*[11] considered the extent to which an application for legal aid was privileged, in circumstances where the information included in the application was said by the Crown to be in furtherance of a crime or fraud and therefore subject to the crime-fraud exception.[12] The Court was asked to consider whether the application for legal aid was subject to privilege. Considering the definition of privilege set out at section 10(1) of the Police and Criminal Evidence Act 1984 (PACE 1984),[13] it was held that the application form was clearly a communication made in contemplation of and for the purpose of litigation.

9.21 Some caution should be exercised when interpreting the decision in *Snaresbrook* as its application in respect of the crime-fraud exception has been questioned in later authorities. Whilst *Snaresbrook* does make clear that an application for legal aid made in good faith is subject to litigation privilege, this is a generous interpretation of the dominant purpose test and a more considered approach would be to treat legal aid applications as confidential documents containing privileged information rather than privileged communications in and of themselves. The distinction is unlikely to serve any material purpose, as the result in either case is that privileged information shared with the Legal Aid Agency will remain privileged as against the rest of the world and therefore be exempt from compelled disclosure, for example to the police investigating the matter for which funding has been sought. The potential caveat to that proposition, however, is that where an application for legal aid is made in circumstances in which there is evidence of dishonesty or bad faith in respect of the application for legal aid itself, the application may engage the crime-fraud exception and therefore not be privileged. This may arise if a defendant dishonestly makes false representations in order to appear eligible for legal aid.

---

[10] [2020] EWCA Civ 35, [2020] QB 1027, confirming that a dominant purpose test applies to legal advice privilege.
[11] [1988] QB 532 (QB).
[12] The crime-fraud exception is examined in detail in ch 2.
[13] See para 3.26.

Advice from Non-Lawyers

The extent to which advice given by non-lawyer advisers can be subject to legal advice privilege was considered in the case of *R (Prudential plc) v Special Commissioner of Income Tax*.[14] It was held that advice from accountants in respect of tax matters was not covered by legal advice privilege and therefore could not be withheld from disclosure to HMRC, re-emphasising what had long been understood, that legal advice privilege is reserved for advice from lawyers only. It ought to be possible, however, for advice of this nature, for example from tax or accountancy experts, to be covered by litigation privilege, assuming the usual criteria for litigation privilege are satisfied.

9.22

3 Engaging with Witnesses

Defence Witnesses

Actual and potential witnesses of fact
The communications between a lawyer on behalf of a defendant in criminal proceedings and a witness of fact will be subject to litigation privilege so long as they are confidential and are made for the dominant purpose of conducting the criminal proceedings, for example to obtain the witness' account. Draft versions of witness statements are privileged and remain so even if the final version of the witness statement is served.[15]

9.23

The service and admissibility of witness statements in criminal proceedings is governed by the Criminal Justice Act 1967 (CJA 1967), section 9 and Crim PR 16. If a defence witness statement is served under the provisions of section 9, the document in its final, served form (as opposed to a draft version) is no longer privileged.

9.24

The CPIA 1996, section 6C makes it a requirement that the defence must notify the prosecution of their intention to call witnesses at trial, and provide the prosecution with the name, address and date of birth of those witnesses.[16] Unless and until such notification is given, the identity of a witness is covered by litigation privilege.[17] In *R (Kelly) v Warley Magistrates' Court*[18] a defendant had been directed by the district judge at a pre-trial review hearing to disclose to the prosecution the names, addresses, and dates of birth of all witnesses he intended to call at trial. Allowing his claim for judicial review, the Divisional Court held that the direction was unlawful and quashed it. It purported to impose an unconditional requirement to provide privileged information, but there was no statutory basis for overriding privilege in this way. It could only have been lawful if it had specified that procedural sanctions would be imposed if advanced disclosure of such matters was not

9.25

---

[14] [2013] UKSC 1, [2013] 2 AC 185.
[15] *Waugh v British Railways Board* [1980] AC 521, 531 (HL).
[16] CPIA 1996, s 6C.
[17] *China National Petroleum Corp v Fenwick Elliott* [2002] EWHC 60 (Ch), [2002] TCLR 19 [45]; *R (Kelly) v Warley Magistrates' Court* [2007] EWHC 1836 (Admin), [2008] 1 WLR 2001 [20].
[18] *R (Kelly) v Warley Magistrates' Court* (n 17).

made. By not specifying a sanction in default of compliance, it was either an unlawful order or it amounted to no more than a request.

9.26 There is no requirement to serve a defence witness statement in advance of calling the witness to give evidence, and so any unserved written statement taken from a defence witness on behalf of the defendant will remain privileged even after the witness has given oral evidence.

Communications with defence witnesses: to whom does the privilege belong?

9.27 In respect of communications with a defence witness, the privilege belongs to the defendant, not the witness.[19] The effect of this is that the information obtained by or on behalf of the defendant can be deployed in the manner of the defendant's choosing, but it is not open to the witness to reveal privileged information which they may have obtained in the course of communicating with the defendant and/or their legal representatives.[20] However, as discussed below, there is no power to stop a witness doing so, and should they choose to do so it is likely that it would amount to an inadvertent waiver of privilege or loss of privilege through loss of confidentiality, and subject to the court determining the relevance of the disclosed information, it could be deemed admissible evidence.[21]

9.28 If the witness has their own legal representation, the witness' communications with their legal advisers will be covered by legal advice privilege, and their status as a non-party will not exclude them from being able to claim their own litigation privilege to the extent that they communicate with third parties for the dominant purpose of obtaining legal advice in connection with the conduct of the litigation in which they are a witness.[22]

Communications with defence witnesses: confidentiality

9.29 It is a condition of litigation privilege that communications between the witness and the party to the litigation and/or their legal adviser are confidential. However, there need not be a legal obligation of confidence on the witness for the defendant to claim privilege over the communications.[23] Whilst the defendant or their legal representative may approach the witness with the intention of the communications between them being confidential, in practice it may not be possible to enforce this requirement.

9.30 In taking a proof of evidence from a witness, it may be necessary to provide the defendant's confidential or privileged information to them. The court may therefore intervene in cross-examination of the witness at trial if it appears that a line of questioning may lead to disclosure of privileged or confidential information. In the event that a defence witness in criminal proceedings chooses to provide privileged material or information obtained in the course of their communications with the defendant's legal representatives to the court or prosecution, it is open to the court to hold that privilege has been waived or confidentiality has been lost.[24]

---

[19] *R (the Health and Safety Executive) v Jukes* [2018] EWCA Crim 176, [2018] 2 Cr App R 9.
[20] *In the Estate of Fuld (deceased) (No 2 A)* [1965] 3 WLR 162 (PDA).
[21] See eg *R v Crozier* (1990) 12 Cr App R (CA).
[22] *Al Sadeq v Dechert LLP* [2024] EWCA Civ 28.
[23] *Istil Group Inc v Zahoor* [2003] EWHC 165 (Ch), [2003] 2 All ER 252. See also para 1.51.
[24] See eg *R v Crozier* (n 21).

9.31 In some cases a defendant may require a witness to sign a non-disclosure agreement (NDA), which, if breached, may provide a contractual remedy to the defendant. The existence of an NDA will not, however, be relevant when considering whether or not the evidence is admissible.

Communications with defence witnesses by the prosecuting authority

9.32 The CPIA 1996, section 6C was intended to abolish 'trial by ambush' and effectively codifies the principle that there is no property in a witness; the defence cannot prevent the prosecution from seeking to obtain information from a witness intended to be called by the defence (it is, however, open to the witness to decline to be interviewed). Whilst the witness must not be asked to reveal any confidential or privileged information to the investigator if interviewed, there is no restriction on the witness providing their factual account, which will not be privileged, to the investigator.

9.33 The Law Society Practice Note entitled 'Defence Witness Notices'[25] sets out the best practice for defence solicitors in respect of obtaining evidence from defence witnesses and in protecting the defendant's interests in the process. If, having notified the prosecution of the intention to call a defence witness under the CPIA 1996, section 6C, the prosecution wishes to speak to them, the witness has to consent to be interviewed by the investigator (on behalf of the prosecution) and the defendant's solicitor is entitled to be present at the interview. A key part of the defence solicitor's presence will be to ensure that the questioning does not encroach on matters concerning the defendant's privilege or confidentiality.

9.34 The requirements and principles remain the same whether applied to defence witnesses of fact or character.[26]

Prosecution Witnesses

Approaching a prosecution witness

9.35 As a continuation of the principle that there is no property in a witness, it remains open to the defence to interview and take statements from any prosecution witness. When communicating with a prosecution witness, if the defendant or their representatives provide the witness with privileged or confidential information or material, the defendant and/or their representative can require the witness to respect the defendant's confidentiality and privilege. However, in the event that the witness does not abide by this request and relays information to the prosecution, there is likely to be little to prevent the information being deployed by the prosecution as the principles of inadvertent waiver will apply.[27] As with defence witnesses, it is necessary to consider the relative benefit of the information the defendant hopes to obtain from the prosecution witness against the potential risk that

---

[25] The Law Society, 'Defence Witness Notices' (3 March 2021) https://www.lawsociety.org.uk/topics/criminal-justice/defence-witness-notices (accessed 10 June 2023).
[26] ibid para 2.5.
[27] See paras 1.104–1.109.

confidential or privileged information may be shared with the prosecution or investigating agency as part of the process.

9.36 There is no practical distinction in the approach that should be taken when seeking to obtain information and/or a witness statement from witnesses who have provided a statement to the prosecution but upon whom the prosecution does not rely (unused witnesses).

Expert Witnesses

Expert witnesses for the defence

9.37 Litigation privilege protects confidential communications between a defendant or their legal representative and an expert witness if the dominant purpose is to obtain information or evidence to be used in or in connection with the conduct of the criminal proceedings. This includes experts upon whose evidence the defence intend to rely in support of their case, but also experts who may provide assistance to the defence in helping them understand or prepare their case but whose evidence will not be served on the prosecution.[28] It also protects the work product of the expert and any drafts of the expert's reports. The final report produced by the expert is privileged until served in the proceedings.[29]

Expert witnesses: whose privilege?

9.38 The privilege attaching to an expert's draft/unserved report(s) and work product belongs to the defendant. Whilst the material is privileged in the hands of the expert, they cannot assert privilege for their own benefit as the privilege remains that of the defendant. In *Schneider v Leigh*[30] the plaintiff commenced an action for libel against a doctor who had acted as an expert witness instructed by a company who were the defendants in a separate personal injury action commenced by the same plaintiff. The defendants in the personal injury action had written to the plaintiff quoting an extract from the expert's report, but not serving the full report. The question arose of whether the expert could rely on privilege to resist disclosure of his report in the libel action. It was held that the expert could not rely on a free-standing claim of privilege to resist disclosure, as the privilege was not the expert's but belonged to the defendant company in the personal injury action. It is not clear from the judgment whether the company was prepared to waive privilege, but an order was made that inspection of the material should take place after the original personal injury claim was disposed of in order not to infringe the company's privilege.

9.39 Whilst it is not open to an expert unilaterally to waive privilege, if an expert chooses to disclose privileged information contrary to their instructions, it will be open to the court to consider the use to be made of the information provided. In the case of *R v Crozier*[31] a psychiatric expert was engaged to assess a defendant who had pleaded guilty to the attempted murder of his sister. The psychiatrist assessed the defendant as suffering from a

---

[28] This reflects the scope of litigation privilege discussed at para 1.60. See also the Irish case *Ahern v Judge Mahon* [2008] IEHC 119, [2008] 4 IR 704.
[29] *Waugh v British Railways Board* (n 15).
[30] [1955] 2 QB 195 (CA).
[31] *R v Crozier* (n 21).

mental illness of a psychopathic nature, warranting detention in a special hospital. The report was not provided to the defendant's counsel and was not deployed on the defendant's behalf. However, at the sentencing hearing the psychiatrist attended expecting to be called as a witness, and upon hearing the judge pass a sentence of nine years' imprisonment, the psychiatrist approached prosecution counsel and made him aware of the contents of his report. The prosecution then invited the court to vary the sentence in light of the psychiatrist's evidence and the court did so, imposing a hospital order. On appeal it was held that it was open to the judge to hear from the psychiatrist and to vary the sentence accordingly, regardless of the propriety of the psychiatrist's actions (which the court did not criticize); the judge could not ignore the evidence once it was before him.

Expert witnesses: distinction between report and opinion

9.40 A defence expert's draft or unserved final report remains privileged, along with their work product. Disclosure of this material cannot be compelled. However, the principle that there is no property in a witness applies equally to expert witnesses.

9.41 In *Harmony Shipping Co SA v Saudi Europe Line Ltd*[32] a handwriting expert inadvertently accepted instructions from both sides in a civil claim in which the authenticity of a handwritten document was a central issue. The expert advised consistently, advising first the plaintiff and then the defendant that the document was not genuine, before realizing that he had already advised on the document. The defendant sought to subpoena the expert to provide this evidence at trial, to which the plaintiffs objected on the basis that their instructions to the expert were privileged. Whilst making it clear that this was a case that turned on its own facts, the Court of Appeal upheld the trial judge's ruling that the expert could be compelled, stating:

> Many of the communications between the solicitor and the expert witness will be privileged. They are protected by legal professional privilege. They cannot be communicated to the court except with the consent of the party concerned. That means that a great deal of the communications between the expert witness and the lawyer cannot be given in evidence to the court. If questions were asked about it, then it would be the duty of the judge to protect the witness (and he would) by disallowing any questions which infringed the rule about legal professional privilege or the rule protecting information given in confidence—unless, of course, it was one of those rare cases which come before the courts from time to time where in spite of privilege or confidence the court does order a witness to give further evidence. Subject to that qualification, it seems to me that an expert witness falls into the same position as a witness of fact. The court is entitled, in order to ascertain the truth, to have the actual facts which he has observed adduced before it and to have his independent opinion on those facts.[33]

A distinction was drawn between the expert's opinion on the issues in the case and what he had said in his report to the plaintiffs.

---

[32] [1979] 1 WLR 1380 (CA).
[33] ibid 1385.

Material provided to the expert

9.42 An issue involving a handwriting expert also arose in the criminal case of *R v King*.[34] The defence instructed a handwriting expert to examine documents which formed part of the prosecution case against the defendant for conspiracy to defraud. The prosecution sought disclosure of documents provided to the expert for comparison and obtained an order compelling the expert to provide the documents upon which his instruction had been based. One of the documents was supportive of the prosecution case and the defendant was convicted. On appeal, it was argued that the material provided to the expert was privileged and the trial judge ought not to have compelled the expert to produce it. This was dismissed on the basis that the communications between the defendant's representatives and the expert were privileged, but the documents provided were not:

> The rule is that in the case of expert witnesses legal professional privilege attaches to confidential communications between the solicitor and the expert, but it does not attach to the chattels or documents upon which the expert based his opinion, nor to the independent opinion of the expert himself.[35]

9.43 The judgment in *King* raises an important issue of the extent to which material provided to an expert can be compelled to be put before the court. This was further considered in *R v R (Blood Sample: Privilege)*,[36] which concerned the issue of whether a blood sample provided by the defence to an expert was a privileged item and whether the expert could be instructed by the prosecution to give opinion evidence based on an analysis of the sample. The defence had provided the expert with a sample of the defendant's blood which had been taken for the express purpose of instructing the expert. The defence ultimately did not seek to rely upon the expert, but she was called by the prosecution to give evidence on her analysis of the blood sample. The defendant was convicted and appealed his conviction on the grounds that the expert's evidence ought not to have been admitted. The Court of Appeal recognized the ability of the prosecution to call an expert previously instructed by the defence to give their opinion, which would be limited by the normal rules of privilege. The issue in this case was that the expert's evidence was based on a blood sample provided by the defendant, in conditions of confidence, so that her advice could be obtained.

9.44 The Court referred to the statutory definition of 'items subject to legal privilege' as set out in PACE 1984, section 10(1):

> Subject to subsection (2) below, in this Act 'items subject to legal privilege' means—
>
> (a) communications between a professional legal adviser and his client or any person representing his client made in connection with the giving of legal advice to the client;
>
> (b) communications between a professional legal adviser and his client or any person representing his client or between such an adviser or his client or any such representative and any other person made in connection with or in contemplation of legal proceedings and for the purposes of such proceedings; and

---

[34] [1983] 1 WLR 411 (CA).
[35] ibid 414.
[36] [1994] 1 WLR 758 (CA).

(c) items enclosed with or referred to in such communications and made—
   (i) in connection with the giving of legal advice; or
   (ii) in connection with or in contemplation of legal proceedings and for the purposes of such proceedings,
when they are in the possession of a person who is entitled to possession of them.

Interpreting 'made' as synonymous with 'brought into existence', the Court of Appeal held that the blood sample was privileged, having been brought into existence on a confidential basis and enclosed with privileged communications for the purpose of the proceedings, thereby satisfying the requirements for litigation privilege. The fact that the sample itself was privileged meant that the expert's opinion (provided to the prosecution) was not admissible as it could not be divorced from the privileged material on which it was based.

9.45 The decisions in *King* and *R* are consistent with the underlying principles in that, in *King*, the item submitted to the expert for comparison was a pre-existing document that was not privileged to begin with and was not created for the purpose of instructing the expert, whereas the blood sample in *R* was brought into existence for that very purpose.[37] It was noted in *R* that if the expert's analysis had been based upon a sample taken lawfully from the defendant by the police, then her evidence would have been admissible as privilege over the sample, if privileged at all, would have belonged to the police/prosecution.

9.46 This position was confirmed in the case of *R v Davies*,[38] which concerned expert psychiatric evidence. The defendant had been assessed by a Dr Cope, whose report did not support the defence of diminished responsibility which he advanced. Another expert, Dr Haldane, produced a report which made reference to Dr Cope's report, and this was served by the defence. The prosecution called Dr Cope to give evidence of her opinion of the defendant's mental state. The Court of Appeal, allowing the appeal against conviction, rejected this approach. It was not open to the prosecution to call Dr Cope, on the basis that this intruded on the defendant's privilege, which had not been waived. The Court held the case to be indistinguishable from *R* as Dr Cope's opinion was based on privileged information:

> In our judgment, the judge was wrong to decide that Dr Cope's opinion resulted from a doctor/patient relationship. There was no question of Dr Cope treating the appellant. The purpose—certainly the dominant purpose—of her visit to him in prison was to form an opinion of his mental state and to report to his solicitors, all for the purpose of enabling them to advise him in relation to his defence in the proceedings in which he was charged and to conduct his defence. Her opinion was based, at least to a material extent, on privileged communications. She received documents from the solicitors, some of which were privileged. She may have observed facts about the appellant which did not depend on him consciously communicating with her. But the occasion of her visit was privileged and his communications to her on that occasion were privileged. In her evidence, she was obliged

---

[37] An authority considered in each of these cases is that of *W v Edgell* [1990] Ch 359 (CA), which was held in both *King* and *R* to be concerned with confidentiality rather than privilege and as such is not considered in this chapter.
[38] [2002] EWCA Crim 85, (2002) 166 JP 243.

to report things which he had said to her. Thus her opinion then was based on privileged material. In so far as it may also have been in part based on mere observation, the opinion was nevertheless inextricably dependent on privileged material. This did not change because she additionally heard the evidence of Dr Haldane. The critical part of her opinion remained inextricably dependent on privileged material.[39]

Privileged material referred to in expert reports

9.47 There is a clear difference between what an expert is required to include in their report in civil proceedings compared to criminal proceedings. Under Civil Procedure Rule 35.10(3), an expert must 'state the substance of all material instructions, whether written or oral, on the basis of which the report was written.' Civil Procedure Rule 35.10(4) states that the instructions in Rule 35.10(3) 'shall not be privileged against disclosure', although the court will not, in relation to those instructions, order disclosure of any specific document or permit questioning in court unless satisfied that there are 'reasonable grounds to consider the statement of instructions given under paragraph (3) to be inaccurate or incomplete.' There is no equivalent in the Criminal Procedure Rules expressly requiring instructions to be stated, only requirements to state 'information which the expert has relied on in making the report' (Rule 19.4(b)) and 'the substance of all facts given to the expert which are material to the opinions expressed in the report, or upon which those opinions are based' (Rule 19.4(c)).

9.48 Notwithstanding these requirements, an expert in criminal proceedings may nevertheless decide to record their instructions in the report and/or make reference to privileged documents provided to them. This carries a risk of waiver.

9.49 There is some doubt over whether there is a different test for waiver in respect of privileged material referred to in an expert report compared to other statements of fact and documents served during the course of litigation.[40] In *Clough v Tameside and Glossop HA*[41] the defendants obtained a statement from a doctor regarding the treatment of the plaintiff and provided it to an expert as part of his instructions for the preparation of a report. The expert's report, which the defendants disclosed, made reference to the fact the expert had been provided with the statement from the doctor. Bracewell J held that this waived privilege over the doctor's statement. It mattered not whether the expert considered the statement material or if they found it unhelpful or even irrelevant; the mere fact it had been provided in order for the expert to consider it as part of the background information in formulating his opinion was sufficient. Bracewell J considered experts to be in a special and unique category of witness. She stated as follows:

> An essential element of the process is for a party to know and to be able to test in evidence the information supplied to the experts, in order to ascertain if the opinion is based on a sound factual basis, or on disputed matters or hypothetical facts yet to be determined by the courts. If an expert has discounted some evidence supplied to him, he may, at the conclusion of the case, be held wrong to have done so and his opinion may thereby be invalidated. Equally, he may have assumed an incorrect significance for a particular piece of

---

[39] ibid [32].
[40] See discussion of waiver of privilege in ch 1, s 5.
[41] [1998] 1 WLR 1478 (QB).

material. It is only by proper and full disclosure to all parties, that an expert's opinion can be tested in court, in order to ascertain whether all appropriate information was supplied and how the expert dealt with it. It is not for one party to keep their cards face down on the table so that the other party does not know the full extent of information supplied. Fairness dictates that a party should not be forced to meet a case pleaded or an expert opinion on the basis of documents he cannot see.[42]

9.50 A number of subsequent authorities have questioned the validity of *Clough* when considering the same or similar issues. This includes several Court of Appeal authorities.[43] In *Lucas v Barking*,[44] although it was suggested that had the case been decided under the law before the introduction of the Civil Procedure Rules (as was the case in *Clough*), Bracewell J's approach would likely have been followed, this was on the basis that, in *Lucas*, the contents of a privileged statement were being *deployed* in the expert evidence. The Court quoted with approval a passage from *Disclosure*[45] that noted that deployment was the key issue for waiver and that 'a mere reference to a privileged document in an affidavit does not of itself amount to a waiver of privilege'. The discussion that followed clearly considered deployment to be the key issue.[46] Similarly, in *Bourns Inc v Raychem Corp (No 3)*[47] Aldous LJ suggested that 'the result reached by the judge in *Clough* was probably correct', but he added: 'I cannot support all her statements as to the law.' He noted that Bracewell J had not been referred to a number of relevant cases.[48] He went on to say that 'mere reference to a document does not waive privilege in that document: there must at least be reference to the contents and reliance'.[49] Swinton Thomas LJ added that he wished to reserve for future consideration whether, even on its own facts, *Clough* was correctly decided.[50]

9.51 *Clough* has also been discussed by the Court of Appeal in a criminal case, albeit the comments were obiter. In *R v Davies*[51] it was not necessary for the Court to determine whether the decision in *Clough* was correctly decided and, if it was, whether it should apply in a criminal context. However, the Court considered that 'It could not, we think, apply absolutely, since the court has a discretion under section 78 of [PACE 1984] to exclude evidence which in fairness ought not to be admitted'. The Court would, if necessary, have adopted the approach in *Phipson on Evidence*[52] 'to the effect that passing reference to another document would not necessarily amount to waiver'.[53]

9.52 It is the view of the authors that were the Court of Appeal to be asked to determine this issue directly in a future criminal case, it would not fully adopt *Clough*. As a first instance

---

[42] ibid 1484.
[43] See also *Sands v Gardiner* [2012] NIQB 29 [9]; *BSA International SA v Irvine* [2009] CSOH 77, 2009 SLT 1180 [16]–[17].
[44] [2003] EWCA Civ 1102, [2004] 1 WLR 220.
[45] Paul Matthews and Hodge Malek, *Disclosure* (2nd edn, Sweet & Maxwell).
[46] *Lucas v Barking* (n 44) [18]–[22].
[47] [1999] 3 All ER 154 (CA).
[48] ibid 164.
[49] ibid 166–67.
[50] ibid 172.
[51] *R v Davies* (n 38).
[52] MN Howard, Peter Crane, and Daniel A Hochberg (eds), *Phipson on Evidence* (14th edn, Sweet & Maxwell 1990).
[53] *R v Davies* (n 38) [37]–[38].

decision, it would not be binding authority, and the doubt cast around its correctness in subsequent authorities, including from the Court of Appeal and, in particular, the obiter comments in *Davies*, would most likely lead to the Court looking instead to the preponderance of other authorities supporting the notion that, for the purposes of waiver, reliance on or deployment of the content or substance of a privileged document is required, rather than mere reference.

9.53 However, even if *Clough* is disregarded, the risk of waiver remains if the nature and extent of an expert's reference to privileged material is such that it crosses the threshold into reliance on or deployment of the content or substance of the material where fairness requires it to be disclosed in full, engaging the waiver principles discussed at paras 1.88–1.93. This will be fact-specific.

9.54 As far as instructions to an expert are concerned, it is common practice for experts to set out in their report the questions they have been asked to address by the instructing party. These will most likely be taken from the letter of instruction or other communication between the defendant's legal representatives and the expert, which will be covered by litigation privilege. As to the effect on privilege of serving the report, it is the view of the authors that merely stating the questions asked in an expert report ought not to result in a waiver of privilege over the whole letter of instruction. It is difficult to characterize this as *reliance* on the content of the privileged document. The expert is not *relying* on the questions; they are merely referring to them and responding accordingly. Furthermore, there is no risk of the court or prosecution being given only an incomplete or inaccurate picture of the questions that have been asked to the expert if the expert has listed them all, so fairness would seem not to require there to be a waiver. Moreover, were the opposite to be true, a defendant would effectively waive privilege automatically whenever serving an expert report if, as will invariably be the case, it contained the questions put to the expert. This would amount to a disproportionate inroad into privilege.

9.55 A different approach might be taken if the expert states other information from the letter of instruction in their report, for example background facts or details of the defence case. If the expert relies on these facts in forming their opinion, there is more scope for arguing that this amounts to reliance on the content of the privileged correspondence, and fairness would likely require disclosure of the full information provided to the expert to allow the court and prosecution to test the reliability of their opinion.

9.56 The practical effect of waiver of privilege on this basis in criminal proceedings is that the prosecution will be entitled to cross-examine the expert on the information or material over which privilege has been waived. As the defence do not have the same disclosure obligations as a party in civil proceedings, arguments about waiver are unlikely to concern the production of documents.

9.57 In many cases the risk of waiver will be unavoidable. Experts need to be briefed on the background to the case and questions have to be put to them. Nevertheless, lawyers should limit the material provided to an expert only to what is necessary in order for them to carry out their function. Highly sensitive privileged documents such as the defendant's proof of evidence should never be provided, and lawyers should think carefully about what they say to an expert.

Expert shopping

In civil proceedings, if, having already instructed one expert, a party instructs a new one, the court may order that the previous expert's report is served. This is to deter 'expert shopping', or the practice of seeking out a new expert where the originally instructed expert's opinion is unfavourable. **9.58**

In criminal proceedings, the disclosure obligations on the prosecution mean that it would be difficult, if not impossible, for the prosecution to engage in 'expert shopping' as material in the prosecution's hands which undermines the prosecution case or supports the defence case, such as an unfavourable expert report, would pass the disclosure test and fall to be disclosed to the defence, even if it was privileged (see discussion in Chapter 8, Section 4). **9.59**

The CPIA 1996, section 6D[54] was drafted with the intention of deterring the defence from engaging in expert shopping in criminal proceedings. However, despite being inserted by the Criminal Justice Act 2003, this provision is still not in force. The defendant in criminal proceedings therefore currently benefits from the protection of litigation privilege over unused expert reports. **9.60**

Joint instructions

Crim PR 19.7 permits the court to direct that expert evidence is given by a single expert jointly instructed by co-defendants (a 'single joint expert'). The manner in which this expert is to be instructed is set out at Crim PR 19.8, which states that each co-defendant who is a party to the joint instruction must provide a copy of their instructions to the expert to each other co-defendant. **9.61**

There is an absence of authority regarding the extent to which co-defendants in criminal proceedings can be compelled to instruct a single joint expert where there is a conflict between their positions. It would seem unlikely from a case management perspective that this would be allowed to arise, given that the sharing of instructions would require sharing of privileged material. **9.62**

4 Communications between Co-defendants

A defendant in criminal proceedings can share privileged information with a co-defendant in the same proceedings without waiving privilege as against the prosecution. **9.63**

---

[54] CPIA 1996, s 6D(1) states as follows: 'If the accused instructs a person with a view to his providing any expert opinion for possible use as evidence the trial of the accused, he must give to the court and the prosecutor a notice specifying the person's name and address.'

This can be done on the basis of common interest privilege or on the basis that privileged information can be shared on a confidential and limited basis without privilege being lost.[55]

9.64 Whilst co-defendants can share privileged material between themselves, it is important to ensure that the appropriate claim to privilege is identified before material is shared. For example, communications with third parties made at the pre-charge stage, when litigation may not have been reasonably in contemplation, might be shared with co-defendants once a prosecution is underway. If a claim to privilege cannot be made over a particular communication, once it is shared there is no restriction on the use the receiving party may make of it.[56]

9.65 The position on waiver of common interest privilege is not entirely straightforward. The authors of *The Law of Privilege*[57] suggest that the original, or primary, privilege holder can waive privilege without the permission of the consent of those with whom privilege has been shared, but there is no English authority which directly addresses the point. The issue of whether one party's waiver of common interest privilege waives privilege for all is likely to be determined as a question of fairness based on the specific circumstances,[58] but again there is no English authority on the point. It therefore appears possible that waiver by one party to common interest privilege may lead to waiver for all of the parties, and it would be wise to advise clients of that potential risk.

5 Seeking Disclosure of Privileged Material

Prosecution Witnesses: Disclosure of Draft and Unused Statements

9.66 As set out at para 9.23, litigation privilege applies to drafts of witness statements, or unserved witness statements taken from defence witnesses. These documents in the hands of the defence are protected from compelled production. Applying the same principles, draft witness statements of prosecution witnesses, and statements taken from unused prosecution witnesses, will also be subject to litigation privilege; they are confidential communications between a party to the proceedings or their legal representative and a third party for the dominant purpose of conducting litigation. However, the fact that they are privileged does not in practice exempt them from disclosure as the prosecution treats its disclosure requirements under the CPIA 1996 as paramount for the conduct of a fair trial and will disclose privileged documents if they meet the disclosure test. For a detailed consideration of the prosecution's ability to claim privilege and the relationship with statutory disclosure obligations, see Chapter 8.

---

[55] See paras 1.77–1.79 and 1.116–1.117.
[56] *WXY v Gewanter* [2012] EWHC 1071 (QB).
[57] Bankim Thanki (ed), *The Law of Privilege* (3rd edn, OUP 2018) paras 6.61–6.62.
[58] See eg *Farrow Mortgage Services Pty Ltd v Webb* (1996) 39 NSWLR 601 (CA NSW); *Patrick v Capital Finance Corporation (Australasia) Pty Ltd* [2004] FCA 1249.

Disclosure and Litigation Privilege: Common Law and CPIA 1996 Duties

9.67 The Attorney General's Guidelines on Disclosure 2022[59] identify categories of material which are likely to meet the test for disclosure. These include any previous accounts made by a complainant or any other witness, and interview records with actual or potential witnesses or suspects.

9.68 The CPIA 1996 governs the disclosure process and applies from the point of a not guilty plea in the magistrates' court. This does not mean that there are no disclosure obligations before this point, as the common law duty of disclosure applies from the point at which a suspect is charged with an offence. The common law duty of disclosure requires a prosecutor to disclose material in accordance with the interests of justice or fairness. The CPS Disclosure Manual states that:

> In all cases, irrespective of anticipated plea, the officer must comply with the common law disclosure obligations and certify that, to the best of the officer's knowledge and belief, no information has been withheld which would assist the accused in the preparation of the defence case, including the making of a bail application. A copy of any material which the investigator considers should be disclosed must be provided to the prosecutor, who will immediately disclose it to the defence if they consider it meets the test. Examples of what should be disclosed are:
>
> - any previous convictions of the victim or a key witness if that information could reasonably be expected to assist the accused when applying for bail;
> - material which might enable an accused to make an early application to stay the proceedings as an abuse of process;
> - material which might enable an accused to make representations about trial venue on a lesser charge; or
> - material which would enable an accused to prepare for trial which may be significantly less effective if disclosure is delayed (e.g. names of eyewitnesses whom the prosecution does not intend to use).
>
> This list is not exhaustive and disclosure prior to the statutory duty arising will not exceed the disclosure which would be required under the CPIA 1996.[60]

9.69 Draft and unused witness statements, and other prosecution material which might be privileged, fall to be disclosed under the CPIA 1996 but are also disclosable under common law principles which apply from the point at which a suspect is charged.[61] The prosecution's obligations to disclose this material are therefore not limited to the obligations under the CPIA 1996. In some cases early disclosure is requested and/or provided under the common law before the CPIA 1996 obligations arise if there are circumstances which require immediate

---

[59] Attorney General's Office, 'Attorney General's Guidelines on Disclosure' (26 May 2022) https://www.gov.uk/government/publications/attorney-generals-guidelines-on-disclosure (accessed 10 June 2023).
[60] CPS, 'Disclosure Manual: Chapter 2—General Duties of Disclosure Outside the CPIA 1996' (21 October 2021) https://www.cps.gov.uk/legal-guidance/disclosure-manual-chapter-2-general-duties-disclosure-outside-cpia-1996 (accessed 10 June 2023).
[61] *R v DPP ex p Lee* [1999] 1 WLR 1950 (QB).

disclosure in the interests of justice or fairness, for example if the material goes to the issue of bail.[62]

No Distinction between Prosecuting Bodies

9.70 The principles of the CPIA 1996 and common law disclosure apply to any individual or body acting as a prosecutor, including a prosecution brought by a private individual.

Third Party's Privileged Material in the Prosecution's Hands

9.71 The CPIA 1996 Code of Practice[63] requires the retention of material of any kind which may be relevant to the investigation, including information and objects. This material should be recorded on the schedule of non-sensitive unused material. If material exists which the disclosure officer believes should be withheld from the defence on the grounds of sensitivity, it should be scheduled on the sensitive material schedule.[64] The CPIA 1996 Code of Practice states that 'the disclosure officer must list on a sensitive schedule any material the disclosure of which he believes would give rise to a real risk of serious prejudice to an important public interest, and the reason for that belief'.[65] It then lists examples of the types of material which may be considered to be sensitive. One example cited is 'material given in confidence', but there is no reference to privileged material. Whilst it is possible that material provided in confidence could include privileged material, in practice privileged items are unlikely to be listed on the sensitive schedule. As explained in Chapter 8, Section 4, the prosecution will usually disclose privileged material that meets the disclosure test. Disclosure will only be withheld if the material is not relevant (and therefore will not be recorded on either the sensitive or non-sensitive schedules) or it is relevant but does not meet the test for disclosure. The fact that the material is privileged will not be a reason for withholding disclosure or treating it as sensitive. For material to be listed on the sensitive schedule, a balancing exercise is required in order to determine whether the risk of serious prejudice to an important public interest outweighs the benefit to the defendant of having sight of the material. This balancing exercise has no application to privilege.[66]

---

[62] See further discussion in CPS (n 60).
[63] 'Criminal Procedure and Investigations Act 1996 (section 23(1)) Code of Practice' (March 2015) https://assets.publishing.service.gov.uk/government/uploads/system/uploads/attachment_data/file/447967/code-of-practice-approved.pdf (accessed 9 October 2023).
[64] CPS, 'Disclosure Manual: Chapter 8—The Sensitive Material Schedule' (21 October 2021) https://www.cps.gov.uk/legal-guidance/disclosure-manual-chapter-2-general-duties-disclosure-outside-cpia-1996 (accessed 9 October 2023).
[65] 'Criminal Procedure and Investigations Act 1996 (section 23(1)) Code of Practice' (March 2015) para 6.15 https://assets.publishing.service.gov.uk/government/uploads/system/uploads/attachment_data/file/447967/code-of-practice-approved.pdf (accessed 9 October 2023).
[66] In *R v Derby Magistrates' Court, ex p B* [1996] AC 487, 508 (HL) it was said that: 'Legal professional privilege and public interest immunity are as different in their origin as they are in their scope. Putting it another way, if a balancing exercise was ever required in the case of legal professional privilege, it was performed once and for all in the 16th century, and since then has applied across the board in every case, irrespective of the client's individual merits.' See further discussion in ch 8, s 4.

9.72 The defence is entitled, having served a defence statement compliant with the CPIA 1996, section 6A, to request disclosure of items on the schedule of non-sensitive unused material which pass the disclosure test. If it appears to the defence that an item listed on the schedule refers to material which is subject to privilege and the privilege does not belong to the prosecution, this does not preclude the ability of the defence to request its disclosure. Depending on the manner in which the material has been provided to the prosecution, privilege over the material may have been lost or waived. Regardless of the basis on which the prosecution hold it, the prosecution's disclosure obligations apply to all material in its possession and disclosure will not be resisted on the grounds of privilege (see paras 7.33–7.35 and Chapter 8, Section 4).

9.73 The rules in respect of the admissibility of privileged material in circumstances where there has been inadvertent disclosure are set out at paras 1.104–1.109. The paramount consideration is the test for exclusion set out in PACE 1984, section 78, namely whether, having regard to all the circumstances, the admission of the evidence would have such an adverse effect on the fairness of the proceedings that the court ought not to admit it. Once waiver has been deemed to have taken place, the fact that the material was once privileged is not relevant to the assessment of admissibility.

9.74 It may be possible for a third party who has inadvertently disclosed privileged material to the prosecution to seek to injunct or restrain its onward transmission. The onus would be on the third party to do so, and unless such an order is made, it is the view of the authors that the prosecution's disclosure obligations will be the paramount consideration and will take precedence over any perceived obligations of confidence to the third party.

Reliance on Part of a Privileged Document

9.75 The general principle is that if disclosure of part of a privileged document results in a waiver, the waiver extends to the whole document unless the document deals with two entirely different subject matters and can effectively be divided into two separate documents each dealing with entirely separate matters.[67]

9.76 What if a document over which privilege purports to have been waived is served or disclosed by the prosecution, but the document contains redactions? In this scenario it may not be immediately clear whether the principle has been correctly applied, and it would be legitimate to seek clarification of the reason for the redaction. For example, a redaction may have been applied for reasons other than a claim of privilege, such as to prevent disclosure of a witness' address or other personal details, in which case no issue is likely to arise.

9.77 If redactions have been applied due to a claim of privilege, this will only be permissible if the privilege relates to an entirely separate incident or matter which is not relevant to the current proceedings or, if it is relevant, the information does not meet the disclosure test under the CPIA 1996. This is because, if the redacted information is relevant and meets the

---

[67] *Great Atlantic Insurance v Home Insurance Co* [1981] 1 WLR 529, 536 (CA).

6 Deploying Defence Privileged Material

9.78 It may be the defence strategy to deploy the defendant's own privileged material in their defence. If this is the case, whilst it should be possible to limit the waiver to the proceedings in question,[68] the principles of collateral waiver will apply and the defendant will be taken to have waived privilege over other material relating to the same issue (see paras 1.94–1.96). This will enable the prosecution (and any co-defendant) to adduce evidence of hitherto privileged matters at trial, whether that be through cross-examination of the defendant or by calling additional witnesses such as a current or former legal representative of the defendant. This issue is discussed further at paras 10.27–10.34 in relation to waiving privilege over previous legal advice, particularly police station advice. It is important to bear in mind that the parameters of collateral waiver will be determined objectively, and whilst the defendant's intentions, and/or that of their advisers, may assist the court in identifying the parameters of the waiver, they are not determinative.

9.79 Careful consideration will be required in the event that the defendant wishes to deploy material which is subject to another party's privilege. Privilege can only be waived by the privilege holder, not by the legal adviser or a third party. In the case of a lawyer who is charged with a criminal offence in relation to a client's matter, the SRA's guidance makes clear that whilst there may be circumstances where confidential client information may be disclosed, privilege is absolute.[69] They would not be permitted to rely upon privileged information as part of their defence unless they had their client's permission.[70]

9.80 Whilst there will be serious professional consequences for a legal professional who breaches a client's privilege, the consequences for a defendant who wishes to breach another party's privilege may be civil or regulatory action.

---

[68] Although a loss of confidentiality over the material during the course of court proceedings will mean that confidentiality, and therefore privilege, is lost in its entirety.
[69] SRA, 'Confidentiality of Client Information' Guidance (30 June 2022) https://www.sra.org.uk/solicitors/guidance/confidentiality-client-information/ (accessed 10 June 2023).
[70] *R v Devani* [2007] EWCA Crim 1926, [2008] 1 Cr App R 4. This case is discussed in detail at paras 10.47–10.60.

10
Court Proceedings

1 Introduction

This chapter considers the particular issues which can arise during court proceedings which may impact on the ability to rely on privilege. There are two potential issues at play: first, matters discussed in open court are no longer confidential, so there is a risk of privilege being lost as a result of confidentiality being lost; secondly, the defendant or their legal representative may disclose privileged material or information in circumstances which expressly or impliedly allow its use by the other party or the court, thereby waiving privilege over that material and potentially all other material relating to the same issue through 'collateral waiver'. The law surrounding loss and waiver of privilege generally is discussed in Chapter 1, Section 5. Much of the focus of this chapter is on the principles of loss and waiver of privilege, whether deliberate or inadvertent, at court during criminal proceedings and the practical implications of decisions which may be taken during the conduct of a trial, in particular during live evidence.

10.01

2 Intentional Disclosure of Privileged Documents

Disclosure by the Prosecution

Privileged documents belonging to a third party
A complainant or cooperating party, whether an individual or a company, may provide privileged material to the police or other investigating agency in order to assist with an investigation and/or potential prosecution. This is particularly common where a corporate entity is under investigation and voluntarily discloses privileged documents to the investigating authority as a mark of cooperation and in the hope of avoiding prosecution (see Chapter 7). This will have the effect of waiving privilege over the material (either expressly or impliedly), but it is possible for the waiver to be limited so that collateral use of the material is prevented. The extent to which the information remains privileged once in the hands of the prosecution will depend on the use that is made of it and the extent to which it remains confidential as against the rest of the world. In the event of a prosecution against one or more third parties, the prosecuting authority will have statutory disclosure obligations and will be required to disclose the privileged material to the defence if it meets the disclosure test. If the material is then read in open court during the course of those proceedings and thereby enters the public domain, confidentiality (and therefore privilege) will be lost (see paras 7.25–7.32), notwithstanding the terms of the original limited waiver.

10.02

The Criminal Procedure and Investigations Act 1996 (CPIA 1996) limits the collateral use that can be made of unused material.[1] Under section 17, a defendant can only use the

10.03

---
[1] See also *Taylor v Director of the Serious Fraud Office* [1999] 2 AC 177 (HL).

material for a purpose unrelated to the proceedings in which it has been disclosed with the permission of the court. However, this does not apply if the information has been 'communicated to the public in open court' (section 17(3)), in which case collateral use of disclosed prosecution material is permissible. This supports the position that confidentiality over a document or the information it contains is lost if it becomes public. It is therefore worth considering how 'communicated to the public' may be interpreted, and the extent to which confidential material can be deployed in a trial without losing confidentiality and privilege.

10.04 In *SL Claimants v Tesco PLC*[2] the claimants sought damages for losses incurred due to the overstatement by Tesco PLC of its trading profits. The Serious Fraud Office (SFO) conducted an investigation and commenced proceedings for fraud and false accounting against various directors and employees of Tesco, which resulted in a criminal trial and a subsequent re-trial. Tesco provided a number of privileged documents to the SFO under a limited waiver. One such document was sought by the claimants in the civil proceedings in an application for specific disclosure. The application was made on the basis that the document had been deployed in open court during the criminal proceedings and was therefore no longer confidential or privileged.

10.05 The document in question was a note of a meeting between an in-house lawyer at Tesco and Tesco's external advisers, Freshfields. Its disclosure to the defendants in the criminal proceedings led to requests for further disclosure in those proceedings, including the note of a similar meeting which had taken place between Tesco's General Counsel and Tesco's external advisers. Tesco declined to waive privilege over this additional note, and therefore it was not in the hands of the SFO. An application was made for a witness summons requiring one of the Freshfields lawyers to produce the note of the meeting with Tesco's General Counsel. The application was made in open court, and in the course of the application, submissions were made by counsel for two of the defendants in the criminal trial which extensively referred to the disclosed note in arguing for disclosure of the other document. Counsel quoted the first paragraph of the disclosed note and then invited the judge to read the first three pages of the note to himself, which he did. Counsel then described the contents of the disclosed note, without quoting any further sections. Counsel for Tesco also made submissions which included reference to the disclosed note and the reading of short extracts from the first three pages of the note. The witness summons application was ultimately unsuccessful, but the issue raised by the claimants in the civil proceedings was that the references to the disclosed note in the course of this application were extensive enough to amount to a loss of its confidentiality and therefore its privileged status.

10.06 The judge determining the claimants' application for disclosure held that the note was not deployed in the criminal proceedings in such a way as to constitute a waiver of privilege and that therefore the only issue to be determined was whether confidentiality in the disclosed note had been lost due to the manner in which it had been referred to in the witness summons application. He drew a distinction between the information in a document and

---

[2] [2019] EWHC 3315 (Ch), [2019] All ER (D) 30 (Dec).

the document itself and was of the view that, in this case, the references made in open court did not amount to a loss of confidentiality in the document itself, only the specific sections quoted. The judge also referred to the ability under the Criminal Procedure Rules for members of the public to apply for access to documents placed before the court and referred to during a hearing through the principle of open justice. The relevant Criminal PD at the time stated that:

> Open justice requires only access to the part of the document that has been read aloud. If a member of the public requests a copy of such a document, the court should consider whether it is proportionate to order one of the parties to produce a suitably redacted version. If not, access to the document is unlikely to be granted; however open justice will generally have been satisfied by the document having been read out in court.[3]

The judge noted that no such application had been made by the claimants and took the view that, had such an application been made in respect of the disclosed note, it would not have succeeded. It was held that the document remained confidential and privileged and disclosure would not be ordered.

10.07 This case examined loss of confidentiality and privilege as regards disclosed unused material. However, the principles are equally applicable to served prosecution evidence. What matters for the purposes of loss of confidentiality is how the material is used in open court rather than what type of material it is.

Disclosure by the Defence

Privileged documents belonging to a third party

10.08 If a defendant seeks to rely upon a privileged document, the issues which arise may vary depending on the status of the privilege holder. If the privilege holder is a third party then the defendant will require the privilege holder's consent to use the document in a way that may lead to privilege being lost or waived. There is a very real risk of this happening if the material is deployed at trial. Whilst the defendant can try to limit the waiver to applying only to those proceedings, waiver is assessed objectively and it will not preclude the court from finding that privilege has in fact been waived more widely. Furthermore, regardless of the terms of any limited waiver, confidentiality will be lost if the document or the information it contains becomes public as a result of being read in open court. This will, of course, be fact-specific, and the defendant and any third-party privilege holder should be advised of the risks accordingly.

10.09 What are the implications if a defendant is in possession of privileged material and the privilege holder does not consent to its use in the proceedings? For example, an ex-employee may be in possession of privileged documents from their time as an employee, but their ex-employer, as the privilege holder, may not consent to disclosure of the material to any third party. The potential consequences of disclosing the privileged material without consent will vary depending on the particular circumstances but could be very

---

[3] Crim PD 2015, 5B.14.

serious. It is inadvisable, and extremely risky, to deploy privileged material without the consent of the privilege holder, and any defendant seeking to do so should be advised accordingly. It may be open to the privilege holder to restrain or injunct against the use of the material, or there may be other contractual or statutory consequences depending on the status of the privilege holder and the relationship between the privilege holder and the defendant.

10.10 Where relevant material is in the possession of a third party and the defendant does not have a copy, it is open to the defendant to seek disclosure of the material via a witness summons which, if granted, would allow for its deployment in the proceedings. However, if the material sought is privileged, it will not be possible to compel its disclosure.[4] The witness summons application will only succeed if the defendant can demonstrate that the documents are not privileged (for example because the crime-fraud exception applies) or that privilege has otherwise been lost or waived. In *R v Derby Magistrates Court ex p B*[5] a defendant in a murder trial made an application for a witness summons against the solicitor of a previously acquitted defendant in respect of the same murder. The application sought production of the attendance notes and proofs of evidence disclosing the factual instructions of the acquitted defendant prepared when he had been charged with the murder. The magistrates' court granted the summons, reasoning that a balancing exercise should be conducted between the privilege of the acquitted defendant on the one hand, and the current defendant's right to a fair trial on the other. On appeal this approach was rejected by the House of Lords, with Millett LJ making clear that once privilege has been established there is no exception to its absolute nature.[6] If it is demonstrated that the material is privileged then its disclosure cannot be compelled. The use to which it might be put if produced is irrelevant.

Privileged documents belonging to the defendant: documents relating to a separate matter

10.11 In circumstances where a defendant seeks to waive their own privilege in order to deploy a privileged document in their defence, it will be necessary to identify with sufficient particularity the issue over which privilege is waived. The extent of the waiver will not be defined by the defendant's intention alone, but by an objective assessment of the issue to which the disclosed material relates. It is unlikely to be confined to a single document.

10.12 A defendant may wish to waive privilege over material that relates to a separate matter and has not been generated in the course of the current criminal proceedings. For example, a defendant in a fraud trial may seek to rely upon advice given by a solicitor in respect of the formation of a company by producing and relying upon a letter of advice from the solicitor setting out the options for structuring the company. Whilst the defendant may choose to waive privilege over the letter from the solicitor only, the issue over which privilege is being waived is the advice sought and received in respect of the company's formation. This will therefore likely permit the defendant, and potentially the legal adviser, to be cross-examined in respect of the instructions given by the defendant and any other information upon which

---

[4] See para 3.31.
[5] [1996] AC 487 (HL).
[6] ibid 508.

the advice was based, as well as other advice on the same issue that is not contained in the letter. The principle of collateral waiver means that a party must not be permitted to 'cherry-pick' by waiving privilege over material which assists their case, whilst maintaining privilege over unhelpful material.[7]

The defendant must therefore be advised that in waiving privilege over a particular document, privilege will be waived over all communications relating to the same issue. In serving or deploying a privileged document on a defendant's behalf, their legal representative should set out, ideally in writing, the defendant's intentions regarding the parameters of the waiver. If the material is served in advance of trial either within a witness statement or exhibited by a witness statement, it would be wise to set out the terms of the limited waiver in the covering letter and/or any exhibiting statement. If it is to be introduced in examination-in-chief, it is similarly likely to assist the parties and the court to set out the parameters of the limited waiver orally before the material is referred to in open court. Whilst this will not be determinative of the extent of the waiver, it makes clear that the decision has been taken in a considered manner and will be a relevant factor which the court will take into consideration if required to determine the issue further. **10.13**

Privileged documents belonging to the defendant: documents relating to current proceedings
Where a defendant seeks to waive privilege over an aspect of the advice given in respect of the current proceedings, it is again important to identify the parameters of the issue over which privilege will be waived. This typically arises in respect of waiving privilege over advice given at the police station, particularly where a defendant seeks to avoid an adverse inference direction and adduces evidence of the instructions given to their legal adviser at the police station (see further below at paras 10.27–10.34) to rebut an assumption of recent fabrication. In these circumstances care should be taken on the defendant's behalf to ensure that the waiver goes no further than is necessary to rebut the assumption. **10.14**

In *R v Hall*[8] one of the defendants in a six-handed murder trial, O'Toole, sought to rebut the assumption that his defence was a recent fabrication by calling his solicitor to give evidence of the instructions he gave at the police station. In advance of being called to give evidence, the defendant's team disclosed copies of the solicitor's police station notes, which were set out on a pro forma document containing their advice, along with other privileged information. It was held on appeal that in disclosing the full notes the defendant had waived privilege over the entire content of the notes, not just in respect of the matters which were relevant to determining when the facts now relied upon were disclosed. The judgment noted that this voluntary waiver was entirely avoidable: **10.15**

> In this case it would have been possible for O'Toole's solicitor to be called to give evidence and asked a series of discrete questions relating to the individual pieces of his evidence which it was suggested had been late fabrications. For example, as affects the appellant, the solicitor could have been asked whether O'Toole had given an account of anything said by the appellant at the relevant times and if so what that account was.

---

[7] See further discussion at paras 1.94–1.96 and *Nea Karteria Maritime Co Ltd v Atlantic & Great Lakes Steamship Corp (No 2)* [1981] Comm LR 138, 139 (QB).
[8] [2015] EWCA Crim 581, [2015] All ER (D) 41 (Apr).

However that was not the course followed. Instead, the attendance notes containing a more extended account from O'Toole were disclosed. In accordance with ordinary principles of waiver of legal professional privilege, summarised in [*R v Seaton* [2011] 1 WLR 623 [43]], privilege was undoubtedly waived in respect of the whole content of the attendance notes.[9]

In voluntarily disclosing the full notes it was therefore permissible for the defendant to be asked questions about other aspects of his account recorded in the notes which the prosecution would otherwise not have been able to ask had there been no waiver of privilege. This demonstrates the extreme care that must be taken when making decisions regarding waiver of privilege, particularly in the course of a trial, when the issues are developing at pace.

3 Inadvertent Disclosure of Privileged Documents

Inadvertent Disclosure by the Defence to the Prosecution

10.16 One of the key areas in which the civil and criminal jurisprudence diverge is the consequences which flow from the inadvertent disclosure of privileged material by, or on behalf of, the defendant. It is possible in civil proceedings to take steps to restrain the use that can be made of privileged material which is disclosed inadvertently. For public policy reasons, this is not the case in criminal proceedings, where the courts have deemed it necessary to allow the prosecution to make use of privileged material even if it has been obtained without the privilege holder intending it to be disclosed or for privilege to be waived over it.[10]

10.17 In the vast majority of cases dealing with the inadvertent disclosure of privileged or confidential material, the issue arises due to acts or omissions on the part of the legal advisers. This serves as a reminder of the importance of safeguarding privileged material, as the courts have made clear that when considering whether a waiver has taken place, the test is an objective rather than subjective one; the intentions of the privilege holder and/or their advisers are not determinative.[11]

10.18 In *R v Tompkins*[12] a privileged note passed from the defendant to his counsel during the course of his criminal trial came into the possession of the prosecution team. The note was found on the courtroom floor by a legal assistant in the prosecuting solicitor's office who was instructing counsel for the prosecution. The legal assistant provided the note to counsel for the prosecution who then handed it to the defendant in the course of cross-examination. Without giving an indication to the jury of the nature or the contents of the note, counsel

---

[9] ibid [22].
[10] *Butler v Board of Trade* [1971] Ch 680 (Ch), approved by the Court of Appeal in *R v Tompkins* (1978) 67 Cr App R 181 (CA), *R v Cottrill* [1997] Crim LR 56 (CA), and *R v K (A)* [2009] EWCA Crim 1640, [2010] QB 343, and more recently by the High Court in *Eurasian Natural Resources Corp Ltd v Dechert LLP* [2022] EWHC 1138 (Comm). See paras 1.104–1.109.
[11] *D (A Child) (Care Proceedings Legal Privilege)* [2011] EWCA Civ 684, [2011] 4 All ER 434.
[12] *R v Tompkins* (n 10).

said to the defendant, 'I want you to look at this piece of paper. Just look at it and think carefully before you answer the next question.'[13]

10.19 It was accepted that this turn of events was fortuitous for the prosecution, but its propriety was not raised as an issue on appeal. The issue considered was simply whether the conviction was safe in light of the prosecution having made use of privileged information. The judge held that the conviction was safe, stating:

> Privilege, in this context, relates only to production of a document; it does not determine its admissibility in evidence. The note, though clearly privileged from production, was admissible in evidence once it was in the possession of the prosecution (*Butler v Board of Trade* [1971] Ch. 680). Admissibility depends essentially on the relevance of the document; the method by which it has been obtained is irrelevant: (*Kuruma, son of Kanui v R* [1955] A.C. 197, per Lord Goddard C.J. at p. 203).[14]

10.20 The case of *Tompkins* predates the Police and Criminal Evidence Act 1984 (PACE 1984), so whilst it would now be open to a defendant in Tompkins' position to make an application under PACE 1984, section 78 to exclude evidence of this nature, the test to be applied is whether admitting the evidence would have such an adverse effect on the fairness of the proceedings that it ought not to be admitted. Whilst the circumstances in which the evidence was obtained should be considered, the fact that the information is, or was, privileged does not give it any exceptional status in an application for its exclusion under this section.

Inadvertent Disclosure by a Third Party to the Prosecution

10.21 Relevant material in the possession of the prosecution must be considered for disclosure to the defence under the CPIA 1996. The obligations set out in the CPIA 1996 are paramount and apply to all material in the hands of the prosecution. It is the view of the authors that this includes privileged material disclosed to the prosecution by a third party inadvertently, which should be treated in the same way as material subject to the prosecution's own privilege, as discussed in Chapter 8, Section 4.

10.22 In circumstances where privileged material belonging to a third party has inadvertently been provided to the prosecution, it may be open to the third party to request its return from the prosecution or to seek to limit or restrain the use which is made of it. The onus is on the privilege holder to do so. Once the material has been disclosed to the defence, the privilege holder's main concern is likely to be to try to prevent the material losing confidentiality and therefore ceasing to be privileged by being read or referred to in open court. The parties may agree to handle the material during the course of the trial in a way that prevents or reduces the risk of it losing its confidentiality, but any measures that might interfere with the defendant's right to a fair trial must not be taken.

---

[13] ibid 183.
[14] ibid 184.

Inadvertent Disclosure by the Prosecution

10.23 In *R v G*[15] the Court of Appeal considered the extent to which a trial judge could restrain the use of material inadvertently disclosed by the prosecution to two of the defendants in a five-handed trial. The material had previously been ruled by the trial judge not to be disclosable to the defence on the grounds that it was covered by Public Interest Immunity (PII). The issues considered therefore do not directly address the inadvertent disclosure of privileged material, but the principle established is likely to be similarly applicable to privileged material. Following the inadvertent disclosure, the judge heard submissions from the Crown at an *ex parte* hearing and made a provisional ruling that the information should not be disclosed to the defence and that no injustice would result to the defence as a result of the lack of disclosure. At a further hearing the judge ruled that there would be a ban on dissemination by any of the lawyers who had received the material, including to their clients, and that they could make no use of the material. As the ruling was made at a preparatory hearing, counsel who had received the inadvertently disclosed material were granted permission to appeal.

10.24 On appeal, the issues which caused the Court of Appeal concern were the impracticality and undesirability of two sets of advisers being ordered not to disclose information to their respective clients and, in addition, requiring them not to communicate the information to their co-defending counsel. The Court observed that whilst it might be possible in some cases to restrain the use of inadvertently disclosed material, in this case the disclosure should not have been restrained. Rose LJ stated:

> There is no reason in principle why a Crown Court, exercising the jurisdiction to which we have earlier referred, should not similarly restrain the use of material inadvertently disclosed, although the particular circumstances of the case which dictate whether justice requires an order, will of course, be different. In a criminal case with more than one defendant, regard must be had to the position both between the prosecution and the defendants and between the defendants. However, the defendants submit, referring to *Archbold, Criminal Pleading Evidence and Practice* (2004) para 12-16, that no comparable remedy is ever available in the event of inadvertent disclosure in criminal proceedings, at least in the case of a public prosecution. The basis of this view in *Archbold* is that cases such as *Kuruma v The Queen* [1955] AC 197 establish that admissibility of evidence depends upon relevance and it is immaterial how the evidence was obtained. We do not accept that reasoning or its conclusion. The approach in *Kuruma v The Queen* applies in civil cases: see *Calcraft v Guest* [1898] 1 QB 759. But a sharp distinction has been drawn between restraining a person from divulging or using confidential information which has come into his possession, including using it in litigation before trial, and preventing its use at trial: see *Lord Ashburton v Pape* [1913] 2 Ch 469, particularly at p 476.
>
> It is not necessary for the purposes of this appeal for us to define the circumstances in which the Crown Court might exercise similar powers to those established in a civil context and restrain use of documents inadvertently disclosed in criminal proceedings.[16]

---

[15] [2004] EWCA Crim 1368, [2004] 1 WLR 2932.
[16] ibid [16]–[17].

10.25 *R v G* did not go so far as to identify the circumstances in which it might be permissible for the Crown Court to exercise powers of restraint in respect of material inadvertently disclosed by the prosecution. However, it is apparent from the judgment that restraint would be unlikely to be ordered in circumstances where it would lead to lawyers being prevented from sharing information with their client or with co-defending counsel. It is therefore possible that in circumstances where inadvertent disclosure was made in a trial involving a single defendant, and that disclosure had been shared with the defendant prior to the inadvertent disclosure being discovered, a judge could order that the material could not be used in the proceedings or disseminated further. This will, of course, be entirely fact-specific and it does not address the issue highlighted in *R v G* that 'use' itself is hard to define as 'the distinction between overt use and inward thoughts is not always easy to maintain'.[17]

4 Oral Evidence

The Position Generally

10.26 The principles governing loss and waiver of privilege apply similarly to evidence given orally as to documentary evidence.

Defendant's Evidence

10.27 Waiver of privilege in oral evidence is most commonly encountered in criminal proceedings when a defendant seeks to rebut an assumption of recent fabrication by reference to what was said to their legal adviser at an earlier stage of proceedings, usually at the police station (see also paras 6.39–6.47 for further discussion of waiver in the context of advice at the police station and in respect of an interview under caution).

10.28 The extent to which a defendant can be cross-examined about what and/or when they told their legal adviser about their defence has been examined in a number of authorities. The interplay between the provisions of the Criminal Justice and Public Order Act 1994 (CJPOA 1994), section 34 and privilege has been considered on several occasions and the position is most comprehensively set out in the Court of Appeal's judgment in *R v Seaton*:

(a) Legal professional privilege is of paramount importance. There is no question of balancing privilege against other considerations of public interest: *R v Derby Justices Magistrates Court, Ex p B* [1996] AC 487.
(b) Therefore, in the absence of waiver, no question can be asked which intrudes upon privilege. That means, inter alia, that if a suggestion of recent fabrication is being pursued at trial, a witness, including the defendant, cannot, unless he has waived privilege, be asked whether he told his counsel or solicitor what he now says is the truth. Such a question would require him either to waive his privilege or suffer criticism for not doing so. If any such question is asked by an opposing party (whether the Crown

---

[17] ibid [13].

or a co-accused) the judge must stop it, tell the witness directly that he does not need to answer it, and explain to the jury that no one can be asked about things which pass confidentially between him and his lawyer. For the same reasons, in the absence of waiver, the witness cannot be asked whether he is willing to waive.

(c) However, the defendant is perfectly entitled to open up his communication with his lawyer, and it may sometimes be in his interest to do so. One example of when he may wish to do so is to rebut a suggestion of recent fabrication. Another may be to adduce in evidence the reasons he was advised not to answer questions. If he does so, there is no question of breach of privilege, because he cannot be in breach of his own privilege. What is happening is that he is waiving privilege.

(d) If the defendant does give evidence of what passed between him and his solicitor he is not thereby waiving privilege entirely and generally, that is to say he does not automatically make available to all other parties everything that he said to his solicitor, or his solicitor to him, on every occasion. He may well not even be opening up everything said on the occasion of which he gives evidence, and not on topics unrelated to that of which he gives evidence. The test is fairness and/or the avoidance of a misleading impression. It is that the defendant should not, as it has been put in some of the cases, be able both to 'have his cake and eat it'.

(e) If a defendant says that he gave his solicitor the account now offered at trial, that will ordinarily mean that he can be cross-examined about exactly what he told the solicitor on that topic, and if the comment is fair another party can comment upon the fact that the solicitor has not been called to confirm something which, if it is true, he easily could confirm. If it is intended to pursue cross-examination beyond what is evidently opened up, the proper extent of it can be discussed and the judge invited to rule.

(f) A defendant who adduces evidence that he was advised by his lawyer not to answer questions but goes no further than that does not thereby waive privilege. This is the ratio of *Bowden*[18] and is well established. After all, the mere fact of the advice can equally well be made evident by the solicitor announcing at the interview that he gives it then and there, and there is then no revelation whatever of any private conversation between him and the defendant.

(g) But a defendant who adduces evidence of the content of, or reasons for, such advice, beyond the mere fact of it, does waive privilege at least to the extent of opening up questions which properly go to whether such reason can be the true explanation for his silence: *Bowden*. That will ordinarily include questions relating to recent fabrication, and thus to what he told his solicitor of the facts now relied upon at trial: *Bowden* and *Loizou*.[19]

(h) The rules as to privilege and waiver, and thus as to cross examination and comment, are the same whether it is the Crown or a co-accused who challenges the defendant.[20]

10.29 In attempting to resist an adverse inference by demonstrating that facts relied upon as part of a defence have not been recently fabricated, a defendant may seek to do one (or both) of

---

[18] *R v Bowden* [1999] 1 WLR 823 (CA).
[19] *R v Loizou* [2006] EWCA Crim 1719, [2006] All ER (D) 215 (Jul).
[20] [2010] EWCA Crim 1980, [2011] 1 WLR 623 [43].

two things: first, they may seek to explain a no comment interview at the police station as being purely based on legal advice (and therefore not because the facts have been recently fabricated); and/or, secondly, they may seek to suggest that the facts relied upon were in fact communicated to their legal adviser at the police station, and therefore have not been recently fabricated. In the first scenario, by simply stating that a no comment interview was advised, the defendant does not waive privilege. This alone may not, however, be enough to resist an adverse inference from being drawn. If a defendant then goes further and explains why they were advised to answer no comment, this waives privilege and permits questioning on the instructions provided which elicited that advice to determine whether the no comment interview was in fact due to the advice. In the second scenario, giving evidence regarding the communication of facts to the legal adviser does not necessarily result in privilege being waived over anything other than what has been disclosed. The authorities rationalize this on the basis that the same facts could have been communicated to any third party; the fact the client happened to provide the information to their legal adviser is treated as incidental.[21] It is therefore possible to adduce evidence that a legal adviser was told of specific facts relied upon without waiving privilege over the entirety of the instructions given and/or advice received at the police station.

R v Condron[22] considered the issue in circumstances where the defendant sought to avoid an adverse inference by relying upon the fact that his solicitor had advised him not to answer questions in interview due to the solicitor's view that at the time of the interview the defendant was unfit to be questioned. This was not the view of the police medical examiner, who had considered the defendant fit to be interviewed. The Court of Appeal considered the extent to which referring to advice given at the police station might amount to a waiver of privilege and the distinction between referring to the fact of advice versus the substance of that advice. Stuart Smith LJ set out clearly the analysis which must be undertaken by the defence in considering whether a waiver of privilege is necessary in attempting to resist an adverse inference: **10.30**

> Communications between an accused person and his solicitor prior to interviews by the police are subject to legal professional privilege. But the privilege can be waived by the client, though not the solicitor. If an accused person gives as a reason for not answering questions that he has been advised by his solicitor not to do so, that advice, in our judgment, does not amount to a waiver of privilege. But, equally, for reasons which we have already given, that bare assertion is unlikely by itself to be regarded as a sufficient reason for not mentioning matters relevant to the defence.
>
> So it will be necessary, if the defendant wishes to invite the court not to draw an adverse inference, to go further and state the basis or reason for the advice. Although the matter was not fully argued, it seems to us that once this is done it may well amount to a waiver of privilege so that the defendant or, if his solicitor is also called, the solicitor can be asked whether there were any other reasons for the advice, and the nature of the advice given, so as to explore whether the advice may also have been given for tactical reasons.

---

[21] *R v Condron* [1997] 1 WLR 827, 837 (CA).
[22] ibid.

However, it should be borne in mind that the inference which the prosecution seek to draw from failure to mention facts in interview is that they have been subsequently fabricated. It is always open to a party to attempt to rebut this inference by showing that the relevant facts were communicated to a third person, usually the solicitor, at about the time of the interview: see *Reg. v. Wilmot* (1988) 89 Cr.App.R. 341. This does not involve waiver of privilege if it is the solicitor to whom the fact is communicated; the solicitor is, for this purpose, in the same position as anyone else.

In the unlikely event, therefore, that the solicitor advised his client to say nothing, even though the client has given him information which amounts to a defence, or affords an innocent explanation of otherwise incriminating evidence, the solicitor can be called to say that he was given that information and this, if accepted, will rebut the inference of subsequent fabrication. Moreover, it is always open to an accused person who has failed to mention some important fact at interview to communicate it to the police at any time before trial; but, unless it is done promptly, it is unlikely to rebut any adverse inference which might otherwise be drawn. In the present case Mr. Delbourgo, having said that the basis of his advice was his perception of his clients' fitness for interview, was asked, inter alia, in cross-examination: 'Coming down to the specifics of the allegation, he was in a sufficiently lucid state to be able to explain to you why it was that he had taken drugs, and to repeat that in interview?' Mr. Delbourgo thereupon claimed privilege and the judge upheld the objection. For the reasons we have given, we are far from satisfied that he was correct to do so since we consider that the appellant, in fact, waived his privilege.

It is probably desirable that the judge should warn counsel, or the defendant, that the privilege may be taken to have been waived if the defendant gives evidence of the nature of the advice.[23]

10.31 This issue was also examined in *R v Bowden*,[24] in which the distinction was drawn between the lawyer as mere recipient of information, evidence of which could rebut an assumption of recent fabrication, and a lawyer giving evidence of the grounds on which advice was given. *Bowden* is considered in more detail at paras 6.42–6.44 as it concerns the extent to which statements made during the police interview itself may give rise to a waiver of privilege. The principle applies similarly to evidence given orally at trial, and it is clear from the judgment that where the defence seeks to rely on the reasons why advice was given not to answer questions, it will not be possible to resist cross-examination on the nature of the instructions provided and the advice given.[25]

10.32 *R v Wishart*[26] further reinforces the principle that the bare assertion that a no comment interview was given on the advice of a solicitor is not sufficient to waive privilege, but if a defendant goes further and explains the basis upon which the advice was given, or a legal representative does so on their client's behalf, this amounts to waiver. In *Wishart*, a central consideration was the extent to which the prosecution is permitted to comment on a lack of waiver. The Court of Appeal held that:

---

[23] ibid 837.
[24] *R v Bowden* (n 18).
[25] ibid 829.
[26] [2005] EWCA Crim 1337.

It is well-established that it is not enough for a defendant simply to assert that he has made a no comment interview on legal advice in order to avoid a section 34 [CJPOA] direction. The defendant's explanation is left to the jury to consider in accordance with the JSB [Judicial Studies Board] standard direction. In a case such as this the judge would obviously remind the jury of the defendant's evidence that he had told his solicitor the facts which he failed to mention in interview and if the solicitor was not called to support the defendant's assertion it would be open to the Crown and the judge in his summing-up to comment upon this omission.[27]

R v Loizou[28] further considered what it is permissible of the prosecution to ask a defendant who seeks to rely upon advice to give a no comment interview at the police station in order to avoid an adverse inference being drawn from their silence. The Court of Appeal made the following observations:

10.33

> The question whether the evidence creates a misleading impression or risks doing so depends on the issue before the finder of fact. In our case that issue is 'the section 34 question'; that is whether the appellant's reason for exercising her entitlement to be silent is the legal advice genuinely given and genuinely accepted or whether it is because she had no or no satisfactory explanation to give: see *Hoare & Pierce* [2004] EWCA Crim 784. Paragraph 54 of the judgment in *Hoare & Pierce* draws a distinction between the defendant's belief in his entitlement to remain silent which may be genuine and his reason for exercising it which may not be reliance on that entitlement. The prosecution submit that the question asked in the case before us goes to the issues of genuineness and reasonableness and to explore whether the appellant's actions were tactical or not: see written submissions, paragraph 11, set out in paragraph 68 of this judgment. Realistically, in this case 'genuineness' is not in issue. The solicitor gave the advice and there does not appear to have been any evidence to put in question the appellant's belief that she was entitled to rely on the advice. In any event, according to *Hoare & Pierce*, it is immaterial to the section 34 question whether the solicitor rightly or wrongly believed that, as a matter of law, the defendant was not required to answer the police officers' questions or whether he or she believed they had a right to rely on the advice of the solicitor: paragraph 56. The question is whether it was the advice rather than the absence of a satisfactory explanation which caused the appellant to make no comment.
>
> It is in our judgment potentially misleading for the jury in considering this issue to have only the appellant's answers in chief before them without further evidence as to the context or, in the language used by this Court in *Bowden*, the factual underpinning of the advice given to her.[29]

Consistent with the other authorities discussed above, the Court took the view that if a defendant gives evidence as to the reasons why they were advised to give a no comment interview, the prosecution will be permitted to cross-examine the defendant (and potentially the legal adviser) about the instructions given and the advice received in order to establish whether the defendant did in fact give a no comment interview in reliance on that advice, or whether they were effectively 'hiding behind' that advice.

---

[27] ibid [23].
[28] *R v Loizou* (n 19).
[29] ibid [80]–[81].

190   LPP IN CRIMINAL INVESTIGATIONS AND PROCEEDINGS

10.34 Defendants giving evidence in respect of police station advice must be advised of the risks of giving evidence which goes beyond the fact of the advice given. It is possible to say, 'I told my solicitor about my alibi but I did not raise it in interview as I was advised to answer no comment to all questions', without waiving privilege. If the defendant goes further than this, by saying, for example, 'I told my solicitor about my alibi but she advised me not to raise it in interview because she did not feel we had been given adequate pre-interview disclosure', this will waive privilege over the instructions provided to the solicitor and the details of the advice given. Cross-examination on these matters will therefore be permissible in order to determine whether this was in fact the reason for not mentioning the alibi.

Evidence adduced by the Prosecution

10.35 As explained at paras 6.39–6.47, if a legal adviser or their client makes a statement during an interview under caution that discloses the reasons for the advice not to answer questions, privilege is effectively waived at that stage as the prosecution is entitled to adduce evidence of this at trial and, as a result, ask the defendant questions about what was said to their legal adviser at the time.[30]

10.36 However, this does not mean that the circumstances in which privilege was waived and how that waiver is sought to be deployed by the prosecution are irrelevant. A defendant may apply for the evidence or a line of cross-examination to be excluded under PACE 1984, section 78, in which case these will be factors the judge must consider. As the Court of Appeal stated in *R v Hall-Chung*: 'A judge must not assume that the Crown is entitled to take advantage of the waiver in every case, where, as a matter of law, it has been waived. He must exercise independent judgment as to whether it is fair to permit the prosecution to exploit that waiver.'[31] However, in most cases where the purpose of the cross-examination is to test the defendant's claim that the reason for not answering questions was because of the legal advice received, this will be permitted.

Defendant's Evidence: Judge's Questioning

10.37 In *R v Pearce*[32] the Court of Appeal quashed a conviction for attempted robbery in circumstances where the judge had asked questions of the defendant during the trial which resulted in the defendant, in answering the questions, disclosing privileged information which he had not waived in examination-in-chief or in cross-examination. There was no transcript of Pearce's evidence, but the judge in his summing up told the jury that Pearce had said: 'I was interviewed on 30 March in the presence of my solicitor. I exercised my

---

[30] *R v Bowden* (n 18) 829; *R v Hall-Chung* [2007] EWCA Crim 3429, [2007] All ER (D) 429 (Jul) [16]–[18].
[31] *R v Hall-Chung* (n 30) [19].
[32] [2013] EWCA Crim 808.

right to go "no comment". I was advised by my solicitor to go "no comment" and to say nothing to the police or to him … The whole scenario was on the CCTV. I provided instructions which were put in a defence statement on 21 June.' There was some debate over whether the words 'or to him' were used, as this wording did not appear in Pearce's counsel's contemporaneous note of the evidence. The judge, however, then asked Pearce a series of questions which included, 'Before you received that advice did you tell your solicitor that you believed that [the complainant] was [a friend]?' and, 'When did you first give your solicitor this information about [the friend]?' Pearce answered the questions and thereby waived privilege.

The Court of Appeal held that in examination-in-chief and cross-examination Pearce had not waived privilege as he gave evidence that he was advised by his solicitor not to answer questions in interview but did not disclose the reasons for that advice. The questions asked by the judge improperly required Pearce to go further and provide information which had the effect of waiving privilege. This rendered his conviction unsafe. **10.38**

A different issue arose in the case of *R v Inglis*.[33] An unrepresented defendant at trial intended to say in evidence that not only had the duty solicitor advised him to answer no comment in his interview under caution, but also that he had made a statement to the solicitor explaining everything. He told the judge about this at the conclusion of his evidence-in-chief and while the jury were out. The judge warned him about the danger of saying this in evidence as it would risk waiving privilege. The defendant decided not to mention it and he was convicted. The Court of Appeal thought that the judge had not made sufficiently clear that the defendant had a choice about whether he waived privilege. The Court of Appeal held that the conviction was unsafe (because of this and another ground relating to admission of hearsay evidence). **10.39**

5 Expert Evidence

Communications with third parties such as expert witnesses are covered by litigation privilege as long as litigation is in progress or reasonable contemplation, the communication is for the sole or dominant purpose of conducting that litigation and the litigation is adversarial[34] (see Chapter 1, Section 3 and para 9.37 for further discussion and analysis). The privilege belongs to the defendant and it is not the expert's to waive.[35] However, disclosure of privileged material by an expert during proceedings, in oral evidence or by disclosure of documents, even if it is without the consent or knowledge of the defendant or their legal representative, will still lead to waiver of the defendant's privilege.[36] **10.40**

---

[33] *R v Inglis* [2021] EWCA Crim 1545, All ER (D) 54 (Nov).
[34] *Three Rivers District Council v Governor and Company of the Bank of England* [2004] UKHL 48, [2005] 1 AC 610 [102].
[35] *Schneider v Leigh* [1955] 2 QB 195 (CA).
[36] *R v Crozier* (1990) 12 Cr App R (CA).

6 Lawyers Giving Evidence

The Position Generally

10.41 There are a range of potential circumstances under which a lawyer may be called by the prosecution or the defence to give evidence. The basic principle remains that privilege belongs to the client and cannot be waived by the lawyer without their client's consent. However, because a legal representative is assumed to have their client's authority in the actions taken on their behalf, it is possible that what they say in evidence or otherwise in court may lead to a waiver of privilege, even if it is without the defendant's consent. There is also the possibility that what the lawyer says causes information to lose confidentiality and therefore also its privileged status.

Confirming the Fact of Advice Given

10.42 Lawyers are required on various occasions to confirm to the court that a defendant has been advised in respect of particular matters, for example credit for a guilty plea or (if applicable) that an adverse inference may be drawn if the defendant does not give evidence. Confirming the fact that advice has been given on a particular matter in response to an enquiry from the court does not waive the client's privilege as it does not involve the defendant relying on the content or substance of the advice to advance their case. However, should the content or substance of the advice be disclosed, this may amount to a waiver of privilege on the client's behalf depending on the nature and extent of the disclosure and its purpose. See paras 10.27–10.34 in respect of the same distinction when a defendant gives evidence.

Lawyers as Prosecution Witnesses

10.43 There is no rule prohibiting the prosecution from calling a defendant's lawyer to give evidence against a client. However, if this does happen, the lawyer will not be permitted to answer questions which intrude on the client's privilege, unless it has been lost or waived or the client has given their consent for the information to be disclosed.

10.44 It is possible that the evidence sought from the lawyer will be neither confidential nor privileged and the fact that the witness is a lawyer is simply incidental, rather than central to the issue. Nevertheless, if this is the case, care must still be taken by all parties to ensure that questioning does not stray into areas which may be covered by privilege. In other circumstances, it may be that the evidence sought from the lawyer is not privileged but is confidential, in which case there is no absolute protection against disclosure.

10.45 Where the evidence sought by the prosecution relates to prima facie privileged matters, such as the client's instructions or the advice given, it will be for the prosecution to establish that the evidence sought is either not privileged due to the crime-fraud exception (see Chapter 2) or because privilege has otherwise been lost or waived. These matters will likely have been argued and determined at an earlier stage of proceedings and therefore ought not to arise for the first time in oral evidence. However, it will remain necessary for all parties to be cognizant of the parameters of the evidence to be given, whether that is on the basis that privilege has been lost or waived or because it is said the evidence sought never was privileged.

Lawyers as Defence Witnesses

10.46 The issues which may arise when a lawyer is called by their own client to give evidence in their defence are discussed at paras 10.27–10.34 in relation to potential waiver of privilege by the defendant. The considerations when calling the defendant's lawyer to give evidence as part of the defence case are likely to centre around whether what is intended to be adduced from the lawyer will result in a waiver of privilege, if so, the extent of the waiver, and ensuring the evidence given goes no further than the intended extent of the waiver. Whilst privilege is for the client to waive, not the lawyer, if the lawyer inadvertently waives privilege without the express consent of their client, the prosecution will be entitled to rely upon that evidence.

Lawyers as Defendants

10.47 It is not permissible for a lawyer suspected of a criminal offence to waive a client's privilege, even if it is to provide evidence which would assist in their defence. This principle is demonstrated by the case of *R v Devani*,[37] which concerned a solicitor accused of conspiring with her client to pervert the course of justice by fabricating evidence in an attempted murder trial in which her client was a defendant. Whilst the essential principle that only the privilege holder can waive privilege is uncontroversial, the case demonstrates the difficulties that privilege issues can present in criminal proceedings.

10.48 It was alleged that Devani, a newly qualified solicitor, had visited her client, Timothy Merchant, at HMP Belmarsh where, during the course of her visit, she took possession of two sealed letters written by him. One was a personal letter to Merchant's girlfriend and the other was a letter to Merchant's co-defendant, Mustafa Abdullah. The letter to Abdullah contained what was alleged to be a plan to create false evidence to deal with part of the Crown's case against Merchant.

10.49 The Crown's case against Devani was that she knew specifically of the contents of the letter to Abdullah and that she and Merchant were both active and willing participants in a plan to fabricate a defence for Merchant. The Crown alleged that, during the conference at HMP Belmarsh, Devani and Merchant discussed perverting the course of justice before she took possession of the letters. Merchant's defence was that he admitted passing the letters to Devani but denied that in doing so he was perverting the course of justice as

---

[37] [2007] EWCA Crim 1926, [2008] 1 Cr App R 4.

the letter to Abdullah contained a true statement of facts which he was simply communicating to him. Devani's defence was that she received from Merchant a folded piece of paper showing a telephone number for Merchant's mother, she had no knowledge that within the folded paper were two sealed envelopes, and she had no knowledge of the contents of either letter.

10.50 Devani was approached by a prison officer as she was leaving HMP Belmarsh. The officer, having seen the paper being passed to her, asked Devani if she had taken anything from Merchant. Devani denied having done so and was subsequently searched. The letters were found, opened, and passed to a police liaison officer. Devani was permitted to return to HMP Belmarsh to continue visiting Merchant, which she did later the same afternoon and then on two separate occasions a few days later. Devani was arrested approximately a month later when she attended the police station to review disclosure material in relation to Merchant's case. A file she was carrying that day was seized by the police and sealed.

10.51 Devani was interviewed under caution on the day of her arrest. In interview she answered questions about communications between herself and Merchant during the morning conference at which the letter was passed. She stated that Merchant had not mentioned the letters to her but had provided her with his mother's contact details for use in preparing his bail application.

10.52 Later, the file she had been carrying when arrested, which had been seized by the police, was provided to independent counsel, who reviewed it and provided relevant documents to Devani. One such document was the note she had made of the conference with Merchant in the afternoon immediately following the seizure of the letters. It contained a note of the account given by Merchant which had also been set out in his letter to Abdullah.

10.53 At trial, Merchant maintained that he did pass the letter to Devani but that its contents were true. He did not claim privilege over the note of the conference with Devani on the afternoon after the letters were handed over, even though it was accepted by the court that he could have done so. He did, however, maintain privilege over his communications with Devani during the course of the morning conference when the letters were alleged to have been passed to her.

10.54 The judge ruled that Merchant could decline to answer any question regarding what was discussed in the morning meeting on the basis of privilege. As he did not waive privilege over the morning conference, Devani was not permitted to rely on the contents of her files to give evidence of communications contained therein, including evidence relating to the morning conference. However, the judge ruled that she was permitted to rely upon the contents of her police interview, in which she had disclosed what was discussed in the morning conference, and the note of the afternoon conference which had been provided to her by independent counsel. The result of this was that the jury was permitted to hear what Devani had said in her police interview about what was discussed in the morning conference with Merchant, but Merchant was permitted not to answer any questions about that same topic on the basis that it was privileged, and Devani could not adduce evidence from her file relating to the morning conference either.

10.55 Devani was found guilty and appealed against her conviction on several grounds, including that she was prejudiced by Merchant's claim to privilege which prevented her counsel from questioning Merchant and prevented her from giving evidence herself about what was said in the morning conference leading up to, during, and after the passing of the folded paper containing the letters, and adducing into evidence the part of her attendance note taken during this part of the conference.

10.56 The Court of Appeal's approach was to assess whether Merchant's claim to privilege caused unfairness to Devani in the presentation of her defence such as to render her conviction unsafe. The position was not considered with reference to the principles of waiver. Devani's counsel did not seek to challenge the judge's approach to Merchant's claim to privilege, and the Court was simply asked to consider whether Devani's case was 'seriously and unfairly prejudiced by those inhibitions'. The analysis centred on the factual position of both Devani's and Merchant's evidence, with the Court concluding that the account likely to be given by Merchant if he had waived privilege would not have assisted Devani's defence (and would likely have undermined it given that he implied that he did discuss the contents of the letter with Devani), and therefore she was not prejudiced by his claim to privilege. The Court also rejected the submission that Devani was disadvantaged by being unable to rely upon the contents of her file, save for the note of the afternoon conference. The position taken by the Court was that certain matters were bound to have been discussed in the conference and that any matters discussed which related to falsifying evidence would not have been noted in any event.

10.57 The conclusion arrived at was that Devani's conviction was safe and that Merchant's claim to privilege did not disadvantage Devani's ability to present her defence. Whilst this conclusion may have been correct, this reasoning tends to approve a rather inconsistent approach to the treatment of privilege by both the defence and the prosecution at trial. The starting point is that the privilege was Merchant's alone to waive, yet Devani answered questions during her police interview regarding the instructions taken from and advice given to Merchant during the morning conference at which the letter had been passed. In doing so, however improperly, Devani had caused Merchant's privilege to be waived when the record of the interview was adduced in evidence at trial. It was open to Merchant to object to this evidence being adduced during the trial, and whilst it is unclear whether he did so, the principle that the actions of a client's legal representative can cause privilege to be waived inadvertently may have caused the judge to permit its introduction. In any event, by allowing Devani to rely on what she had said in the police interview, privilege had been waived over the instructions given by Merchant and advice provided to him in the morning conference when the letter was passed. On this basis, questioning of Merchant on the discussions during the morning conference ought to have been permitted. Whether further questioning on this matter would have assisted Devani in the presentation of her case is difficult to predict, but, as a matter of law, the approach taken was inconsistent with the established principles of waiver of privilege.

10.58 Separately, it was potentially open to the prosecution to frame the interaction between Merchant and Devani as one to which the crime-fraud exception applied.[38] Communications in furtherance of a criminal purpose cannot be privileged, and the case of *R (Hallinan Blackburn Gittings & Nott) v Crown Court at Middlesex Guildhall*[39] illustrates the circumstances in which it is permissible to obtain and adduce evidence from a legal representative's file where there is free-standing and independent evidence of a conspiracy to pervert the course of justice and material from the file is said to be relevant to the issues. The *Hallinan* case, discussed in more detail at paras 2.20–2.21, concerned a production order for certain documents from a solicitor's file in circumstances where the solicitors were said to have been unwittingly used to fabricate evidence in support of a defence to drugs, firearms, and driving offences. The crime-fraud exception was held to apply to these documents as they were relevant to the production of allegedly false witness evidence and were therefore generated in furtherance of a criminal purpose. It was certainly arguable on the facts of *Devani* that there was free-standing and independent evidence of a conspiracy to pervert the course of justice (for example, the letter from Merchant to Abdullah and Devani's false denial when asked by the prison officer whether she had taken anything from Merchant), which was separate from the issues to be determined in respect of the attempted murder, and as such it could have been argued that communications between Devani and Merchant in respect of the letter were not privileged.

10.59 This position could have been advanced regardless of whether the prosecution's case was that Devani was a willing co-conspirator or an innocent dupe. This would have had the effect of allowing Merchant and Devani to be questioned on all communications regarding the letter as well as permitting disclosure of all attendance notes and correspondence in relation to this particular issue. In the Court of Appeal's judgment, Kay LJ appeared to suggest that the crime-fraud exception was not engaged during the trial because Merchant had not been convicted of the offences at that time, and therefore the issue of whether the communications were in furtherance of a criminal purpose was still being determined. This is not consistent with *Hallinan* or the later case of *R v Minchin*,[40] which also concerned production of material from a solicitor's file in circumstances where a conspiracy to pervert the course of justice was alleged. The judge granting the production order in *Minchin* followed *Hallinan* and his decision was upheld by the Court of Appeal.

10.60 It therefore appears that on more than one analysis of the facts of *Devani*, Merchant ought not to have been permitted to claim privilege over his communications with Devani.

---

[38] See ch 2 for a detailed examination of the crime-fraud exception.
[39] [2004] EWHC 2726 (Admin), [2005] 1 WLR 766.
[40] [2013] EWCA Crim 2412. See further discussion about this case at paras 2.22–2.24.

7 Costs Applications

In *Medcalf v Mardell*[41] counsel faced a wasted costs order which it was argued he could not properly contest given that the information he sought to rely upon was subject to his client's privilege. The Court recognized the punitive nature of a wasted costs order against counsel and held that courts should proceed with extreme care in making wasted costs orders against counsel in circumstances where it is not possible to hear the full facts due to a client's refusal to waive privilege. Accordingly, the benefit of the doubt had to be given to counsel and the wasted costs order was quashed.

10.61

8 Interlocutory Hearings

The principles of loss and waiver of privilege apply equally to interlocutory hearings as they do at trial unless it is possible for a waiver in some way to be limited to the interlocutory issue only. This will be fact-specific. The guiding principle was set out in *Dunlop Slazenger International Ltd v Joe Bloggs Sports Ltd*:

10.62

> If in interlocutory proceedings a party has waived privilege … then, that is a waiver for all purposes and the cherry picking principle applies. Whether that will always be right is a matter that I would reserve for future decisions. It is not necessary to say that that will always be right to dispose of this case. If there is to be an exception to that principle it would need to be framed in the following way. It would need to be argued that since it was only for the purpose of the interlocutory proceedings and in relation to an issue in those proceedings that the waiver had taken place the waiver was in some way limited.[42]

---

[41] [2002] UKHL 27, [2003] 1 AC 120.
[42] [2003] EWCA Civ 901 [17].

11
Appeals

1 Introduction

There are specific considerations concerning waiver of privilege which arise on appeal against conviction and/or sentence. This chapter will focus on the implications for privilege which arise when a convicted defendant appeals to the Court of Appeal against their conviction or sentence in the Crown Court and the extent to which these principles similarly apply in appeals from the magistrates' court to the Crown Court.

11.01

2 Appeals to the Court of Appeal

Appeals against Conviction: *McCook* Requirements

An appeal against a conviction in the Crown Court is made to the Court of Appeal Criminal Division. Permission to appeal is required and Crim PR 39.3(1) and 39.2(2) set out the information which must be provided in an application for permission to appeal, which is made by way of Form NG. As part of the declaration to be completed by solicitors and counsel on Form NG there is a requirement to confirm that any new representatives have complied with their obligations under *R v McCook*.[1] These obligations require a representative who is instructed in an appeal against conviction or sentence who was not the representative at the trial to make specific enquiries of the legal representative(s) who acted at the trial in order to ensure that the factual basis for the grounds of appeal is correct. If the trial representatives fail to respond to enquiries within a reasonable time, the fresh representatives should seek to obtain other objective evidence to substantiate the factual basis for those grounds. Crim PD 10.4.4 sets out the obligations on new legal representatives.

11.02

These requirements have implications for privilege and confidentiality, which are considered in further detail below. The requirement to confirm compliance with the obligations set out in *McCook* applies regardless of the nature of the grounds of appeal. However, there are certain grounds which are likely to engage the issues in *McCook* more directly. Where an appeal is based on criticism of previous representatives or on the availability of fresh evidence, the obligations are of particular significance. Appeals on these grounds also carry an increased likelihood that a waiver of the appellant's privilege will be required in order to support the grounds of appeal.

11.03

The guidance note to Form NG states in respect of the *McCook* obligations:

11.04

---

[1] [2014] EWCA Crim 734, [2016] 2 Cr App R 30.

The Court stated in *R v Achogbuo* [2014] EWCA Crim 567 that it is the fundamental duty of advocates and solicitors to exercise due diligence when making applications to the Court. The guidance by the Lord Chief Justice in the case of *R v McCook* [2014] EWCA Crim 734 makes clear that in any case where fresh representatives are instructed, it is necessary for them to approach the solicitors and/or counsel who acted at trial to ensure that the factual basis upon which the grounds are premised is correct.[2]

11.05   In *R v Clinton* it was stated that:

> Errors on the part of advocates may lead to a conviction being found to be unsafe. If the decision of the advocate is taken in good faith, having weighed the competing considerations and having consulted the client where appropriate, the Court of Appeal is much less likely to interfere than where the decision is taken in defiance of instructions and without reference to the client.[3]

11.06   It is therefore necessary in cases where the actions of previous representatives are being criticized for the Court to have the necessary information to determine the extent to which decisions taken by counsel and/or solicitors were based on instructions given by the client. This will require enquiries to be made about the content of privileged conversations and, where it supports the grounds of appeal, the privileged information to be put before the Court.

McCook Requirements: Development of the Principle

11.07   The Court of Appeal is particularly concerned to limit the number of appeals which are based on unsustainable or unfounded criticism of legal advisers. The introduction of the requirement for new representatives to confirm that they have made enquiries of previous solicitors and counsel when applying for permission to appeal in *R v McCook* was preceded by a number of cases that addressed this issue.

11.08   In *R v Achogbuo*[4] an application for leave to appeal based on criticism of previous solicitors and counsel was deemed to be frivolous or vexatious, according to the Criminal Appeal Act 1968, section 20. The appellant lodged an application for leave to appeal on the basis that hearsay evidence had been incorrectly admitted into evidence at trial. The Court of Appeal obtained the transcript of the summing up which was sent to the new solicitors and it was conceded by them that no such hearsay application had been made or granted and no such hearsay evidence admitted. The new solicitors accepted that the appeal was misconceived. Four months later, a further application for leave to appeal was made by the same solicitors, who submitted that the appellant had been negligently advised by his previous solicitors not to waive privilege over the advice given at the police station with regard to his no comment interview. The application also asked for permission to appeal out of time, but made no reference to the previous application. The Court wrote to the appellant's previous solicitors, in

---

[2] Form NG guidance note https://assets.publishing.service.gov.uk/government/uploads/system/uploads/attachment_data/file/945344/ng-guidance.pdf (accessed 10 June 2023).
[3] [1993] 1 WLR 1181 (CA).
[4] [2014] EWCA Crim 567, [2014] 2 Cr App R 7.

response to which they stated that the notes of advice given at the police station showed that the appellant had said that he denied the offences and could not think of any reason why the allegations were being made. It was noted that he had been advised about the possibility of an adverse inference being drawn from his silence in interview.

The Court of Appeal stated: **11.09**

> Of late it has become the habit for a number of cases to be brought on appeal to this court on the basis of incompetent representation by trial solicitors or trial counsel. As in this case, many such cases proceed without any enquiry being made of solicitors and counsel who acted at trial. That means that the lawyer who brings such an application acts on what is, ex hypothesi, the allegations of a convicted criminal—and in this case a convicted paedophile. For a lawyer to put forward such allegations based purely on such a statement, and without enquiry, is in our view impermissible. Before applications are made to this court alleging incompetent representation which is based upon an account given by a convicted criminal, we expect lawyers to take proper steps to ascertain by independent means, including contacting the previous lawyers, as to whether there is any objective and independent basis for the grounds of appeal.
>
> As long ago as 1997 in *R. v Doherty and McGregor* [1997] 2 Cr. App. R. 218, this court drew attention to the fact that it was proper for fresh representatives as a matter of courtesy to speak to former counsel before grounds of appeal are lodged. Today circumstances have changed. The frequency of this kind of appeal makes it clear to us that counsel and solicitors would be failing in their duty to this court if they did not make enquiries which would provide an objective and independent basis, other than complaints made by the convicted criminal, as to what had happened.[5]

This issue was considered further in *R v McCook*,[6] in which the application for leave to appeal was also found to be frivolous and vexatious. McCook had been convicted of robbery despite advancing a defence, supported by medical evidence, that his medical condition would have prevented him from committing the offence. He successfully appealed against his conviction on the basis that the list of convictions adduced as evidence of his bad character was incorrect. A retrial was ordered and directions were given in respect of medical evidence to be obtained by the defendant. At the retrial, more extensive medical evidence than was adduced at the first trial was relied upon, but the defendant was again convicted. He was given negative advice on his prospects of succeeding with an appeal against conviction by both trial solicitors and counsel. He instructed new solicitors and counsel who prepared an application for leave to appeal and advanced grounds that there had been a failure to call proper medical evidence in the first trial. The Court drew the new solicitors' attention to the fact that the conviction arising from the first trial had been overturned, leading to counsel returning the case on the basis that he had not been given the relevant information and therefore the grounds could not be sustained. The solicitors attempted to withdraw the appeal but did not lodge the appropriate forms. **11.10**

---

[5] ibid [16].
[6] *R v McCook* (n 1).

11.11 The Court summarily dismissed the appeal and set out the procedure to be followed in cases such as these:

> This case illustrates, however, two matters. First, it is always desirable to consult those who have acted before in a case where fresh counsel and solicitors have been instructed. In *R v Achogbuo* [2014] EWCA Crim 567 we stated that it was necessary to do so where criticisms of previous advocates or solicitors were made, or grounds were to be put forward where there was no basis for doing so other than what the applicant said. Second, it is clear from this case that we must go further to prevent elementary errors of this kind. In any case where fresh solicitors or fresh counsel are instructed, it will henceforth be necessary for those solicitors or counsel to go to the solicitors and/or counsel who have previously acted to ensure that the facts are correct, unless there are in exceptional circumstances good and compelling reasons not to do so. It is not necessary for us to enumerate such exceptional circumstances, but we imagine that they will be very rare.[7]

Implications of *McCook* on Privilege

11.12 The obligations on new legal representatives instructed on appeal, as imposed by *McCook*, are set out in Crim PD 10.4.4:

> Fresh representatives must comply with the duty of due diligence explained in *R v McCook*. To ensure compliance with this duty:
>
> a. New legal representatives must confirm within the grounds of appeal that the duties set out in *McCook* and associated authorities have been complied with.
> b. If privileged information is included within, or as an attachment, to the grounds of appeal (including but not limited to, explicit or implied complaints about the conduct of trial representatives), then a signed waiver of privilege must also be lodged with the grounds of appeal.
> c. If trial representatives fail to respond to inquiries within a reasonable time, fresh representatives should instead seek other objective independent evidence to substantiate the factual basis for the grounds as far as they are able. A statement confirming that the trial representatives have failed to respond to their *McCook* inquiries must be lodged with the grounds of appeal, along with a signed waiver of privilege.
> d. Fresh representatives must consider obtaining other objective independent evidence if the information provided by the trial representatives contradicts the appellant's instructions.
> e. A signed waiver of privilege must also be lodged by new legal representatives in all fresh evidence cases, following the guidance in *R v Singh*.[8]

11.13 The Crim PD require an express waiver of privilege to be provided if privileged information is included within the grounds of appeal. Strictly speaking, as a matter of law, this is not necessary in order for there to be a waiver of privilege, given that the inclusion of

---

[7] ibid [11].
[8] [2017] EWCA Crim 466, [2018] 1 WLR 1425.

privileged material in/with the grounds will amount to a waiver of privilege over those matters by implication in any event. However, this is an important procedural requirement that provides clarity over the appellant's position. The Crim PD do not specify the form the waiver should take, but it would be wise to provide the waiver in a form which identifies with some particularity the issues over which privilege is waived. The principles of waiver, and in particular collateral waiver, are relevant and are set out at paras 1.80–1.96. Collateral waiver means that waiver extends to all material relating to the same issue, as a matter of fairness and to prevent 'cherry picking'. This means that it will not be possible to limit the waiver of privilege to specific documents which assist the appeal; privilege will be waived over any other documents or information relevant to the same issue.

11.14 Notwithstanding the fact that there is a duty on new legal advisers to make the enquiries as set out in *McCook*, the client must still consent to their new advisers doing so, and the client must also provide consent to their former legal representatives to allow them to disclose matters which are subject to confidentiality and privilege to their new representatives. This is not a waiver of privilege but rather consent to the confidential sharing of privileged information between two sets of lawyers who are/have been instructed by the same client.[9] If this consent is given by the client, then discussions with previous legal advisers regarding confidential matters will remain confidential, and privileged matters will remain privileged unless or until privilege is waived.

11.15 The Bar Council's practice note, 'Criminal Appeals: Duties to the Court to Make Enquiries',[10] provides further guidance to counsel newly instructed. The issues identified include the interplay between fulfilling these obligations and respecting the client's privilege. The guidance states:

> This means that you cannot accept instructions to act on a criminal appeal if:
>
> a) Your client will not permit you to discuss even non-confidential matters with his former legal representative(s); or
> b) Your client will not permit you to discuss confidential matters with his former legal representatives, save in exceptional circumstances.[11]

11.16 If a client gives permission for those discussions to take place and privileged or confidential information is shared, it will require the new solicitors and counsel to consider the use to be made of that information. In some circumstances the privileged or confidential discussions may assist in determining that there are no grounds for appeal, in which case it would be unlikely that there would be a requirement for the information to be shared more widely. In these circumstances a waiver of privilege would not be required.

---

[9] See further at paras 1.41 and 1.77–1.79 for a discussion of the ways in which privileged and confidential information can be shared without waiving privilege overall.

[10] Bar Council, 'Criminal Appeals: Duties to the Court to Make Enquiries' (June 2016) (Bar Council Appeals Guidance) https://www.barcouncilethics.co.uk/wp-content/uploads/2017/10/Criminal-appeals-Duties-to-the-Court-to-make-enquiries-3.pdf (accessed 10 June 2023).

[11] Bar Council Appeals Guidance (n 10) para 8. The Bar Council uses the case of *R v Lee* [2014] EWCA Crim 2928 as authority for this proposition.

11.17 Where the content of the privileged or confidential material lends support to the grounds of appeal, the client will be required to waive privilege over the issue which is to be relied upon in order to advance the grounds. This is particularly likely to be the case in situations where an appeal is based on criticism of previous legal representatives, and also in fresh evidence cases where it may be necessary to explain why the evidence was not deployed previously.

11.18 It is important to note that nothing in the case law or Crim PD compels the client to waive privilege. The Bar Council guidance and the relevant case law set out the steps that must be taken in order to ascertain that appeals against conviction are based on an accurate understanding of the position at trial and of the actions taken by the client's representatives at first instance. Once the new representatives have satisfied themselves that they are fully apprised of the facts, it is a separate matter to consider whether there are grounds for appeal and whether settling grounds will require the client to waive privilege.

Fresh Evidence

11.19 Crim PD 10.4.4.e makes clear that a signed waiver of privilege must be lodged by new legal representatives in all fresh evidence cases. The guidance refers to the case of *R v Singh*,[12] in which criticism was made of fresh representatives who sought leave to appeal against a conviction for money laundering. The appeal was on the basis of fresh evidence, but privilege was not waived as the new representatives did not deem this necessary given that no criticism was being made of the previous solicitors. The Court of Appeal enquired further about the position and privilege was eventually waived, but at a late stage of proceedings, which caused the new representatives to seek an adjournment to the appeal in order to consider the information provided by the previous representatives. This application to adjourn was refused, as was the initial application for leave to appeal. The Court of Appeal made clear that the requirements set out in *Achogbuo* to make enquiries of previous solicitors had not been complied with:

> No exceptional circumstances arise here [to justify enquiries not being made]. It is difficult to envisage a case where they will arise when fresh representatives seek to adduce fresh evidence. A waiver of privilege will be required in most, if not all cases, so that the court can be satisfied that the provisions of section 23(2)(d) of the Criminal Appeal Act 1968[13] have been adequately addressed.[14]

11.20 The issue in *Singh* was the initial failure to make enquiries of the previous representatives. Having failed to make the enquiries, the new representatives were not in a position to consider whether their appeal could be sustained on the grounds submitted or to adequately consider whether a waiver of privilege was required. The judgment in *Singh* makes clear that, regardless of whether there are criticisms of previous solicitors, the obligations under *McCook* apply.

---

[12] *R v Singh* (n 8).
[13] Criminal Appeal Act 1968, s 23(2)(d) provides that, in considering whether to receive any evidence, the Court of Appeal shall have regard in particular to whether there is a reasonable explanation for the failure to adduce the evidence in the proceedings from which the appeal lies.
[14] *R v Singh* (n 8) [25].

11.21 The Bar Council's guidance also clearly advises that the requirements set out in *McCook* apply in fresh evidence cases as it is necessary for the previous legal representatives to explain why the evidence was not available at trial.[15]

11.22 In practice, the position may be slightly more nuanced in that fresh evidence cases will not always involve new representatives, and therefore the *McCook* requirements (and the requirements in Crim PD 10.4.4.e) may not automatically be engaged if there is no change of representation. However, it will be necessary to consider whether a waiver of privilege may still be required in order to explain why the fresh evidence was not available at trial.

Appeals against Sentence

11.23 An appeal against sentence is made using Form NG (Sentence), which sets out a similar declaration in respect of compliance with the obligations prescribed by *McCook*.[16]

Implications of an Express Waiver of Privilege

11.24 The obligations on new representatives as set out in *McCook* are limited to the enquiries that must be made *before* applying for permission to appeal. There is no requirement in *McCook*, or any authority, for a client to waive privilege in order to apply for permission to appeal. It will be a question of fact whether a waiver of privilege is required in order to advance the grounds of appeal. Crim PD 10.4.4.b states that a waiver is required 'if privileged information is included within, or as an attachment, to the grounds of appeal (including but not limited to, explicit or implied complaints about the conduct of trial representatives)', and Crim PD 10.4.4.e requires a signed waiver of privilege to be lodged in all fresh evidence cases where new legal representatives are instructed.

11.25 The Bar Council guidance notes that it is a matter for counsel as to whether a waiver of privilege is required in the context of an appeal:

> Whether and when a waiver of privilege is needed is a matter of law for you to consider. The Bar Council cannot advise you on this. In simple terms, however, this is most likely to arise where criticisms are being made of former legal representatives. The Court of Appeal has indicated that a failure to waive privilege will usually mean that the single judge and/or the court will be unable to determine whether complaints made against former legal representatives constitute an arguable ground of appeal, and such grounds may be dismissed on that basis: see, for example, R. v. Frost-Helmsing [2010] EWCA Crim 1200 at [14]–[15].[17]

---

[15] Reference is made in the Bar Council Appeals Guidance (n 10) to *R v Grant-Murray* [2017] EWCA Crim 1228, [2018] Crim LR 71.

[16] See *R v Roberts* [2016] EWCA Crim 71, [2016] 1 WLR 324 [40]; *R v Lea* [2021] EWCA Crim 65, [2021] 4 WLR 38 [43].

[17] Bar Council Appeals Guidance (n 10) para 34; similar guidance can be found in 'The Court of Appeal Criminal Division Guide to Commencing Proceedings' (July 2021) https://www.judiciary.uk/wp-content/uploads/2021/07/Blue-guide-July-2021-Final-1.pdf (accessed 10 June 2023).

11.26 Whilst the form of waiver to be provided by the appellant's new representatives is not stipulated, the Bar Council guidance states:

> If a waiver of privilege is necessary, then you must advise your client fully about the need for waiver and the consequences of that waiver.
>
> He will need to be made aware that a general waiver of privilege removes all confidentiality from the communications that he had with his former legal representatives. He will need to understand that, as a consequence of this, those former representatives will be free to respond to what he says about his case in the way that they see fit, to communicate directly with the court and, if required, to give evidence, all without any constraint on what they are allowed to tell the court about their privileged dealings and discussions with him. This will permit his former legal representatives to deal directly with any criticism that he may make of them. It will also mean that your communications with those former representatives will no longer be protected by privilege or confidentiality.[18]

11.27 This suggests that the client should be advised that in waiving privilege they are permitting their previous representatives to disclose any privileged communications to the court. This appears to be somewhat qualified by the guidance on the form of the waiver, which states: 'If, having been so advised, your client instructs you to waive privilege, then you should obtain a written waiver of privilege, signed by him, and covering all *relevant* communications with, instructions to and advice given by each of the affected former legal representatives.'[19]

11.28 The reference to 'relevant' communications is an important qualification which suggests that the waiver to be drafted is limited rather than general in its form. This is consistent with the established principles in respect of waiver in which, even when waiver is implied rather than express (unlike in this context), the extent of the waiver is governed by the principles of fairness such that the implied waiver is limited to the material required for the court to assess the issue to which the privileged material relates.

Form of Waiver

11.29 Whilst there is no guidance which specifically addresses the form of the waiver to be provided, a properly considered limited waiver which goes no further than is necessary to allow the issues to be determined on appeal, and for the appeal to be properly arguable, would appear to be the most prudent approach.

Refusal of Waiver

11.30 A refusal to waive privilege in the context of an appeal does not necessarily preclude an application for permission to appeal being lodged, but it is likely to hinder its prospects. The Bar Council guidance sets out clearly the issues to be considered should a client refuse to waive privilege: first, to consider as a matter of law the effect of a refusal to waive on the

---

[18] Bar Council Appeals Guidance (n 10) paras 39–40.
[19] ibid para 42 (emphasis added).

points to be argued; and, secondly, as a matter of professional conduct whether the appeal is properly arguable in the absence of a waiver of privilege:

> If your client declines to waive privilege, you should make a contemporaneous note of that decision. It would be best practice to ask the client to sign that note.
>
> You should then consider the effect of the refusal on the Grounds of Appeal. The court's inability to know information that a waiver of privilege would otherwise have enabled it to consider may affect whether it would be proper for you to settle particular grounds of appeal (for example, grounds which criticise former legal representatives). The effect of the absence of a waiver of privilege is a question of law, and you are referred to paragraph 36 above[20] in this regard. The question for you, as a matter of professional conduct, is whether the affected grounds of appeal are properly arguable in the absence of a waiver of privilege. In reaching a view about this, you might be assisted by considering the matters set out in sub-paragraphs 49(a)-(c) below.[21] You would also need to ensure that the court is not misled: see paragraph 47 below.[22]
>
> If you consider that, despite the absence of a waiver, you are able to submit proper grounds, then you must draw the refusal to the court's attention in the Grounds of Appeal.[23]

11.31 It is important to distinguish between the requirement to make enquiries as set out in *McCook* and the consideration of waiver. Even if a client refuses to waive privilege, this does not negate the requirement to make enquiries of previous solicitors. The enquiries of previous solicitors do not require a waiver of privilege, but they do require the permission of the client in order for privileged or confidential information to be shared with the new advisers. If a client refuses to permit these enquiries to be made, the Bar Council guidance states that counsel cannot accept instructions, save for in exceptional circumstances.[24]

Can Waiver of Privilege Be Implied by the Grounds of Appeal?

11.32 If an appellant refuses expressly to waive privilege for the purposes of an appeal, it is possible that privilege could in any event be impliedly waived by the lodging of grounds of appeal criticizing the advice given by previous solicitors. In practice, this issue is unlikely to arise as the Court of Appeal is more likely simply to reject the appeal or refuse to grant leave if there is no express waiver. The guidance and case law refer to the fact that a waiver is required in order to allow the single judge and/or the court to determine the issues on appeal. If there is no express waiver of privilege then the appeal can be dismissed on that basis

---

[20] ibid para 36, which states: 'A waiver of confidentiality is likely to be implied if confidential material is referred to in the Grounds of Appeal or in open court. Where privilege is not involved, the Court of Appeal is unlikely to require any further confirmation. The Court of Appeal does, however, need to know expressly whether privilege is being waived.'
[21] The Bar Council Appeals Guidance (n 10) refers to paras 49(a)-(c), but the relevant reference is para 50(a)-(c), which refers to the requirement to consider what objective information should be sought in circumstances where a previous legal representative refuses or fails to assist in response to enquiries made of them.
[22] ibid para 47, which states: 'A decision by your client not to waive privilege does not affect your duty to make inquiries of former legal representatives. A waiver of privilege is concerned with what the court can know, not what you can know.'
[23] ibid paras 44-46.
[24] ibid para 27.

alone.²⁵ Similarly, the Bar Council guidance suggests that in the absence of a waiver it is for the advocate to consider whether the grounds of appeal are properly arguable.

11.33 In the unlikely event that waiver by implication is an issue, parallels may be drawn with the position which arises when a client sues a former legal adviser. In *Paragon Finance PLC v Freshfields*²⁶ it was held that a client bringing an action for negligence against a former solicitor was asking the court to determine issues stemming directly from the confidential relationship between them. By doing so, confidentiality was lost by the issue being determined in open court, and therefore this led to an implied waiver of privilege so far as needed for resolution of the claim.

11.34 The Court in *Paragon Finance* endorsed an earlier case, *Nederlandse Reassurantie Groep Holding NV v Bacon & Woodrow (No 1)*, in which Colman J explained the rationale in the following terms:

> The true analysis of what the courts are doing in such cases of so-called implied waiver of privilege is, in my judgment, to prevent the unfairness which would arise if the plaintiff were entitled to exclude from the court's consideration evidence relevant to a defence by relying upon the privilege arising from the solicitor's duty of confidence. The client is thus precluded from both asserting that the solicitor has acted in breach of duty and thereby caused the client loss and, to make good that claim, opening up the confidential relationship between them and at the same time seeking to enforce against that same solicitor a duty of confidence arising from their professional relationship in circumstances where such enforcement would deprive the solicitor of the means of defending the claim. It is fundamental to this principle that the confidence which privilege would otherwise protect arises by reason of the same professional relationship between the parties to the litigation. The underlying unfairness which the principle aims to avoid arises because the claim is asserted and the professional relationship opened for investigation against the very party whose duty of confidence is the basis of the privilege. It is against the unfairness of both opening the relationship by asserting the claim and seeking to enforce the duty of confidence owed by the defendant that the principle is directed.²⁷

11.35 In order to afford fairness to the party defending the claim, the confidential relationship that existed between them and their former client is opened up and the previous legal adviser cannot be prevented from relying on privileged communications between the parties in the conduct of their defence.

11.36 There is no authority for the proposition that an appeal based on criticism of previous legal representatives automatically amounts to an implied waiver of privilege where no express waiver has been agreed. In principle, there may be some similarities between the position where a former legal adviser is sued and that of legal representatives whose advice is subject to criticism on an appeal against conviction or sentence. A situation may even arise

---

[25] *R v Frost-Helmsing* [2010] EWCA Crim 1200.
[26] [1999] 1 WLR 1183 (CA).
[27] [1995] 1 All ER 976, 986 (Com Ct).

where previous legal advisers are both criticized in grounds of appeal and sued for professional negligence. However, the principles engaged in each case are not identical and the need to afford fairness to the legal advisers defending a claim for professional negligence is not analogous to the position of the Court of Appeal in considering the merits of an appeal. The previous legal advisers are not a party to the proceedings in an appeal against conviction or sentence, and the issue being litigated is not whether they have discharged their duties towards their former client; it is the safety of the conviction and the extent to which the advice given by the previous legal advisers affects this. The court is therefore concerned to establish the facts as they relate to the instructions provided by the appellant and the advice given at first instance in order to establish whether the conviction is safe. A client's refusal to waive privilege brings no unfairness to the former legal advisers, as a non-party.

11.37 There is, however, more similarity between the two different types of claim if the issue is looked at from the perspective of the court. An appellant appealing against conviction on the basis of criticism of previous advisers will on the one hand be asking the Court of Appeal to find that the criticism is well-founded and that, as a result, the conviction is unsafe, whilst on the other hand refusing to substantiate that criticism by waiving privilege over the relevant material. The court may take the view that, considering the underlying principle for waiver is fairness, it would be unfair to allow the appellant to adopt this position and for the court to determine the appeal without knowledge of the relevant information. The court could therefore hold that privilege has been waived and that the appellant must produce the relevant privileged material in order to continue with the appeal.

Collateral Waiver

11.38 The principle of collateral waiver (see paras 1.94–1.96) is likely to apply should attempts to limit the waiver of privilege hinder the determination of any relevant issue. In circumstances where a limited waiver of privilege is provided which the court deems does not permit a proper examination of the issues, it will be open to the court to consider whether the grounds of appeal give rise to a collateral waiver of privilege over other material. If the court considers that the waiver of privilege amounts in any way to 'cherry-picking' of the issues over which privilege is claimed, the court will be entitled to consider the waiver as extending to other privileged material relating to the same issue. This will, of course, be fact-specific, but it is possible to envisage the court making enquiries regarding advice given and received which may be wider than the appellant and their representatives would wish. For example, it may arise in circumstances where the court seeks to understand when an issue was first raised with a legal representative, which could lead to enquiries regarding instructions given at the police station. Clients should therefore be aware that even in circumstances where an express limited waiver has been provided, the principles of collateral waiver could extend the parameters of the waiver should it be deemed necessary by the court to ensure fairness in the proceedings.

Appeals to the Crown Court from the Magistrates' Court

11.39 Appeals against conviction from the magistrates' court to the Crown Court take the form of a complete rehearing of the facts, and the conduct of previous legal representatives is not relevant. Appeals do not require permission and there is no restriction on the introduction of fresh evidence. This means that the obligations as set out in *McCook* are not relevant and the privilege issues discussed in this chapter do not arise in the same way as with an appeal to the Court of Appeal.

3 The Criminal Cases Review Commission

11.40 The Criminal Cases Review Commission (CCRC) has the power to investigate suspected miscarriages of justice and to refer cases back to the Court of Appeal in certain circumstances. The CCRC's powers are set out in the Criminal Appeal Act 1995 (CAA 1995). The CCRC's powers to investigate include a wide-ranging power to require documents to be produced from both public bodies and private individuals. Section 17 gives the CCRC the power to obtain documents from those serving in public bodies, including documents for which 'any obligation of secrecy or other limitation on disclosure' would otherwise prevent their disclosure or production.[28] Section 18A provides similar powers in respect of documents held by those not serving in public bodies, although in this case the procedure requires judicial oversight as the CCRC has to apply to the Crown Court for an order requiring the production of the material. As with section 17, an order under section 18A can be granted in respect of material for which 'any obligation of secrecy or other limitation on disclosure' would otherwise prevent its disclosure or production.[29]

11.41 Although not expressly stated, it is the authors' view that these provisions allow privileged material to be obtained and are therefore a rare example of a statutory abrogation of privilege. As discussed at paras 1.09–1.10, in the absence of express words, privilege can only be overridden if an intention to do so appears by 'necessary implication' from the wording of the relevant statutory provision.[30] Here, it is clear from the use of the words '*any* obligation of *secrecy* or other limitation'[31] that Parliament must have intended it to incorporate privilege, especially considering the context is one in which privileged material held by lawyers is very likely to be relevant to the CCRC's consideration of a case. It is perhaps unsurprising that Parliament included this provision considering the CCRC's purpose is to correct miscarriages of justice, which can be contrasted to investigating agencies seeking to obtain potentially incriminating material. There are also important safeguards concerning privilege contained in the CAA 1995 that are discussed below.

11.42 Section 25 states that where material is obtained under sections 17 or 18A and disclosure of the material would otherwise have been prevented by an obligation of secrecy or other

---

[28] Criminal Appeal Act 1995, s 17(4).
[29] ibid s 18A(6).
[30] *R (Morgan Grenfell & Co Ltd) v Special Commissioners of Income Tax* [2002] UKHL 21, [2003] 1 AC 563.
[31] Emphasis added.

limitation on disclosure, the person providing the information is permitted to require that the CCRC obtains their consent before any onward disclosure is made:

(1) Where a person on whom a requirement is imposed under section 17 or by an order under section 18A notifies the Commission that any information contained in any document or other material to which the requirement relates is not to be disclosed by the Commission without his prior consent, the Commission shall not disclose the information without such consent.
(2) Such consent may not be withheld unless—
   (a) (apart from section 17 or 18A) the person would have been prevented by any obligation of secrecy or other limitation on disclosure from disclosing the information to the Commission, and
   (b) it is reasonable for the person to withhold his consent to disclosure of the information by the Commission.
(3) An obligation of secrecy or other limitation on disclosure which applies to a person only where disclosure is not authorised by another person shall not be taken for the purposes of subsection (2)(a) to prevent the disclosure by the person of information to the Commission unless—
   (a) reasonable steps have been taken to obtain the authorisation of the other person, or
   (b) such authorisation could not reasonably be expected to be obtained.

11.43 This provides an important safeguard against the requirement to share privileged information with the CCRC, in that it affords the person sharing the privileged information the opportunity to request the CCRC not to disseminate or share it without their prior consent, a request with which the CCRC must comply. Consent may only be withheld in circumstances where disclosure would otherwise be prevented by an obligation of secrecy or other limitation (as would be the case with privileged information) and it is reasonable to withhold consent.

11.44 Section 25(3) makes clear that it is not sufficient to rely upon a lack of consent from another person to limit disclosure unless reasonable steps have been taken to obtain the other person's consent or it would be unreasonable to expect consent from that person to be obtained. This is particularly relevant where the material requested by the CCRC is a client file held by a lawyer.

11.45 What are the practical implications of these provisions on solicitors who may be required by the CCRC to share privileged material relating to clients or former clients? If an order has been obtained from the Crown Court that the material be produced, then refusal is likely to amount to contempt. It will not be permissible to resist production of the material to the CCRC even if the client does not consent; section 25 only limits onward disclosure once the CCRC has the material. The client should nevertheless be notified of the request and production, and it is imperative that the person providing the material expressly states that they require the CCRC to obtain their permission before any onward disclosure. Failure to do so will permit the CCRC to disclose the information without notifying the person providing the information.

11.46 If the CCRC is notified that they must seek permission before disclosing the information, then once notification of intended disclosure has been given by the CCRC, it will afford an opportunity for the person providing the material to obtain the consent of their client.

11.47 Section 25 applies equally to those providing information on behalf of a public body, although there are likely to be some differences in these circumstances, in that it may be the public body's own privilege which requires protection. This may affect the issue of who can give consent before onward disclosure can take place. In any event, there should always be careful consideration of the material being provided under any request from the CCRC and the provision of material should be accompanied by a covering letter or note stipulating clearly the requirements that must be satisfied before onward disclosure can take place.

11.48 The basis on which these provisions can be considered an abrogation of privilege is discussed above. However, it is worth considering their potential reach and whether the powers given to the CCRC to override privilege are proportionate to the function they perform. The wording of the statute permits the CCRC to obtain privileged information from any individual, and the holder of the privilege does not need to be the person who would benefit from the intervention of the CCRC. For example, the legislation as drafted would potentially permit the CCRC to obtain the file of an applicant's co-defendant's solicitor in order to examine the issues raised by the applicant. This would appear to be a far wider abrogation than one might imagine to be proportionate and, on its face, at odds with the fundamental principles of privilege as set out in *R v Derby Magistrates Court*.[32] In *Derby Magistrates*, the House of Lords held that a witness summons could not be issued in order to compel the production of documents subject to privilege which had not been waived. The documents in question were the proofs and attendance notes held by the solicitor of an acquitted defendant in a murder trial which were sought by a defendant facing trial for the same murder. It would appear that the position now follows that if a defendant in the same position as the defendant in *Derby Magistrates* was convicted and successfully applied to the CCRC, the CCRC would, in theory, have the power to obtain the privileged material to which the House of Lords held the defendant was not entitled. Whilst there is a distinction between the material being in the hands of the defendant and in the hands of the CCRC, the CAA 1995 does appear to confer unusually wide-ranging powers on the CCRC to obtain privileged material.

---

[32] [1996] AC 487 (HL).

12
Internal Investigations

1 Introduction

Privilege in the context of internal investigations has attracted a great deal of attention in recent years. A number of decisions have examined and clarified its scope, whilst authorities such as the Serious Fraud Office (SFO) have repeatedly emphasized the importance and benefits of waiving privilege over internal investigation material in order to be seen as cooperative in criminal investigations (see Chapter 7). The question of whether privilege applies to an internal investigation is complex and highly fact-specific, and it should certainly not be assumed that privilege will apply whenever lawyers are instructed to carry out an investigation.

Internal investigations take many forms and can examine a wide range of issues. This chapter is principally concerned with corporate[1] investigations carried out by lawyers (as opposed to other types of professional advisers) that consider issues potentially giving rise to criminal liability, and which may, therefore, take place in the shadow of a possible criminal investigation and/or prosecution. However, the issues under examination in an internal investigation will often not be confined solely to questions of criminal liability, and it is not uncommon for investigations also to consider related regulatory or employment issues or potential civil proceedings.

This chapter begins by looking at the application of legal advice privilege to internal investigation material before then considering how litigation privilege may apply. The final section of the chapter provides practical guidance on a number of important issues that may arise in the course of an investigation.

2 Importance of Privilege to Investigations

There is a fundamental disparity between the protection privilege affords an individual suspected of wrongdoing and the protection afforded to a company in a similar position. An individual suspected of wrongdoing is able to consult freely with their legal adviser, providing them with as much factual material as is necessary to enable advice to be obtained on their position. The same is not true of a corporate body. This is in large part due to the restrictive definition of 'client' within a corporate context that was established by *Three Rivers District Council v Governor and Co of the Bank of England* (*Three Rivers (No 5)*)[2],

---

[1] Internal investigations are usually carried out on behalf of a corporate entity, but the same principles apply to all types of organization. In this chapter, 'corporate' is used for consistency but should be read to include all types of organization.
[2] [2003] EWCA Civ 474, [2003] QB 1556, confirmed as correct law by the Court of Appeal more recently in *The Director of the Serious Fraud Office v Eurasian Natural Resources Corporation Limited* (*SFO v ENRC Ltd*) [2018] EWCA Civ 2006, [2019] 1 WLR 791 [123].

the effect of which is that legal advice privilege can only apply to communications between a company's lawyers and a small group of individuals within the company who have the requisite level of authority to engage the lawyers. In large corporations in particular, this has a significant impact on the ability to confidentially communicate with legal advisers, undermining the very basis for legal advice privilege. Information that is relevant to the legal advice that has been sought is extremely unlikely to be held solely by those few individuals who make up the client group according to the narrow *Three Rivers (No 5)* definition. Key information and evidence are far more likely to be held by a wide range of officers and employees of different levels of seniority across the whole company. The effect of *Three Rivers (No 5)* is that those individuals are treated as third parties and are not able to communicate with their employer's legal advisers in a way that attracts the protection of legal advice privilege.

12.05 The impact as far as internal investigations are concerned is that deciding whether to investigate potential wrongdoing and, if so, the extent of the investigation requires a careful assessment of the benefits versus the risks. The obvious risk is that incriminating evidence may be uncovered and will not be protected from seizure or compelled production if the authorities decide to investigate and wish to obtain the material. This may be enough to persuade a company not to initiate an internal investigation in some cases, which in turn impacts the quality of legal advice a company can receive. An individual client, however, does not face this dilemma. They can provide potentially incriminating information to their lawyer, and receive the best possible legal advice in return, safe in the knowledge that what has passed between them will not be disclosed to any other person without their permission.

12.06 Lawyers involved in internal investigations must therefore balance the competing objectives of identifying the issues on which a company requires advice and protecting the company from generating material which may be used to incriminate it. This is why the issues discussed in this chapter are of such importance and why they will continue to come before the courts for determination until the disparity between individual and corporate clients is remedied.

3 Legal Advice Privilege

Relationship between Client and Investigating Lawyer(s)

12.07 If a company instructs an external lawyer to carry out an investigation, their relationship will be one of client and lawyer (unless the lawyer is performing an 'independent' investigator role more akin to an expert than a legal adviser; as to which, see para 12.10) and confidential communications that pass between them will be covered by legal advice privilege if they are made for the dominant purpose of giving or obtaining legal advice. The same position applies if a solicitor instructs counsel to conduct the investigation. As set out at paras 1.25–1.26, 'legal advice' has a broad meaning for the purposes of privilege. As long as the lawyer's role includes providing related advice that has a 'relevant legal context', such as advice consequent on the findings of the investigation or on any matters related to the issues under investigation (which will almost certainly be the case), legal advice privilege will apply to the vast majority of communications with their client, including those that only contain factual findings from the investigation. Privilege attaching to investigation reports is discussed further at paras 12.29–12.35.

In *Al Sadeq v Dechert LLP*[3] Popplewell LJ rejected an argument that certain activities carried out by Dechert as part of its wide-ranging investigation on behalf of its clients (governmental departments in the Emirate of Ras Al Khaimah) into alleged fraud and misappropriation of public assets, and the related communications between Dechert and their clients, did not have a relevant legal context. It was suggested that at least some of the work carried out by Dechert was investigative work in which they were not being consulted in their capacity as lawyers. Popplewell LJ did not accept this, holding instead that Dechert were 'engaged in the investigatory process to bring their lawyers' skills to that process and to conduct it through lawyers' eyes', and that this was 'against the background of being instructed to provide legal advice in relation to suspected fraud'.[4] He considered that the work undertaken by Dechert had a relevant legal context. At first instance, Murray J had rejected the same submission and dismissed as 'unrealistic and artificial' the distinction between 'investigatory work' on the one hand and legal advice and assistance on the other, stating that: 'Where lawyers are engaged to conduct an investigation, it is a reasonable and fair assumption that the engagement encompasses the investigatory work and related legal advice and assistance as part of a continuum of legal service. It would take strong evidence to rebut this.'[5]

12.08

For these reasons, it is far preferable that lawyers carry out an internal investigation rather than the company itself or professional advisers who are not lawyers. This will ensure that the investigation report and other communications or documents containing the findings of the investigation will be covered by legal advice privilege (if the other requirements are satisfied as well), which will not be the case if produced by somebody who is not a lawyer.

12.09

It is sometimes the case that a lawyer, usually a barrister in chambers, is instructed as an 'independent' investigator to conduct a fact-finding investigation and to present their findings in a report. Rather than being instructed by a client or solicitor in the usual way, they are appointed under terms of reference and are not considered to have a lay or professional client. Their role is limited to investigating facts and they do not provide any legal advice. As such, they perform a function that is more akin to that of an expert rather than a legal adviser. Although in practice it may not always be easy to distinguish between the roles with precision, where such an arrangement is established, communications between the investigator and the organization commissioning the investigation and/or its legal advisers will not be covered by legal advice privilege. This is because the communications will not be between a client and their legal adviser and, in any event, the investigator will not be providing legal advice.

12.10

---

[3] [2024] EWCA Civ 28.
[4] ibid [229].
[5] *Al Sadeq v Dechert LLP* [2023] EWHC 795 (KB) [136]–[137].

Witness Interviews

Witnesses are likely to be third parties

12.11 For the purpose of legal advice privilege, when dealing with a corporate client, only those employees and officers of the corporate who are tasked with seeking and receiving legal advice on behalf of the corporate entity can have privileged communications with the corporate's lawyers. This is not the same as employees who are only authorized to speak to the company's lawyers or to provide information to them. This is the consequence of the narrow definition of 'client' in a corporate context adopted by the Court of Appeal in *Three Rivers (No 5)*.

12.12 This has important ramifications for internal investigations, particularly witness interviews. It means that, unless the interview is with an employee who can properly be considered part of the client group according to the narrow *Three Rivers (No 5)* definition, the interviewee will be a third party for the purposes of privilege and the interview will not attract legal advice privilege.

12.13 In reality, employees and officers of the type envisaged by *Three Rivers (No 5)* are unlikely to be interviewed as witnesses. It is common practice for a company to designate a small client group to provide instructions to and receive advice from the lawyers on the corporate's behalf in the course of an internal investigation (see paras 12.120–12.122), and these individuals will usually be chosen because they have no association with the matters under investigation or are as far removed from the issues as possible. As such, they are unlikely to hold relevant information that could be provided in a witness interview. Those who do hold such information will more likely fall outside the client group and therefore be third parties for the purposes of privilege. It should be noted, however, that with some investigations, particularly those involving smaller companies, it may not be possible for the client group to be entirely independent of the matters under investigation.

12.14 This narrow definition of 'client' was fatal to RBS' claim of legal advice privilege over witness interview notes in *The RBS Rights Issue Litigation (RBS)*.[6] The notes related to interviews conducted with a total of 124 individuals across a number of divisions, locations, and levels of seniority within RBS, both current and former employees. The interview notes were prepared variously by RBS' in-house lawyers, its external lawyers, and non-lawyers within the RBS Group Secretariat (as agents for the external lawyers). The basis of RBS' claim was that each of the interview notes recorded a communication between a lawyer and a person authorized by RBS to give instructions to its lawyers. The purpose of the interviews was to collect relevant factual information to enable RBS to obtain legal advice from its external lawyers, and there was no dispute that RBS had indeed authorized each of the interviewees to participate in the relevant interviews. RBS submitted that the communication of factual information (which was evidenced in the interview notes) gathered by or for the purpose of being provided to its lawyers was privileged, as long as the person providing and communicating the information was authorized to do so by RBS.

---

[6] [2016] EWHC 3161 (Ch), [2017] 1 WLR 1991.

12.15 Hildyard J rejected this argument. Relying on one of the facets of the decision in *Three Rivers (No 5)*, namely that legal advice privilege does not extend to information provided by (non-client) employees and ex-employees to or for the purpose of being placed before a lawyer, he was of the view that:

> [T]he Interview Notes, albeit that they record direct communications with RBS's lawyers, comprise information gathering from employees or former employees preparatory to and for the purpose of enabling RBS, through its directors or other persons authorised to do so on its behalf, to seek and receive legal advice. It is clear from the judgment in *Three Rivers (No 5)* that 'information from an employee stands in the same position as information from an independent agent' (see p1574H). The individuals interviewed were providers of information as employees and not clients: and the Interview Notes were not communications between client and legal adviser.[7]

12.16 Similarly, in *The Director of the Serious Fraud Office v Eurasian Natural Resources Corp Ltd* (*SFO v ENRC Ltd*)[8] ENRC's solicitors had conducted interviews with current and former employees or officers of the company and its subsidiaries, their suppliers and other third parties regarding suspected corruption and financial wrongdoing. Ultimately, the Court of Appeal did not need to decide whether the internal investigation interviews were covered by legal advice privilege since it found that litigation privilege applied. However, the Court expressed, obiter, that had it been necessary to decide the issue, it would have been bound to follow the narrow definition of 'client' established by *Three Rivers (No 5)*.[9] The Court would therefore have held that the interview notes were not covered by legal advice privilege, on the basis that '[t]hose documents did not contain information that was communicated to ENRC's solicitor by anyone authorised to seek or receive legal advice on behalf of ENRC or its subsidiaries'.[10]

Interview notes as lawyers' working papers

12.17 As explained at paras 1.36–1.37, legal advice privilege can cover a lawyer's working papers, such as their own confidential notes and documents relating to the matter on which they are instructed.

12.18 Unsuccessful attempts have been made at extending this principle to internal investigation witness interview notes made by a lawyer. In *RBS*, the bank made an alternative claim to legal advice privilege over the interview notes (save for those produced by the RBS Group Secretariat) on the basis that they constituted lawyers' working papers and were therefore privileged. Reviewing the relevant authorities on this issue, Hildyard J noted that, because verbatim transcripts of unprivileged interviews would themselves not be privileged, RBS had to demonstrate 'some attribute of or addition to the relevant Interview Notes which distinguishes them from verbatim transcripts or reveals from an evident process of selection the trend of legal advice being given, and is such as to trigger their protection as lawyers'

---

[7] ibid [93].
[8] *SFO v ENRC Ltd* (n 2).
[9] Although, if it had been open to the Court to depart from *Three Rivers (No 5)*, it would have been in favour of doing so as it could see much force in the arguments that the case was wrongly decided (*SFO v ENRC Ltd* (n 2) [124], [130]).
[10] *SFO v ENRC Ltd* (n 2) [133].

working papers'.[11] RBS' evidence was that the purpose of the interview notes was not to create transcripts of the interviews but rather 'documents that would assist in providing legal advice to RBS'. It was said that they were therefore not 'simply verbatim recitals' of the interviews but 'impressions of the lawyer with a view to advising the client'. RBS claimed that the interview notes:

> [R]eflect the lawyers' impressions in the sense that they reflect both the work undertaken in preparation for the interviews (ie they reveal the lawyers' train of inquiry), and in the sense that they are a note not a transcript, and therefore to some greater or lesser extent reflect a selection by the author of the points to be recorded.

The notes stated on their face that they reflected external counsel's 'mental impressions'.[12]

12.19 Hildyard J considered the question ultimately to be: 'has the likelihood sufficiently been demonstrated that the [Interview] Notes would by reason of the legal input they reflect give a clue as to legal advice (or some aspect of the legal advice) given to RBS?' In determining the answer, he took full account of the fact that: 'Any notes of an interview, as distinct from a bare transcript, are likely to reflect, even if only to a limited extent, the particular interests, lines of inquiry and perception of the relative importance of the points covered (including those omitted) of the person making the note.' He also acknowledged that: 'To that extent at least, such notes may be taken to reflect the note-maker's "mental impressions"', and he noted RBS' evidence about the purpose of the notes and what the documents stated on their face.

12.20 However, in his judgment, 'the mere fact that a note is not verbatim, and therefore may betray some selection or line of enquiry', does not suffice. What is required is 'Something more … to distinguish the case from the norm'. RBS had offered 'nothing beyond mere conclusory assertion'. For example, RBS' evidence did not show anything substantial of its legal team's analysis of the documents or give examples of the sort of legal input said to justify and be capable of justifying the claim of privilege. Even the reliance on the fact that the notes stated on their face that they reflected 'mental impressions' was not backed up by any assertion that the notes did in fact, 'upon careful review, contain material that would or could reveal the trend of advice'. As such, the basis for RBS' claim was not sufficient and the claim was rejected. Hildyard J added that his conclusion was 'reinforced by the consideration that there is a real difference between reflecting "a train of inquiry" and reflecting or giving a clue as to the trend of legal advice'.[13]

12.21 The issue was examined by the High Court again in the first instance decision in *SFO v ENRC Ltd*.[14] Whilst much of Andrews J's decision was subsequently overturned by the Court of Appeal, the Court declined to give an opinion on this particular issue as its conclusion that the notes were covered by litigation privilege meant that the issue did not require determination.

---

[11] *RBS* (n 6) [105].
[12] ibid [109].
[13] ibid [121]–[126].
[14] [2017] EWHC 1017 (QB), [2017] 1 WLR 4205.

12.22 ENRC had claimed that the internal investigation witness interview notes taken by its external lawyers were covered by legal advice privilege on the basis that they constituted lawyers' working papers. Rejecting the claim, Andrews J endorsed the approach taken by Hildyard J in *RBS*, holding that, 'A claim for privilege over lawyers' working papers will only succeed if the documents would betray the trend of the legal advice'. That could not be the case here because the documents were 'merely notes of what the lawyers were told by the witnesses'. Andrews J relied on *Parry v News Group Newspapers*,[15] in which Bingham LJ, having acknowledged that a note of a conversation taken by a solicitor inevitably involved a process of distillation and selection, nevertheless stated that, 'A bare record of what passed is in my view entitled to no legal professional privilege, whether it is a solicitor's memorandum, a transcript, or an exchange of letters'. Andrews J rejected ENRC's submission that, because the notes were taken by a lawyer, the process inevitably represented the work of the lawyer's mind and their selection of what should be written down, so that, taken as a whole, the matters inevitably gave a clue as to the trend of the advice. This was contrary to Bingham LJ's approach in *Parry* and had 'no principal foundation'. Andrews J was not satisfied that the evidence established, on the balance of probabilities, that the notes would give a clue as to legal advice or any aspect of legal advice given to ENRC. There had been no suggestion that the notes included ENRC's lawyers' 'qualitative assessment of the evidence, or any thoughts about its importance or relevance to the inquiry, or even indications of further areas of investigation that the lawyer making the notes considered might be fruitful in consequence of what the witness had said', although it was noted that 'the betrayal of further lines of inquiry would not in itself have been sufficient in any event'. As in *RBS*, the evidence relied on by ENRC failed to show 'anything substantial of its legal team's analysis of the documents' and failed 'to give examples of the sort of legal input into the document that would justify a claim to privilege'. The evidence consisted of 'no more than conclusory statements that fell well short of what would suffice to make out a claim for working papers privilege'.[16]

12.23 Andrews J's implied suggestion that, in order for privilege to apply to lawyers' working papers, the documents in question must betray the tenor of legal advice regardless of the type of document (ie not just interview notes) is not, in the authors' view, an accurate reflection of the law.[17] However, so far as notes of non-privileged internal investigation interviews that simply record what was said are concerned, the authors consider the approach taken by Hildyard J and Andrews J to be correct. The claims in both cases were ambitious; fundamentally, they concerned interviews which were not themselves privileged, but the parties were attempting to make notes of those interviews privileged merely because they had been prepared by a lawyer and inevitably involved some form of selection and distillation. It seems that the reliance on the working papers principle in both cases was driven more by necessity than anything more compelling, given the courts' adoption of the narrow definition of 'client' from *Three Rivers (No 5)*. The judges' reasoning did not mean that information that would otherwise have been privileged lost its privileged status. Rather, it was simply that information which was not privileged to begin with did not *become* privileged merely because it was recorded by a lawyer.

---

[15] [1990] NLJR 1719.
[16] *SFO v ENRC Ltd* (n 14) [178]–[180].
[17] See discussion at para 1.37.

12.24 What the two cases do not rule out, however, is that interview notes *could* be privileged as lawyers' working papers in the right circumstances. Andrews J's comments imply that such a claim might succeed if the notes contain 'qualitative assessment of the evidence, or any thoughts about its importance or relevance to the inquiry, or even indications of further areas of investigation that the lawyer making the notes considered might be fruitful in consequence of what the witness had said'. In the context of an internal investigation, this could include the lawyer's comments on whether what has been described by the witness amounts to a criminal offence or contributes to the corporate's potential liability, how credible the witness' evidence is, possible lines of further enquiry or points to discuss with the client in light of the evidence, and other points that are likely to feed into the advice being given to the client.

12.25 Whether these sorts of comments would mean that the *whole* note was privileged, however, is another matter. Considering that the interview itself would not be privileged, it is the authors' view that, were the issue to be litigated, a court would most likely attempt to separate the lawyers' comments from the witness' evidence and treat only the former as privileged. In most cases, they could be redacted without impacting the non-privileged parts. This would of course defeat the whole purpose of structuring a note in such a way, as the witness' evidence itself would not be protected. Indeed, in *R (AL) v Serious Fraud Office*, the Divisional Court indicated that a suggestion that 'the inclusion within the interview notes of lawyers' musings etc served to cloak the interview notes themselves in privilege' was flawed. The Court suggested that any genuinely privileged entries could be redacted in the usual manner.[18]

12.26 Moreover, structuring interview notes in this way risks undermining their value as an account of what a witness has said. The more analysis and annotation a lawyer adds to a note in order to try to make the document privileged, the further away it becomes from serving as a clear and complete account of what the witness has said, as such an approach is likely to cause some of the witness' evidence to be lost or obscured.

12.27 For these reasons, it would be unwise for lawyers to assume that the working papers principle provides a sound basis for claiming legal advice privilege over internal investigation interview notes. This is particularly important considering that agencies such as the SFO are very likely to challenge such a claim if asserted against them. Before interviews take place, and particularly in cases where litigation privilege does not arise, clients should be advised that the notes are unlikely to be covered by legal advice privilege and that any such claim is very unlikely to be accepted by investigators or prosecutors.

12.28 Finally, it should also be borne in mind that, even if a note of a witness interview is privileged, the witness' own knowledge of relevant facts will not be, and there is no property in a witness. There is therefore nothing to prevent an investigator from speaking to a witness to obtain their account as part of a criminal investigation.

---

[18] [2018] EWHC 856 (Admin), [2018] 1 WLR 4557 [111]. This case is examined in more detail at paras 7.21–7.24, 7.52, and 7.54.

Investigation Reports: A Need for More than Just a Factual Report?

In *SFO v ENRC Ltd*, one of the categories of documents over which privilege was claimed included slides and notes from meetings at which one of ENRC's external lawyers presented factual evidence from the internal investigation to the board and the Nomination and Corporate Governance Committee. ENRC claimed that the documents also contained or revealed advice by the lawyer as to potential allegations of criminality and the steps the company should take in respect of those potential allegations. **12.29**

At first instance, the SFO argued that the advice ought to be redacted, but that, insofar as the lawyer was presenting the findings of the internal investigation to the board, those aspects of the documents could not be privileged. Andrews J concluded that: 'If the solicitor had simply been reporting his fact findings to the board, and there was no legal advice involved, the minutes recording what transpired at the meeting at which the fact findings were reported to the client would not be subject to legal advice privilege.' However, in this instance, the evidence relating to the meetings for which the slide presentation was prepared indicated that the lawyers had been instructed to give legal advice to the board about certain specific matters consequential on their findings. This meant that the slides prepared by the lawyers for the specific purpose of giving legal advice to ENRC were privileged, even if reference was made in them to factual information or findings from the internal investigation that would otherwise not be privileged. They were part and parcel of the confidential solicitor-client communication. Likewise, anything said by the lawyer at the meetings to elaborate on what was on the face of the slides as part of the background to or foundation for the advice given as to what the client should do next, and any record of it, would also be privileged, even if referring to information which would not otherwise be privileged.[19] **12.30**

Summarizing the issue, Andrews J held that: **12.31**

> The results of [ENRC's external lawyers'] investigations, any reports, any fact-findings made by them, and the underlying data upon which they are based, would not be subject to LPP outside this specific context. It is only if they are properly to be characterised as a record of the confidential solicitor-client dialogue for the purpose of giving and receiving legal advice that they would be subject to legal advice privilege. So, any [external lawyers'] report of its investigation into Africa and the underlying materials used by [one of ENRC's external lawyers] and his colleagues to produce it will not be privileged; the privilege extends only to what he said to his client at the meeting(s) in March 2013 at which that slide presentation was made and any record of what he said on that occasion.[20]

On this basis, the documents were covered by legal advice privilege.

As has been pointed out by other commentators,[21] this is not an accurate reflection of the law. It is not correct to say that an internal investigation report produced by a lawyer which contains factual findings but no advice on the law will not be privileged. This is inconsistent **12.32**

---

[19] *SFO v ENRC Ltd* (n 14) [181]–[185].
[20] ibid [186].
[21] See eg Colin Passmore, *Privilege* (4th edn, Sweet & Maxwell 2020) para 2-319.

with the broad scope of legal advice privilege established by earlier (and more authoritative) decisions. In the vast majority of cases, lawyers carrying out an internal investigation will be instructed not only to investigate and to establish the facts, but also to advise on matters arising from the findings of the investigation, such as the company's potential criminal liability and actions to be taken, and other matters related to the issues under investigation. Conducting the investigation and reporting the findings to the client will be necessary in order for the legal advice to be provided, and both functions will be intertwined and core aspects of the lawyer's retainer. In these circumstances, a lawyer presenting the factual findings of an investigation to their client, either in writing or orally, will be expected to provide legal advice as appropriate, just as their client will be expected to ask for advice on any issues arising.

12.33 This falls squarely within the 'continuum of communication' between a solicitor and their client described in *Balabel v Air India*:

> Where information is passed by the solicitor or client to the other as part of the continuum aimed at keeping both informed so that advice may be sought and given as required, privilege will attach. A letter from the client containing information may end with such words as 'please advise me what I should do'. But, even if it does not, there will usually be implied in the relationship an overall expectation that the solicitor will at each stage, whether asked specifically or not, tender appropriate advice.[22]

It is also consistent with the broad scope of legal advice privilege established by *Minter v Priest*[23] and referred to with approval by Lord Carswell in *Three Rivers District Council v Governor and Co of the Bank of England (Three Rivers (No 6))*:

> [A]ll communications between a solicitor and his client relating to a transaction in which the solicitor has been instructed for the purpose of obtaining legal advice will be privileged, notwithstanding that they do not contain advice on matters of law or construction, provided that they are directly related to the performance by the solicitor of his professional duty as legal adviser of his client.[24]

12.34 It is therefore the authors' view that as long as the lawyer's role includes, either expressly or impliedly, providing related advice that has a 'relevant legal context', such as advice on matters consequent to the factual findings of the investigation or on any other matters related to the issues under investigation (as will invariably be the case), any communications between the lawyer and their client containing the findings of the investigation, including the investigation report, will be covered by legal advice privilege in their entirety, even if they contain nothing else. This proposition is supported by *Al Sadeq v Dechert LLP*,[25] discussed at para 12.08.

12.35 Where this may not be the case, as far as investigation reports are concerned, is if the report is prepared for an intended readership that includes third parties outside the client group. Depending on the circumstances, this may mean that the report cannot

---

[22] *Balabel v Air India* [1988] Ch 317, 330.
[23] [1930] AC 558 (HL).
[24] [2004] UKHL 48, [2005] 1 AC 610 [111].
[25] *Al Sadeq v Dechert LLP* (n 3).

be considered a confidential communication between the lawyer and their client for the dominant purpose of giving or obtaining legal advice. This is different, however, to a report that is prepared only for the client but is later shared with third parties, in which case the report may be privileged to begin with but privilege is either waived or lost subsequently.

4 Litigation Privilege

Introduction

12.36 In the context of internal investigations, litigation privilege is most relevant to witness interviews, which will usually involve lawyers speaking to individuals who fall outside the client group and who are therefore third parties, meaning that legal advice privilege cannot apply.

12.37 The question of whether litigation privilege applies to an internal investigation is highly fact-specific and it is difficult to draw principles of general application from the case law relating to this. Nevertheless, an analysis of the reported cases does reveal some points of interest which may assist lawyers in making the determination. What follows is a discussion of those points, first in relation to the question of whether litigation can be said to be in progress or reasonably in contemplation at the time of the investigation, and then in relation to whether the dominant purpose of the investigation is the conduct of litigation. Not all of the cases relate to criminal litigation, but the points they raise are of some assistance nevertheless.

Litigation in Progress or Reasonably in Contemplation

12.38 As noted in the introduction to this chapter, there are many types of litigation that will engage litigation privilege in the context of an internal investigation, but this chapter is primarily concerned with criminal litigation. Criminal litigation means a prosecution, not an investigation, although litigation privilege can apply pre-charge if a prosecution is reasonably in contemplation.[26]

12.39 Note that some regulatory investigations which begin as pure fact-finding inquiries into suspected wrongdoing can change in character to become sufficiently adversarial to engage litigation privilege. This was found to be the case in *Tesco Stores Ltd v Office of Fair Trading*,[27] which concerned an Office of Fair Trading (OFT) investigation into suspected anti-competitive practices. The investigation began with the OFT obtaining documentation and interviewing witnesses in a manner that was purely inquisitorial. However, the OFT subsequently issued statements informing Tesco of its proposed finding that the company had infringed certain prohibitions. The procedure to be followed after the issuing of the statements was that Tesco would have the right to make representations in response,

---

[26] See paras 1.54 and 1.58.
[27] [2012] CAT 6, [2012] Comp AR 188.

following which the OFT would decide whether the prohibitions had in fact been infringed. The Competition Appeal Tribunal held that, following the issuing of the OFT statements, the proceedings were no longer simply an inquiry to get to the bottom of the facts. They had become confrontational and Tesco stood accused of wrongdoing. The tribunal felt that the proceedings were, by that stage, no less confrontational than ordinary civil proceedings involving the same alleged infringements. Furthermore, the OFT was about to decide Tesco's liability under the relevant legislation. Whilst the outcome was by no means certain, there was a serious risk that Tesco could be found liable for the alleged infringements and fined a substantial sum.[28]

12.40 It would seem that the key factor in this case was that the proceedings in question were going to conclude with the OFT making a final determination as to the facts and Tesco's liability, with the possibility of imposing mandatory legal obligations for Tesco in the form of a fine. This can be contrasted with a criminal investigation, where the assessment of evidence and liability goes no further than determining whether there is a realistic prospect of conviction should the matter go to court.

12.41 Whatever the type of litigation, it must either be in progress or reasonably in contemplation in order for litigation privilege to apply. 'Reasonably in contemplation' is not clearly defined, but it has been suggested that the following will *not* suffice:

- a 'mere possibility' of litigation;
- a 'distinct possibility that sooner or later someone might make a claim'; or
- a 'general apprehension of future litigation'.[29]

Indications from investigators or prosecutors

12.42 Relevant to the question of whether litigation is reasonably in contemplation will be any indications as to the likelihood of litigation commencing that a potential adverse party to the prospective litigation has given. In a criminal context, it is necessary to consider any signs that investigators or prosecutors have given as to the possibility of charges being brought and to ask whether those indications are enough to cross the threshold of a prosecution being more than a mere possibility. If the authorities are not yet aware of the issues under investigation, it will likely be difficult to reasonably contemplate a prosecution, unless it is anticipated that they will become aware at a future point, for example if a self-report is contemplated. This will often be the case with whistle-blowers who raise concerns internally rather than directly to the authorities or in a public forum such as the media. It is particularly important to look for these external signs in criminal cases as it will be the prosecution authorities who decide whether to commence litigation, not the company that has commissioned the internal investigation. This can be contrasted with civil proceedings, where the company that initiates the internal investigation may be the party who decides whether to bring proceedings.

12.43 A number of cases helpfully demonstrate the importance of this point, most notably *SFO v ENRC Ltd*.[30] Key to the Court of Appeal's decision that litigation privilege applied in *SFO*

---

[28] ibid [44]–[45].
[29] *United States of America v Philip Morris Inc* [2004] EWCA Civ 330, [2004] 1 CLC 811 [68]. See para 1.56 of this work.
[30] *SFO v ENRC Ltd* (n 2).

v ENRC Ltd was the nature and timing of the SFO's communications with the company around the time of the internal investigation.

The privilege dispute that arose between ENRC and the SFO related to documents generated as part of an internal investigation into suspected corruption and financial wrongdoing within a subsidiary company owned by ENRC. This was triggered by an email from a whistle-blower in December 2010. Relevant documents included notes of interviews that ENRC's solicitors conducted with current and former employees and documents relating to a 'books and records review' carried out by a firm of forensic accountants. On 10 August 2011, ENRC received a letter from the Chief Investigator of the SFO which referred to 'recent intelligence & media reports concerning allegations of corruption and wrongdoing by [ENRC]'. The letter urged ENRC carefully to consider the SFO's Self-Reporting Guidelines whilst undertaking its internal investigation and invited ENRC's General Counsel to meet with the SFO to further discuss matters. The letter also said that the SFO wished to discuss with the General Counsel 'ENRC's governance and compliance programme and its response to the allegations as reported'. The letter concluded by saying that the SFO was not carrying out a criminal investigation into ENRC at that stage. On 19 August 2011, ENRC's General Counsel replied to the SFO accepting its invitation to meet. He said that he was happy to discuss ENRC's governance and compliance programme and its response to the allegations reported in the press, that ENRC understood the merits of self-reporting and that he looked forward to discussing the topic with the SFO at the meeting.

12.44

At first instance, Andrews J held that ENRC had failed to establish that at the time of the 19 August 2011 letter to the SFO, it was 'aware of circumstances which rendered litigation between itself and the SFO a real likelihood rather than a mere possibility'.[31]

12.45

On appeal by ENRC, the Court of Appeal reached a different view and decided that, as at the date of the ENRC response, the company was aware of circumstances that rendered litigation in the form of a prosecution by the SFO a real likelihood rather than a mere possibility. The reasons for the Court's conclusion included the following:

12.46

- By March 2011, information the General Counsel had received from his GC100 contacts made him think that ENRC was firmly on the SFO's radar and that an investigation would be opened in due course. This had caused him to upgrade ENRC's dawn raid procedures.
- In April 2011, ENRC's head of compliance predicted a dawn raid before the end of summer.
- In April 2011, communications between ENRC's lawyers noted that the conduct under review in the internal investigation was potentially criminal in nature and that adversarial proceedings might occur as a result of the investigation. As such, one of the lawyers stated that 'both criminal and civil proceedings can be reasonably said to be in contemplation'.
- When the SFO wrote to ENRC on 10 August 2011, although it said that a criminal investigation was not being carried out, it asked ENRC to consider the Self-Reporting

---

[31] *SFO v ENRC Ltd* (n 14) [149].

Guidelines[32] very carefully. The guidelines expressly said that, 'no prosecutor can ever give an unconditional guarantee that there will not be a prosecution', and participation in the self-reporting process would increase 'the prospect (in appropriate cases) of a civil rather than a criminal outcome' by reducing the likelihood that the SFO would discover corruption itself.[33]

12.47 Whilst the Court was satisfied that litigation was reasonably in prospect by 19 August 2011, it also referred to several subsequent events, including:

- At a meeting with its lawyers on 22 September 2011, ENRC was advised that, if it engaged in the voluntary disclosure regime with the SFO, it would lose privilege in relation to the documents that it provided. This advice assumed at that time that privilege would otherwise attach to those documents.
- At the first meeting between ENRC and the SFO in October 2011, the SFO said that it could give no assurance that it would not prosecute.
- By June 2012, the SFO expressed concern to ENRC that it had not yet made a self-report. ENRC was told that: 'If the investigation had stalled or been obstructed this would be regarded very negatively. For a civil settlement to be entertained, it was essential that the investigation findings were disclosed in the near future.'
- In December 2012, ENRC's lawyers wrote to the SFO and asked for confirmation that 'if an equitable settlement [were not] reached between the SFO and ENRC ... that it [was] accepted that the report [would] not be used by the SFO as evidence of any wrongdoing or in any criminal proceedings against either ENRC, any subsidiary of ENRC or any employee or director of ENRC or its subsidiaries'. The SFO's reply gave no such assurances.[34]

12.48 These factors meant that 'the whole sub-text of the relationship between ENRC and the SFO was the possibility, if not the likelihood, of prosecution if the self-reporting process did not result in a civil settlement'.[35] Whilst the Court was 'not sure that every SFO manifestation of concern would properly be regarded as adversarial litigation', and it rejected an argument that once an SFO investigation is reasonably in prospect so too is a prosecution, it stated that 'when the SFO specifically makes clear to the company the prospect of its criminal prosecution (over and above the general principles set out in the Guidelines), and legal advisers are engaged to deal with that situation ... there is a clear ground for contending that criminal prosecution is in reasonable contemplation'.[36]

12.49 The SFO's reference to the Self-Reporting Guidelines was significant because, as far as companies are concerned, the self-reporting regime is about avoiding prosecution. The SFO may take the fact of a self-report into consideration as a public interest factor tending against prosecution. That the SFO was making explicit reference to the self-reporting regime in its August 2011 letter strongly indicated that a prosecution was on its radar at that

---

[32] See extracts of relevant sections of the Guidelines in the judgment at [18].
[33] *SFO v ENRC Ltd* (n 2) [92].
[34] ibid [92].
[35] ibid [93].
[36] ibid [96]–[97].

stage. It did not matter that the SFO had not yet commenced a formal criminal investigation or that ENRC's internal investigation was not complete; the indication from the SFO, combined with the other factors highlighted by the Court of Appeal in its judgment, was sufficient to give rise to a reasonable contemplation of prosecution.

12.50 *SFO v ENRC Ltd* can be contrasted with another criminal case, *R v Jukes*,[37] in which the relevant prosecutor, the Health and Safety Executive (HSE), had at the relevant time given no indication that a prosecution was likely, beyond commencing a criminal investigation. The case concerned an incident in which an employee of a waste and recycling company suffered a fatal accident whilst at work. The appellant was alleged to have had responsibility for health and safety and maintenance of the machine that had caused the employee's death and to have failed to take reasonable care for the safety of employees. He was convicted of a health and safety offence.

12.51 On appeal against conviction, one of the issues raised was the admissibility of a statement which the appellant had made to the company's solicitors as part of their investigation a few weeks after the incident. This had been relied upon by the prosecution at trial as it undermined the prepared statement he had later given to the HSE and the police, the contents of which he had repeated in his defence statement. The appellant argued that the statement was covered by litigation privilege and as such should not have been relied upon by the prosecution.

12.52 The Court of Appeal rejected this argument. At the time the statement was made, the HSE was investigating the matter but no decision to prosecute had been taken. The appellant was not interviewed by the HSE and police until sixteen months later. There was no evidence that at the time the investigation by the company was taking place, anybody:

> [H]ad enough knowledge as to what the investigation would unearth or had unearthed when the Health and Safety Executive concluded its investigations, that it could be said that they appreciated that it was realistic to expect the Health and Safety Executive to be satisfied that it had enough material to stand a good chance of securing convictions.

It was not enough simply to say, as the appellant did, that where there is a death and on the face of it a breach of duty, the HSE normally prosecutes. There was no evidence as to the state of mind of any of the people who were subsequently prosecuted, nor any evidence from the HSE as to the stage of its investigation at the time the appellant made his statement in the course of the internal investigation.[38]

12.53 It was suggested on behalf of the appellant that the fact the statement was drafted in a form that made reference to the Criminal Justice Act 1967, section 9 and included the usual declaration that begins, 'If it is tendered in evidence I shall be liable for prosecution', was relevant to the question of whether litigation was in reasonable contemplation. The Court did not agree. This was insufficient to establish, without more, that a criminal prosecution was in reasonable contemplation, and the Court was not willing, in the absence of evidence from

---

[37] [2018] EWCA Crim 176, [2018] 2 Cr App R 9.
[38] ibid [23]–[24].

the company's lawyers, simply to assume from the fact that experienced solicitors used this form that it could be said that criminal proceedings were in reasonable contemplation.[39]

12.54 Although this case was decided before the Court of Appeal overturned the first instance judgment in *SFO v ENRC Ltd*, the Court of Appeal in *SFO v ENRC Ltd* did not consider its reasoning to be at odds with *Jukes*, emphasizing that *Jukes* was a decision on the facts.[40] The key difference between the two cases was that, in *SFO v ENRC Ltd*, there was a significant indication from the SFO that a prosecution was a real possibility, by virtue of the fact that explicit reference was being made to the self-reporting regime and ENRC was being asked to consider the guidelines very carefully. In *Jukes*, there was no equivalent indication. The HSE was investigating the incident but had not communicated anything which alluded to how it might deal with the case once its investigation was complete.

12.55 In *The State of Qatar v Banque Havilland SA & Another*[41] the fact of a regulator's investigation into potential financial misconduct at Banque Havilland SA was not sufficient to give rise to a reasonable contemplation of litigation. The nature of the regulator's involvement and dealings with the bank did not suggest that the matter would go beyond the investigation stage. The bank and the second defendant, a former employee of the bank, were alleged to have been participants in a conspiracy to cause financial damage to the Qatari economy. The case against them was principally based on the preparation by the second defendant, while employed at the bank, of a seven-page slide presentation entitled 'Distressed Countries Fund' and its subsequent alleged dissemination. The presentation was featured substantively in a lengthy online news article on 9 November 2017 and the article explained that the metadata for the presentation identified the second defendant as its creator. The second defendant resigned from the bank on the same day as the article was published.

12.56 In the immediate aftermath of the online article, the bank, through its Luxembourg lawyers, instructed PwC to carry out what was described at the time as a 'forensic' or 'IT' investigation. The bank notified the Luxembourg regulator, the CSSF (the bank was incorporated in Luxembourg), about the issue and that it was investigating it as a matter of priority. The CSSF asked for full clarity on the issue. PwC's terms of engagement, contained in a letter from PwC to the bank's lawyers dated 20 November 2017, included the following:

> Following a trigger event indicating a disclosure of a confidential file that allegedly was created by an employee of the Bank, You have been selected to investigate on this context in accordance with a contract between You and the Bank. You would now like us to proceed, as subcontractor under legal privilege, with the capture of the professional computers or any other electronic device of the suspected individuals, and perform a deep analysis to retrieve information around the data leakage and file creation.
>
> …
>
> In close collaboration with You, our objective will be to help You to investigate and understand how the file in scope of the investigation, and any potentially linked files or aspects, have been created and potentially shared from systems of the Bank with external or internal

---

[39] ibid [25].
[40] *SFO v ENRC Ltd* (n 2) [100].
[41] [2021] EWHC 2172 (Comm).

parties. We will investigate, to the extent possible in the given IT environment of the Bank, the life cycle of the file on the suspect's assets, or any other asset involved in the investigation, will be supported by factual evidence.

The terms of engagement stated that PwC would be reporting directly to, and taking direction exclusively from, the lawyers, and, as such, 'all of PwC's work pursuant hereto, including its communications with You and with BH personnel, shall be subject to legal privilege and confidential to the maximum extent provided by the attorney-client, the work-product doctrine, and any other applicable privilege'. It was stated that all documents created by PwC and all communications in the matter would be marked "'Legally Privileged and Confidential" to reflect the privileged nature of the engagement'. PwC issued its investigation report on 7 June 2018.

12.57 In the course of the litigation between Qatar and the defendants, Qatar sought disclosure of the PwC report, but the bank refused to disclose it on the grounds that it was covered by litigation privilege. Rejecting the bank's privilege claim, David Edwards QC (sitting as a judge of the High Court) said that the most important point in time for the purposes of litigation privilege was the position on 13 November 2017 when PwC was instructed to carry out its work and to produce its report.[42] Whilst the online article and disclosure within it of the presentation were regarded by the bank as a serious matter, the fact that it was felt at the time that this 'could have significant ... regulatory and legal consequences' was far too general to support a claim for litigation privilege. The bank recognized that the fact and content of the article were matters that needed to be brought to the attention of the CSSF as the primary regulator. The judge accepted the bank's evidence that it was sure the CSSF would want to investigate the matter and that, as part of that investigation, it would ask questions. But, as at 13 November 2017, or indeed in the period thereafter prior to publication of the report in June 2018, there was 'little in the evidence to suggest that the CSSF's position was, or was regarded by the bank as, hostile, or that adversarial regulatory proceedings were, or were regarded by the bank, as reasonably in contemplation'. On the contrary, the evidence suggested that the tone of discussions with the CSSF had been 'fairly positive' and the CSSF seemed to be reassured. The CSSF, it was said, was 'convinced that the bank was not involved with the plan'. The questions the CSSF had asked the bank about the article were, the judge said, 'not particularly aggressive or adversarial', and the CSSF did not threaten proceedings. Nothing in the bank's subsequent communications with the CSSF suggested that the regulator was adopting an adversarial position towards the bank.[43]

12.58 Even allowing for the fact that, in some cases, what may start as an investigation might develop into adversarial proceedings, as in *Tesco Stores Ltd v Office of Fair Trading*,[44] and the CSSF was likely to have enforcement powers, including the power to impose fines, the judge did not consider the CSSF's involvement to have gone beyond the investigative stage, nor was there anything to suggest that it would do so.[45]

---

[42] ibid [162].
[43] ibid [164]–[169].
[44] *Tesco Stores Ltd v Office of Fair Trading* (n 27). See paras 12.39–12.40.
[45] *Qatar v Banque Havilland SA & Anor* (n 41) [170]–[172].

12.59 The second body whom the bank suggested might commence adversarial proceedings was the FCA (the second defendant had worked out of the bank's London branch). However, the bank had had no contact with the FCA prior to 13 November 2017 and the FCA was not notified until 14 November 2017. In February 2018, the FCA wrote to the bank seeking information about the creation of the presentation and whether the second defendant had worked at the bank's London branch. Whilst the judge did not doubt that this 'emphasised the importance … of obtaining PwC's findings to allow the bank to respond effectively to the FCA', it fell far short of an anticipation of adversarial proceedings.[46]

12.60 As far as litigation with Qatar was concerned, there was no evidence of any communication between Qatar and the bank, or of any intimation or fear of a claim by Qatar against the bank, prior to when PwC was instructed. The first contact was in December 2017 when a lawyer acting on behalf of the Qatar Central Bank wrote to the bank asking it to preserve documents 'in connection with potential claims that our client may have'. Despite the reference to potential claims, the judge considered it to stop some way short of suggesting that the bank did, in fact, anticipate a claim by Qatar. There was no evidence of any further communication with Qatar prior to June 2018.[47]

12.61 The indications from the CSSF in this case were markedly different to those given by the SFO in *SFO v ENRC Ltd*, hence why the claim to litigation privilege failed.

Contemplation of several sets of proceedings

12.62 It is possible that the requirement for litigation to be reasonably in contemplation can be satisfied by anticipating more than one set of proceedings. This is demonstrated by the case of *FM Capital Partners Ltd v Marino*.[48] An internal investigation was triggered after FM Capital Partners Ltd received a letter from the Libya Africa Investment Portfolio, a sovereign wealth fund whose assets it managed, making a number of serious complaints about its management of those assets. The letter alleged breaches of duty and unlawful conduct by the CEO of FM Capital. In response, the company's lawyers appointed the accountancy firm BDO to investigate, and this was followed shortly afterwards by the suspension of the CEO. A disciplinary hearing was scheduled to take place but the CEO failed to attend. He was then dismissed for gross misconduct. FM Capital subsequently issued proceedings against the CEO (and several other defendants) alleging various dishonest breaches of duty.

12.63 In the course of the proceedings, one of the other defendants sought disclosure of documents created as part of BDO's investigation, including BDO's interim report. This was resisted by FM Capital on the basis that the documents were covered by litigation privilege. The evidence from FM Capital's lawyers was that, when BDO was instructed and during its investigation, litigation was seriously contemplated in a number of forms. First, the letter of complaint from the Libya Africa Investment Portfolio expressly threatened proceedings and made it likely that court proceedings would be brought on the basis of the allegations made in the letter. Second, the allegations in the letter raised serious questions about the former CEO's conduct which created a real prospect that FM Capital would

---

[46] ibid [173].
[47] ibid [174]–[175].
[48] [2017] EWHC 3700 (Comm), [2017] All ER (D) 140 (Dec).

wish to bring proceedings against him (as in due course did indeed happen). Third, it was contemplated that the former CEO might himself issue proceedings against FM Capital in relation to his suspension. Seeing no reason to doubt FM Capital's evidence on this point, Leggatt J held that litigation was indeed reasonably in prospect at the time of BDO's investigation.[49]

The case is of note for the fact that the litigation that was held to be reasonably in contemplation was three separate sets of proceedings, but that did not prevent the claim of litigation privilege being made out. The key factor was that they all related to the same issue: the mismanagement of the Libya Africa Investment Portfolio's assets and misconduct by the CEO. It will often be the case that an internal investigation examines issues that give rise to the possibility of more than one set of proceedings. An investigation into suspected fraud will raise questions of criminal liability, but if the organization is regulated, there may also be regulatory consequences to consider, as well as possible employment proceedings against employees suspected of wrongdoing and perhaps also civil claims by defrauded shareholders or investors. What *FM Capital* helpfully demonstrates is that uncertainty as to the precise form the litigation will take is not necessarily fatal to a claim of litigation privilege, as long as litigation of some kind is reasonably contemplated (and the dominant purpose test is satisfied as regards that anticipated litigation). **12.64**

Uncertainty as to what will be uncovered
A common problem with privilege claims in this context is that internal investigations are often, by their very nature, fact-finding inquiries whose purpose is to establish what has happened, in circumstances where there is limited understanding of the veracity of the allegations or suspicions and therefore whether they are likely to give rise to litigation. If so little is known about the issues under investigation that it cannot be said that there is more than a 'mere possibility' of litigation, litigation privilege will not apply. **12.65**

This was partly the reason why the claim to litigation privilege failed in *R v Jukes* (discussed at paras 12.50–12.54), and it was also a problem in another case, *Starbev GP Ltd v Interbrew Central European Holding BV*,[50] which is discussed below. However, in *SFO v ENRC Ltd*, the Court helpfully noted that just because there is uncertainty as to the facts and whether there is any substance to the suspicions or concerns that have been raised, that does not mean litigation cannot reasonably be in contemplation. Where there is potential criminal liability, litigation privilege can arise before a party knows the full details of what is likely to be unearthed or a decision to prosecute has been taken.[51] The Court of Appeal commented that: **12.66**

> [W]hilst a party anticipating possible prosecution will often need to make further investigations before it can say with certainty that proceedings are likely, that uncertainty, in our judgment, does not in itself prevent proceedings being in reasonable contemplation ... An individual suspected of a crime will, of course, know whether he has committed it. An international corporation will be in a different position, but the fact that there is uncertainty does not mean that, in colloquial terms, the writing may not be clearly written

---

[49] ibid [5]–[6].
[50] [2013] EWHC 4038 (Comm), [2014] All ER (D) 116 (Jan).
[51] *SFO v ENRC Ltd* (n 2) [98], [100].

on the wall. We think [Andrews J at first instance] was wrong to regard the uncertainty as pointing against a real likelihood of a prosecution. The reasoning in paragraphs 162–163 of her judgment[52] could not outweigh the clear indications of a likely prosecution contained in the documents to which we have referred.[53]

12.67 Similarly, two other cases, *AXA Seguros SA de CV v Allianz Insurance Plc (T/A Allianz Global Risks)*[54] and *Collidge v Freeport Plc*,[55] both discussed below, indicate that it may be sufficient if there is a reasonable prospect of the investigation uncovering a particular issue which will likely result in litigation. In those cases, it seems that the existence of that particular issue and the commencement of litigation were inextricably linked so that reasonable contemplation of one meant reasonable contemplation of the other.

12.68 In *AXA Seguros SA de CV v Allianz Insurance Plc (T/A Allianz Global Risks)*[56] the claimant had provided insurance to a Mexican bank responsible for various highways in Mexico. The claimant's risk in respect of this was covered by a reinsurance contract with the defendant. The reinsurance contract applied only to roads constructed to 'internationally acceptable standards', and, within a reasonable time from inception of the reinsurance contract, surveys were to be carried out to confirm the acceptability of the quality of construction and maintenance of the roads. The claimant duly instructed a company to survey all the roads covered by the insurance to determine their value and to report on their condition. Their report was delivered to the defendants. The response from the lead underwriter was that the report did not contain the level of detail they would expect from such a document and the reinsurance policy would therefore be endorsed to include a 'reverse onus of proof clause', imposing on the claimant an obligation to show that the roads were up to the correct standard.

12.69 In 2001, a hurricane in Mexico caused considerable damage to one of the highways covered by the insurance, and a claim was made under the policy against the claimant by the insured party. Payment was made by the claimant, following which the claimant sought an indemnity from the defendant pursuant to the reinsurance contract. The defendant denied that it was liable to pay an indemnity, leading to the commencement of proceedings between the parties. The claimant applied for inspection of all reports and associated documents produced by an engineering firm which had been appointed by the defendants to inspect the damage to the highway. These documents included a preliminary report and an additional studies report. The defendants resisted the application on the basis that the documents were covered by litigation privilege. The defendants claimed that they were obtained and prepared for the dominant purpose of obtaining legal advice in connection with litigation reasonably in prospect.

12.70 Clarke J held that, at the relevant time, there was a reasonable expectation of litigation between the claimant and the defendants. Of relevance were the conditions of the reinsurance

---

[52] *SFO v ENRC Ltd* (n 14).
[53] *SFO v ENRC Ltd* (n 2) [98].
[54] [2011] EWHC 268 (Comm), [2011] Lloyd's Rep IR 544.
[55] [2007] EWHC 645 (QB).
[56] *AXA Seguros SA v Allianz Insurance Plc* (n 54).

contract and the fact that surveys had taken place but had not confirmed the acceptability of the roads to the satisfaction of the defendants. In the circumstances, there could be said to have been:

> [W]hat can properly be described as a reasonable prospect that the reports from [the engineering firm instructed by the defendants to inspect the damage] would reveal that the reason why the Claimant had not fulfilled its obligation to provide surveys which confirmed the acceptability of the roads, was because they were not constructed to an acceptable standard, with the result that the Defendants would reject the claim and litigation would inevitably follow. There was also a reasonable prospect of litigation if the … report left the acceptability of the Roads unclear, on the basis that, according to the Defendants, it was for the Claimant to prove fulfilment of the condition [that the roads be constructed to internationally acceptable standards].[57]

The claimant argued that, when the engineering firm was instructed, the defendants did not know either way whether the road had been constructed in accordance with international standards and that a doubt as to whether it had been so constructed was not the same as a reason to believe that it had not been. Rejecting this argument, Clarke J noted that:

> The fact that one or more conditions have to be fulfilled in order for a dispute to arise which requires the commencement of litigation in order to resolve it does not necessarily mean that litigation is only a possibility. Much may depend on what, at the relevant time, is the prospect that the conditions will be fulfilled.[58]

In this case, therefore: **12.71**

> [A] reasonable prospect of litigation does not depend solely on knowledge of the facts that justify rejection of the claim (in which case rejection and hence a dispute would be almost certain) but on what was reasonably to be regarded as in prospect, upon which question the failure of the claimants to produce the confirmation promised was highly material. Such failure was, in my judgment, one of the factors that took the prospect of litigation beyond that of a mere possibility.[59]

Ultimately, however, the privilege claim failed as the judge did not consider the defendants to have established that the reports were produced for the dominant purpose of the anticipated litigation (see the discussion at para 12.86). **12.72**

In *Collidge v Freeport Plc*[60] concerns regarding the claimant's (Executive Chairman of Freeport) conduct arose and, following a confrontation with him at a board meeting, he chose to resign, subject to a compromise agreement. Under the terms of the agreement, the claimant warranted that there were no circumstances of which he was aware or ought reasonably to have been aware which would constitute a repudiatory breach on his part of his contract of employment, which would have entitled the company to terminate his employment without notice. The defendant set up an investigation into the claimant's conduct **12.73**

---

[57] ibid [44]–[45].
[58] ibid [43].
[59] ibid [46].
[60] *Collidge v Freeport Plc* (n 55).

in order, it claimed, to enable the board, in conjunction with the company's solicitors, to satisfy itself that the claimant's warranty that he had not been guilty of any serious misconduct was true. The defendant was unwilling, on the basis of a bare denial by the claimant, to authorize a large severance payment to him in circumstances where serious allegations had been made about his conduct. If the allegations were found to be true, the defendant would potentially have no liability to pay him. The defendant's evidence was that, in reality, it had no option but to conduct an investigation. It was intended that the defendant's solicitors would scrutinize the findings of the investigation and advise the board on its rights and obligations, in particular whether the claimant was in breach of his warranty or not, and, if he was, whether the defendant was legally entitled to refuse to pay the termination monies and other benefits otherwise due.

12.74 In subsequent proceedings between the parties, the claimant sought disclosure of certain documents which the defendant withheld on the basis of litigation privilege. One such document was a witness statement taken by the defendant as part of the investigation, four days after the claimant's resignation. It was highly critical of the claimant and formed the basis of the defendant's pleaded case of breaches of the warranty in the compromise agreement. The claimant argued that the investigation was akin to any other internal inquiry that an employer might carry out to determine facts in dispute, and the fact that litigation might result at some stage thereafter, whether in the form of an action for wrongful dismissal or otherwise, was not sufficient to give rise to privilege.

12.75 Upholding the defendant's claim to privilege, Nigel Wilkinson QC (sitting as a deputy judge of the High Court) was in no doubt that the particular circumstances of the case enabled the defendant successfully to claim litigation privilege in respect of the underlying documents gathered for the purpose of the investigation into the claimant's conduct. The judge agreed with the defendant's submission that no other purpose could be identified or at any rate sensibly argued as being separable from the purpose of litigation. Litigation was inevitable in light of the results of the investigation, which was designed to establish if there was evidence that the claimant had been guilty of conduct capable of amounting to a repudiatory breach of his employment contract.[61]

12.76 Although not expressly stated in the judgment, it is assumed that this was a case in which there was a reasonable prospect that the investigation would find that the allegations were true, that this would lead to the defendant not paying the claimant and that the claimant would then issue proceedings against the defendant.

12.77 A different approach was taken in *Starbev GP Ltd v Interbrew Central European Holding BV*.[62] Starbev had acquired a brewing business from the defendant, ICEH, which Starbev had then sold to another company. A dispute arose as to whether and to what extent ICEH was entitled to a share of the sale proceeds under the terms of the original contract between Starbev and ICEH. In the course of the proceedings, Starbev challenged ICEH's withholding inspection of two categories of documents on the grounds that litigation privilege applied. The first category related to advice received from ICEH's advisors, Barclays

---

[61] ibid [11]–[12].
[62] *Starbev GP Ltd v Interbrew Central European Holding BV* (n 50).

Capital, concerning the structuring of the consideration for the sale of the business by Starbev. ICEH suspected that Starbev had deliberately structured the sale in order to eliminate the payment due to ICEH. They asked Barclays to advise on what steps were available to them to challenge this. ICEH claimed that litigation with Starbev was reasonably anticipated and that the dominant purpose of instructing Barclays was in connection with that litigation.

Rejecting ICEH's privilege claim, Hamblen J considered the evidence to amount to ICEH having a suspicion concerning the sale of the business and instructing Barclays to investigate in order to see if there was substance to that suspicion, but nothing more. Barclays' role was investigatory, and 'Unless and until they confirmed that there was substance to [the] suspicion there was no real reason to anticipate litigation'.[63] The individual within ICEH who was involved in seeking Barclays' advice said in his statement that 'it occurred to me that ICEH would end up in another dispute with Starbev'. This, so thought Hamblen J, suggested no more than such a dispute being a possibility. It did not 'connote that it was reasonably anticipated both that there would be such a dispute and that it would result in litigation. Whether or not it would do so was unlikely to be known until Barclays investigated and reported'.[64] **12.78**

That Barclays' role was purely investigatory was borne out by a number of contemporaneous documents which referred to their role as one of checking the position and calculating the payment that might be likely to come to ICEH as a result of the sale. The fact that Barclays' advice was to be and was in fact shared with ICEH's corporate solicitors took the matter little further. They may well have been part of the investigatory exercise, but that is all it was at that stage.[65] **12.79**

The courts' approach in *SFO v ENRC Ltd*, *AXA Seguros v Allianz Insurance*, and *Collidge v Freeport Plc* helpfully demonstrates that litigation can still be in reasonable contemplation even if the full facts are not yet known, as will so often be the case when an internal investigation is commenced. The cases establish a helpful line of reasoning that takes a pragmatic approach to the situation in which many companies will find themselves when allegations or suspicions first come to light. However, *Jukes* and *Starbev* show that there must nevertheless be at least some understanding of the facts before litigation can reasonably be contemplated. **12.80**

Dominant Purpose of Conducting Litigation

If litigation is in progress or reasonably in contemplation, litigation privilege will only apply to internal investigation witness interviews (if the witness is a third party) and other communications between the client or their lawyer and a third party if the sole or dominant purpose of the relevant communication or document is: **12.81**

---

[63] ibid [19].
[64] ibid [20].
[65] ibid [21], [23].

1. to enable legal advice to be sought or given in connection with the conduct of the litigation;
2. to obtain evidence or information to be used in or in connection with the conduct of the litigation; or
3. to conduct or aid in the conduct of the litigation (insofar as not covered by the above).[66]

12.82 If an internal investigation is carried out in circumstances where litigation is in progress or in reasonable contemplation, it is unlikely that the purpose of the investigation will be entirely unrelated to that litigation. However, a mere connection with the litigation is not sufficient for litigation privilege to apply, nor is the fact that evidence and information gathered in the course of the investigation may be used in that litigation. The conduct of the litigation must be at least the *dominant* purpose of the investigation.

Conduct of litigation is of no more than equal importance to one or more other purposes

12.83 If the conduct of litigation is not the only purpose of an investigation, this does not automatically mean litigation privilege cannot apply. However, if it is of no more than equal importance to the other purpose(s), the dominant purpose test will not be satisfied. The case that established this principle was *Waugh v British Railways Board*,[67] a case that involved a fatal accident on the railway. Two days after the accident, two officers of the railway board prepared a 'joint inquiry report' which incorporated statements of witnesses. In litigation brought by the wife of the deceased against the railway board, disclosure of the report was resisted on the basis that it was covered by litigation privilege. The board's evidence was that it was standard practice whenever an accident occurred on the railway for officers of the board to produce a report on the causes of the accident and for the officers to forward it to their superiors. It was said that such reports were also made equally for the purpose of 'being submitted to the board's solicitor as material upon which he can advise the board upon its legal liability and for the purpose of conducting on behalf of the board any proceedings arising out of such accidents'. In this particular case, it was anticipated from the very outset that a claim for damages would almost certainly ensue.

12.84 The House of Lords held that litigation was not the dominant purpose of the report and therefore litigation privilege could not apply. In the Court's view, the report had a dual purpose: for 'railway operation and safety purposes' in order to ascertain 'whether the working system was defective and could be improved so as to obviate such accidents', and 'for the purpose of obtaining legal advice in anticipation of litigation'. The first purpose was more immediate than the second, but both were described as being of equal rank or weight.[68]

12.85 Lord Edmund-Davies thought that: '[T]he claims of humanity must surely make the dominant purpose of any report upon an accident (particularly where personal injuries have been sustained) that of discovering what happened and why it happened, so that measures

---

[66] See para 1.60.
[67] [1980] AC 521 (HL).
[68] ibid 531, 533.

to prevent its recurrence could be discussed and, if possible, devised.' He believed the dominant purpose test would be difficult to satisfy 'when inquiries are instituted and reports produced automatically whenever any mishap occurs, whatever its nature, its gravity, or even its triviality'.[69]

12.86 The existence of a dual purpose was also fatal to the claim for litigation privilege in *AXA Seguros SA de CV v Allianz Insurance Plc (T/A Allianz Global Risks)* (discussed at paras 12.68–12.72). Although Clarke J found that litigation was reasonably in contemplation at the relevant time, he did not consider the defendants to have established that the reports were produced for the dominant purpose of anticipated litigation between them and the claimant. Instead, he considered there to be a dual purpose: (i) assessing whether the highway had been constructed to internationally acceptable standards, and (ii) determining to what extent any damage had been caused by the hurricane and verifying the correctness of quantum figures for remedial work. The first issue bore on the question whether there was cover under the reinsurance at all. The second set of issues concerned whether and to what extent there was liability under the original insurance, and thus the reinsurance. As between the two purposes, neither purpose was predominant. Insofar as the engineering firm was instructed in relation to the quantum of the insurance claim against the claimant, the interests of the claimant and the defendants were common, not adverse. There was no evidence of any issue on quantum as between the claimant and the defendants or that the engineering firm's work was in any way directed to any such issue.[70] The claim to litigation privilege over the reports was therefore rejected.

12.87 Similarly, in *Price Waterhouse v BCCI Holdings (Luxembourg) SA*,[71] litigation was held to be just one of several purposes of an investigation. The claimant performed several different functions in relation to the Bank of Credit & Commerce International SA and its associated companies (BCCI). One of these functions was that, from October 1990, partners of Price Waterhouse were members of a special committee of investigation initially established by the government of Abu Dhabi, representing the controlling shareholders, and later reconstituted as an internal committee of BCCI to investigate certain problem loans made by companies in the group. Price Waterhouse received notices requiring the production of specified documents to the SFO and the Bank of England, prompting it to seek a declaration that it was not precluded from complying with any such notice by any claim made by the defendants that relevant documents were subject to privilege. The question was very narrowly drawn and was concerned only with documents which came into existence for the purpose of the investigation. The question for the court was therefore whether the circumstances in which the investigating committee was established and carried out its functions were such as to give rise to privilege for the documents which it generated. The documents in question consisted of drafts, reports, notes, and working papers of the investigating teams (comprising staff of Price Waterhouse and Ernst & Young) and/or the investigating committee.

---

[69] ibid 544.
[70] *AXA Seguros SA v Allianz Insurance Plc* (n 54) [49].
[71] [1992] BCLC 583 (Ch).

12.88 It was accepted that possible litigation for the recovery of at least some of the problem loans was in contemplation in or about October 1990 when the investigating committee was first established. It was also accepted that one of the purposes of the investigation was to obtain legal advice in connection with or to prepare for such litigation. However, Millett J held that this was not the dominant purpose; rather, it was 'a very subsidiary purpose indeed'. He considered that:

> The primary concern was to establish the amount of the possible losses which had resulted from the problem loans, in order to enable proper provision to be made for them in the 1990 accounts, and to quantify the amount of further financial support which was required from the controlling shareholders. A further, though possibly subsidiary, purpose was to ascertain whether the conditions under which the promised support would be forthcoming (ie that there had been no fraud or other impropriety) were satisfied. Another, and certainly subsidiary purpose, was to recommend improvements in management control.
>
> The board of BCCI, the auditors, and the regulatory authorities all needed to know what was the true financial position of BCCI, and this required an investigation in order to establish the facts. If BCCI itself or its controlling shareholders did not set an investigation in motion, it was feared that the regulatory authorities would. BCCI's financial position depended, in part at least, on the recoverability of the problem loans and that might require legal advice as to the prospects of success if resort had to be made to legal proceedings. But just as in *Waugh v British Railways Board* the board needed to establish the facts whether or not litigation ensued, so the board of BCCI, the auditors and the controlling shareholders needed to establish BCCI's financial position whether or not recovery proceedings were necessary.
>
> …
>
> In the present case it was necessary to determine the extent to which the problem loans were recoverable, in order to establish BCCI's financial position and to decide whether recovery proceedings should be taken. But the two purposes were quite independent of each other. There was nothing of merely academic interest in the former; it was of vital concern not only to BCCI, but also to the controlling shareholders, the auditors, and the regulatory authorities. I am satisfied that this was the dominant purpose of the investigation, and was quite independent of the possible need to take recovery proceedings, and that accordingly the documents in question do not attract legal professional privilege.[72]

12.89 *London Fire and Emergency Planning Authority (LFEPA) v Halcrow Gilbert & Co Ltd*[73] involved a similar issue to *Price Waterhouse*, in that litigation was a distinct and not immediate purpose of an inquiry. The case involved a dispute between LFEPA and Halcrow in relation to the construction of a fire house at LFEPA's training centre. The project suffered severe delays and costs were over budget. Halcrow had been retained by LFEPA as its project manager. In light of the delays and escalating costs, LFEPA instructed a claims consultant to carry out a 'technical audit' to ascertain what had caused the delays and overspend. The consultant carried out interviews with Halcrow employees and examined various categories of documents. At the conclusion of the audit, he produced a report for

---

[72] ibid 589–91.
[73] [2004] EWHC 2340 (TCC), [2005] BLR 18.

LFEPA. Just over two months after the report was produced, LFEPA gave formal notice that it intended to make claims against Halcrow and outlined in a 24-page letter the nature of the claims that were to be made. Draft particulars of claim were not served until almost seven months later.

In the course of the proceedings between LFEPA and Halcrow, Halcrow sought disclosure of the claims consultant's report. LFEPA resisted disclosure on the grounds that it was covered by litigation privilege, the dominant purpose of the report having been for use in litigation against Halcrow and at least some of the contractors. LFEPA did not claim privilege over the interviews and seemed to accept in final submissions that they had a dual purpose, but this was said by LFEPA to be irrelevant. In any event, LFEPA maintained that the dominant purpose was for use in litigation, even if a subsidiary purpose may have been the audit required by LFEPA's elected members. 12.90

Rejecting LFEPA's claim to litigation privilege, HHJ Toulmin QC held that the immediate purpose of instructing the consultant was to investigate the cause of the delay and the increased cost of the project, to provide answers for LFEPA's elected members and to provide an answer to the question of whether LFEPA should continue with the project or not. The 'more distant purpose' was to obtain an analysis which would be helpful in the event of litigation. The judge noted that, although the letter which gave formal notice of LFEPA's intention to make claims against Halcrow was served two months after the consultant's report, it was described as an 'initial letter', and the 'detail which is required for litigation'—the draft particulars of claim—was not provided until almost ten months after the consultant's report was produced.[74] 12.91

Investigation would have been carried out anyway
Waugh and *Price Waterhouse* are both notable for the fact that the investigations would have been required regardless of whether or not there was litigation. In *Waugh*, the evidence showed that it was standard practice whenever an accident occurred on the railway for officers of the board to produce a report on the causes of the accident and to forward it to their superiors. Similarly, in *Price Waterhouse*, the board of BCCI, the auditors and the controlling shareholders needed to establish BCCI's financial position whether or not recovery proceedings were necessary. 12.92

It follows, therefore, that where an internal investigation is required irrespective of the possibility or threat of litigation, it will be difficult to claim that litigation is the dominant purpose of the investigation. 12.93

Several purposes may form part of a single purpose of preparing for litigation
The cases discussed above highlight the fact that investigations with more than one purpose will not satisfy the dominant purpose test if the conduct of litigation is of no more than equal importance to the other purpose(s). However, in some cases, what may at first appear to be distinct purposes may actually be aspects of one single overall purpose of preparing for litigation, such that litigation privilege can apply. This more nuanced approach has been taken in a number of cases and involves careful consideration of the full 12.94

---

[74] ibid [51]–[52].

context to the investigation. A fact-finding inquiry if considered in isolation may not appear to be directly related to litigation, but if one asks what the purpose of establishing the facts is, this may reveal that fact-finding and preparing for litigation are effectively one and the same.

12.95 This was the approach taken in *Re Highgrade Traders*.[75] Highgrade Traders Ltd was a wholesale supplier of cloth to the clothing trade and its stock and assets were insured against fire and consequential loss. Very shortly after the company had substantially increased the insurance cover on its stock, a serious fire broke out in the premises occupied by the company, destroying all of the stock and gutting the premises. A claim was made under the insurance policy. The insurer instructed a firm of chartered loss adjustors and surveyors to investigate and report, resulting in a preliminary report four days later. The report disclosed a number of suspicious circumstances suggesting the fire had been deliberately caused. The police carried out an investigation and an employee of Highgrade was charged with arson. The insurer's solicitors, who had been instructed in relation to the claim, advised the insurer that they considered the case to be one in which litigation was likely to ensue and asked their client to obtain from their loss adjustors a fully detailed report. The report was prepared shortly thereafter and provided to the solicitors, who advised the insurer that the claim ought to be resisted.

12.96 The employee who had been charged with arson was subsequently acquitted and this led to Highgrade pressing the insurer for the claim to be dealt with. Highgrade's loss adjustors wrote to the insurer's loss adjustors complaining about the delay in settling the claim and said that it was hoped the insurer 'will not be party to a policy which can only result in our clients being forced either into liquidation or into litigation to secure the proper settlement of their claim'. This, Oliver LJ believed, clearly conveyed a threat of possible litigation.[76] The insurer's solicitors instructed a firm of chartered accountants to investigate and report on the financial position of the company at the date of the fire and prior thereto. In their report, the accountants concluded that the company's business was no longer viable at the time of the fire. A forensic expert was also instructed on behalf of the insurer to prepare a formal report as to the cause of the fire. After receiving the reports and consulting with counsel, the insurer took a firm decision to repudiate liability under the policies. It wrote to Highgrade confirming that it was satisfied that the fire was deliberately started by or with the connivance of the company and the claim would therefore not be met. Highgrade went into liquidation soon after.

12.97 On the application of the liquidator, the Registrar of the Companies Court made an order requiring a representative of the insurer to be examined on oath and to produce the reports prepared by the insurer's loss adjustors, chartered accountants, and forensic expert. The representative of the insurer applied to discharge the order on the basis that the three reports were covered by litigation privilege, but this was rejected. The decision was appealed and the matter came before the Court of Appeal. The Court considered it to be unarguable that litigation was not in reasonable prospect at the time the reports were commissioned and brought into being.[77] As to the purpose of the reports, the judge at first instance had

---

[75] [1984] BCLC 151 (CA).
[76] ibid 158.
[77] ibid 173.

found a duality of purpose: the insurers wanted not only to obtain the advice of their solicitors but also to ascertain the cause of the fire. However, on appeal, Oliver LJ found these purposes to be 'quite inseparable', stating that:

> The insurers were not seeking the cause of the fire as a matter of academic interest in spontaneous combustion. Their purpose in instigating the enquiries can only be determined by asking why they needed to find out the cause of the fire. And the only reason that can be ascribed to them is that of ascertaining whether, as they suspected, it had been fraudulently started by the insured. It was entirely clear that, if the claim [under the insurance policy] was persisted in and if it was resisted, litigation would inevitably follow. The claim had been made and there was no indication that it was not going to be pressed, particularly after [the Highgrade employee's] acquittal [of arson]. It is, as it seems to me, entirely unrealistic to attribute to the insurers an intention to make up their minds, independently of the advice which they received from their solicitors, that the claim should or should not be resisted. Whether they paid or not depended on the legal advice which they received, and the reports were prepared in order to enable that advice to be given. The advice given would necessarily determine their decision and would also necessarily determine whether the anticipated litigation would or would not take place.[78]

12.98 Oliver LJ disagreed with the first instance judge's reading of *Waugh v British Railways Board* (discussed at paras 12.83–12.85), that it was only if the documents were brought into existence for the dominant purpose of actually being used as evidence in the anticipated proceedings that privilege could attach and that the purpose of taking advice on whether or not to litigate was some separate purpose which did not qualify for privilege. This was 'to confine litigation privilege within too narrow bounds'. In the present case:

> No doubt the purpose was 'dual' in the sense that the documents might well serve both to inform the solicitors and as proofs of evidence if proceedings materialised. But, in my judgment, the learned judge failed to appreciate that the former purpose was itself one which would cause the privilege to attach.

Unlike in *Waugh*, where the documents in question would have had to have been produced in any event for the board's internal purposes in connection with railway safety, in the present case there was no purpose for bringing the documents into being other than that of obtaining the professional legal advice which would lead to a decision whether or not to litigate. That was 'a sufficient purpose on its own to entitle them to privilege quite apart from any subsidiary purpose which they might serve in any litigation which might ensue as a result of the decision'.[79] As such, the reports were covered by litigation privilege.

12.99 A similarly nuanced approach was taken in *SFO v ENRC Ltd*. Having found that litigation was reasonably in prospect (see paras 12.43–12.49), the Court of Appeal had to decide whether it was reasonable to regard ENRC's dominant purpose as being to investigate the facts to see what had happened and deal with compliance and governance or to defend the proceedings which were reasonably in prospect.

---

[78] ibid 173–74.
[79] ibid 174.

12.100 As well as urging careful consideration of its self-reporting guidelines, the SFO's letter of 10 August 2011 had said that it wanted to discuss 'ENRC's governance and compliance programme and its response to the allegations as reported'. The Court held that:

> [I]n this case, the answer can be achieved by unpacking the words 'compliance' and 'governance'. Although a reputable company will wish to ensure high ethical standards in the conduct of its business for its own sake, it is undeniable that the 'stick' used to enforce appropriate standards is the criminal law and, in some measure, the civil law also. Thus, where there is a clear threat of a criminal investigation, even at one remove from the specific risks posed by the SFO should it start an investigation, the reason for the investigation of whistle-blower allegations must be brought into the zone where the dominant purpose may be to prevent or deal with litigation.[80]

12.101 On this basis, the Court held that the notes of interviews with former and current employees and the product of the books and records review were brought into existence for the dominant purpose of resisting or avoiding a criminal prosecution against ENRC or its subsidiaries or their employees. Whilst there may have been a need to investigate the existence of corruption from a compliance and corporate governance perspective, that was just a subset of the defence of contemplated legal proceedings as opposed to a 'distinct purpose that prevented the possible litigation being the dominant purpose'. The Court considered this to be similar to the need to identify the cause of the fire in *Highgrade*. Andrews J at first instance had made an error of law in stating that documents prepared for the purpose of settling or avoiding a claim are not created for the dominant purpose of defending litigation.[81]

12.102 *Bilta (UK) Ltd v Royal Bank of Scotland*[82] was another case in which the court was willing to take a similar approach. Indications from another state authority—in this case, Her Majesty's Revenue & Customs (HMRC), albeit exercising a civil tax function—had triggered an internal investigation. HMRC had written to RBS indicating a possible issue with almost £90 million of VAT that RBS had reclaimed and which HMRC was now investigating. In the months that followed, RBS provided documents and information to HMRC. Approximately two years after HMRC's first letter, HMRC wrote to RBS indicating for the first time that there might be grounds to deny RBS' VAT reclaim. The letter analysed the information RBS had provided and concluded that, 'HMRC's view is that we have sufficient grounds to deny RBS £86,247,876 of input tax on the basis that they knew or should have known that their transactions were connected with fraud'. It said that if a decision to deny was made at a later date, HMRC would have to consider the matter of penalties for inaccuracies. RBS was invited to give its views on whether input tax should be denied before the issue of penalties was considered (if appropriate). HMRC also said that, if, after receiving a response from RBS, HMRC remained of the view that any input tax should be denied, RBS would receive a further letter 'giving an appealable decision and ... would have 30 days to request a review or appeal this'. Whilst waiting for RBS' response, HMRC issued a protective interim assessment for an amount totaling just over £86 million, in

---

[80] *SFO v ENRC Ltd* (n 2) [109].
[81] ibid [113]–[114], [118]–[119].
[82] [2017] EWHC 3535 (Ch), [2018] Lloyd's Rep FC 202.

order to avoid being time-barred. HMRC said it was not intended to be a final decision and discussions would continue.

HMRC's letter indicating that there might be grounds to deny the VAT reclaim led almost immediately to managing legal counsel in RBS' litigation and investigations team taking over conduct of the matter internally, and, approximately two weeks later, RBS instructed external lawyers. An internal investigation commenced, and, in an interim update to HMRC, RBS explained that: **12.103**

> The purpose of the investigation is to gather and review the available evidence in order to analyse whether, based on the information available to the business at the time, the business should have concluded that the only reasonable explanation for the circumstances of individual trades was their connection with actual fraud (not a risk of fraud) and to prepare a report in response to [HMRC's letter].

RBS told HMRC that, 'the work product of [the] investigation is privileged'. Almost two years after the letter from HMRC that had triggered the internal investigation, RBS provided HMRC with its final report, which was prepared by its external lawyers. The report included a detailed point-by-point response to HMRC's letter and concluded by inviting HMRC to withdraw the assessment. Several months later, RBS appealed HMRC's decision to issue the assessment to the First Tier Tribunal (Tax Chamber).

In the separate litigation that gave rise to this privilege issue, RBS disclosed the investigation report to the claimant but claimed litigation privilege over other documents created as part of the investigation, including transcripts of twenty-nine interviews with key RBS employees and ex-employees. The claimant accepted that litigation was in reasonable contemplation at the relevant time, that litigation being a threatened assessment by HMRC against RBS in respect of the overclaimed VAT, but it did not accept that the dominant purpose was the conduct of litigation. **12.104**

Upholding RBS' claim to litigation privilege, Sir Geoffrey Vos C considered the HMRC letter to amount to a 'watershed moment'. In his judgment: **12.105**

> Following an investigation into the facts, which had lasted more than two years, HMRC stated for the first time in the HMRC letter that it considered that it had sufficient grounds to deny RBS nearly £90 million by way of input VAT. The HMRC letter analysed the relevant law and applied the law to the facts as they understood them before asking for RBS's comments on those facts. It was, therefore, similar in nature ... to a letter before claim. Moreover, since HMRC had to prove no more ... than that RBS knew or ought to have known that the relevant transactions were connected with fraud, it was highly likely at this point that an assessment would follow. That the assessment was highly likely is the evidence of [one of RBS' external lawyers] and is also the business and revenue reality. It was hardly very likely that RBS would persuade HMRC to drop altogether a claim for many millions of pounds on the basis of a solicitor's report, however persuasive that report might turn out to be when HMRC had already determined expressly that it had evidence supporting the case that RBS 'knew or ought to have known' of the VAT fraud.[83]

---

[83] ibid [60].

12.106 It was argued on behalf of the claimant that the purpose in creating the report and conducting the interviews was to maintain a good relationship with HMRC and to do as RBS had said it would do, namely to respond to HMRC's letter. RBS, it was said, was providing information to HMRC in accordance with its duties as a taxpayer, its own codes of practice and in order to persuade HMRC to change its mind. However, Sir Geoffrey Vos C took the view that all those purposes were 'effectively subsumed under the purpose of defeating the expected assessment'. The report provided to HMRC was closely comparable to a response to a letter before claim in ordinary commercial litigation.[84] Furthermore:

> The commercial reality here was that RBS had to comply with its own protocols and its statutory duties to cooperate with HMRC. The discussions were conducted in an entirely appropriate collaborative and cooperative manner but that did not change the fact that the overwhelming probability was that an assessment would follow the HMRC letter and that RBS knew as much. RBS took steps to protect its position which were only consistent with its overarching purpose being preparation for the litigation in the FTT that it fully expected to be necessary to contest the assessment it expected. It instructed its litigation solicitors effectively to resist HMRC's position and to promote its own in the expected litigation.[85]

12.107 The fact that RBS' interactions with HMRC after the HMRC letter were ostensibly collaborative and cooperative did not change the position. It is commonplace for HMRC to canvass the views of large corporate taxpayers prior to formally issuing an assessment, and RBS was seeking extensions to the deadline for filing its formal written response, so it was unsurprising that RBS met several times with HMRC and provided updates on the progress of its investigation. Such cooperation did not preclude the investigation being conducted for the dominant purpose of litigation, nor did it mean that the interviews conducted were not fully and primarily intended to provide the material to resist the expected assessment by a challenge in the FTT.[86]

12.108 Sir Geoffrey Vos C likened the case to *Highgrade*, in that, just as the insurers in that case were not determining the cause of the fire as a matter of academic interest, RBS was not spending large sums on legal fees in the hope that HMRC would be dissuaded from issuing an assessment. If that was properly to be regarded as a purpose of the investigation at all, 'it was obviously a very subsidiary purpose'.[87] 'Fending off the assessment was just part of the continuum that formed the road to the litigation that was considered, rightly, as it turned out, to be almost inevitable.'[88]

12.109 Referring to the first instance decision in *SFO v ENRC Ltd* (which had not yet come before the Court of Appeal), Sir Geoffrey Vos C highlighted the fact-specific nature of these sorts

---

[84] ibid [63]–[64].
[85] ibid [65].
[86] ibid [62], [67].
[87] Interestingly, this case was decided after the first instance decision in *SFO v ENRC Ltd* (n 14) but before that judgment was largely overturned by the Court of Appeal, including Andrews J's contention that attempts to settle or avoid litigation did not amount to the conduct of litigation. Had *Bilta* been decided after the Court of Appeal decision in *SFO v ENRC Ltd* (n 2), the fact that one of the purposes of the internal investigation may have been to persuade HMRC not to issue an assessment ought not to have presented any problems for RBS' claim to litigation privilege.
[88] *Bilta (UK) Ltd v Royal Bank of Scotland* (n 82) [66].

of issues: 'one cannot simply apply conclusions that were reached on one company's interactions with the Serious Fraud Office in the very different context of another company's interactions with HMRC'. Rather, one must take 'a realistic, indeed commercial view of the facts'.[89]

Similarly, in *FM Capital Partners Ltd v Marino*,[90] having found that litigation was reasonably in contemplation (see paras 12.62–12.64), Leggatt J could see no reason to doubt FM Capital's evidence about the dominant purpose of the BDO investigation. The evidence was that it was in order to ascertain the rights and liabilities of FM Capital and to find out the facts in connection with those potential proceedings that BDO was instructed, or at any rate this was the dominant purpose of their instruction. It was suggested on behalf of the defendant seeking disclosure that the disciplinary process pursued against the CEO was inherently likely to have been at least an equal purpose of the investigation, in which case litigation privilege could not apply. Leggatt J did not agree, observing instead that:

12.110

> I would have thought it inherently less likely that a company faced with serious allegations and a serious potential claim against it from one of its clients would be predominantly or even equally concerned with disciplining its own employee as opposed to preparing to defend litigation being threatened against it and to pursue a claim potentially against its employee.[91]

As regards the interim report specifically, the judge could see no reason to doubt FM Capital's lawyer's evidence that the dominant purpose, as with the investigation as a whole, was the contemplated litigation, 'albeit that the report was used as a vehicle for informing [the CEO] in the context of the disciplinary process of the allegations against him and of the evidence relied on in support of those allegations'.[92]

12.111

Establishing facts to answer a regulator's or investigator's questions

We saw at paras 12.55–12.61 that in the case of *The State of Qatar v Banque Havilland SA & Another*,[93] the Court rejected the bank's claim that litigation was reasonably in contemplation. However, even if it had been the case that the bank reasonably contemplated adversarial litigation when PwC was instructed on 13 November 2017, or at some later stage prior to production of the report in June 2018, the judge was not satisfied that PwC's instruction, or the bank's request that PwC should produce a report, was for the dominant purpose of anticipated litigation. He considered there to be a number of purposes behind PwC's instruction: 'The two most prominent, and dominant, purposes were (a) to find the facts, including how a copy of the Presentation had been obtained from the bank's files, and (b) to satisfy the CSSF and put the bank in a position where it could answer the CSSF's questions.' The evidence was somewhat uncertain, but it appeared that the suggestion of a 'forensic' or 'IT' investigation may have come from the CSSF itself. However, even if it had not been requested by the CSSF, it was plain that one of the principal purposes of the

12.112

---

[89] ibid [59], [66].
[90] *FM Capital Partners Ltd v Marino* (n 48).
[91] ibid [6].
[92] ibid [7].
[93] *Qatar v Banque Havilland SA & Anor* (n 41).

investigation was to enable the bank to answer the CSSF's questions, which did not amount to conducting litigation.[94]

12.113 This decision is of relevance to criminal cases as there will be many internal investigations whose purpose is to establish facts in order for a company to respond to a regulator's or investigator's enquiries. It may be the case that the purpose of answering those enquiries is to avoid a prosecution or some other form of litigation, in which case the internal investigation ought to be covered by litigation privilege. But if the purpose of answering the questions is merely because the company is required to do so and the purpose goes no further than discharging that obligation, the dominant purpose test is unlikely to be satisfied (and litigation is unlikely to be in reasonable contemplation in any event).

Instructing Third Parties

12.114 The principles concerning litigation privilege discussed in this chapter apply equally to internal investigation interviews as to communications with other non-witness third parties in the course of an investigation. For example, lawyers conducting an investigation may require specialist assistance from an expert, such as an accountant, in order to understand the matters under investigation. Whilst each communication must be considered separately, if litigation privilege applies to the investigation as a whole, this will include the vast majority of communications with third parties such as experts.

Whose Privilege Is it?

12.115 So far, this chapter has looked at the privilege position from the perspective of the company or organization at whose behest the internal investigation is carried out. But what about the position of a witness interviewed as part of the investigation? Are they able to rely on the company's litigation privilege?

12.116 This question was addressed in *R v Jukes*.[95] As discussed at paras 12.50–12.54, the appellant in the case claimed that a statement he had given to his employer as part of its investigation into a fatal accident was covered by litigation privilege. Having rejected the privilege claim on the basis that litigation was not reasonably in contemplation at the time he gave the statement, the Court went on to say that, even if it had decided that the statement was privileged, it was not the appellant's privilege to claim but rather that of the company. As the maker of a statement given to a party who was entitled to rely upon privilege, the appellant was 'at best a potential witness' who was not entitled to rely upon the company's privilege for his own benefit. In what the Court considered to be 'one of the striking aspects of this case', the company had never claimed privilege over the statement. The Court stated:

---

[94] ibid [176]–[183].
[95] *R v Jukes* (n 37).

Privilege does not simply float in a vacuum; nor can it just be inferred ... Unless the other party to litigation accepts a claim to privilege, a party has to claim privilege. If the company ... had ever sought to claim privilege, they would have had to provide appropriate evidence. The claim could then have been properly tested, if necessary through cross-examination.

The Court did not accept the argument that it mattered not whose privilege it was. The fact that the company might have claimed privilege over the document was not in itself a reason for excluding it if it was otherwise admissible and probative.[96]

12.117 This is an important reminder that a third party cannot rely upon somebody else's privilege in circumstances where that privilege could be claimed by the privilege holder but has not in fact been claimed. In an internal investigation, this point will be most relevant to witnesses. This is a separate issue to the entitlement of a non-party to litigation being able to claim their own litigation privilege, as confirmed in *Al Sadeq v Dechert LLP*.[97]

5 Practical Guidance

12.118 This section looks at a number of practical points of which lawyers should be aware when conducting internal investigations, drawing on the legal points discussed earlier in this chapter.

Determine Extent of Lawyer's Role

12.119 As discussed at paras 12.29–12.35, an investigation report that purely sets out the factual findings of an internal investigation will be privileged as long as the lawyer's role includes providing related advice that has a 'relevant legal context', such as advice on matters consequent to the findings of the investigation or any other matters relating to the issues under investigation. Whilst this can be implied rather than expressly stated, in the event that any subsequent claim to legal advice privilege is challenged, it will assist if the terms of engagement explicitly state that this is part of the lawyer's role.

Setting up a Client Group

12.120 The effect of *Three Rivers (No 5)*[98] is that only communications between lawyers and employees and officers of a company who are tasked with seeking and receiving legal advice on behalf of the company will be capable of attracting legal advice privilege. This has obvious consequences on the ability to claim legal advice privilege over witness interviews, as discussed at paras 12.11–12.16, but it also creates a risk of generating non-privileged communications between employees of the company and its lawyers that the company

---

[96] ibid [26]–[29].
[97] *Al Sadeq v Dechert LLP* (n 3). See para 1.57 of this work.
[98] *Three Rivers (No 5)* (n 2).

would prefer not to be disclosable in the event of any subsequent litigation or potentially seized by the authorities in a criminal investigation.

12.121   It is therefore of vital importance that when lawyers are first appointed to conduct an internal investigation (and indeed whenever a corporate client instructs external lawyers), the company appoints a 'client group' comprising a limited number of senior personnel who will serve as the representatives of the company for the purpose of communicating with its lawyers. It is common practice for this arrangement to take the form of an investigation committee appointed by the board. In order to preserve the integrity of the investigation and to prevent any potential conflicts of interest arising, it is preferable for the individuals who make up the client group to be as far removed from the issues under investigation as possible. These individuals must have sufficient authority to seek and receive legal advice on behalf of the company, in accordance with *Three Rivers (No 5)*. Merely stating that a particular employee has such authority does not mean that, when assessed objectively, they do in fact have such authority. In reality, it is likely only to be senior personnel who will be capable of meeting these requirements. However, this does not mean that a person cannot be appointed specifically to carry out this role, as long as they are given the requisite degree of authority. In smaller companies, for example, it is sometimes the case that an external third party is appointed for this purpose.

12.122   Lawyers should ensure that the names of all members of the client group are expressly set out in a written document when first instructed. If possible, this should be supported by a board resolution or endorsed by the board and evidenced some other way. The document should also set out the procedure to be followed if it is proposed that an additional member is to be added to the client group. It is advisable also to include the identity of the client group in the lawyer's engagement letter.

File Note of Assessment of Litigation Privilege

12.123   Because the question of whether litigation privilege applies is based on the position at the time of the relevant communication, in circumstances where there may be an arguable claim to litigation privilege and the company wants to structure the investigation on this basis (the dangers of which are discussed at paras 12.129–12.131), lawyers should prepare a memorandum to be kept on the file that clearly sets out the factual basis for asserting litigation privilege. This will assist if, at a later stage, the privilege claim is challenged. Whilst it will ultimately be an objective question for the court to determine, highly relevant to that question will be the state of mind of the company and its advisers at the time of the investigation, and a file note will provide a contemporaneous record of this.

12.124   The note should identify the litigation that is said to be reasonably in contemplation and the basis for believing that there is more than a mere possibility of that litigation commencing, pointing to specific facts, events, communications with law enforcement agencies (if applicable), knowledge of the issues to be investigated and the potential liability for the company. It should also clearly explain the purpose of the investigation and how this satisfies the requirement for the sole or dominant purpose to be the conduct of litigation.

12.125 In some cases, the circumstances may be such that litigation privilege cannot be asserted at the outset of the investigation but subsequent developments mean that a claim later arises from a certain point onwards. A file note should be prepared at that stage. In *SFO v ENRC Ltd* (discussed earlier in this chapter), the Court of Appeal recognized that the dominant purpose of an internal investigation can change over time. The Court noted that, 'even if litigation was not the dominant purpose of the investigation at its very inception, it is clear from the evidence that it swiftly became the dominant purpose'.[99]

12.126 In other cases, there may be a development which could potentially give an adverse party a basis for challenging a claim to litigation privilege at a later stage. For example, an investigator might communicate something to the company that suggests that a prosecution is less likely than first anticipated. If this happens but the lawyer considers that litigation privilege still applies, the file note should be updated to record this.

12.127 Part of the Court of Appeal's reasoning in holding that a prosecution by the SFO was reasonably in contemplation in *SFO v ENRC Ltd* was the fact that communications between ENRC's lawyers noted that the conduct under review in the internal investigation was potentially criminal in nature and that adversarial proceedings might occur as a result of the investigation. One of the lawyers had stated that 'both criminal and civil proceedings can be reasonably said to be in contemplation'.[100] This highlights the value of a contemporaneous record.

Marking Documents as Privileged

12.128 Following on from the point above, it is advisable to add a note to any privileged documents that makes clear that they are subject to privilege, for example: 'Confidential and subject to legal professional privilege'. This is particularly important for any documents over which a privilege claim could later be challenged, such as interview notes and other investigation documents. Marking documents in this way will not be determinative of whether or not they are privileged, but it demonstrates the party's state of mind and may be a factor the court takes into account if the privilege claim is disputed.

Risk of Structuring an Investigation on a Weak Privilege Claim

12.129 Lawyers have a duty to advise clients about any possible claim to privilege that may exist and to assert it if there is a reasonable basis for doing so and the client has not decided to waive it. However, this does not mean that where there is an arguable claim to litigation privilege over an internal investigation, the investigation should automatically proceed on the basis that litigation privilege will apply. Such an approach could be seriously detrimental to the client's interests if the claim was later challenged successfully. In the current climate, authorities such as the SFO are likely to challenge privilege claims over witness interviews in

---

[99] *SFO v ENRC Ltd* (n 2) [111].
[100] ibid [92].

particular, and, as the discussion in this chapter has shown, there will be many cases where such a challenge would succeed. This could result in notes of interviews with witnesses who have given information which is highly damaging to the company ending up in the hands of the authorities.

12.130 There is nothing wrong in principle with a lawyer advising their client that there is a properly arguable claim to litigation privilege over the investigation but that it could be successfully challenged, and for the client then to instruct their lawyer to proceed with the investigation on the basis that litigation privilege does apply. As long as the client is aware of the likelihood and consequences of the claim being successfully challenged, the lawyer has discharged their duty.

12.131 Where there is uncertainty over whether litigation privilege applies, the investigation may be conducted differently to how it would be if the privilege claim was stronger. For example, lawyers may suggest that fewer witnesses should be interviewed and/or that witnesses should be interviewed about fewer topics in order to limit the potential evidence that the authorities may obtain in the event of an unsuccessful privilege claim. Similarly, the company may decide not to instruct a third party such as an accountant to assist with the lawyers' conduct of the investigation if there is a chance that the communications with and material produced by that third party will not be covered by litigation privilege. However, as noted at para 12.28, a witness's knowledge of relevant facts will not be privileged and there is no property in a witness. There is therefore nothing to prevent the authorities from speaking to a witness to obtain their account in connection with a criminal investigation.

Handling Pre-Existing Privileged Material

12.132 Large-scale investigations involving significant volumes of data are likely to result in pre-existing privileged documents being obtained or handled by the investigation team and/or third parties such as e-discovery companies. As long as this is handled in such a way that its overall confidentiality is preserved, privilege will not be lost, even if it is seen by people other than the privilege holder or their legal advisers. Note, however, the guidance at paras 12.136–12.137 regarding the loss of confidentiality (and therefore privilege) that will result from making the material public.

Privilege Reviews

12.133 Internal investigations will often involve a review of potentially privileged material to identify which specific documents are privileged. This may be necessary if, for example, relevant documents are to be shared voluntarily with an investigating authority but a waiver of privilege has not been agreed. Detailed practical guidance on how to conduct privilege reviews can be found in Chapter 4.

Dissemination of Privileged Information Outside Client Group

It is likely that during the course of an internal investigation and/or at its conclusion, privileged (or potentially privileged) information such as status updates, investigation plans, factual findings and legal advice relating to the findings will be shared outside the group that constitutes the client for the purposes of legal advice privilege. It may be necessary, for example, to share this information with other groups within the company, such as the board or a particular committee. As explained at paras 1.77–1.79, it is possible to share privileged material with third parties on a confidential basis without losing privilege more widely. As long as the circumstances of the disclosure carry an obligation or expectation of confidence, as will almost certainly be the case where information is shared within a company, privilege will be maintained as against the rest of the world. **12.134**

Communications with Insurers

In some cases, a company that has commissioned an internal investigation may seek to recover its costs under an insurance policy. This is likely to require certain information which may be privileged being shared with the insurer. This issue is discussed in the context of defendants in criminal proceedings at para 9.17, but the same principles apply where it is a corporate entity seeking insurance cover or other third party funding for an internal investigation. **12.135**

Public Statements on Findings of Investigation

The circumstances surrounding an internal investigation will sometimes attract public attention. Allegations might first emerge in the press, triggering an internal investigation (and potentially a criminal investigation by the authorities), or the company commissioning the investigation might choose to publicize allegations that have been made against it, or it may be obliged to do so. In these circumstances, the company might provide periodic public updates or announce the findings of the investigation once complete. **12.136**

If privileged information is made public in this way, it will no longer be confidential and privilege will be lost. However, the loss of confidentiality will be limited to what has actually been publicized rather than any additional undisclosed privileged information or material, as collateral waiver does not result from loss of confidentiality.[101] Loss of privilege as a result of loss of confidentiality is examined in more detail at paras 1.73–1.79. **12.137**

---

[101] See Hodge Malek (ed), *Phipson on Evidence* (20th edn, Sweet & Maxwell 2021) paras 26-01, 26-03.

Index

abrogation of privilege 1.09–1.10, 8.23, 11.41, 11.48
abuse of process 3.92–3.93, 3.96, 6.13–6.14
  prosecution privilege 8.15, 8.28
account freezing/forfeiture orders 1.54, 1.55
accountants 9.22, 12.114, 12.131
  forensic 7.64, 12.44
  internal investigations, conducting 12.62–12.63, 12.110
admissibility
  inadvertent disclosure 1.105, 1.108, 9.73, 10.19, 10.24
  unlawfully obtained evidence 6.14
adversarial proceedings 1.47, 1.54–1.55, 9.01–9.02, 12.39, 12.48, 12.57–12.59
adverse inference drawn from silence 1.84, 1.95, 10.14, 10.29–10.30, 10.33
  lawyers giving evidence 10.46
  police station and interviews under caution 6.37, 6.39, 6.44–6.45
affidavits 1.99
agents and agency principle 1.24, 6.21, 6.25, 6.26
Airbus SE 7.65
Airline Services Ltd (ASL) 7.67
alibi
  assertion of 2.19
  false 2.22, 2.24
Amec Foster Wheeler Energy Ltd 7.68
anti-competitive practices 12.39
appeals 11.01–11.48
  Criminal Cases Review Commission (CCRC) 11.40–11.48
  Crown Court from Magistrates' Court, appeals to 11.39
  see also Court of Appeal
appointment record 1.42
appropriate adults 6.26–6.28, 6.33
artificial intelligence (AI), use of 4.36–4.40, 4.51, 7.62
  see also machine learning
assertions of privilege, blanket 3.89
Association of Chief Police Officers' (ACPO) guidance 6.50
attendance note 1.34, 1.42, 2.23, 6.38
Attorney General's Guidelines on Disclosure 4.10–4.11, 4.13, 9.67
audit, technical 12.89

bad faith 9.21
balance of probabilities test 2.13
Bank of England 12.87

Bar Council
  'Criminal Appeals: Duties to the Court to Make Enquiries' practice note 11.15, 11.18, 11.21, 11.25–11.26, 11.30–11.32
  independent counsel 3.64, 4.29–4.30
  professional obligations 2.29
Bar Standards Board 4.15
  Handbook 1.02 n.4
Barclays 7.27–7.28, 12.77–12.79
blanket assertions of privilege 3.89
blocked access to seized/compelled material 4.06
blood samples 9.43–9.45
'blue bagged' disputed items 3.64
Bluu Solutions Ltd (BSL) 7.69
board meeting 1.34
'books and records review' 12.44
bulk interception warrant 3.103

cartel cases 7.79–7.80
carve-outs 7.09–7.11, 7.32
case management forms 9.11–9.13
case progression form 9.12
caution, interviews under *see* interviews under caution at police station
character witnesses 1.52
'cherry-picking' and waiver 1.91, 1.94, 8.18, 10.12, 10.62, 11.13, 11.38
child welfare/child protection procedures 6.27–6.28
civil proceedings 1.99
  covert surveillance and interception of communications 3.108
  crime-fraud exception 2.04, 2.06, 2.18
  expert witnesses and evidence gathering/preparing for court 9.41, 9.47, 9.56, 9.58
  file note of assessment of litigation privilege 12.127
  inadvertent disclosure of privileged documents 1.104, 10.16, 10.24
  intentional disclosure of privileged documents 10.04–10.05
  internal investigations 12.02
  limited waiver and voluntary disclosure 7.08, 7.11, 7.27–7.28, 7.30–7.31
  litigation privilege in internal investigations 12.39, 12.42, 12.46–12.47, 12.64
  prosecution privilege 8.05–8.06
  search warrants 3.56
  waiver and collateral waiver 1.97
civil recovery investigations 3.08
'cleansing' and immunity/leniency 7.78

client
  care or engagement letter 1.42
  corporate 1.20, 12.11
  definition 1.19–1.20
  group 12.13, 12.120–12.122
  lawyer relationship 1.21, 12.07–12.10
  name, address and telephone number 1.42, 3.29–3.30
  prospective 1.21
  sharing legal advice with partner or family member 1.79
Codes of Practice (RIPA 2000 and IPA 2016) 3.100, 3.102, 3.105–3.108
co-defendants 1.116, 9.61–9.65
collateral waiver 1.71, 1.81, 1.94–1.103, 1.109
  Court of Appeal 11.13, 11.38
  court proceedings 10.01
  defence privileged material, deployment of 9.78
  intentional disclosure of privileged documents 10.12
  interviews under caution 1.103
  limited waiver and voluntary disclosure 7.28
  prosecution privilege 8.18–8.20
  public statements on investigation findings 12.137
committal hearing 9.12
committee meeting 1.34
Commodity Futures Trading Commission (US) 7.09
common interest privilege 1.112–1.113, 1.116–1.117, 9.63, 9.65
  co-defendants, between 1.116, 9.63
common law
  compared to statutory definition of privilege 3.29, 5.09
  duty of disclosure 9.68–9.69
communications
  between co-defendants 9.63–9.65
  between lawyers 1.41
  continuum of 1.28
  during interview under caution 6.37–6.38
  legal advice privilege 1.13–1.14, 1.28–1.30
  litigation privilege 1.49–1.50
  overseas-related 3.103
  see also interception of communications
company
  joint interest privilege with directors and/or senior employees 1.115
  privilege and compelled interviews 5.17
compelled interviews 5.01–5.25
  during interview 5.13–5.19
  failure to comply without reasonable excuse 5.11–5.12
  with lawyers 5.20–5.25
  main powers 5.02–5.05
  no right to silence 5.01, 6.04
  privileged information, exclusion of 5.06–5.10
  section 2 CJA 1987 5.13–5.14, 5.23
compelled material *see* search and seizure, compulsion, surveillance and interception

Competition and Markets Authority (CMA) 3.99, 5.05, 5.10, 7.79–7.83
Competition Appeal Tribunal (CAT) 12.39
compromise agreement 12.73–12.74
compulsion *see* search and seizure, compulsion, surveillance and interception
computers, mobile phones and other electronic devices 3.01, 3.72, 3.81–3.82, 4.39, 7.62, 12.56
  additional powers of seizure 3.14, 3.22–3.23
  document review platforms 4.42
  privilege reviews 4.12, 4.24, 4.27, 4.36, 4.42, 4.45
  search terms 4.15
  search warrant application 3.34, 3.40–3.41, 3.44, 3.47–3.48, 3.52, 3.58–3.59
  seized/compelled material 4.05–4.06, 4.23–4.24
conduct
  police impropriety 3.96, 6.13–6.14
  professional 11.30
  of trial, instructions on 3.92
  unlawful 3.96, 6.13–6.14, 12.62
conducting litigation *see under* litigation privilege
confidence *see under* confidentiality
confidentiality 1.02, 1.15–1.16, 1.51, 1.73
  business records 3.04
  communications with the court 9.10
  compelled interviews 5.13, 5.21
  covert surveillance and interception of communications 3.106
  crime-fraud exception and overlap with special procedure material 3.50
  defence witnesses 9.29–9.31
  express 1.78
  implied 1.78
  legal advice privilege 1.15–1.16
  limited waiver and voluntary disclosure 7.09, 7.17
  litigation privilege 1.51
  obligation or expectation of 1.78
  police station and interviews under caution 6.06–6.07, 6.16–6.17, 6.22–6.24, 6.26–6.27, 6.33, 6.37, 6.47
  prosecution privilege 8.27 n.35
  third parties and evidence gathering/preparing for court 9.07
  see also loss of confidentiality
confiscation proceedings 1.54
consent
  express 1.80, 1.83
  implied 1.80, 1.83
  informed 1.02 n.4
  jointly waived privilege 1.114
conspiracy to pervert the course of justice 2.20–2.21, 2.23–2.25, 3.92, 6.51, 10.47, 10.49, 10.58–10.59
  'free-standing and independent evidence' 2.21, 2.23–2.24, 10.58
continuum of communication 1.28
conviction
  appeals against 11.02–11.06
  unsafe 10.39, 11.05
cooperation *see* waiver of privilege and cooperation

INDEX

cooperation credit *see under* waiver of privilege and cooperation
Core Duty of solicitor 7.40
corporate cooperation *see under* waiver of privilege and cooperation
corporate entity 1.20, 10.02
corporate investigations *see* internal investigations
corruption
    of solicitor 3.46
    investigating for compliance purposes 12.101
cost drafting service 3.58
costs applications 10.61
court, preparing for *see* evidence gathering and preparing for court
Court of Appeal 11.01–11.40
    collateral waiver 11.13, 11.38
    conviction, appeals against 11.02–11.22, 11.24–11.38
    express waiver of privilege, implications of 11.24–11.28
    fresh evidence 11.19–11.22
    McCook requirements 11.02–11.18, 11.20–11.24, 11.31
    sentence, appeals against 11.23
    waiver, form of 11.29
    waiver of privilege implied by grounds of appeal? 11.32–11.37
    waiver, refusal of 11.30–11.31
    see also criticism of legal advisers on appeal
court proceedings 10.01–10.62
    costs applications 10.61
    expert evidence 10.40
    inadvertent disclosure of privileged documents 10.16–10.25
        defence to prosecution, by 10.16–10.20
        prosecution, by 10.23–10.25
        third party to prosecution, by 10.21–10.22
    interlocutory hearings 10.62
    lawyers giving evidence 10.41–10.60
        confirming fact of advice given 10.42
        defence witnesses, lawyers as 10.46
        defendants, lawyers as 10.47–10.60
        general position 10.41
        prosecution witnesses, lawyers as 10.43–10.45
    oral evidence 10.26–10.39
        defendant's: judge's questioning 10.37–10.39
        defendant's 10.27–10.34
        general position 10.26
        prosecution, evidence adduced by 10.35–10.36
    see also intentional disclosure of privileged documents during court proceedings
covert surveillance *see* search and seizure, compulsion, surveillance and interception
crime-fraud exception 2.01–2.29
    consultation in presence of third parties 6.30, 6.32
    covert surveillance and interception of communications 3.102, 3.107
    R v Cox and Railton 2.05–2.07
    criminal cases 2.15–2.25

    'free-standing and independent evidence' 2.19, 2.21, 2.23–2.24, 10.58
    iniquitous conduct and issues to be determined at trial, overlap between 2.19–2.25
    'ordinary run' 2.15–2.18
    general principles 2.04–2.14
        cases in which exception applies 2.04
        conduct engaging exception 2.05–2.09
        expanded scope 2.08–2.09
        standard of proof 2.13–2.14
        whose conduct engages exception 2.10–2.12
    independent counsel 4.30
    innocent dupe 2.10
    lawyers giving evidence 10.45, 10.58–10.59
    legal aid application 9.20–9.21
    PACE 1984 definition 3.27–3.28
    practical considerations 2.26–2.29
        establishment of whether exception applies 2.27–2.28
        professional obligations 2.29
        when exception arises in practice 2.26
    seizure and compelled production of privileged material 3.27–3.28
    and special procedure material overlap 3.50–3.56
    third parties and evidence gathering/preparing for court 9.20–9.21
    third parties and witness summons 10.10
Criminal Cases Review Commission (CCRC) 11.40–11.48
Criminal Justice Act 1987 3.06, 3.12, 3.29, 3.88, 5.02, 5.07, 5.11, 5.13
Criminal Justice and Police Act 2001 3.14–3.23, 3.35, 3.67–3.82, 3.85–3.87
criminal law advice, application of legal advice privilege to 1.27 n.39
criminal liability
    internal investigations 12.02
    joint interest privilege 1.115
    legal advice privilege in internal investigations 12.32
    litigation privilege in internal investigations 12.64, 12.66
Criminal Procedure and Investigations Act (CPIA) 1996
    collateral use of unused material 7.06, 10.03
    defence obligations 9.14–9.15, 9.25, 9.32–9.33, 9.60
    prosecution obligations 7.22, 7.33, 8.12–8.13, 8.17, 8.21–8.29, 9.66–9.72, 9.77, 10.21
criticism of legal advisers on appeal 11.03, 11.07–11.08, 11.11, 11.17, 11.19–11.20, 11.25–11.26, 11.36–11.37
    unsustainable or unfounded 11.07
cross-examination 9.56, 9.78, 10.12, 10.28, 10.31, 10.33–10.34, 10.36–10.38
Crown Court 3.04, 3.07, 3.11, 3.85, 4.33, 11.39–11.40, 11.45
    appeals to from Magistrates' Court 11.39
    application for disclosure 7.22, 7.24

Crown Prosecution Service (CPS)
　compelled interviews 5.03
　compelled production 3.09
　disclosure to third parties 8.08
　deferred prosecution agreement (DPA) 7.01
　Disclosure Manual 4.11, 8.14–8.15, 9.68
　letter of representation 1.38, 1.63
　privilege assertion in response to compulsion powers 3.89
　prosecution privilege 8.06, 8.08–8.11, 8.14–8.16
　seized/compelled material 4.11
　SOCPA 2005 compulsion powers, guidance on 3.89
　SOCPA 2005 and Sentencing Act 2020, agreements under 7.78
CSSF 12.56–12.58, 12.61, 12.112
current proceedings, waiver over documents relating to 10.14–10.15
cursory tests of obviousness 7.54
cut-throat defence 7.20

deception of solicitors 2.18
defence
　applications for prosecution disclosure 8.22
　case statement 1.38, 1.99, 9.14–9.16
　cut-throat 7.20
　disclosure by 10.08–10.15
　　defendant, privileged documents belonging to relating to current proceedings 10.14–10.15
　　defendant, privileged documents belonging to relating to separate matter 10.11–10.13
　　third parties, privileged documents belonging to 10.08–10.10
　disclosure to 10.05–10.07
　independent counsel, disagreement between, and 4.31–4.35
　privileged material, deployment of 9.78–9.80
　role of with seized/compelled material 4.23–4.28
　to prosecution, inadvertent disclosure by 10.16–10.20
　witnesses 1.63
　　lawyers as 10.46
　　see also under evidence gathering and preparing for court
defendants
　lawyers as 10.47–10.60
　oral evidence 10.27–10.34
　　judge's questioning 10.37–10.39
　privileged documents belonging to
　　relating to current proceedings 10.14–10.15
　　relating to separate matter 10.11–10.13
deferred prosecution agreements (DPAs) 7.43–7.75
　Code of Practice 7.44–7.45, 7.47
　see also under waiver of privilege and cooperation
definition of legal professional privilege 1.01–1.05
deleted files 4.27
denial of having committed a crime 2.19
Department of Justice (US) 7.09

deployment
　of content or substance of privileged advice/document 1.88–1.89, 9.50, 9.52–9.53
　of defence privileged material *see under* evidence gathering and preparing for court
　intentional disclosure of privileged documents 10.11, 10.13
devices belonging to lawyer 4.20
digital material *see* computers, mobile phones and other electronic devices
Digital Review System (DRS) 4.12
direct access counsel 1.18
Director of Public Prosecutions (DPP) 3.09, 7.11, 7.43, 7.77
　prosecution privilege 8.05, 8.07, 8.27 n.35
disclosure
　continuing duty of 8.22
　defence applications for 8.22
　of draft and unused statements 9.66
　full and frank, duty of 3.42–3.44
　inadvertent *see* inadvertent disclosure
　initial duty of 8.22
　notices
　　compelled interviews 5.03, 5.08
　　privilege assertion in response to compulsion powers 3.89–3.90
　　search and seizure and compulsion 3.09
　obligations *see* statutory disclosure obligations; *see also under* prosecution privilege
　onward, to overseas authorities 7.36–7.37
　order 3.07
　partial 1.83–1.84,1.101–1.102
　of privileged information during interviews under caution 6.41
　of privileged material to third parties by the prosecution 8.08
　prosecution 8.12–8.29
　required or permitted by law or client consents 1.02
　to defendants in criminal proceedings and reference in open court 7.25–7.35
　types of 1.83–1.84
　voluntary *see* voluntary disclosure
　of whole of privileged document 1.83, 1.100–1.101
　withholding prosecution 8.21–8.28
　see also intentional disclosure of privileged documents during court proceedings; privileged material, seeking disclosure of *under* evidence gathering and preparing for court
dishonest application for legal aid 9.21
disputed items, 'blue bagged' 3.64
dissemination of privileged information outside client group 1.34, 12.134
doctor/patient relationship 9.46
doctors as expert witnesses 9.49
document review platforms 4.42–4.47, 4.60–4.61
documents
　copied 1.69
　draft 1.38
　draft, interviews under caution and 6.49

hard copy 3.83, 4.06, 4.42
indicating substance of advice 1.40
lawyers' working papers 1.36–1.37
legal advice privilege 1.35–1.40
litigation privilege 1.50
prepared by client 1.39
production and admissibility distinction 1.108
see also pre-existing documents
dominant purpose test
  failure to satisfy 4.56
  file note of assessment of litigation privilege 12.124–12.125
  legal advice privilege 1.31–1.33
  litigation privilege 1.60, 1.62, 1.64
  litigation privilege in internal investigations 12.81–12.113
  multi-addressee emails 4.63
  see also under internal investigations; litigation privilege
draft documents and interviews under caution 6.49
draft statements, disclosure of 9.66
draft witness statements 8.11, 8.15, 9.23, 9.68–9.69
duality of purpose 1.62, 12.83–12.91, 12.97–12.98
due diligence 11.04, 11.12
duty to advise on privilege 7.40–7.42

'early advice' 8.08, 8.11
eavesdropping
  deliberate or unlawful 3.96, 6.13
  inadvertent 6.11
  police station 6.09, 6.13
e-discovery companies 4.43–4.44, 12.132
egregious conduct 3.96, 6.14
electronic devices *see* computers, mobile phones and other electronic devices
emails
  attachments 4.66
  chains 4.60–4.62
  concerning compliance, anti-money laundering and other 'on-boarding' matters 1.42
  multi-addressee/multi-recipient 1.33, 4.63–4.65
employment contract, repudiatory breach of 12.75
employment issues/proceedings 12.02, 12.64
enforcement agencies and powers of compulsion 1.02
see also search and seizure, compulsion, surveillance and interception
ENRC 3.88, 7.41–7.42, 7.50, 12.16, 12.22, 12.29–12.31, 12.43–12.50, 12.54, 12.99–12.101, 12.127
European Convention on Human Rights (ECHR) 3.100–3.101
evidence
  admissible 1.107–1.108, 6.14, 9.12, 9.27, 9.31, 9.73, 10.19
  blood samples 9.43–9.45
  experts 10.40
  fabrication 10.58
  false 2.18, 2.25, 10.48
  false witness 10.58
  fresh 11.19–11.22
  lawyers giving *see under* court proceedings
  medical 11.10
  see also evidence gathering and preparing for court; oral evidence; witness evidence
evidence gathering and preparing for court 9.01–9.80
  co-defendants
    communications between 9.63–9.65
    single joint expert 9.61–9.62
  defence privileged material, deployment of 9.78–9.80
  defence witnesses 9.23–9.34
    confidentiality 9.29–9.31
    privilege belonging to defendant not witness 9.27–9.28
    prosecution authority, communications by 9.32–9.34
    witnesses of fact, actual and potential 9.23–9.26
  expert witnesses 9.37–9.62
    confidentiality obligations 9.07
    defence 9.37
    expert shopping 9.58–9.60
    joint instructions 9.61–9.62
    material provided to 9.42–9.46
    privileged material referred to in expert reports 9.47–9.57
    report and opinion distinction 9.40–9.41
    whose privilege? 9.38–9.39
  privileged material, seeking disclosure of 9.66–9.77
    disclosure and litigation privilege: common law and CPIA 1996 duties 9.67–9.69
    privileged document, reliance on part of 9.75–9.77
    prosecuting bodies, no distinction between 9.70
    prosecution witnesses: disclosure of draft and unused statements 9.66
    third parties' privileged material in prosecution's hands 9.71–9.74
  third parties, engaging with 9.05–9.22
    communication regarding funding 9.17–9.21
    communications with court and case management forms 9.09–9.13
    defence statements 9.14–9.16
    generally 9.05–9.08
    invoices and fee notes 9.18
    Legal Aid Agency 9.19–9.21
    non-lawyers, advice from 9.22
  witnesses, engaging with 9.23–9.62
    defence witnesses 9.23–9.34
    expert witnesses 9.37–9.62
    prosecution witnesses 9.35–9.36
examination and return of property seized under Criminal Justice and Police Act 2001 3.71–3.74
examination warrant, targeted 3.103
examination-in-chief 10.37–10.38
Excel spreadsheets 4.45
exceptional and compelling circumstances
  covert surveillance and interception of communications 3.106, 6.36

excluded material
    inextricably linked property 3.77, 3.79
    privileged material, obligation to return 3.77
    search warrants 3.04, 3.39, 3.43–3.45, 3.47–3.48
exclusion of evidence, test for 9.73
expert(s) 1.52
    accountants 9.22
    doctors 9.49
    evidence 10.40
    handwriting 9.41–9.42
    prosecution, instructions to 8.15
    litigation privilege 1.52
    litigation privilege in internal investigations 12.114
    psychiatric 1.63, 9.39, 9.46
    reports 1.63
        privileged material referred to in 9.47–9.57
        unused defence 9.60
        unused prosecution 8.15
    search terms 4.19
    shopping 9.58–9.60
    tax or accountancy 9.22
    witnesses, *see also under* evidence gathering and preparing for court
    witnesses 1.72, 9.07
express exclusion of privileged material from seizure *see under* search and seizure, compulsion, surveillance and interception
express waiver of privilege
    appeals 11.13, 11.24–11.28
    limited 1.85
    voluntary disclosure 10.02
extradition proceedings 1.55, 8.09–8.10

fabrication
    of evidence 10.58
    recent/subsequent 10.27–10.28, 10.30–10.31
fact of advice versus substance of that advice, distinction between 10.30
failure to comply without reasonable excuse 5.11–5.12
fair trial
    balancing exercise 10.10
    disclosure of draft and unused prosecution statements 9.66
    impact of seizure on 3.92–3.96
    inadvertent disclosure of privileged documents 10.22
    limited waiver and voluntary disclosure 7.33
    prosecution privilege 8.13, 8.24, 8.28–8.29, 9.66
fairness
    inadvertent disclosure 1.109
    interviews under caution 6.45
    prosecution privilege 8.14, 8.18
    waiver and collateral waiver 1.88, 1.91, 1.94, 1.96–1.97, 1.101–1.103
    see also in the interests of justice or fairness
false alibi 2.22, 2.24
false case 2.18
false diary entry 2.20
false evidence 2.18, 2.25, 10.48

false information 2.20
false representations 9.21
false statement in compelled interview 5.01
false witness evidence 10.58
family and friends of the party to litigation 1.52
fatal accident 12.50, 12.83, 12.116
fee notes 9.18
filters for privileged material 4.10–4.11, 4.15, 4.44
filters for relevant material 3.81, 4.06
Financial Conduct Authority (FCA) 3.10, 7.84–7.85, 7.77, 12.59
    compelled interviews 5.04, 5.09, 5.15
    covert surveillance and interception of communications 3.99
    Enforcement Guide 7.15, 7.35, 7.84
    interviews under caution 6.02
financial investigator, accredited 3.07
financial misconduct 12.55
financial penalty reduction/discount 7.62–7.69, 7.71–7.72, 7.77, 7.79
Financial Services and Markets Act 2000 3.10, 3.12, 3.30, 5.04, 5.09, 5.11
financial wrongdoing 12.16, 12.44
foreign lawyers 1.17
forensic accounting 7.64, 12.44
form MG3 8.08
Form NG 11.02, 11.04, 11.23
fraud
    claims for reimbursement of legal costs to HMCTS 3.58
    intentional disclosure of privileged documents 10.12
    legal advice privilege in internal investigations 12.08
    litigation privilege in internal investigations 12.64
    see also crime-fraud exception
'free text' comments box 4.46, 4.59, 4.61
fresh evidence 11.19–11.22
frivolous or vexatious application for leave to appeal 11.08, 11.10
FTT 12.106
full and frank disclosure duty 3.42–3.44
funding
    communication regarding 9.17–9.21
    Legal Aid 9.19–9.21
    third party 12.135

G4S Care & Justice Services (UK) Ltd 7.66
general waiver of privilege 7.04
giving 'notice', by CPS to police 8.08
Glencore Energy UK Ltd 7.75
good faith 2.08
gross misconduct 12.62
guilty plea, credit for 9.11, 9.13, 10.42
Gürlap Systems Ltd (GSL) 7.73–7.74

handwriting experts 9.41–9.42
harassment 1.65, 2.12
hard copy documents 3.83, 4.06, 4.42

Health and Safety Executive (HSE) 5.05, 5.10, 6.19, 8.17, 12.50–12.52
hearings
　committal 9.12
　interlocutory 10.62
　Newton 9.01
High Court 3.88
　compelled interviews 5.07–5.08
　definition of privilege 3.29, 3.75, 3.88, 3.90, 5.07–5.08
His Majesty's Courts and Tribunals Service (HMCTS), fraudulent claims for reimbursement of legal costs to 3.58
His Majesty's Revenue and Customs (HMRC)
　artificial intelligence, use of by 4.39
　compelled interviews 5.03
　covert surveillance and interception of communications 3.99, 3.103
　litigation privilege in internal investigations 12.102–12.109
　search and seizure and compulsion 3.03, 3.07, 3.09, 3.12, 4.24
Hong Kong Court of Appeal 7.12, 7.37
Hong Kong Department of Justice 7.12–7.13, 7.18
Hong Kong Securities and Futures Commission (SFC) 7.12–7.13, 7.18, 7.37
hospital order 9.39
human rights 1.01, 3.100–3.101

immigration officers 3.07
immunity from prosecution 7.77, 7.79
implied waiver of privilege 1.71, 1.85, 7.04–7.06, 1.110–1.111, 10.02, 11.28, 11.32–11.34, 11.36
in the interests of justice or fairness 7.50, 8.28, 9.68–9.69
inadvertent disclosure 1.104–1.109, 5.25
　during evidence gathering/preparing for court 9.73–9.74
　limited waiver and voluntary disclosure 7.17
　police station and interviews under caution 6.10–6.11
　see also under court proceedings
inadvertent eavesdropping at police station 6.11
inadvertent loss of privilege 1.04, 5.20, 9.27, 10.01
inadvertent seizure 4.11
inadvertent waiver 1.04
　defence witnesses and evidence gathering/preparing for court 9.27
　police station 6.11
　lawyers giving evidence 10.57
　prosecution witnesses and evidence gathering/preparing for court 9.35
inadvertently obtained privileged material through interception/surveillance 3.108
incompetent representation by trial solicitors or trial counsel 11.09
independent counsel
　Competition and Markets Authority (CMA) 7.81–7.83
　crime-fraud exception 2.26, 2.28
　and defence, disagreement between 4.31–4.35
　deferred prosecution agreements (DPAs) and cooperation with SFO 7.45, 7.58–7.59, 7.62–7.64, 7.69
　lawyers as defendants 10.52, 10.54
　privilege assertion in response to compulsion powers 3.89
　privilege reviews 4.01, 4.52
　search warrants 3.58, 3.60, 3.62–3.66, 3.89, 4.11
　seized/compelled material 3.81, 3.83, 4.06, 4.10–4.13, 4.14, 4.26–4.27, 4.29–4.33, 4.35
independent investigator 12.10
inextricably linked material 3.72, 3.78–3.81, 3.85, 3.87, 4.05, 4.34–4.35
inference as to substance of advice 1.40
informed consent 1.02 n.4
in-house lawyer 1.18, 1.32, 5.20, 5.23
in-house technical staff 4.07, 4.13, 4.32
iniquitous conduct 2.01 n.1, 2.08, 2.10, 2.12–2.13
　and issues to be determined at trial, overlap between 2.19–2.25
iniquity exception *see* crime-fraud exception
initial duty of disclosure 8.22
injury, personal 9.38
innocent dupe 2.10
instructions to prepare legal document 1.43
insurers, communications with 12.135
intelligence services 3.99, 3.103
intentional disclosure of privileged documents during court proceedings 10.02–10.15
　defence, disclosure by 10.08–10.15
　　defendant documents relating to current proceedings 10.14–10.15
　　defendant documents relating to a separate matter 10.11–10.13
　　third parties, privileged documents belonging to 10.08–10.10
　prosecution, disclosure by 10.02–10.07
　　third parties, privileged documents belonging to 10.02–10.07
interception of communications
　see under search and seizure, compulsion, surveillance and interception
interception warrant, bulk or targeted 3.103
interception-related material and prosecution privilege 8.22, 8.24
interlocutory hearings 10.62
internal investigations 12.01–12.137
　deferred prosecution agreements (DPAs) and cooperation with SFO 7.47
　fact-finding 12.10, 12.31, 12.65, 12.94
　interviews 6.05, 12.11–12.28
　non-privileged 1.37
　legal advice privilege 12.03–12.04, 12.07–12.35, 12.119–12.120, 12.134
　　client and investigating lawyer(s) relationship 12.07–12.10
　　investigation reports 12.29–12.35
　　witness interviews 12.11–12.28

internal investigations (*cont.*)
  limited waiver and voluntary disclosure 7.07
  litigation privilege 1.59, 12.03, 12.16, 12.21, 12.36–12.117, 12.123–12.127, 12.129–12.131
    dominant purpose 12.81–12.113, 12.124–12.125
    conduct of litigation of no more than equal importance to one or more other purposes 12.83–12.91
    establishing facts to answer a regulator's/investigator's questions 12.112–12.113
    investigation would have been carried out anyway 12.92–12.93
    several purposes may form part of single purpose of preparing for litigation 12.94–12.111
  litigation in progress or reasonably in contemplation 12.38–12.80
    contemplation of several sets of proceedings 12.62–12.64
    investigators or prosecutors, indications from 12.42–12.61
    uncertainty as to what will be uncovered 12.65–12.80
  third parties, instructing 12.114
  whose privilege is it? 12.115–12.117
  practical guidance 12.118–12.137
    client group, setting up 12.120–12.122
    insurers, communications with 12.135
    lawyer's role, determination of extent of 12.119
    litigation privilege, file note of assessment of 12.123–12.127
    pre-existing privileged material, handling 12.132
    privilege claim, weak, risk of structuring investigation on 12.129–12.131
    privilege reviews 12.133
    privileged, marking documents as 12.128
    privileged information, dissemination of outside client group 12.134
    public statements on investigation findings 12.136–12.137
  privilege, importance of 12.04–12.06
  privilege reviews 4.02, 12.133
  reports 12.29–12.35
    draft 7.41
    factual 12.29–12.35
    limited waiver and voluntary disclosure 7.35
interpreters 6.24–6.25
interview notes as lawyers' working papers 12.17–12.28
interview records with actual or potential witnesses or suspects 9.67
interviews
  internal investigation *see under* internal investigations
  with lawyers 5.20–5.25
  see also compelled interviews; interviews under caution at police station
interviews under caution at police station 6.01–6.51
  client consultation in presence of third parties 6.22–6.36

appropriate adults 6.26–6.28
interpreters 6.24–6.25
statutory surveillance of privileged consultation 6.35–6.36
during interview 6.37–6.51
  communications 6.37–6.38
  prepared statements 6.48–6.50
  references to reasons for advice given 6.39–6.47
initial engagement and instruction 6.06–6.21
  contact from police station 6.06–6.14
  third party instructions 6.15–6.21
location of interview 6.03
oral evidence and waiver 10.27–10.39
voluntary attendance 6.03
waiver and collateral waiver 1.103, 6.39–6.47, 10.27–10.39
see also no comment interviews
investigation committee 12.121
investigation findings, public statements on 12.136–12.137
investigation team 12.132
investigation/prosecution, assistance with 7.05–7.15
investigator, independent 12.10
Investigatory Powers Act (IPA) 2016 3.103–3.108
Investigatory Powers Commissioner 3.108
investigatory work/legal advice and assistance distinction 12.08
invoices 3.58, 9.18
Irish Stock Exchange 7.11
isolation of privileged material 3.81–3.82, 4.06, 4.10–4.14, 4.23, 4.27, 4.34–4.35

joint inquiry report 12.83
joint instructions (expert witnesses) 9.61–9.62
joint interest privilege 1.112–1.115
joint retainer 1.114
Jones Lang LaSalle 7.69
journalistic material held in confidence 3.04
judge's questioning 10.37–10.39
Judicial Commissioner 3.103
judicial oversight 11.40
judicial review
  crime-fraud exception 2.20–2.21, 2.27
  defence witnesses and evidence gathering/preparing for court 9.25
  limited waiver and voluntary disclosure 7.23–7.24
  prosecution privilege 8.09
  search warrants 3.51
  seized/compelled material 4.34
Judicial Studies Board (JSB) standard direction 10.32
justices of the peace (JP) 3.04, 3.06, 3.09–3.10, 3.39–3.41, 3.51

keyword searches 3.81, 3.83, 4.15–4.22

Law Society 2.29, 5.14, 7.57
  'Defence Witness Notices' Practice Note 9.33
lawyers
  attendance of for search warrants 3.66

communications between 1.41
deception 2.18
defined 1.17–1.18, 1.53
foreign 1.17
fraud 2.18
giving evidence *see under* court proceedings
in-house 1.18, 1.32, 5.20, 5.23
interviews with 5.20–5.25
offices
   covert surveillance and interception of communications 3.101
   statutory surveillance of privileged consultation 6.35
   prevention of harm to 6.29–6.30
role of in internal investigations 12.34, 12.119
and third parties 1.52–1.53
unlawful violence inflicted against 2.09
see also legal advisers
legal advice 1.25–1.27
   and assistance, distinction between investigatory work and 12.08
   in connection with conduct of litigation 1.60
   dissemination within company 1.79
   relevant legal context 1.25–1.27
   sharing with client's non-legal advisers 1.79
   see also legal advice privilege
legal advice privilege 1.05, 1.11–1.46
   agents 1.24
   client (defined) 1.19–1.20
   client and lawyer relationship 1.21
   communications 1.13–1.14, 1.28–1.30
   between lawyers 1.41
   confidentiality 1.15–1.16
   continuum of communication 1.28
   corporate clients 1.20
   crime-fraud exception 2.04
      criminal law advice 1.27 n.39
   defence witnesses and evidence gathering/preparing for court 9.28
   dissemination of privileged information outside client group 1.79, 12.134
   documents 1.35–1.40
      draft 1.38
      prepared by client 1.39
   dominant purpose 1.31–1.33
   evidence gathering and preparing for court 9.04
   in-house lawyers 1.18
   instructions to do something 1.43
   items not covered by 1.42–1.46
   joint interest privilege and common interest privilege 1.112
   lawyer (defined) 1.17–1.18
   legal advice 1.25–1.27
   limited waiver and voluntary disclosure 7.21
   litigation privilege distinction and 1.47
   multi-addressee emails 1.33, 4.63
   non-lawyer 1.23, 9.22
   privilege reviews 4.54
   privileged communications, evidence of 1.34

   prosecution privilege 8.02–8.04, 8.11, 8.29
   relevant legal context 1.25–1.27
   subject matter of legal advice 1.44–1.46
   substance of advice, documents indicating 1.40
   third parties 1.22–1.23
   working papers, lawyers' 1.36–1.37, 12.17–12.28
   see also under internal investigations
legal advisers
   suing 1.110–1.111
   unsustainable or unfounded criticism of 11.07
   see also criticism of legal advisers on appeal
Legal Aid Agency funding 9.19–9.21
Legal Sector Affinity Group 5.12 n.5
Leniency policy, Competition and Markets Authority (CMA) 7.79–7.83
letter of representation to CPS 1.38, 1.63
liability *see* criminal liability
libel action 9.38
limited waiver of privilege 1.85–1.87, 7.04
   advising clients on 7.38–7.42
   assistance with investigation/prosecution 7.05–7.15
   Court of Appeal 11.29, 11.38
   deferred prosecution agreements (DPAs) and cooperation with SFO 7.43, 7.62–7.69, 7.75
   express 1.85, 7.06, 11.38
   implied 7.05–7.06
   intentional disclosure of privileged documents 10.02, 10.04, 10.08, 10.13
   risks 7.16–7.37
      disclosure to defendants in criminal proceedings and reference in open court 7.25–7.35
      onward disclosure to overseas authorities 7.36–7.37
      use of material against privilege holder 7.16–7.17
      waiver more extensive than intended 7.18–7.24
   summary of main principles 1.85–1.87, 7.04
litigation 1.54–1.55
   in progress or reasonably in contemplation *see under* internal investigations
   see also adversarial proceedings; litigation privilege
litigation privilege 1.05, 1.47–1.64
   between party or lawyer and a third party 1.52–1.53
   communications 1.49–1.50
   conducting litigation 1.47, 1.52, 1.60–1.61
   confidentiality 1.51
   crime-fraud exception 2.04
   defence witnesses and evidence gathering/preparing for court 9.23, 9.25, 9.29
   disclosure, prosecution 9.66–9.69
   dominant purpose 1.60, 1.62, 1.64
   dual purpose 1.62
   evidence gathering and preparing for court 9.02, 9.04
   expert evidence/witnesses 9.37, 9.44, 9.54, 9.60, 10.40
   file note of assessment of 12.123–12.127
   joint interest privilege and common interest privilege 1.112
   legal advice privilege distinction and 1.47

litigation privilege (*cont.*)
   Legal Aid Agency 9.20–9.21
   limited waiver and voluntary disclosure 7.21
   litigation 1.54–1.55
   non-party 1.57
   police station 6.16–6.20
   prosecution privilege 8.02–8.04, 8.10–8.11, 8.29, 9.66–9.69
   purpose 1.60–1.64
   reasonably in contemplation 1.56–1.59
   investigation stage, at 1.58
   risk of structuring investigation on weak privilege claim 12.129–12.131
   search terms 4.15
   third parties and evidence gathering/preparing for court 9.07, 9.21–9.22
   third party instructions 6.16–6.20
   see also under internal investigations
loss of confidentiality 1.73–1.79
   defence witnesses, communications with 9.27
   handling pre-existing privileged material 12.132
   interview under caution 1.103
   investigating authority, as against 1.100
   limited waiver, risks associated with 7.26, 7.30–7.31, 7.39
   public statements on investigation findings 12.137
   references in open court 1.75–1.76, 7.26, 7.30–7.31, 7.39
   third parties, confidential disclosure to 1.77–1.79
   waiver and collateral waiver 1.98, 1.103
   waiver distinction and 1.80
loss of privilege 1.04, 1.70–1.111
   court proceedings 10.01
   defence witnesses, communications with 9.27
   deliberate 10.01
   disclosure, inadvertent 1.104–1.109
   inadvertent 5.20, 10.01
   interlocutory hearings 10.62
   interviews under caution 6.39
   lawyers giving evidence 10.45
   limited waiver and voluntary disclosure 7.18, 7.26, 7.31–7.32, 7.36
   oral evidence 10.26
   police station 6.12
   prosecution, disclosure to 9.72
   see also inadvertent disclosure; loss of confidentiality; waiver of privilege
loss of witness evidence 12.26
lying to solicitor about key factual issue 2.19

McCook requirements 11.02–11.06, 11.20–11.22–11.24, 11.31
   development of principle 11.07–11.11
   implications on privilege 11.12–11.18
machine learning 4.37–4.38, 4.51
   supervised 4.37–4.38
   unsupervised 4.37–4.38
Magistrates' Court, appeals to Crown Court from 11.39

manual review 3.83
material, use of against privilege holder 7.16–7.17
medical evidence 11.10
medical records 3.04
mental health issues of defendant 9.39
mere rumour 2.14
Metropolitan Police 3.103
Ministry of Justice 7.64, 7.66
miscarriages of justice 11.40–11.41
misleading court 2.17
misleading impression/understanding and waiver 1.91, 1.101, 6.45, 8.19, 10.28, 10.33
misleading statement 5.01
mobile phones *see* computers, mobile phones and other electronic devices
money laundering 2.11, 3.07, 3.52, 5.12 n.5
multi-addressee/recipient emails 1.33, 4.63–4.65
mutual legal assistance (MLA) 3.12, 3.32

National Crime Agency (NCA) 3.03, 3.09, 3.12, 3.99, 3.103, 5.03
national security, in interests of 3.106
'necessary implication', abrogation of privilege by 1.09–1.10, 3.33, 8.23, 8.26, 11.41
negotiation over disputed material 3.89
Newton hearing 9.01
no comment interviews 6.39, 6.43–6.44, 10.29, 10.32–10.34, 11.08
no-action applications 7.80
non-criminal conduct and crime-fraud exception 2.08
non-disclosure agreement (NDA) 9.31
non-lawyers, advice from 9.22
non-legal issues 1.32
non-privileged internal investigation interviews 1.37
non-sensitive unused material, schedule of 9.71–9.72
non-waiver agreements, express confidential 7.09
not guilty plea 9.68
not obviously invalid test 7.54
'notice', CPS giving to police 8.08
notice, written 3.06, 3.67, 5.02

obligation of confidentiality, qualified 1.02
obscured witness evidence 12.26
obviousness, cursory tests of 7.54
Office of Fair Trading (OFT) 7.80, 12.39–12.40
'once privileged, always privileged' maxim 1.70
onward disclosure to overseas authorities 7.36–7.37
open court
   collateral use of unused material 10.03
   Court of Appeal 11.33
   loss of confidentiality 1.75–1.76, 7.26–7.27, 7.29–7.31, 7.38–7.39, 9.10, 10.02, 10.04–10.07, 10.08, 10.22, 11.33
open justice 1.76, 7.26, 7.30, 10.06
oral evidence 10.26–10.39
   defence witnesses and evidence gathering/preparing for court 9.26
   defendant's, judge's questioning 10.37–10.39

defendant's 10.27–10.34
see also under court proceedings
oral opinion of independent counsel 3.64
oral statement in interview under caution 6.48–6.49
oral summaries of witness interviews 7.53
'ordinary run' of criminal cases *see under* crime-fraud exception
originals and facilitation of copies or images 3.69
overriding privilege by statute 1.02, 1.09–1.10
see also abrogation of privilege
overseas authorities
  obtaining evidence located in UK 3.12
  onward disclosure to 7.36–7.37
overseas-related communications 3.103

paraphrasing 1.34
Parquet National Financier (France) 7.65
part 8 claim 4.34
partial disclosure 1.83, 1.101–1.102
partially quoted privileged advice 1.83
partly privileged documents 4.57–4.59
perjury 2.17
personal injury 9.38
persons, searches of (PACE 1984) 3.05
persons, searches of (section 51 CJPA 2001) 3.18–3.23
pervert the course of justice *see* conspiracy to pervert the course of justice
Plea and Trial Preparation Hearing (PTPH) 9.11
police
  compelled interviews 5.03
  confidentiality 1.16
  covert surveillance and interception of communications 3.99
  potential witnesses and police, communications between 8.11
  privilege *see* prosecution privilege
  search and seizure and compulsion, powers of 3.03–3.07, 3.09–3.10, 3.12, 3.22–3.23, 3.25
  seized/compelled material 4.24, 4.26–4.27
  tape recording of privileged conversations by police 3.96
  see also police stations
Police and Criminal Evidence Act 1984 (PACE 1984)
  crime-fraud exception 2.11, 2.20, 3.50, 3.53
  definition of privilege 2.11, 2.20, 3.26, 9.20, 9.44
  exclusion of evidence (s78) 1.106, 1.108, 4.35, 6.41, 7.17, 9.51, 9.73, 10.20, 10.36
  interviews under caution 6.01, 6.37–6.51
  mutual legal assistance 3.12
  search and seizure and compulsion 3.03–3.05, 3.25, 3.36, 3.39–3.48, 3.57–3.58, 3.69, 3.72, 3.80
  see also section 8 (PACE 1984) warrants; section 9/schedule 1 (PACE 1984) warrants/production orders
police stations
  advice
    defence privileged material, deployment of 9.78

intentional disclosure of privileged documents 10.14–10.15
  oral evidence 10.27
confidentiality 1.16
covert surveillance and interception of communications 3.101, 6.35
search and seizure and compulsion 3.05
statutory surveillance or privileged consultation 6.35
see also interviews under caution at police station
pre-charge stage 9.64, 12.38
pre-existing documents 1.65–1.69
pre-existing privileged material, handling 12.132
pre-hearing information form 9.11
premises, searches of (section 50 CJPA 2001) 3.18–3.23
premises, searches of (PACE 1984) 3.05
  see also search and seizure and compulsion *under* Police and Criminal Evidence Act 1984 (PACE 1984)
prepared statements and interviews under caution 6.48–6.50
pre-trial review hearing 9.25
previous accounts made by complainant or other prosecution witness 9.67
prima facie case 2.13
prisons
  covert surveillance and interception of communications 3.101
  statutory surveillance or privileged consultation 6.35
private law 1.25
private prosecutions 8.29
privilege against self-incrimination 9.15
privilege reviews 3.63–3.64, 4.01–4.66, 12.133
  artificial intelligence 4.36–4.40
  document review platforms 4.42–4.47
  document types and practical issues 4.52–4.66
    email attachments 4.66
    email chains 4.60–4.62
    emails, multi-addressee 4.63–4.65
    individual documents 4.54–4.56
    redactions and partly privileged documents 4.57–4.59
  first-tier 4.47, 4.50
  independent counsel, by 3.63–3.64, 4.29–4.35
  internal investigations 12.133
  management of 4.48–4.51
  oversight and consistency 4.48
  search terms 4.15–4.22
  second-tier 4.47, 4.50
  seized/compelled material 4.01, 4.05–4.40
    artificial intelligence (AI) 4.36–4.40
    defence's role 4.23–4.28
    independent counsel 4.29–4.30
    independent counsel and defence, disagreement between 4.31–4.35
    procedure 4.05–4.14
    search terms 4.15–4.22

privileged communications, evidence of 1.34
privileged consultation, covert/statutory surveillance of 3.100–3.101, 3.106, 6.35–6.36
privileged conversations, tape recordings of by police 3.96
privileged, marking documents as 12.128
privileged material, seizure and compelled production of *see* search and seizure, compulsion, surveillance and interception
Proceeds of Crime Act 2002 3.07–3.08, 3.30, 3.75, 5.12 n.5
production orders 3.04, 3.07, 3.12, 4.34
   crime-fraud exception 2.11, 2.20–2.24, 2.26–2.27, 2.29, 10.58–10.59
   ex parte 2.27
   litigation privilege 1.55
   privilege assertion in response to compulsion powers 3.88
   privilege reviews 4.02, 4.41
   return of material application 3.86
professional conduct and appeals 11.30
professional confidence, duty of 1.23 n.28
professional ethics 2.29
professional negligence 1.72, 11.33, 11.36
professional obligations 2.29
proffer sessions 7.21–7.22, 7.24, 7.72
proffer summaries, oral 7.53–7.54
proof of evidence 9.30, 9.57
property obtained in consequence of commission of offence 3.77
prosecuting bodies, no distinction between 9.70
prosecution
   authority, communications with defence witnesses by 9.32–9.34
   disclosure by, third parties, privileged documents belonging to 10.02–10.07
   disclosure, defence applications for 8.22
   evidence adduced by 10.35–10.36
   inadvertent disclosure by 10.23–10.25
   litigation 1.54
   private 8.29
   see also prosecution privilege; prosecution witnesses; prosecution *under* disclosure
prosecution privilege 8.01–8.29
   availability of 8.02–8.10
   disclosure obligations 8.12–8.28
      approach taken in practice 8.13–8.17
      consequences of disclosure 8.18–8.20
      consequences of withholding disclosure on grounds of privilege 8.28
      withholding disclosure 8.21–8.27
   examples 8.11
   private prosecutions 8.29
prosecution witnesses 9.35–9.36
   approaching, by defence 9.35–9.36
   disclosure of draft and unused statements 8.15, 9.66
   instructions regarding 3.92
   lawyers as 10.43–10.45
   prosecution privilege 8.04, 8.11, 8.15, 9.66

prosecutor and prosecution counsel, communications between 8.11
prosecutor and prosecution expert witness, communications between 8.11
protected items 3.30, 5.09
psychiatric experts 1.63, 9.39, 9.46
psychopathic defendant 9.39
public authorities 3.105–3.106
public domain 1.75, 7.36, 7.38, 10.02
public interest 1.03
   covert surveillance and interception of communications 3.106
   deferred prosecution agreements (DPAs) and cooperation with SFO 7.44, 7.49, 12.49
   inadvertent disclosure 1.105
   litigation privilege 1.63
   prosecution privilege 8.24–8.25, 8.26 n.35
   search warrants 3.47
   schedule of sensitive unused material 9.71
   see also public interest immunity (PII)
public interest immunity (PII) 8.09, 8.14, 8.22, 8.24–8.25, 10.23
public law 1.25
public policy
   contrary to 2.08, 7.08
   crime-fraud exception 2.08–2.09
   inadvertent disclosure of privileged documents 10.16
   prosecution privilege 8.05
public statements on investigation findings 12.136–12.137
'put on legal spectacles' 1.25, 1.32

qualified right 1.23 n.28
quality control dip-sampling 4.37
quasi-legal issues 1.32
question of fact and degree 2.18

rationale for privilege 1.06–1.08
RBS 7.09, 12.14–12.15, 12.18–12.20, 12.102–12.108
reasonable excuse, failure to comply without 5.11–5.12
reasonably in contemplation
   litigation privilege 1.56–1.59
      file note of assessment 12.124, 12.127
      in internal investigations 12.38–12.82, 12.86, 12.104, 12.110, 12.112
receipt acknowledgements 1.42
records
   proper 4.10
   showing dates and times of calls and meetings 1.42
redactions
   email chains 4.61
   email headers and footers 4.62
   legal advice privilege 1.34, 12.25
   limited waiver and voluntary disclosure 7.07
   multi-addressee emails 4.64–4.65
   partly privileged documents 4.57–4.59
   privilege reviews 4.57–4.59

prosecution disclosure 9.76–9.77
references in open court 1.75–1.76, 7.25–7.35
references to reasons for advice given (interviews under caution) 6.39–6.47
Regulation of Investigatory Powers Act (RIPA) 2000 3.98–3.102, 3.105–3.108
regulatory consequences 12.64
regulatory issues 12.02
report and opinion distinction (expert witnesses) 9.40–9.41
representations
　false 9.21
　independent counsel, to 4.06
repudiatory breach of employment contract 12.75
retention 7.73
　of seized material 3.37, 3.81, 3.86, 4.05–4.06
return of material
　application for 3.85–3.87, 4.33
　inadvertent disclosure, following 10.22
　seized/compelled material 3.71, 3.74–3.81, 3.92–3.93, 4.05–4.06, 4.12, 4.14, 4.23, 4.35
　voluntary disclosure, following 7.08, 7.12
review of material to remove privileged items prior to voluntary disclosure 4.02
right, inviolable 1.02
Rolls-Royce 7.53, 7.62
rule of law 1.06, 6.13

safeguarding privileged material 10.17
Sarclad Ltd 7.21–7.24, 7.53–7.54, 7.71–7.72, 7.74
search and seizure, compulsion, surveillance and interception 1.10, 3.01–3.108
　additional powers of seizure (CJPA 2001) 3.14–3.23, 3.37
　covert surveillance and interception of communications 3.02, 3.97–3.108, 6.35–6.36
　　directed surveillance 3.98–3.100
　　intrusive surveillance 3.98–3.101
　　Investigatory Powers Act (IPA) 2016 (interception of communications) 3.103–3.108
　　Regulation of Investigatory Powers Act (RIPA) 2000 (covert surveillance) 3.98–3.102, 3.105–3.108
　　safeguards 3.105–3.108
　　unauthorized/unlawful 6.13
　crime-fraud exception 2.26
　Criminal Justice and Police Act 2001 3.14–3.23, 3.67–3.87
　exclusion of privileged material
search warrant, wording of 3.34, 3.57–3.60
statutory 1.108, 3.13, 3.24–3.34
　fair trial, impact of seizure on 3.92–3.96
　following arrest 3.05
　inadvertent seizure 4.11
　police powers see search and seizure and compulsion, powers of under police
　police station, at 3.05
　post-seizure 3.70–3.87
　　examination and return of property 3.71–3.74
　　inextricably linked property, use of 3.79–3.80

privilege reviews 4.01–4.40, 4.52–4.66
privileged material, application for return of 3.85–3.87
privileged material, handling 3.81–3.84
privileged material, obligation to return 3.75–3.78
powers of search and seizure and compulsion 3.03–3.13
　Criminal Justice Act 1987 3.06
　Criminal Justice and Police Act 2001 3.14–3.23
　Financial Services and Markets Act 2000 3.10
　mutual legal assistance (MLA) 3.12
　Police and Criminal Evidence Act 1984 3.03–3.05
　privileged material, seizure of 3.13
　Proceeds of Crime Act 2002 3.07–3.08
　Serious Organised Crime and Police Act 2005 3.09
　witness summons 3.11
privilege, asserting in response to compulsion powers 3.88–3.91
search of person 3.05, 3.18–3.23
search of premises 3.05, 3.18–3.23
search and seizure warrant 3.04, 3.07
'seize and sift' powers 3.15
whilst lawfully on premises 3.05
　see also privileged material, seizure and compelled production of; search warrants
search terms 4.15–4.22, 7.64
　devices belonging to lawyer 4.20
　document review platforms 4.44
　false positives 4.22
　generic 4.15, 4.17, 4.22
　refining 4.21–4.22
　seized/compelled material 4.06, 4.08, 4.10–4.13
　specific 4.15, 4.18–4.19
　see also filters
search warrants
　application for 3.38–3.60
　　applications not mere formalities 3.45–3.49
　　crime-fraud exception and overlap with special procedure material 3.50–3.56
　　full and frank disclosure duty 3.42–3.44
　　Police and Criminal Evidence Act 1984 section 8 warrants 3.39–3.41, 3.65
　　privileged material exclusion in wording of warrant 3.57–3.60
　balancing exercise 3.47
　crime-fraud exception 2.26
　disclosure notice, as an alternative to 3.89
　disputed material 3.89
　execution of 3.61–3.69
　　independent counsel 3.62–3.65
　　lawyers, attendance of 3.66
　　obligations when exercising Criminal Justice and Police Act 2001 powers 3.67–3.69
　litigation privilege 1.55
　see also section 2 (CJA 1987) warrant; section 8 (PACE 1984) warrants; section 9/schedule 1 (PACE 1984) warrants/production orders
secondary data from communications 3.103

secrecy, obligation of 11.40–11.43
Secretary of State 3.12, 3.99, 3.103
section 2 (CJA 1987) compelled interview 5.13–5.14, 5.23
section 2 (CJA 1987) production notice 3.06
section 2 (CJA 1987) warrant 3.06
section 8 (PACE 1984) warrants 3.04, 3.39–3.41, 3.44, 3.50, 3.52–3.53, 3.65
section 9/schedule 1 (PACE 1984) warrants/production orders 3.04, 3.22, 3.42–3.43, 3.45–3.48, 3.50, 3.53, 3.58
section 9 witness statements 2.23, 9.24, 12.53
   'seize and sift' powers 3.15
   see also additional powers of seizure (CJPA 2001) *under* search and seizure, compulsion, surveillance and interception
seizure *see* search and seizure, compulsion, surveillance and interception
self-incrimination
   privilege against 9.15
   risk of 6.37
self-reporting process 6.20
   internal investigations 12.42, 12.44, 12.46, 12.48–12.49, 12.54, 12.100
   privilege reviews 4.41
   waiver and cooperation 7.21, 7.41–7.42, 7.44, 7.47–7.48, 7.70
sensitive material schedule 9.71
sentencing 9.01
   appeals against 11.23
   reduction or review for defendants assisting prosecution 7.77–7.78
Sentencing Act 2020 7.77–7.78
separate matter, documents relating to 10.11–10.13
Serco Geografix Ltd 7.64
Serious Fraud Office (SFO)
   artificial intelligence (AI) 4.39
   compelled interviews 5.07, 5.13–5.14, 5.20, 5.23, 5.25
   Corporate Cooperation Guidance 7.45, 7.49, 7.55, 7.58
   covert surveillance 3.99
   Director 3.06, 3.12, 5.02, 7.77
   file note of assessment of litigation privilege 12.127
   General Counsel 7.48, 7.52
   intentional disclosure of privileged documents 10.04
   internal investigations 12.01
   legal advice privilege 12.27, 12.30
   litigation privilege 12.43, 12.45–12.49, 12.54, 12.61, 12.87, 12.100, 12.109, 12.129
   interviews under caution 6.02, 6.20
   limited waiver and voluntary disclosure 7.01–7.02, 7.21–7.24, 7.27–7.29, 7.31, 7.34, 7.40, 7.41–7.42, 10.04
   Operational Handbook 4.12
   privilege assertion in response to compulsion powers 3.88, 3.90
   seized/compelled material 3.07, 4.12–4.13, 4.24

Self-Reporting Guidelines 12.44, 12.46, 12.49
   see also deferred prosecution agreements (DPAs); section 2 (CJA 1987) compelled interview; section 2 (CJA 1987) production notice; section 2 (CJA 1987) warrant; *see also under* waiver of privilege and cooperation
Serious Organised Crime and Police Act 2005 3.09, 3.30, 3.89, 5.03, 5.08, 5.11, 7.77–7.78
sharp practice 2.08
silence
   no right to 5.01, 6.04
   see also adverse inference drawn from silence; no comment interviews
social workers 6.28
sole or dominant purpose of conducting litigation *see* dominant purpose *under* litigation privilege
solicitors *see* lawyers
Solicitors Regulation Authority (SRA) 4.15, 9.79
   Code of Conduct 1.02
special procedure material
   crime-fraud exception 2.29, 3.50–3.56
   inextricably linked property 3.79
   privileged material, obligation to return 3.77
   search and seizure and compulsion 3.04, 3.39–3.41, 3.43–3.45
Standard Bank 7.53, 7.70–7.71
standard of proof 2.13–2.14
statements
   of case 1.99
   defence 9.14–9.16
   defence case 1.38, 1.99
   draft and unused prosecution, disclosure of 9.66
   false or misleading 5.01
statutory disclosure obligations 7.25, 7.33–7.34, 8.12–8.29, 9.66–9.72
   prevent/restrict compliance with 7.35
statutory surveillance of privileged consultation *see* privileged consultation, covert/statutory surveillance of
stay case, refusal to 3.92–3.93
subject matter of legal advice 1.44–1.46
substance of advice, documents indicating 1.40
suing legal advisers 1.110–1.111, 11.33–11.36
summarized form, legal advice/privileged material in 1.34, 1.83
surmise and conjecture 2.14
surveillance *see* covert surveillance; search and seizure, compulsion, surveillance and interception
surveillance agents 2.12
suspects *see* interviews under caution at police station
suspects, interview records with actual or potential 9.67
suspicion and assumption 2.14

tape recordings of privileged information 3.96, 6.13
targeted examination warrant 3.103
targeted interception warrant 3.103
tax experts 9.22
technical audit 12.89

INDEX

technical staff, in-house 4.07, 4.13
terrorist attack 3.106
Tesco 7.29–7.31, 7.63, 10.04–10.05, 12.39–12.40
Tetris Projects Ltd (TPL) 7.69
text recognition 3.83
third parties
   client groups, setting up 12.121
   co-defendants and evidence gathering/preparing for court 9.64
   common interest privilege 1.116–1.117
   compelled interviews 5.17
   confidential disclosure to 1.77–1.79
   crime-fraud exception 2.10–2.11
   defence witnesses and evidence gathering/preparing for court 9.28
   disclosure of privileged material to 8.08
   evidence gathering and preparing for court 9.02, 9.04
   expert evidence 10.40
   funding 12.135
   inadvertent disclosure by, to prosecution 9.74, 10.21–10.22
   internal investigations 12.04, 12.11–12.16, 12.35–12.36, 12.81, 12.114, 12.117, 12.131, 12.134
   interviews under caution 6.51
   legal advice privilege 1.22–1.23, 1.25, 1.34
   limited waiver and voluntary disclosure 1.87, 7.06, 7.09, 7.11–7.12, 7.15, 7.31, 7.33
   litigation privilege 1.47, 1.52–1.53, 1.63
   loss of confidentiality 1.77, 1.80, 1.87
   loss of privilege 1.72, 1.77, 1.80, 1.87
   non-privileged documents 1.69
   oral evidence 10.29–10.30
   police station 6.07, 6.09
   pre-existing documents 1.66
   pre-existing privileged material, handling 12.132
   privilege assertion in response to compulsion powers 3.91
   privilege reviews 4.49
   privileged documents belonging to 10.02–10.10
   privileged documents disclosed in entirety 1.83
   privileged information outside client group, dissemination of 12.134
   privileged material in prosecution's hands 9.71–9.74
   prosecution privilege 8.03–8.04, 8.10, 8.29, 9.66
   redactions and partly privileged documents 4.57
   search terms 4.15, 4.17, 4.19
   search warrants 3.42 n.22
   waiver 1.72, 1.83, 1.87
   weak privilege claim, risk of structuring investigation on 12.131
   witness summons 3.91, 10.10
   witnesses likely to be 12.11–12.16
   see also under evidence gathering and preparing for court; interviews under caution at police station; third party instructions
third party instructions 6.15–6.21
   agency principle 6.21
   general position 6.15–6.16
   litigation privilege, availability of 6.16–6.20
threat to life or limb 3.106
'trial by ambush', avoidance/abolition of 9.15, 9.32

unfair trial 1.106
United States 7.21, 8.09
   Attorneys General 7.09
   Department of Justice 7.48
   Securities and Exchange Commission 7.09
unlawful conduct by police 6.14
unlawful violence, infliction of 6.29–6.30, 6.32
   against solicitors 2.09, 6.29
unsafe conviction 10.39, 11.05
unused material, non-sensitive, schedule of 9.71–9.72
unused statements, disclosure of 8.15, 9.66, 9.69
urgent circumstances 3.108

voluntary attendance at police station 6.03
voluntary disclosure
   review of material to remove privileged items prior to 4.02
   see also under waiver of privilege

waiver of privilege 1.02, 1.04, 1.70–1.73, 1.80–1.103
   appeals to Court of Appeal 11.01, 11.12, 11.19, 11.22, 11.29
   circumstances in which advice has been revealed 1.89
   compelled interviews 5.22
   content or substance of advice or document 1.88–1.89
   content/effect distinction 1.88–1.90
   court, communications with the 9.10–9.11, 9.13
   defence witnesses and evidence gathering/preparing for court 9.30
   deployment or reliance placed on content or substance 1.88–1.89
   disclosure, different types of 1.83–1.84
   effect of advice or document 1.88–1.89
   expert evidence/witnesses 9.48–9.57, 10.40
   fairness 1.88, 1.91, 1.94, 1.96–1.97, 1.101–1.103
   intentional disclosure *see* voluntary disclosure
   interlocutory hearings 10.62
   interviews under caution 6.40–6.42, 6.44–6.46
   lawyers giving evidence 10.42, 10.45–10.46, 10.57
   and loss of confidentiality distinction 1.80
   nature of what has been revealed 1.89
   objective basis, assessment on 1.82
   occurrence of waiver and collateral waiver 1.97–1.103
   oral evidence 10.26–10.32, 10.34–10.39
   prosecution privilege 8.06, 8.13, 8.18–8.20, 9.75–9.76
   reference/reliance distinction 1.88–1.90
   refusal of in Court of Appeal 11.30–11.31
   test for 1.88–1.93
   third parties, privilege belonging to 9.72
   true 1.80, 1.100

waiver of privilege (*cont.*)
  unintentional 9.16
  voluntary disclosure 1.80, 7.04–7.85, 9.16, 10.13, 10.15, 12.47
  see also 'cherry-picking' and waiver; collateral waiver; express waiver of privilege; general waiver of privilege; implied waiver of privilege; inadvertent waiver; limited waiver of privilege; loss of privilege; waiver of privilege and cooperation
waiver of privilege and cooperation 7.01–7.85
  cooperation credit 7.45, 7.55, 7.57
  cooperation with authorities other than SFO 7.76–7.85
    Competition and Markets Authority (CMA) 7.79–7.83
    Financial Conduct Authority (FCA) 7.84–7.85
    Sentencing Act 2020, agreements under 7.77–7.78
    Serious Organised Crime and Police Act (SOCPA) 2005, agreements under 7.77–7.78
  corporate cooperation 7.01, 7.45, 7.49, 7.55–7.60
  deferred prosecution agreements (DPAs) and cooperation with SFO 7.01–7.03, 7.14, 7.21, 7.23, 7.43–7.75
    companies, impact/pressure on 7.56–7.60
    expectations to waive privilege 7.45–7.55
    what happens in practice? 7.61–7.75
  see also limited waiver and voluntary disclosure; financial penalty reduction/discount
warrants
  interception of privileged communications, authorizing 3.103–3.104
  bulk interception 3.103
  targeted examination 3.103
  targeted interception 3.103
  see also search warrants
wasted costs order 10.61
whistle-blowers 12.42, 12.44
withholding disclosure 8.21–8.28
witness accounts, disclosing to SFO 7.07, 7.45, 7.47–7.49, 7.52–7.58, 7.60, 7.63, 7.69
witness evidence
  false 10.58
  lost or obscured 12.26
  see also witness statements
witness interviews
  client group, setting up 12.120
  internal investigations 12.11–12.28
  interview notes as lawyers' working papers 12.17–12.28
  litigation privilege 12.36, 12.81
  third parties, witnesses likely to be 12.11–12.16
  notes and transcripts 12.14
  risk of structuring investigation on weak privilege claim 12.129
  see also witness accounts, disclosing to SFO
witness statements
  draft 8.11, 8.15, 9.23, 9.66, 9.68–9.69
  intentional disclosure of privileged documents 10.13
  internal investigations 6.19, 12.74
  prosecution privilege 8.11, 8.15, 9.68–9.69
  prosecution witnesses and evidence gathering/preparing for court 9.36
  service and admissibility 9.24
  unserved 9.26, 9.66
  unused 8.15, 9.69
  waiver and collateral waiver 1.99
  see also draft witness statements; section 9 witness statements
witness summons 3.11, 3.31
  application by defendant for third party material 10.05–10.06, 10.10
  compelled interviews 5.05–5.06
  deferred prosecution agreements (DPAs) and cooperation with SFO 7.45
  exclusion of privileged material 3.24, 3.31, 3.33
  privilege assertion in response to compulsion powers 3.91
witness(es)
  additional 9.78
  character 1.52
  credibility 7.78
  evidence gathering and preparing for court 9.02
  expert, *see also under* evidence gathering and preparing for court
  expert 1.72
  of fact, actual and potential 9.23–9.26
  of fact 1.52
  identity 4.62 n.19
  interview records with actual or potential 9.67
  see also defence witnesses; witness accounts, disclosing to SFO; *under* evidence gathering and preparing for court; prosecution witnesses
working papers, lawyers' 1.36–1.37
  interview notes 12.17–12.18, 12.22–12.24, 12.27
written notice *see* notice, written